HAUNTED BY HITLER

Haunted by Hitler

LIBERALS, THE LEFT, AND THE
FIGHT AGAINST FASCISM
IN THE UNITED STATES

CHRISTOPHER VIALS

University of Massachusetts Press ◆ *Amherst & Boston*

Copyright © 2014 by Christopher Vials
All rights reserved
Printed in the United States of America

ISBN 978-1-62534-130-3 (paperback); 129-7 (hardcover)

Designed by Jack Harrison
Set in Adobe Minion Pro
Printed and bound by Sheridan Books, Inc.

Library of Congress Cataloging-in-Publication Data

Vials, Chris.
Haunted by Hitler : liberals, the left, and the fight against fascism in the United States / Christopher Vials.
    pages cm
Includes bibliographical references and index.
ISBN 978-1-62534-130-3 (pbk. : alk. paper) —
ISBN 978-1-62534-129-7 (hardcover : alk. paper)
1. Fascism—United States—History—20th century.   2. National socialism.
3. United States—Politics and government—1945–1989.   I. Title.
E743.5.V53 2014
335.6097309'04—dc23
                            2014021802

British Library Cataloguing-in-Publication Data
A catalogue record for this book is available from the British Library.

For my parents, Judy and Peter Vials

CONTENTS

Acknowledgments ix

Abbreviations xi

Introduction: Antifascism and the United States 1

1. European Precedents, American Echoes: Fascism in History and Memory 12

2. From Margin to Mainstream: American Antifascism to 1945 30

3. Beyond Economics, Without Guarantees: *Faschismustheorie* in the United States 70

4. Resuming the People's War: HUAC, Joe McCarthy, and the Antifascist Challenge of the 1950s 90

5. Brownshirts in the Twilight Zone: Antifascism in the Liberal Moment of the Early 1960s 126

6. United Front against Genocide: African American Antifascism, the Black Panthers, and the Multiracial Coalitions of the Late 1960s 159

7. Queer Antifascism: Pink Triangle Politics and the Christian Right 194

Epilogue: Antifascism in Strip Mall America 233

Notes 237

Index 271

ACKNOWLEDGMENTS

Haunted by Hitler has been inspired by the antifascist writers, artists, and organizers who, for almost a century now, have struggled to ensure that we all have the space to keep writing and thinking. Some of them were kind enough to share their time and their stories with me, including Avram Finkelstein, Charles Kreloff, and another who, owing to experiences during the McCarthy period, still does not want to be named. I am deeply indebted to Brian Halley at the University of Massachusetts Press, whose confidence in this project, editorial guidance, savvy advice, and endless patience allowed me to acknowledge these people's contributions to democracy with far more precision than I originally envisioned. I am also honored by scholars of the American left who encouraged this project at various stages, including Paula Rabinowitz, Julia Mickenberg, Benjamin Balthaser, Bill Mullen, Cheryl Higashida, Aaron Lecklider, Rachel Rubin, Rachel Peterson, Jim Smethurst, and Mary Helen Washington. A very special thanks goes to Alan Wald and Judy Smith, whose generous letters of support enabled me to acquire the time and funding I needed to complete this manuscript. Alan's singular mentorship and guidance have, throughout the whole process, been priceless. The Humanities Institute at the University of Connecticut (UCHI), the James and Sylvia Thayer Research Fellowship at the UCLA Library Special Collections, and the UConn Research Foundation provided generous funds for my research. It is not an exaggeration to say that I could not have completed this book without the time allowed by the Fellowship at the UCHI, which also came with the lively encouragement and thoughtful advice of my peers at the Institute.

Several journals and edited collections provided a home for material on antifascism that could not fit into the manuscript, and I am deeply thankful for the sharp editorial work of a number of individuals whose feedback on these pieces also informed the larger arguments of this book: above all, Joseph Ramsey, Robbie Lieberman, Derek Royal, Andrew Lawson, and Dianne Feeley. This project would not have been possible without the archivists at the Bancroft Library at UC-Berkeley, the Special Collections at Stanford University, the Peace Collection at Swarthmore College, the New York Public Library, the San

Francisco Public Library, the Tamiment Library and Robert F. Wagner Archives at NYU, the UCLA Special Collections, the Babbidge Library and Thomas J. Dodd Research Center at UConn, and the National Association for Armenian Studies and Research (NAASR). Marc Mamigonian at NAASR deserves singular praise for his support. Beyond the archives, the generous hospitality of my friends Todd Evans and Dielly Diaz made my extended research trip to the Bay Area much richer than I thought possible; the same is true for Charles Schlund and Rita Kampalath during my trip to Los Angeles. I also am grateful to audiences at annual conferences of the American Studies Association, the Asian American Studies Association, and the Modern Language Association for their highly informative feedback.

Closer to home, Betty Heiss, David Markowitz, Jim Duffy, Daniel Weiner, and the audience at the Center for Learning in Retirement shared wonderful insights on mid-twentieth-century America which helped shape this book. I would especially like to thank the members of the Americanist Writing Group ("the ARG") at UConn for their intricate feedback on so many chapters of the manuscript: Martha Cutter, Kate Capshaw Smith, Shawn Salvant, and Sharon Harris. Conversations, intellectual stimulation, and emotional support from other stellar colleagues at UConn were invaluable: special thanks here go to Bob Hasenfratz, Clare King'oo, Alexis Boylan, Jason Oliver Chang, Mark Overmyer-Velasquez, Gaye Tuchman, Brendan Kane, Gregory Semenza, Alenda Chang, Kathleen Tonry, Clare Eby, Matt McKenzie, Jeffrey Ogbar, Micki McElya, Albert "Hap" Fairbanks, Charles Mahoney, Margaret Breen, Wayne Franklin, Anna Mae Duane, Dwight Codr, Tom Long, Heather Turcotte, Tom Deans, Brenda Murphy, Delia Aguilar, and E. San Juan Jr. I learned a great deal from graduate students, most notably Karen Renner, Patrick Lawrence, and Joseph Darda. The insights of my dear friends Mary Gallucci and Jerry Phillips guided this book from the very beginning: Jerry's expansive erudition, shared on long dog walks through the woods, was more precious than he realizes.

Finally, I am indebted to my parents, Judy and Pete Vials, whose love and support have always been foundational and whose observations of American society shaped my thinking in this book profoundly. My in-laws, Charles and Ginko Schlund, provided wonderful encouragement and personal insights on the subject of war. My sister, Jan Sheehy, encouraged my writing from a very early stage, and without her love and mentorship I might not even be writing these words. Last but certainly not least is my wife, Cathy Schlund-Vials, a tireless advocate, sharp editor, and inspirational scholar who continually reminds me why our relationships to the past matter.

ABBREVIATIONS

ALAWF	American League Against War and Fascism
ALPD	American League for Peace and Democracy
ASQ	*American Socialist Quarterly*
BP	*The Black Panther* (newspaper)
BPP	Black Panther Party
CP	Communist Party
CPUSA	Communist Party of the United States
CRC	Civil Rights Congress
HAW	Homosexuelle Aktion Westberlin
HUAC	House Committee on Un-American Activities
KPD	Communist Party of Germany
NM	*New Masses*
NR	*New Republic*
NSDAP	National Socialist German Workers' Party (Nazi Party)
NYT	*New York Times*
OFF	Office of Facts and Figures
OWI	Office of War Information
SPD	Social Democratic Party (Germany)
SWP	Socialist Workers Party
WHK	Wissenschaftlich-humanitäre Komitee

HAUNTED BY HITLER

INTRODUCTION
Antifascism and the United States

> The problem is that we have this event—Germany, Hitler, the Holocaust—which we have made into THE standard of absolute Evil—well and good, as standards of Evil go, it's not bad—but then everyone gets frantic as soon as you try to use the standard, *nothing* compares, *nothing* resembles—and the standard becomes unusable and *nothing* qualifies as Evil with a capital E.... how come the only people who ever say "Evil" anymore are southern cracker televangelists with radioactive blue eyeshadow?
>
> The character Zilla in Tony Kushner's play *A Bright Room Called Day* (1985)

From the beginning of her vice presidential candidacy in 2008, Sarah Palin was marketed by the Republican Party as a paradoxical combination of the quotidian and the visionary, of frontier vigor and suburban normalcy that came together, barely, under the label "hockey mom." Little did party officials realize, however, that this packaging helped land her in a much darker history: fascism. While most Democratic strategists and professional pundits studiously avoided this political label, ordinary people did not, and the letters they wrote to newspaper editorial boards across the country reveal how broad swaths of the public continued to read a particular strand of the political right in terms of fascism.[1] What caused letter writers and some journalists to reach for the fascist label to describe Palin were a number of consistent motifs: her attempt to ban books when she was mayor of Wasilla, her ability to stir up xenophobic and even racist crowds with a rhetoric of violence, her anti-cosmopolitanism, her retrograde anticommunism, her unorthodox Christianity—all of which she brought together in a homespun brand of intolerant nationalism. Paradoxically, it was the very *ordinariness* of the persona that brought together all these things—its undeniable and unmistakable Americanness—which seemed to tie her to European regimes and movements of seventy years ago. One Palin detractor in Pittsburgh rebuked her with a quotation he attributed to the novelist Sinclair Lewis: "When fascism comes to America it will be wrapped in the flag and carrying a cross." Jeffrey Feldman, the editor in chief of the liberal *Huffington Post,* noted that many individuals he encountered viewed Palin not as an actual Blackshirt fascist per se but saw her politics as a step on the road to fascism that needed to be stopped before it was too late.[2]

To be sure, it is premature to label Palin a fascist. Though her public statements echo some of fascism's signature elements, she does not stand at the head of an integrated, cohesive fascist movement or party. But at the same time, it is too easy to denounce the words of her critics as hyperbolic political rhetoric and to fall into the contemporary, relativizing habit—so wonderfully captured by Tony Kushner—of claiming that "*nothing* compares, *nothing* resembles." Palin emerged from a theocratic strand of the Christian right which, as I will argue, is the closest functional equivalent to a fascist movement in mainstream American politics. And her use of a particular controversial quotation underscores very real connections to historical fascism among the American hard right. In accepting the vice presidential nomination at the Republican National Convention, Palin cited an unnamed writer who had said, "We grow good people in our small towns, with honesty and sincerity and dignity." The statement was innocuous in itself, but when its source was revealed and its larger context considered, it confirmed for critics that her Capra-esque worldview concealed something much darker. Her source, the syndicated newspaper columnist Westbrook Pegler (1894–1969), was a forerunner of the kind of right-wing populism embodied by Palin. One of the country's best-known columnists in the 1930s and 1940s, Pegler often wrote through an alter ego named George Spelvin, a plainspoken, middle-class conservative who never finished high school and detested snobbery. Speaking through his proxy Spelvin, Pegler once wrote a four-page tribute to the hot dog.[3]

Unlike many others on the right during the 1930s, Pegler did not support fascism. But after the war his rightward shift took on more alarming dimensions. He openly embraced racism and bigotry, and, on one occasion, identified himself as a fascist. At a gathering held in his honor in February 1964 he contended that Jews "suckered" Americans into fighting "their war" and, trying to make a joke, said that the Jews who died in the Holocaust "didn't count" because they were communists.[4] Shortly after Palin's speech, Robert F. Kennedy Jr. asked why she had quoted "the fascist writer Westbrook Pegler," who had once called for the murder of his father with the words, "[I hope] some white patriot of the Southern tier will spatter his spoonful of brains in public premises before the snow flies."[5] Palin's speechwriter, Matthew Scully, very likely encountered Pegler's testimonial to small towns in Pat Buchanan's memoir *Right from the Beginning* (1990). In the section of his book that references it, Buchanan waxes nostalgic for Pegler and recalls fondly how his father, who was a supporter of America First, of the profascist Charles Lindbergh, and of General Francisco Franco, read Pegler's columns to him when he was a child.[6] Buchanan, whose anti-Semitism and disturbing apathy toward Nazi brutalities are quite well known, thus gleaned his politics directly from the profascist right of the 1930s. And it was he who is likely responsible for passing along Pegler's words to the Palin camp, words charged with an anti-cosmopolitan, *volkish* nationalism bearing a disturbing genealogy.

This book is not driven by the fear of a future Fourth Reich in the United States: an irony-driven consumer culture, the post–civil rights institutionalization of multiculturalism, and the absence of a highly visible, fear-inspiring, radical left make that difficult to imagine. It does contend, however, that the functional equivalent of fascist movements and fascist currents have been on this side of the Atlantic since the 1920s; these have palpably impacted American culture and individual lives at a number of critical junctures and continue to haunt American politics. The most notable of these currents are the Coughlinite movement of the 1930s, George Wallace and the American Independent Party in the late 1960s (the racial politics of which were co-opted by the Republican Party), and, since the 1970s, the Christian right. The cultural forces brought together under the banner of McCarthyism in the 1950s also held tremendous potential for congealing into an organized, neofascist politics.

Yet the larger focus of this book is ostensibly more affirming. As revealed by the rhetoric surrounding Palin in 2008, these dark currents have been met, if not fully checked, time and again by a vigorous antifascist tradition. A particular voice accessed by Palin's critics is a testament to its longevity. Sinclair Lewis's portrait of homespun fascism is indicative of the kinds of politics advocated by what I call antifascism. Much like Palin's detractors, Lewis saw nothing unusual about considering fascism an American political phenomenon when he published his novel *It Can't Happen Here* in 1935. A book more often evoked than read, its very title called into question the presumed foreignness of fascism. Indeed, his novel, in many ways the urtext of American antifascism, told a story that would have been quite familiar to both Palin's and George W. Bush's detractors seventy-five years later. It describes the transformation of the country under the regime of Buzz Windrip, a politician who defeats Roosevelt in the election of 1936, quickly bans all political parties but his own and creates a fascist state. Windrip is a folksy populist whom Lewis describes as "vulgar, almost illiterate, a public liar easily detected, and in his 'ideas' almost idiotic . . . his humor the sly cynicism of a country store." Anti-cosmopolitanism pervades his political rhetoric. Uncannily anticipating Pegler and Palin, he exclaims, "In the little towns, ah, there is the abiding peace that I love, and that can never be disturbed by even the noisiest Smart Alecks from those haughty megalopolises like Washington, New York, & etc." His wife "was so edifyingly devoted to their two small children and Bible study that she couldn't be coaxed to come East."[7]

Lewis takes pains to show how bankers and industrialists support Windrip because of his promise to restore order and crack down on "Reds." The rich understand his populism only as a ruse to secure power, and their intuition is correct. Yet he also emphasizes that middle- and working-class white men are agents in this process and that capitalists themselves do not always direct the regime. The character Shad Ledue, who stands in for Windrip's plebeian supporters, eagerly supports the state and becomes its chief representative in his small town because it taps into his hatred of blacks and elites (not the rich per se, but Jews, communists, and sophisticates). Though it does restore capitalism, the Windrip regime successfully interpolates people like Ledue because its driving logics are not strictly economic. Ultimately, its rhetoric is fueled by a complex desire for national renewal based on racial homogeneity, militarism, white Christian supremacy, patriarchy, and a simplistic cult of tradition. Once in power, it intensifies all existing social hierarchies by means of extreme violence, including concentration camps for Jews and leftists. *It Can't Happen Here* uses antifascism to explore how racism and religious bigotry can be mobilized through nationalist rhetoric in ways that bring short-term gains to working- and middle-class white men and, whether intentionally or not, how capitalism can benefit in the process.

Lewis sought not just to label American fascism but also to explain it, and he did so in far greater, more elaborate detail than any critic of Palin in the twenty-first century. His use of antifascism as a frame to interpret populist, right-wing nationalism—presenting it as a force with the potential to violently harden social hierarchies despite its deceptive vapidity—was a move that has been repeated by left and liberal writers, activists, and scholars time and again since the 1930s. A vast archive largely ignored by scholars, such antifascist cultural work is still audible in the American public sphere, though one must increasingly strain to hear it. But the disturbing continuities in right-wing political rhetoric, transmitted from the thirties straight to Buchanan and then onto Palin, suggest it is worth listening to. For the links between elements of the American right and fascism are as real as the left's links to communism, though increasingly unfashionable to acknowledge.

I argue here that many of the warnings from the 1930s ring like the warnings of 2008 for a reason. The ease with which many Americans, primarily but not exclusively liberals, were able to tag Palin with the fascist label was the result of an almost century-long discursive history of antifascism in American culture. Long before scholars discovered Giorgio Agamben's "state of exception," Michel Foucault's biopolitics, Carl Schmitt's notion of sovereignty, and current discussions of corporate sovereignty, antifascism was a pervasive discourse used by intellectuals, writers, activists, and others to describe the structural tendency of Western liberal societies to slide into ever more undemocratic forms and to deliver the antithesis of their universalist promises. Antifascism in the sense I use the term does not refer to just any aversion to Nazis, Blackshirts, and their perceived American equivalents. The antifascism I trace is a more specific modality, more familiar to Europeans than to North Americans, marked off from other rejections of fascism by its intensity and historicity. By *intensity* I mean it is not a reflex aversion, nor does it use *fascist* as a casual slur. For antifascists, fascism is not one problem among many but a force so menacing and so present that it requires concentrated effort to check. It is an urgency that inspires the creation of serious, detailed cultural work aimed at revealing its social bases and possible sites of emergence in civil society. And what I call antifascism possesses historicity in the sense that it comes within range of accurately identifying its target. By these criteria, Steven Spielberg's classic *Raiders of the Lost Ark* would not be properly antifascist: it casts Nazis as villains but does not reflect on the meaning and roots of fascism; neither would Jonah Goldberg's book *Liberal Fascism* (2008), rhetorical conflations of George H. W. Bush and Adolf Hitler, or the U.S. bombing of North Vietnam vis-à-vis the German bombing of Poland, all of which miss their mark so widely that they actually obscure their putative object.

The figure of the fascist continues to serve as the other to American pluralism, but antifascism is more than a mere language that Americans of all political stripes have used to render their antithesis. Throughout the twentieth century, liberals and the left were more deeply haunted by the problem of fascism than those in the center or to the right, and by relentlessly placing their anxieties within the public sphere they played a crucial role in defining the terms through which it was remembered and discussed.[8] One marker of this influence was the popular common sense that whereas communism was the extreme of the left, fascism was the extreme of the right, a consensus that has diminished in the twenty-first century. As recently as twenty-five years ago, liberals, moderates, and even some conservatives seemed quite at ease when evoking the Third Reich and the memory of the Second World War to discuss not only the extreme right, but also the structural inequalities of American society in general—and they did so in mainstream, public forums. Examples abound. At the Republican National Convention in 1984, for instance, Ronald Reagan invoked Hitler to caution his audience about the dangers of moving too far to the right; almost two decades earlier, the conservative icon William F. Buckley and the erstwhile moderate Robert Novak used the term *fascist* to describe George Wallace;[9] in the 1950s and 1960s, leading Cold War liberal academics such as Daniel Bell, David Riesman, Seymour Martin Lipset, and Nathan Glazer explicitly drew on the history of fascism to interpret Joe McCarthy and the new American right;[10]

highly visible writers and intellectuals in the fifties and sixties, ranging from Rod Serling, Arthur Miller, Betty Friedan, Bobby Seale, Elmer Davis, and William Shirer, used the memory of fascism to highlight injustices in their own country, and they did so in venues that often reached audiences numbering in the millions; in the 1980s, gay and lesbian activists made the pink triangle, a reminder of the presence of gay men in Nazi concentration camps, one of their primary symbols, attesting to the continued resonance of antifascism in new social movements forty years after the end of the Second World War. All in all, such efforts undermined but did not entirely displace the Cold War discourse of totalitarianism (the conflation of communism and fascism), preserving the idea of fascism as a unique political force requiring discussion in its own right.

While conservatives also employed the term *fascism* against their political enemies—from Pegler's denunciations of the New Deal as fascist in the late 1930s, through George H. W. Bush's conflation of Saddam Hussein and Hitler, to George W. Bush's discourse of Islamofascism—their usages rarely rose above the merely polemical, offering audiences sustained, elaborate social analyses.[11] The right-wing Tea Party's cries of liberal fascism in the twenty-first century, while not unprecedented on the right, carry a degree of investment new to that side of the spectrum. Yet even recent uses of the term by the Tea Party movement are informed by an understanding of fascism first popularized by the left. The real novelty of recent comparisons between President Barack Obama and Hitler lies in the place they have assumed in the cultural field: they can be heard more loudly because left-wing antifascism has diminished in volume the more the social movements that produced and sustained it recede from memory.

These movements came into their own during the Depression years, the environment that produced Lewis's *It Can't Happen Here*. In the United States, official ideas of fascism in the thirties and forties were shaped in no small measure by the international left. Many left-wing organizers and cultural producers, whose efforts had pushed the New Deal in much more ambitious directions by the late thirties, saw antifascism and antiracism as inseparable parts of their struggle to build a workers' economy. Writers, artists, filmmakers, and activists affiliated with a dynamic social movement of the era, a left-liberal coalition often termed the Popular Front, were at the forefront of a vast effort to make fascism antithetical to American common sense. As a result of their impact on the public sphere in the 1930s and their work in federal agencies during the Second World War, their vision of the war informed the rhetoric of "Why We Fight." Indeed, waging war against fascism, an enemy embodying strict hierarchies of class, race, gender, and sexuality that rallied crowds around the slogan "Death to Communism," had been a tricky and perilous enterprise for those struggling to return the United States to its prewar social order. Postwar reconversion would require the exorcism of the radical energies unleashed by the conflict.

After the Second World War, cultural producers working within the tradition of antifascism would continually disrupt the ideological project of reconversion. In 1944 Vice President Henry Wallace had stated that "fascism is an international disease" and "a spiritual condition," adding that it would likely pose its greatest threats *after* the war and from within the United States.[12] Each in its own way, and long after military hostilities had ceased, future generations would answer his call to keep fighting fascism even after it had been defeated on the battlefield. *Haunted by Hitler* looks at the shifting ways in which writers, artists, filmmakers, scholars, and activists articulated what they saw as nascent fascism in American life. As my examples will demonstrate, Jewish American cultural producers in particular have been central in maintaining antifascism as a critical discourse.

Oppositional narratives of fascism first generated in the 1930s remained in American culture, creating troubling and damning associations which have haunted reactionary social movements in the public sphere. This book primarily examines their surprising legacies in American popular culture after the war. Antifascism in the thirties and forties was never a unitary narrative to which all factions of the left consented, nor was it something that persisted in undiluted form. But it did set in motion a palpably coherent discourse that serves as the focus of this book. In short, American antifascism has accessed the specter of the fascist and the memory of the Second World War to destabilize the anticosmopolitanism and exclusionary nationalism inherent in rightist notions of belonging, in the United States and abroad. It has possessed a dissonant quality, disrupting nationalist memories that claim the war as a victory for American exceptionalism, seeing, more often than not, the nightmare of history in crowds which too vigorously wave a flag. Though the variants of American antifascism are many, it generally posits fascism as a force slumbering in the very bones of all modern nations, a menace that arises as reactionary social movements create vast public spaces for those who overidentify with the dominant hierarchies. Though originating in the 1930s, it has changed shape over time to meet new historical conditions and has resisted full incorporation into the celebratory narratives of the Greatest Generation and the American way.

From *It Can't Happen Here* to Chris Hedges's exposé of Christian fundamentalism, *American Fascists* (2008), what American antifascist cultural production has mostly attempted to describe and explain is political reaction. Yet its analysis has not stopped there. It has also tried to didactically seize reaction by the roots by untangling the web of complex motivations and social forces behind its American incarnations, from Charles Coughlin and Joe McCarthy to

George Wallace to the televangelist Pat Robertson. Central to this task has been the effort to identify and critique the ground from which such figures emerge, namely, the culture of Enlightenment liberalism, rooted in the nation-state and historically dependent on a dense network of social hierarchies. Indeed, the threat of fascism necessitated a discourse that could articulate the relationship between race, class, gender, sexuality, and empire, and antifascists rarely met this challenge on all levels. But with unexpected frequency they did craft an intersectional analytic, even before the birth of the Popular Front in 1935. The very word *racism,* for instance, began to be widely used in English owing to transatlantic antifascism. Thus in its best incarnations, antifascist cultural work challenges political reaction in order to lodge a much wider, more innovative social critique. The careful reading of this body of work over the decades—a reading that searches for patterns in its analyses across time and extracts the necessary lessons—is a job yet to be undertaken.

Complicating such a task is the fact that the term *antifascism* is not legible in contemporary American political discourse. By contrast, in Germany and in sections of Europe to this day it is generally understood as one among many causes of the political left, one preoccupied with the fight against right-wing extremism and its institutional pillars. One of the basic contentions of this book is that antifascism has, in fact, constituted a coherent body of cultural work in the United States. Those who have taken up its call have been in dialogue with one another and have built on each other's insights since the 1930s, even when they do not call themselves antifascists and even though they are not always conscious of their intellectual roots (all too often, however, they are quite aware of them). To more fully recognize the contributions of this work as well as its limitations one must begin to call it by its name.

The artists, writers, and activists of this tradition have been in dialogue not merely with one another but also with much broader publics. The more detailed articulations of fascism by cultural producers like Lewis helped to channel the more casual usage of the term *fascism* by a wider segment of the population, for whom the term existed as a much looser "structure of feeling," in Raymond Williams's sense. That is, for a broad swath of the population, including most critics of Palin, antifascism was not a well-formed, elaborate, or consistent position but a general portrait which they refracted through their political culture and applied to their own experiences; as Williams puts it, they forged "meanings and values as they are actually lived and felt."[13]

By and large, this book traces antifascism in the United States chronologically. Chapter 1 surveys key traits of historical fascism relevant to this study and outlines the theoretical frames which help one to evaluate antifascist memory work after the war. Chapters 2 and 3 trace the origins of American antifascism in the 1930s and 1940s: its constitutive campaigns, the various theories of fascism it generated, and its relationship to the conservative views of the European dictators Hitler, Franco, and Benito Mussolini. Chapter 4 examines McCarthyism as the first major challenge for postwar antifascism. It demonstrates the frequency with which politicians and mainstream journalists in the 1950s applied the word *fascism* to McCarthy and the anticommunist repression. Such figures as Robert Sherwood, Hannah Weinstein, Arthur Miller, Theodor Adorno, and Paul Robeson set the tone for reading McCarthy and his supporters within the terms of antifascism, and they did so in ways still clearly marked by the pre-1945 left. In so doing, they undermined an emerging Cold War conflation of fascism and communism.

Chapter 5 contends that the early 1960s marked the postwar high point of antifascism, as the fall of McCarthyism allowed a long-delayed critical discussion of Nazism to resume. It argues that antifascism was substantially transformed in this period, not only by the Eichmann trials but also by the larger civil rights movement that helped to make race and racism causal factors driving historical events. Deemphasizing social class yet retaining a critical edge, antifascism, like the public at large, retroactively began to emphasize the Holocaust and Nazi racial ideology as the primary reason "Why We Fought" the Second World War. Figures like Serling, Shirer, Friedan, and Stanley Kramer ruptured the amnesia necessary to the Cold War project of elevating America's West German ally to its status as a beacon of freedom and of placing the West in a moral universe separate from that of communism.

Chapter 6 focuses on the late 1960s and early 1970s to highlight the ways in which radical activists of color further transformed antifascism by developing what I call a spatial metaphor of fascism, one deeply attentive to its historical relationship with social death under a dual system of liberal rights. It centers on the National Committees to Combat Fascism (NCCFs), founded by the Black Panther Party in 1969, which emerged from a context of white backlash in the late sixties. Modeled after the Popular Front, the Panthers intended the NCCFs to create a multiracial coalition of whites, Latinos, Asian Americans, and others united in a common front to combat a racial backlash personified by George Wallace, a backlash which indeed originated from some of the darkest corners of American political life.

Chapter 7 shows how, by the mid-1980s, gay and lesbian activists had become the primary demographic to employ antifascism. In adopting the pink triangle worn by gay men in German concentration camps, the gay and lesbian movement became the only major postwar political constellation to evoke the memory of fascism in one of its primary symbols. It drew on new archives of "the gay Holocaust" opened up by post-Stonewall historiography and deployed the memory of gay men in concentration camps as they confronted the AIDS crisis and the religious right. Through the prominence of Nazism as a trope in the activism of the lesbian, gay, bisexual, and transgender community, gay writers and activists—most notably Tony Kushner, Richard Plant, Martin Sherman, and the members of the Silence = Death Project—injected into liberal America a notion of the Christian right as the new face of fascism.

The epilogue, titled "Antifascism in Strip Mall America," argues that because of the twenty-first-century uses of antifascism by the political right, ownership of the term *fascism* is now contested as never before. Rather than open new possibilities, the contestation may very well create a relativism in the broader public which renders the word unusable. "Antifascism in Strip Mall America" speaks to the difficulty of maintaining a critical language of antifascism in a cultural space and time so far removed from the events of the 1930s and 1940s, when the mass movements necessary for creating and maintaining an oppositional, anti-exceptionalist memory are no longer in motion.

Fascism and the Second World War have received thorough scholarly attention, and nonacademic presses continue to publish a range of titles on these popular topics. And scholars of the Holocaust have produced no shortage of excellent works dealing with America's memory of the Nazi genocide.[14] Surprisingly, however, outside of Holocaust studies no book-length study has outlined the postwar memory of fascism in the United States; and no book to date has examined the postwar legacy of left and liberal antifascisms of the thirties and forties. Works in Holocaust studies have skillfully traced the evolution of Holocaust consciousness in American culture and have used the genocide as a site to examine how Jewishness and Jewish identity have been mediated in American life. In many ways, they have productively illuminated the evolving American understandings of Nazism that have informed this book. But generally speaking they have focused on images of American fascism drawn from a shared ethnoreligious frame, not from a shared vocabulary of the political left.

Antifascism is also an important topic of study partly because the figure of the fascist remains one of the primary villains of American pluralist discourse. The word *fascism* is still in continuous use because the era that produced it, the 1930s and 1940s, is a time to which Americans constantly return, whether to evoke the Depression and the lessons its offers for handling contemporary economic crises or to relive the defeat of Hitler on the battlefields of the Second World War. For better or worse, American popular culture returns to the thirties and forties as a foundational moment of national identity even more than to the American Revolution, the Civil War, or the Industrial Revolution: indeed, 1929 and 1941 seem to have become the new 1776. A number of scholars in American studies have traced how the political left shaped American common sense during the Depression and war decades, and my book adds to this dialogue by using narratives of fascism to illustrate the continuing influence of the 1930s on postwar culture.[15]

Revisiting this history carries a particular urgency in the twenty-first century. The recent attempt by the American far right to redefine and co-opt antifascism is novel in its relentlessness and scope.[16] Referring to fascism, the philosopher Walter Benjamin famously wrote in 1940, "In every era the attempt must be made anew to wrest tradition away from a conformism that is about to overpower it."[17] His warning now applies to antifascism itself, and the task of defense is long overdue. Rightist fusions of Obama and Hitler may not win many adherents, but they nonetheless trivialize the history of antifascism in the United States, threatening not only to sever it from its international roots but also to eclipse the memory of the movements that produced it. At the same time, the critiques of Palin illustrate how Americans often use the term *fascism* algebraically, even when they aim it in the correct general direction. That is to say, they see the silhouette of their target but are often unable to fill in the specifics to form a concrete portrait of fascism in an American context. To see their object more concretely, they must be able to recognize and cite a particular history that has always been present, hiding in plain sight: the American tradition of antifascism.

CHAPTER **1**
European Precedents, American Echoes
Fascism in History and Memory

> While fascism's potential for creating a *regime* may be safely regarded as extinguished with the defeat of the Axis powers in the Second World War, as a *political ideology* capable of spawning new movements it should be treated as a permanent feature of modern political culture.
>
> ROGER GRIFFIN, *The Nature of Fascism* (1991)

In 1969 Ernest Mandel wrote, "The history of fascism is at the same time the history of the theoretical analysis of fascism."[1] How its opponents understood fascism, in other words, has played a material role in its history. Mandel, a Jewish Marxist imprisoned at Dora concentration camp for his work in the Belgian underground during the Nazi occupation, learned this insight the hard way. He saw the inadequate theories of fascism pushed by the main organizations of the European left as more than just sloppy analysis: in misrecognizing the enemy, they diverted vital political energy necessary to stop Hitler's rise, indirectly contributing to countless tragedies. Many of his fellow survivors on the left accessed the antifascist resistance more positively, and one must be careful not to overvalue the transformative powers of theory. Yet Mandel's observation underscores the significance of antifascism, a terrain where recognition—and misrecognition—hold the potential to shape a history of intense political violence.

To evaluate the actors covered in this book, I must consider the extent to which they properly identified their foe, mainly by revisiting the now-venerable question, what is fascism? From there, one can address other matters specific to their location, namely, how applicable is fascism to the United States, particularly after 1945? and when does calling its name needlessly divert political energy? To this end, I want to first review pertinent elements of historical fascism in Europe: its demographic basis, its nationalism and ideology, the nature of its violence, its relationship to elites, and its reliance on a broader range of Western hierarchies. Since postwar antifascism typically wages its battles in reference to vanquished regimes, one must also theorize the efficacy of rooting one's struggles in relation to a past formation. While cautioning prudence, I conclude the chapter by asserting that those concerned about an American fascism have had a rational basis for their fears. The contradictions of Enlightenment liberalism, which continue to generate far right movements, unfortunately guarantee that in certain situations "calling fascism" has been warranted in the United States before and after 1945. In the process, I will illuminate why those who have called it most intensely have tended to the political left.

Historians have come to no consensus on the definition of fascism. What's more, fascist historiography is a highly contentious field, one in which the major definitions do not even begin to converge. As Roger Griffin has noted, the diversity of fascist movements across so many national contexts has led some historians to question even if the term should be applied outside of Italy.[2] Though I draw on this historiography to fashion a working definition of fascism, the intent of my book is not to intervene in this debate. Rather, I will refer to major historians in the field to outline some of the features of fascism that are germane to this study and to consider aspects of its nationalism that are crucial to the questions posed above. The working definition of historical fascism I use is as follows: Fascism was a set of far right political movements, finding their fullest expression in Italy and Germany from the 1920s to the 1940s, that destroyed democratic space and violently hardened social hierarchies through a militarist, anti-Marxist, racist, symbol-laden cultural project of national rebirth. Though enabled and sustained by the support of the upper class, it differs from conservative authoritarianism in that its primary agents were not traditional elites but middle-class upstarts animated more by visions of national renewal than by economic logics. Leon Trotsky distinguished between fascism and so-called classic elite dictatorship, using the term *Bonapartism* to indicate the latter, and he was not the only prewar Marxist to differentiate along these lines.[3]

Historians have univocally disproven the vulgar Marxist notion that Hitler and Mussolini were simply front men for more powerful business interests that manipulated them from behind the scenes. Rather, fascism was disproportionately middle class, and its leaders were largely petit bourgeois upstarts with their own agenda of national renewal. This agenda involved the militarization of the entire society, the staging of symbolic rituals of national unity, and a complete cultural purge of cosmopolitanism, intellectualism, and leftist internationalism. In Germany its purge of the national body involved the physical extermination of Jews, Roma, homosexuals, the disabled, and other perceived undesirables. Unlike the elite right, composed of free-market liberals and traditional conservatives, both of whom aimed to politically demobilize the population, the fascist right of the National Socialist German Workers' Party (NSDAP) and the Partito Nazionale Fascista (PNF) actively mobilized the public in a kind of cultural revolution. Elsewhere in Europe, for example, in Romania, Hungary, and Austria, conservative dictatorships emerged under the firm control of established ruling classes which jailed or killed their opponents and dismantled parliamentary authority without resorting to fascist mass mobilization and its particular transformation of civil society.[4]

While historians dismiss the idea that the upper classes were puppet masters pulling the strings of fascist leaders, there is consensus among them that the seizure of power by Hitler and Mussolini was directly enabled by the weight of established elites, including industrialists, financiers, large landowners, the civil service, and the military officer class. Politically, many of these elites were conservatives, but liberals, in the European sense of those who desire a society of open markets free of clerical control, were also complicit. Although there was not an identity of interests between fascists and representatives of elite interests, they formed an active partnership in Germany and Italy that remained in force until the tide of war turned definitively against the Axis.[5] What initially caused the influential sections of the establishment to rally behind fascism was a desire to maintain their political power, which was threatened by the strength of the political left. Germany and Italy had been home to some of the largest, most radical movements of workers in Europe. The Red Years of 1919–20 were still fresh in the memory of Italian landowners and industrialists when Mussolini took power in his famous March on Rome in 1922. In the German elections of November 1932, shortly before the aristocrat Paul von Hindenburg rescued Hitler by naming him chancellor, the Communists had picked up seats in the Reichstag while the Nazis lost votes, political momentum, and even financial viability.[6]

Owing to the strong presence of the left, the hegemony of ruling groups in Germany and Italy was weakened; they needed the help of the fascist newcomers much more than their peers in Japan, Romania, and Hungary. What the Nazis and the Blackshirts offered their coalition partners on the right were not only the votes to form parliamentary majorities: in the wake of the First World War and the economic calamities that followed, they also offered fresh young faces to a public weary of a venerable establishment. Fascism appealed especially to people in the middle classes, including farmers, shop owners, and white-collar employees, who were disillusioned with established authorities yet rejected left-wing alternatives and clung to the idea of the nation. Before taking power it even co-opted pieces of the left's platform. The first meeting of Italian fascists called for the introduction of the eight-hour workday and progressive taxation, while in Germany the spelled-out title of the Nazi Party—the National Socialist German Workers' Party—reflected some of the party's plebeian origins.[7] Once installed in power, however, fascists broke almost every socialist-sounding promise of reform; contrary to their earlier rhetoric, fascist states restored the shop floor hierarchies compromised by labor and the left, though not under circumstances fully controlled or always preferred by business leaders.[8] Fascism thus functioned to restore profits to some of the most influential sectors, even if capitalists, as a class, were not directing policy.

But fascism was much more than a class coalition or a mere restoration of profits. It was a socially transformative form of reaction leveled against the very existence of workers' movements. Geoff Eley, a historian of the European left, writes that, in comparison with workers' organizations in eastern Europe,

> labor movements in Italy and north-central Europe were incomparably stronger. They were larger, better organized, and deeply integrated into the social life and public cultures of their countries. Uprooting the Left from this historic embeddedness in complex civil societies required a comprehensive assault on the status quo. . . . [Fascism] "sought to disenfranchise, in the fullest sense, the working classes, and to destroy political and labor market gains that had been generations in the making." This required a different kind of regime, one that systematically attacked the given bases of political life.[9]

In Germany and Italy attacking the "given bases of political life" involved the use of the most modern forms of mass communication to rally the chosen people away from cosmopolitanism and class-consciousness toward a new national identity that explicitly fused race and nation. As Hitler wrote in *Mein Kampf*, "The folkish state . . . must set race in the center of all life."[10]

Mussolini uses the words *race* and *nation* interchangeably throughout his autobiography *My Rise* (1928), and he did so in order to posit a notion of citizenship based on Italian blood.[11] But the language of race was much more pronounced and sharpened in Nazism. Nazi ideology strove to wean its subjects away from the international, class identity of Marxism toward a national and individual identity that was essentially racial. As Hitler wrote, "The Jewish doctrine of Marxism rejects the aristocratic principle of Nature and replaces the eternal privilege of power and strength by the mass of numbers. . . . Thus it denies the value of personality in man, contests the significance of nationality and race, and thereby withdraws from humanity the premise of its existence and its culture."[12] This passage contains two central tropes of Nazi nationalism: first, the belief in fixed hierarchies rooted in nature and, second, the willful conjoining of Jews and Marxists into one enemy that threatens the cohesion of the nation. Cohesion was to be achieved not only through the elimination of Jews and Marxists but also through the collective, affirmative recognition of the Aryan as the paragon of races. Nazi policy reconfigured citizenship so that being German was not a function of one's place of birth but an explicit function of one's racial status as a physically healthy, genetically sound Aryan.

Fascism's second attack on the "given bases of political life" was its militarization of the national culture. Walter Benjamin saw the cult of the warrior as essential to fascism because it elevated violence and war as the highest of virtues while aestheticizing blood, martyrdom, and sacrifice.[13] Like many of their most ardent followers, both Hitler and Mussolini were profoundly shaped by their experiences in the First World War. They "found themselves" in the fraternal bonding of the battlefield, and their political awakening came when they realized that their uniformed brotherhood had been "stabbed in the back" by socialists, parliamentarians, and other traitors at home.[14] When fascism was officially born at a meeting in Milan in March 1919, the young movement called itself the Fasci di Combattimento, or, approximately, "fraternities of combat." The most honored of its members were war veterans called the *arditi*, Italian commandos who symbolized action, decisiveness, bravery, and the spirit of national sacrifice; the black shirt of their uniforms became the signature of Italian fascist style.[15]

To Hitler, the army was a school of virtue, and the nation was to be remolded in its image. In *Mein Kampf* he wrote,

> What the German people owes to the army can be briefly summed up in a single word, to wit: everything. The army trained men for unconditional responsibility at a time when this quality had grown rare and evasion of it was becoming more and more the order of the day, starting with the model prototype of all irresponsibility, the parliament.... it was the school that still taught the individual German not to seek the salvation of the nation in lying phrases about an international brotherhood between Negroes, Germans, Chinese, French, etc., but in the force and solidarity of our own nation. The army trained men in resolution while elsewhere in life indecision and doubt were beginning to determine the actions of men.[16]

In effect, the militarization of civil society meant that the agent of fascism was male. As Klaus Theweleit argued, the feminine was the antithesis of virtue in the fascist lexicon—it was pacifistic, unclear, disruptive to male unity—and had to be purged through overt misogyny. Meanwhile, the class identity of the left, predicated on "lying phrases" of international and interracial solidarity, was to be made obsolete through the violent reality of war, which naturally elevates the virtues of race and nation; in Nazism, war is the natural means of expression for the Aryan, who constantly strives to expand his living space through conquest of lesser races.[17] War, in other words, is the most effective vehicle for forging a national identity because it works to efface alternative forms of affiliation, melding a class-divided nation into a singular race. Not uncoincidentally, the *fasces,* the original symbol of fascism, was an axe surrounded by a bundle of rods, an ancient Roman icon signifying the unity of the people around the violent authority of the state. Yet the military model allowed this race to remain internally differentiated and unequal, its chain of command—commander, officers, noncommissioned officers, enlisted men—preserving a transparent hierarchy in which each member knows his place. This warrior cult was institutionalized through the staging of martial virtue in mass rituals, a punitive campaign against homosexual men, an educational system that emphasized physical activity over intellect, and universal male conscription during the war itself.

Whether imperial Japan was a fascist state has been heavily contested. Most European and American historians reject the label as an apt descriptor of this regime, while many of their Japanese colleagues have insisted on its applicability. Arguments against its application to Japan tend to hinge on the claim that its authoritarian system was elite driven and hence does not possess a close family resemblance to the regimes of Italy and Germany. Other scholars, while not denying imperial Japan's elite leadership, point to ideological similarities between its government and those of the other Axis powers that are close enough to justify labeling it fascist; implicitly, these scholars call for a new definition of fascism that de-centers European models.[18] While I am persuaded by the latter argument, in this book I focus on Europe, not Asia, when discussing fascism outside the United States because, to Americans, imperial Japan was only sporadically legible as a fascist state. Asian left-wing partisans who fought the Japanese occupation of their countries, including Luis Taruc, Ho Chi Minh, and Mao Zedong, regularly used the term to describe their enemy, and the designation of the occupiers as fascist passed into the official language of the Chinese state after the revolution. In the United States, the American League for Peace and Democracy (ALPD) in the late 1930s viewed China as one of the world's most important battlegrounds, second only to Spain. Yet even members of the league disagreed on whether the Japanese state was fascist or whether it should be regarded as a related form of militarism. The confusion persisted into the war years and beyond, the phrase "Japanese militarism" becoming a common resolution.[19]

Far from trying to present an exhaustive or complete account of historical fascism, I wanted to give a sense of the political characteristics that are critical to understanding both its presence in the United States and its survival after the Second World War. For the purposes of this book, it is also necessary to briefly consider how major historians have dealt with the possibilities of its reincarnation after 1945 inside and outside Europe. In short, the idea that fascism survived the Second World War is no longer a controversial idea among historians; however, as might be expected, there is no consensus as to which national arena, if any, presents the ripest conditions for its full rebirth. In the early 1960s the German historian Ernst Nolte asserted that fascism was effectively buried in 1945, and other eminent scholars followed suit. But by the 1990s this assessment of the European scene changed in light of ethnic cleansing in the Balkans, the decline of social democracy, and the mainstreaming of radical right parties.[20]

In considering the continuity of fascism after the Second World War, one must distinguish between two things: the existence of fascist or fascist-like movements within ostensibly nonfascist states and the nightmarish reconstitution of a fully fascist government. As to the first, no one any longer denies that neofascist groups as well as mainstream radical right parties that draw inspiration, ideas, and personnel from such groups are a reality of modern and postmodern societies across the world and will be for some time. In 1991 Griffin wrote, "As a *political ideology* capable of spawning new movements [fascism] should be treated as a permanent feature of modern political culture."[21] Since then, the heirs to historical fascism have entered mainstream politics in a number of European countries. The first neofascist party to participate in a European majority government was the Italian Movimento Sociale Italiano (MSI), founded in 1946 as the direct heir of Mussolini's PNF. In 1994 the conservative Silvio Berlusconi emerged as the leader of a coalition government when the MSI joined other conservative and rightist parties to form a parliamentary majority.[22] Relying primarily on anti-immigrant sentiments, the Front National in France, Jörg Haider's Freiheitspartei in Austria, the National Front in Britain, the Jobbik party in Hungary (clad in the symbols of the fascist Arrow Cross party from the Second World War), and, more recently, the Golden Dawn in Greece have also moved from margin to mainstream in recent decades.

The larger question here is the continued existence of such groups outside of Europe and whether any of them could ever rebuild an actual fascist state. Major historians are univocal in their doubts about the formation of a future Fourth Reich in Western Europe, as a deepening belief in parliamentary democracy since 1945 has ensured that neofascist parties will remain single-issue movements driven by a narrowly anti-immigrant agenda.[23] It is outside of Western Europe where some scholars urge vigilance. The politically conservative Stanley Payne, for instance, sees the Middle East, Eastern Europe, and Africa as the most likely grounds for a resurgent fascism, and he largely agrees with the assertion of George H. W. Bush in 1990 that Saddam Hussein represented the "Hitler of Our Time."[24] From a liberal perspective, Robert Paxton agrees that the Middle East and Eastern Europe could be future sites, but Paxton sees the United States as a possible danger as well. Though he argues that fascism will never again appear in its exact, pre-1945 form, he urges us to beware of its "functional equivalent." The functional equivalent would not be an "exact repetition" of the NSDAP or PNF but would create fresh symbols to organize the population around national regeneration, encouraging citizens to "give up free institutions" in the process.[25] Paxton describes a potential incarnation in the United States as follows:

> No swastikas in an American fascism, but Stars and Stripes (or Stars and Bars) and Christian crosses. No fascist salute, but mass recitations of the pledge of allegiance. These symbols contain no whiff of fascism in themselves, of course, but an American fascism would transform them into obligatory litmus tests for detecting the internal enemy. . . . Around such reassuring language and symbols and in the event of some redoubtable setback to national prestige, Americans might support an enterprise of forcible national regeneration, unification, and purification.

To Paxton, Americans are well on their way to fascism when jittery conservatives begin looking for "tougher allies" and when establishment politicians appeal to the same mobilizing passions as these brutish allies, giving up "the due process of law" to organize the public around racist and nationalist demagoguery.[26]

But given the legal codification of the Japanese American internment, slavery, Jim Crow, the extermination of Native Americans, and the Naturalization Law of 1790, which made whiteness the basis of U.S. citizenship until its effective repeal in 1952, one could rightly ask whether Paxton's analysis valorizes the due process of law in the United States. If intense racialization has occurred under the normal auspices of the country's liberal democratic system, why single out fascism as a singular threat? Can paying too much attention to fascism help to normalize and render invisible the workings of a more established mode of injustice? For centuries the West has perpetrated racialized mass death without the help of fascist demagogues: examples include the millions dead as a result of the African slave trade, the extermination of indigenous peoples through settler colonialism, and the preventable famines of European imperialism, which, as Mike Davis has recently estimated, claimed at least thirty million lives in three late nineteenth-century catastrophes alone.[27] This dark history made many African Americans and colonial subjects apathetic toward Allied wartime rhetoric, at least initially (see chapter 6).

Since the eighteenth century these crimes have been perpetrated not under fascism but under the auspices of what can be termed liberalism. When I refer to liberals in this book, I rely on the American sense of the word, that is, people whose politics are left of center yet who, unlike leftists, do not wish to radically reshape the given bases of society. But when I use the terms *liberalism* and *the liberal state,* I evoke their European meanings, which do not indicate a distinct left/right orientation. This liberalism commonly refers to a representative system of government grounded in the Enlightenment, one which guarantees its citizens the freedoms of speech, press, and association. Yet because it was championed by the bourgeois founders of modern states in western Europe and the Americas, many of its iterations have linked human freedom with the capitalist marketplace. But capitalist exploitation, which requires hierarchy and political exclusion for its smooth reproduction, undercuts liberalism's leveling impulses. In the attempt to resolve this contradiction, the Western imperial powers created a dual system consisting of both a body of free citizens with constitutionally protected rights of life, liberty, and property and a set of spaces for those outside the social contract who are excluded as political subjects but included as objects of political power and sources of exploited labor.[28] The German conservative Carl Schmitt called attention to this dynamic, arguing that Western democracy offers an internally homogenous "equality of equals" that always depends on the exclusion of the foreign, both internally and externally.[29]

Yet the histories of violence shared by fascism and liberalism do not make the two systems moral equivalents, and the fact that both have tended to preserve capitalist social relations does not make them, in essence, the same. Viewed in the context of liberalism's dual system, fascism is a specific mode of denying formal political rights such as multiparty elections, free speech, and free press to almost all of its subjects and of forcibly closing any space for nonhierarchical, democratic mobilization, actual or potential. After all, a strand within socialism, namely, social democracy, has argued that liberalism is not the exclusive property of its bourgeois originators and can be repurposed for working-class ends; indeed, working-class and subaltern organizing is largely responsible for the extension of political rights to the lower ranks. Further, fascism accelerates and intensifies the violence of the societies from which it sprung. Given the more than sixty million dead in nine years of war, fascist regimes led to the deaths of more people than the dominant liberalism over any equivalent time span. In fascism, the space of social death, reserved only for some in the liberal capitalist state, grows in size to the point that it encompasses the social whole, while at the same time those marginalized in the old regime face intensified repression, even extermination (intellectuals of color drew most closely on this spatial model of fascism).

Scholars and cultural commentators often exalt liberalism as a bulwark against fascism. Weak or failed liberal states are fertile ground for fascist organizing, the argument goes, and thus any people with a broad-based faith in liberal freedoms can be counted on to keep the Blackshirts in check. But given the way it has been historically institutionalized under the auspices of capitalism, as a means to secure a range of social hierarchies, neither I nor most of the figures discussed in this book see liberalism as a ward against fascist mobilization. The dual system created by Enlightenment political thought, combined with the hierarchies required by capitalism, create a set of possessive investments among the privileged polity, investments which, when threatened under particular conditions, can become a truly demonic force. In 1951 Aimé Césaire wrote that Hitler was the demon inside every white, Christian bourgeois and that the defeated dictator "applied to Europe colonialist procedures which until then had been reserved exclusively for the Arabs of Algeria, the coolies of India, and the blacks of Africa."[30] As Césaire shrewdly observes, the possessive investments of the French, English, and Americans can take the form of those of the Germans precisely because Germans share a cultural field with other Western nations from which they cannot be neatly extricated. Indeed, Nazism was fueled by a biological racism begotten of colonialism that hardened across the West in the late nineteenth and early twentieth centuries. It is often forgotten that the Nazis learned eugenic theory from England and the United States: the Nazis' Law on Preventing Hereditarily Ill Progeny, for instance, was modeled on legislation from the State of California.[31] For this reason American antifascist cultural production did not simply miss its mark when ascribing fascism to a society whose main crimes arise from liberalism. Rather, it worked to check liberalism from further degenerating into the nightmare of its own contradictions. Laboring under the banner of antifascism, cultural producers went on the offensive, attacking the very ground of fascism by showing how it can emerge from the hierarchies and dual political spheres of the dominant liberalism.

This book is not guided by a fear that retrograde militarists will establish the functional equivalent of a fascist government in the United States: an irony-driven consumer culture, the post–civil rights institutionalization, however flawed, of multiculturalism, and the absence of an anxiety-producing, organized left make an American Reich hard to imagine at present. But conditions change, and the rise of such a state is not impossible. More pressing, however, is that key historical and institutional dynamics in the United States have persistently facilitated the emergence of fascist and fascistoid groups. The country has its own cult of the warrior fueled by a history of frontier violence, empire building, and, since the Cold War, vast outlays of military spending that have helped to create a permanently militarized culture. Add the venerable racialized dual system of liberalism and a surprisingly tenacious streak of anticommunism to which the American warrior cult is linked, and you have very real foundations for would-be fascists to build on as their relative social privileges become threatened. Consequently, in the United States, as in Europe, there are actors on the political stage who represent neofascist functional equivalents, and they have shifted the political center at a number of critical junctures, as the following chapters will attest.

To begin to recognize these actors and to discern which movements are likely to be animated by a possessive investment in relative social privilege, one must acknowledge something once widely regarded as self-evident: fascism's status as a right-wing movement. Curiously, there is little debate among scholars, including scholars on the left, that even the worst communist regimes are left wing in nature. Such consensus is no longer the case with regard to fascism and the right. Although the recent historiography of fascism is in full agreement that it is not a left-wing movement, there is a debate about whether it constitutes a properly right-wing phenomenon, and consequently contemporary historiography has often been out of synch with a popular majority on this issue, particularly in Europe. While many historians, including Griffin, still feel comfortable describing fascism as a right-wing movement, others, like Payne, Zeev Sternhell, and D. S. Lewis, prefer to place it outside the categories of left and right, mainly because of its eclectic economic policy.[32] Yet in Europe and in the United States for much of its history fascism has often been synonymous with the far right among the public at large.[33] To cite a personal example, when I lived in Germany and was learning the language, I once asked a friend there if a certain politician from the Christian Democratic Party was right wing (*rechts*). Taken aback, he politely informed me that conservative politicians prefer to be called *conservativ* because in Germany *rechts* is generally associated with Nazis.

No major scholar in this field has attempted to actually define the terms *left* and *right* when assigning fascism to a place on the political spectrum. Left and right first appeared as terms of political cartography during the French Revolution of 1789, when supporters of the revolution seated themselves to the left of the National Assembly while those backing the king gathered to the right. After the Bourbon Restoration in the 1820s, the usage of the terms as political markers gradually spread beyond the French context.[34] As political designations, left and right are positional: they do not encompass a consistent set of policies and ideologies across space and time; the belief in free markets and a rejection of statism, for example, have not been dependable markers of the political right over the past two centuries. Rather, left and right are relational terms whose specific contents change over time within diverse national contexts. As the Italian political scientist Norberto Bobbio has argued, however, this does not mean they are simply "empty vessels" that can be filled with any random content; rather, there are broad epistemological assumptions that consistently distinguish left- and right-wing thought.[35] Drawing on Bobbio, the French historian Marcel Gauchet, and the American studies scholar Nikhil Pal Singh, one could synthesize the following definitions of left and right in the West, at least insofar as each position conceives the nation. In short, what places one to the left or to the right is not one's stance toward big government versus small government (this view projects contemporary debates in the United States backward in time and across oceans). More fundamentally, it is our views on social hierarchy and human equality, and how we map these views onto the nation, that position us to the left or to the right.

For a starting point, consider Bobbio's claim that as one moves to the left, people are seen as more equal than unequal, and that as one moves to the right, people are seen as more unequal than equal. In regard to the national arena, the political left tends to see division arising from hierarchies and inequalities which are unnecessary and unjust; it calls attention to structural divides within the nation in the hope of bringing about eventual reconciliation. Those who are slightly to the left, American liberals, for instance, might see some social hierarchies as being unchangeable, but on the whole and like others to the left, they see human beings as more equal than unequal. The right, on the other hand, tends to see social hierarchies within the nation as unavoidable, even natural or desirable, and works toward a nation that is organically unified with many of its inequalities intact, a nation wherein each person acknowledges his or her proper position. The right certainly acknowledges the existence of internal division but sees it as harmful and artificial, something created by those who do not recognize the nation's fundamental unity. Unlike the left, the right therefore tends to locate the ultimate threat abroad.

For the hard right, all this is sharpened: domestic elements that do not fit its narrative of the nation are rendered as foreign, and fatal disunities plaguing the national body are attributed to these alleged outside elements.[36] In other words, the epistemology of the hard right, past and present, is characterized by an often racialized fear of foreignness and by a tendency to render domestic groups as foreign in its drive for a national unity fully compatible with social hierarchy. If one listens carefully, antifascism reveals how the far right brazenly uses nationalism as a means of organizing social hierarchies, and how it does so by making rigid distinctions between the domestic and the foreign, ultimately de-naturalizing those who do not fit their sense of the nation. One early twenty-first-century example is the American who renders Barack Obama foreign by claiming he is a Muslim and has no birth certificate—in actuality, because he does not fit a particular narrative either of the United States or of what an allegedly true American looks like. Rightist American sympathizers of Hitler, Mussolini, and Franco in the 1930s likewise insisted that Franklin D. Roosevelt was actually a Jew and referred to him as "Frankly Deceitful Rosenvelt"[37] (fig. 1). In itself, the claim that Obama is Muslim does not prove the contemporary Islamophobe to be a fascist: rather, it illustrates why she or he (as well as the anti-Semite of the thirties) are both situated on the hard right. They are placed there because they share a deep structure of thought spanning a century and an ocean, one which, to be sure, has intersected with actual fascism.

This example illustrates a potential danger as well. When a conservative labels a liberal a communist or when a leftist calls an ordinary conservative a fascist, they often engage in a behavior one could call tilting the scale. That is to say, if someone's politics are slightly to the left or the right, they are erroneously moved to the extreme of the pole. This can also apply to the mislabeling of specific events or policies, for example, when universal health care is characterized as communistic or the bombing of Hanoi as fascist. To minimize this problem, historians of fascism developed the concept of the fascist minimum, often a bulleted list of benchmarks which someone or something must meet in order to be considered fascist. Such an approach makes it more difficult to apply the label to a contemporary phenomenon on the basis of a single trait it may share with the evils of the past (for example, Hillary Clinton supported after-school programs, Hitler supported after-school programs, therefore . . .). Thus in the example above, to observe that the nationalism of Tea Party Islamophobes and the NSDAP "overlap"—in that both are marked by the epistemology of the political far right—is not to say they are both fascist. The range of ideological beliefs in which an utterance is embedded is what moves its speaker into fascist territory. In the case of Gerald Winrod, a Hitler supporter who adamantly proclaimed FDR's Jewishness in the 1930s, these conditions certainly were present, as his wider belief system met a consistent fascist pattern. Be that as it may, one is justified in raising the alarm when a number of fascist traits converge, even if they are not in their most fully developed form.

Prudence dictates that one should also make clear when modern political actors with xenophobic tendencies are *not* fascist. Many constituents of the Tea Party coalition, for example, are strongly guided by a belief in parliamentary democracy and are preoccupied with economics. So long as these elements predominate, it is not a fascist movement per se, but one that sharpens the exclusionary dual system of rights within liberalism. Yet while liberals and the left use the term *fascism* imprecisely when they apply it to any manifestation of conservatism, there is a strand of the American right that indeed constitutes a functional equivalent of fascist mobilization, one in which too many hallmark traits converge to be ignored. Antifascisms directed at this particular strand of reaction are the focus of this book.

Even if one agrees that calling fascism still has its place, one is left to explain the politics of haunting, that is, how one's relationship to a disturbing, even traumatic, past can be socially generative. Two theories of memory fittingly high-

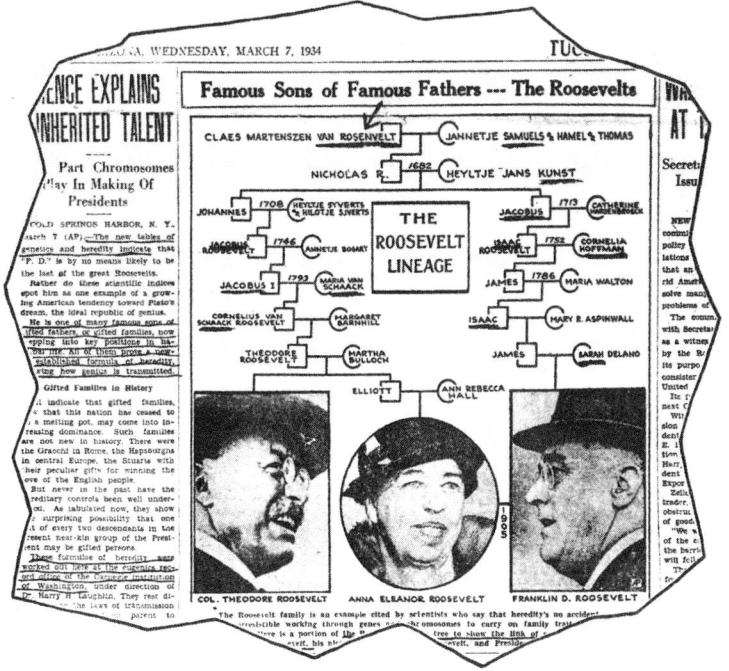

FIGURE 1. Front page of Gerald Winrod's profascist newspaper *The Revealer*, October 15, 1936. Courtesy Avedis Derounian/John Roy Carlson Collection, National Association for Armenian Studies and Research.

light the stakes of antifascism in the postwar United States: those of Raymond Williams and Walter Benjamin.

Antifascism, as I have argued, was one of the main "causes" of the American left from the 1930s through the Second World War. Many of the writers and activists who produced work in the 1950s and 1960s and whom I discuss here—Arthur Miller, William Shirer, Betty Friedan, Rod Serling, William Patterson, Harry Hay—were adults during the Second World War. Whether or not they were politically active at the time, their worldviews were indelibly stamped by the antifascist discourses of their generation. Others, like Bobby Seale, Chris Hedges, Philip Roth, and the activists of the AIDS Coalition to Unleash Power, or ACT UP, were children during the war or were born after 1945. They absorbed the antifascism of the Old Left secondhand, mediated by the sociohistorical dynamics of the postwar period: the Cold War, civil rights, and a mass consumer society. Some, like Avram Finkelstein and Charles Kreloff of the Silence = Death Project in the 1980s, absorbed it more directly from their parents (see chapter 7). In their hands, antifascism was further transformed. While antifascism is not a static discourse, but one continuously updated to meet new social challenges, its primary reference points for writers and activists after the Second World War always lay in the past. To write of Joseph McCarthy, Barry Goldwater, George Wallace, or Jerry Falwell as mobilizing fascist passions, for example, is to situate them in relation to a bygone struggle. While the spirit of fascism may never die, to speak its name in the postwar world is ultimately to allude to the thirties and forties, a time when actual fascist states threatened the very possibility of a future democratic society.

Revisiting Williams's concept of "residual culture" is helpful in theorizing the politics of such gestures. Williams introduced the categories of dominant, emergent, and residual culture to provide a level of historical specificity not offered by the older Marxist concept of stages, for example, feudalism and monopoly capital. Williams's idea of dominant culture is based on Antonio's Gramsci's notion of the hegemonic: it is the culture that results when a historic bloc, a particular coalition of social forces, wins consent by successfully injecting their version of common sense into the public consciousness for a period of time. For example, the left and liberal Popular Front of the thirties and forties greatly influenced the dominant culture of the time but never attained complete hegemony. Its influence derived from the role it played in the larger cultural alliance of the New Deal, which was the real hegemonic force of this period.[38] In the decades after 1945 the values and policies of the Cold War—initially pushed by an elite alliance of liberal and conservative policymakers and almost immediately adopted by the American business and military establishment—rapidly became the dominant culture of the United States.

But older cultural modes do not simply exit the historical stage when new ones take their place. Williams uses the concept of residual culture to describe this phenomenon:

> The residual, by definition, has been effectively formed in the past, but it is still active in the cultural process, not only and often not at all as an element of the past, but as an effective element of the present. Thus certain experiences, meanings, and values which cannot be expressed or substantially verified in terms of the dominant culture, are nevertheless lived and practiced on the basis of the residue—cultural as well as social—of some previous social and cultural institution or formation. It is crucial to distinguish this aspect of the residual, which may have *an alternative or even oppositional relation to the dominant culture,* from that active manifestation of the residual which has been wholly or largely incorporated into the dominant culture [emphasis added].[39]

Residual culture, in other words, can take two forms. First, it can be a kind of collective memory, undigested within the dominant order, which serves as a reservoir for oppositional energies in the present. Second, it can be an earlier set of no-longer-hegemonic values incorporated within a new dominant culture. A given residue can serve both functions at once. Williams discusses the example of the organic rural community, which can be used to imagine alternatives to urban, industrial capitalism or can be employed in the escapist imagery of real estate advertising.

Likewise, the defeat of historical fascism in 1945, one of the crowning achievements of the New Deal, dominant culture, has served both of these ends in the postwar United States: the oppositional and the conservative. One need not look far into contemporary American popular culture to find memories of the Second World War severed from antifascism: for example, conflations of Hitler and Stalin, vague accounts of the war as a time of national unity, History Channel homages to D-Day and the military technologies of the war, and so forth. All of these are ways in which the Second World War has been incorporated into later, dominant cultures of American exceptionalism and often without a trace of Henry Wallace or Sinclair Lewis. But for the writers and activists discussed in this book, the experience of the 1930s and 1940s, mediated by the cultural work of the Popular Front, also lingered in the 1950s and beyond. The antifascisms of the Popular Front and New Deal formed a residual culture which they used to articulate their opposition to later, dominant cultures. And they often looked backward precisely because the earlier struggle against fascism—culminating in a military victory that seemed to spell the end of right-wing nationalism—augured hope for a better world which they felt was forgotten or even betrayed in the America of the Cold War years that followed. Theirs was the oppositional form of residual culture, driven by a sense of broken promises, lost opportunities, and devalued experiences. As Williams writes, this sense entails "a reaching back to those meanings and values which were created in actual societies and actual situations in the past, and which still seem to have significance because they represent areas of human experience, aspiration, and achievement which the dominant culture neglects, undervalues, opposes, represses, or even cannot recognize."[40]

Benjamin helps complete the circuit, offering a model of how residual culture can be turned to emancipatory ends; his work is pertinent as well because it is directly informed by the fight against fascism. In his famous essay "Theses on the Philosophy of History" (1940) Benjamin offered his notion of "messianic time" (*messianisch*), which he contrasted with "homogenous, empty time" (*eine homogene und leere Zeit*).[41] The latter is the teleological temporality held by bourgeois historicism and social democrats. It is homogenous because teleology renders all historical periods the same by welding them into a common upward trajectory; and empty because it drains history of contemporary import by positioning all prior moments as having already spent their relevance through their contributions to the present. The historical materialist, who operates on messianic time, feels that the past lives in the present because he recognizes that the victories and defeats of bygone eras have yet to be redeemed. "Nothing that has ever happened," Benjamin writes, "should be regarded as lost for history. Only a redeemed mankind receives the fullness of its past—which is to say, only for a redeemed mankind has its past become citable in all its moments." The historical materialist, accordingly, must work to make the past "citable" and do so by taking the materials and the eras she examines and "blasting" them out of "homogenous, empty time."[42] In the early postwar decades, the victory over fascism and the millions of lives consumed in the process were felt by many antifascists, in the United States and elsewhere, to be an unredeemed struggle they tried to make present, or citable, through their works. Some antifascists arguably gleaned a messianic sense of time ("the past as charged with the time of the now," to quote Benjamin) from their lived experience of dashed hopes, lost comrades, and devalued aspirations.

Productive antifascism, as I have suggested, is always at least grounded in history, however difficult it is to access, and because of this enables effective social action. The antifascists I discuss in this book certainly define fascism more flexibly than many historians, seeing it as manifest in a broader range of situations than many of their academic counterparts. But their notion of fascism is generally grounded, even if un-honed, by scholarly research. When equipped with a more than facile knowledge of fascism and guided by a general sense of its real nature, those who labored to describe living continuities between postwar

U.S. politics and historical fascism essentially reignited an earlier struggle in the hope of redeeming the past and securing the future. The following chapters illuminate how social critics on the left have put their fears of fascism to use, and, in so doing, they reveal instances of both insight and hyperbole. Uncovering this past will, I hope, serve as a guide to those in the present who are properly disturbed by the political scene unfolding about them but are unsure of what to name it.

CHAPTER **2**
From Margin to Mainstream
American Antifascism to 1945

> So far from any longer regarding it as a menace ... or invidiously comparing it with democracy or parliamentary rule, the world outside Italy is now interested only in the fact that fascism works.... Nearly seven years ago a parallel was drawn in this column between the then comparatively new fascist system in Italy and a receivership for a corporation. That parallel still holds good.
> Wall Street Journal, October 29, 1932

> Whether or not America goes fascist depends on who gets organized first.
> American League Against War and Fascism, 1936

The *Chicago Daily Tribune*, owned and edited by a retired colonel named Robert McCormick, was one of the leading conservative American dailies of the 1930s. Along with the Hearst Press and the newspapers of Eleanor "Cissy" Patterson, it was known for its vehement critiques of the New Deal, the labor movement, and world communism. Yet the *Tribune*'s editorial views on U.S. military deployments abroad may come as a surprise to those familiar with the thrust of postwar conservatism. In 1938, in an editorial titled "The War Mongers," the paper lashed out against antifascist demonstrators in London who protested Neville Chamberlain's appeasement policy:

> There were no munition makers, no captains of industry and no international bankers in the crowd which demonstrated in London for continued opposition to Hitler. The demonstrators were recruited from the Labor party and the groups to the left of it. Much the same picture is presented in France. There the outspoken criticism of the Chamberlain-Daladier policy comes from the Socialist and communist press. The left wingers, not only in Europe but also in this country, prefer the risks of war to the risks of peace. Left wing and pacifist are no longer synonymous, as they were twenty years and even ten years ago. The left wing has given its full support to preparations for war in all the important democratic countries and today, by and large, it is whooping for war and characterizing the refusal of Chamberlain and Daladier to resort to arms as both stupid and craven. ... The left wing is bellicose. It foresees a war and hopes to engage the United States in the conflict to save the world for bolshevism.[1]

Likely written by McCormick himself, these words serve as a proper introduction to the upside-down political world of the late thirties, a world in which conservatives could label those on the left war mongers while promoting a small-sized military at home and a cautious diplomatic strategy in foreign affairs. To be sure, the charge of war monger is overstated here. Throughout the decade of the Depression the American left was critical of the deployment of U.S. troops abroad and worked against the creation of a militarist culture at home. And after the outbreak of general war in Europe following the invasion of Poland in September 1939, many conservatives advocated an enlarged military to guard American borders. But in its broad strokes the *Tribune*'s portrait is correct. In the 1930s leftists and left-liberals in North America and Europe were the main forces urging their governments and their fellow citizens to take strong action against the regimes of Italy, Germany, and Japan, while agitating against what they saw as fascist fifth columns in their own countries (the very phrase *fifth column* entered the English language by way of the antifascist struggle of the Spanish Civil War).[2] Unlike later conservative uses of the term, left and liberal warnings of a fifth column in the United States were metaphoric, a reference not to a foreign-financed force or one alien in spirit but to a dangerous antidemocratic impulse quite native to the soil, born of domestic injustices and acting in tandem with nightmarish equivalents in other lands.

In recollecting the 1930s, scholars and popular commentators often overlook the general left–right divide on the issue of fascism, perhaps out of fear of seeming partisan. However, lurking under the *Tribune*'s charge that antifascists wished to "save the world for bolshevism" is the reality that many conservatives and rightists recognized in fascism the rudiments of a shared worldview: the need for a muscular response to Marxism and organized labor; a desire to restore national honor and an organic national unity; and the overall urge to maintain order, that is, social hierarchy, without regard to democratic process. Open admiration for Hitler was uncommon among American conservatives after his first year in power, unlike the widespread good feelings about the Nazis within the British Conservative Party, which persisted up to 1938. But the American business press and right-of-center Americans generally lauded Mussolini's experiment, along with other European fascisms, up until the middle of the decade. Even after many conservatives in the United States soured on fascism after the invasion of Ethiopia in 1935, their earlier recognition of a mutual worldview led them to see fascism as a singular threat not to world civilization but to economic predictability. Later in the decade they may have fretted that FDR's New Deal was a step toward dictatorship, but they were not the ones urging a dramatic cultural, political, and even military campaign focused on stopping fascism at home and abroad. And influential figures on the right, most notably Father Charles Coughlin, the country's first right-wing radio personality, continued to describe Hitler, Mussolini, and Franco as "defense mechanisms against communism" up until the bombing of Pearl Harbor. It should come as no surprise that the volunteers who fought and died against the proxy armies of Hitler and Mussolini in the Spanish Civil War (1936–39) were not drawn from their ranks.

Most Americans did not become averse to fascism in the thirties merely because their political culture made them immune to its appeals. Rather, to paraphrase the epigraph above, an antifascist common sense emerged, in part, because of "who got organized first." In the decade before Pearl Harbor there was, perhaps for the last time in the nation's history, a real debate as to who constituted America's real enemies abroad. Was the enemy the Soviet Union, the fascist bloc, or both in equal measure? And given the debacle of the First World War, were the British really our friends? Even as early as the Spanish Civil War it was clear that the majority of Americans were listening more to one side of the debate than to the others. Data from the Gallup Polls, established in 1935, reveal that by the late 1930s the broad public agreed with liberals and the left about who was friend and foe abroad. When asked in December 1938, "Who would you want to see win if war broke out between Russia and Germany?," 83 percent said Russia and only 17 percent said Germany. That same year, by contrast, only 65 percent said they would support Britain and France if war broke out with Germany and Italy, with 32 percent favoring neither side. Similarly, 75 percent favored the Spanish loyalists throughout the late thirties, and 74 percent favored the Chinese in the struggle with Japan by June 1939.[3] Hitler and Mussolini were far more aggressive in foreign affairs than Stalin, and this no doubt helped to decide the issue. Nevertheless, public opinion swayed as it did despite a loud campaign emphasizing the singular danger of the communist menace in the United States and abroad, one waged by the National Association of Manufacturers and other business organizations, the Liberty League, the House Committee on Un-American Activities (HUAC), and conservative Catholics and Protestants.

After Hitler's accession to power in 1933, liberals and the left were at the forefront of the campaign against fascism because they recognized it, correctly, as a far-right movement that threatened their very existence. And the thirties, as Michael Denning has argued, was the moment in which the left was at the height of its influence in American history. The vast majority of the public shared the left–liberal view that a "moral economy" was needed to tame the devastation of laissez-faire capitalism.[4] In this milieu, liberals and the left saw fascism as a malign force at home and abroad, one which made a moral economy impossible. Fascism's cultural revolution, centered on race and nation, worked to destroy the left's very cultural ground by violently etching domestic hierarchies in stone and severing the national polity from a global humanity. For this reason, antifascism was not one campaign among many for the left in the thirties. Rather, to many of its activists and cultural producers it conceptually unified a wide range of struggles, including the campaign to organize unions and to create a social safety net, the battle against racial injustice and imperialism, and the fight for gender equality in the workplace and beyond. It served so many political ends at once because antifascists felt that to wean their contemporaries away from their enemy's appeal, the public needed to experience the benefits of a world without strict social hierarchies.

The next two chapters historicize the politics and cultural impact of left-liberal antifascism in the United States from the early 1930s up to 1945. This chapter examines the evolution of its strategies and campaigns, emphasizing its efforts to build consensus around the idea that fascism constituted a singular menace in world affairs. Unlike many studies of midcentury American radicalism, mine evaluates the left's influence by situating its ideas and programs within the broader public sphere, mapping their relationship to evolving notions of fascism exhibited in the center and to the right of the political spectrum. Identifying points of convergence between left antifascism, mainstream political opinion, and public policy allows us to see antifascism as something that never became hegemonic within U.S. foreign policy but yet was engrained in the cultural common sense of broad publics. The strength of the social forces aligned against antifascism as well as the fissures within it ensured that the Second World War was not the genuinely antiracist and social democratic People's War envisioned by the left. Yet in defining fascism as a singular threat and outlining its contours, the antifascist cultural work of the 1930s and the war years would help build the labor movement, solidify the New Deal as a structure of feeling, provide important cultural groundwork for antiracist struggles, and create a remarkably tenacious political grammar that would help place the hard right on the defensive for a generation.

I break down the antifascist front of the 1930s and 1940s into three major streams. First, I consider the communist left, centered around the Communist Party U.S.A. (CPUSA), which enjoyed an influence far wider than party membership numbers suggest. Founded in 1919, the CPUSA remained relatively small in the 1920s. But during the Depression, as many Americans looked to the seemingly stable Soviet Union as an answer to the economic crisis, the CPUSA rapidly eclipsed the older Socialist Party to become the most dynamic organization on the left. Its thousands of organizers did not just "soap-box" for communism; rather, they were a major organizing force for racial justice, labor unions, a social safety net, and an anti-imperial foreign policy. The party initiated a number of broad, united front groups expressly devoted to antifascism, including the American League Against War and Fascism (ALAWF; later, the American League for Peace and Democracy), the Hollywood Anti-Nazi League, the Harlem-based Provisional Committee for the Defense of Ethiopia, the Joint Anti-Fascist Refugee Committee, the American Student Union, and the National Council of American-Soviet Friendship. I discuss these umbrella groups under the heading of the communist left even though many of their members and affiliates were not communists and their positions did not always coincide with other party-generated organizations. The ALAWF was the most significant of these CPUSA-initiated organizations insofar as it received a shocking degree of support from noncommunists, including members of the Roosevelt administration.

A second major formation I consider is the socialists, a diffuse but still notable strand of the left in the 1930s. The American Socialist Party, founded in 1901 and led during its peak years by Eugene V. Debs, was truly a mass movement before the First World War, with a press of over three hundred periodicals enjoying several million readers across the country. By the thirties, however, despite the leadership of the charismatic, well-respected Norman Thomas, its membership had dwindled dramatically. Its remaining constituents split into factions: the so-called Old Guard, closely associated with the American Federation of Labor (AFL), the "Militants" grouped around Thomas, and a Trotskyist faction that arose in the mid-1930s and later split to form the Socialist Workers' Party (SWP) in 1938. Before the formation of the SWP, the small but vibrant Trotskyist movement operated through the Communist League of America (1928–34) and the Workers' Party of the United States (1934–36). Though quite diverse in terms of ideology and strategy, the socialists were united both in their desire to create a socialism independent of the Stalinist model and in their highly critical stance toward the policies of the USSR (indeed, they were even more critical than the liberals).[5] The Old Guard, through the Jewish Labor Committee (JLC), helped to bring antifascism into the mainstream to a degree not adequately acknowledged in broader histories of the Depression-era left.

Third, there were the liberals, many of whom were part of the state apparatus in the 1930s and 1940s. Some produced their work directly under the auspices of the New Deal state, where they were guided by immediate political considerations and compromises, while others worked through pressure groups and publications intended to influence public opinion. The former included President Roosevelt and other high-level public officials such as Henry Wallace, Harold Ickes, and Frances Parkman; those who produced for state cultural organizations like the Federal Theater Project; and, during wartime, those working in state agencies like the Office of Facts and Figures (OFF), the Office of War Information (OWI), the Office of Strategic Services, and the State and Treasury Departments. Outside the official bodies of the New Deal state, the liberal journals the *New Republic,* the *Nation, Christian Century,* and *Common Sense* published a substantial amount of antifascist commentary and reportage by such writers as Lewis Mumford, Bruce Bliven, Malcolm Cowley, and Waldo Frank, some of whom developed close ties to the Roosevelt administration. The radio work of Norman Corwin and Archibald MacLeish also marked crucial interventions. Finally, liberal pressure groups such as the Friends of Democracy, AJC, the American Committee Against Fascist Oppression, Samuel Untermyer's Non-Sectarian Anti-Nazi League, the American Council Against Nazi Propaganda, the American Civil Liberties Union (ACLU), the academic-led Institute for Propaganda Analysis, and the later Committee to Defend America by Aiding the Allies all engaged in antifascist lobbying and organizing. While African American intellectuals and activists engaged in politics in ways that could be characterized as either liberal, socialist, or communist, they produced a brand of antifascism distinctly marked by a diasporic anti-imperialism and an experience of racial abjection in the United States. Hence I discuss the antifascisms of the *Pittsburgh Courier,* the *Chicago Defender,* and the *Crisis,* of figures such as W. E. B. Du Bois, William Patterson, and George Padmore independently, in these chapters and in chapter 6.

The prominence of communists—communists who praised Stalin's Soviet Union—in a coalition devoted to fighting authoritarianism is one of the ironies of history. Communists outside the USSR were tragically blind to the horrors transpiring in the Soviet Union in the 1930s, and their advocacy of that state worked to silence the suffering of Stalin's victims. However, one should not reduce all their efforts to such blindness. American-based communists and noncommunists worked together, for a time, to forge a democratic politics which alleviated domestic injustices, particularly those based on class and race, and in a manner that did not even begin to mirror Stalin's horrors. Communists figured prominently in a force from below that pressured Roosevelt and Congress to adopt some of the more dramatic legislation of the New Deal, including the Wagner Act (1935), the Social Security Act (1935), and the Fair Labor Standards Act (1938). Their activists built the unions of the Congress of Industrial Organizations that would increase the standard of living of working people in the United States.[6] Unlike American rightist supporters of fascism, their efforts at home and in foreign arenas outside the USSR worked to lessen human suffering, not to widen it—they tended to practice, in other words, what they did not always preach. That said, their uncritical marriage to a particular nation-state, albeit an adoptive one, inevitably placed them on a collision course with true human rights and in the process tarnished the moral legitimacy of the left by the close of the Depression.

Restoring Order: American Support for Fascism before Pearl Harbor

In October 1922 the Italian Partito Nazionale Fascista (PNF) engaged a show of force in Rome. Led by Mussolini, a political unknown outside Italy, twenty-five thousand PNF *squadristi,* colloquially known as Blackshirts, descended on the city armed with clubs. Though a coup d'etat was not their intent, it turned out to be the result. The police and the army units stationed in the city outnumbered and outgunned the squadristi, yet King Victor Emmanuel refused to declare martial law. The government promptly resigned, and on October 29 the king invited Mussolini to lead a parliamentary coalition. What came to be known in party mythology as the March on Rome was a complete success. Within three years Mussolini managed to consolidate his power, rendering political parties obsolete and vesting all political authority in himself. By January 1925 the first fascist state was firmly in place.[7]

After Il Duce's consolidation of power, many Americans expressed admiration for the new leader and the fresh concept of fascism he represented. Such praise did not noticeably diminish until more than a decade later, when Mussolini's troops invaded Ethiopia in October 1935. Surprisingly, there has been no comprehensive study of the American public's reaction to fascism abroad in the 1930s; despite the shelves of literature on Nazi Germany and the Second World War, there is to date no broad, book-length survey of American reactions to Hitler.[8] This absence begs for an explanation: given that the evidence shows the only real support for Hitler to be on the right side of the political spectrum, it underscores a possible unwillingness among post-Holocaust scholars to politicize what became the universal index of evil.

While a more comprehensive study of this issue will need to be undertaken, I offer a few observations about American sympathy for fascism abroad before Pearl Harbor. In the 1920s some old-line Progressives and a handful of liberals, including Charles Beard, Horace Kallen, Samuel Gompers, Ida Tarbell, and Lincoln Steffens, offered apologias for Italian fascism. This support, however, came from a minority of liberals and was relatively short-lived among their ranks.[9] Overwhelmingly, odes to fascist Italy came from conservatives and, perhaps most disturbing of all, from those in the business community. Discounting the brazenly fascist, uniformed, rabidly anti-Semitic emulators on the fringe of political life (for example, William Pelley's Silver Shirts, the German American Bund, and the New York– and Pennsylvania-based Khaki Shirts), the three most influential groups to lend a socially meaningful degree of moral support to Hitler, Franco, and Mussolini before December 1941 were the business community, socially conservative Catholics, and what I call the law-and-order right. Their moral support of controversial European regimes was uneven, some fascisms being more palatable than others (Hitler, for instance, did not win nearly as much favor as Mussolini and Franco). These three groups, all on the political right, were united ideologically by anti-Marxism and a sympathetic deportment toward fascist national renewal, yet they were otherwise too divergent in their mobilizing passions to come together in a solid coalition. And approval of the European dictatorships was never as deep in the business community as in the latter two groups: capitalist enthusiasm for fascist experiments abroad waned considerably in the second half of the Depression.

American business writers praised the Italian regime for turning what they called a basket-case nation into an exemplary economy and society. Mussolini, they argued, revived trade, established law and order, disciplined labor, ended strikes, stabilized the lira, and restored efficient management to both public and private sectors. Perhaps best of all, he unleashed a pride of nation and industriousness among the people. Some admirers of the free market, including Herbert Hoover, were highly impressed with his abolition of the inheritance tax.[10] Even after 1926, when fascist economics took a statist turn with the announcement of the corporate state, the support of the American economic establishment remained undiminished. Well into the Depression the American business press presented Mussolini's government as spurring economic activity, not limiting it. Lowering taxes, advocating lower tariff walls, firing lazy public sector workers, helping struggling industries, improving profitability through centralization: all of these were actions any good manager would take. As a reporter from *Business Week* observed in 1933, "Whatever else Benito Mussolini may be, he is both shrewd and capable. He runs Italy like a great company. There is labor; there is capital; there is the management whose duty it is to coordinate the functions of these 2 elements. Mussolini is the management."[11] In light of such statements, it is not surprising that many on the American left came to view fascism as a conspiracy of monopoly capital.

Business attitudes toward Mussolini soured in 1935, at the same time he lost much of the sympathy he enjoyed among the American public at large.[12] His invasion of Ethiopia, reviled by people of color across the globe, made clear to many in the white, mainstream press of the United States that Mussolini was dangerous. The major business periodicals upheld the right of Europeans to colonize Africa. But it was the first time a European nation had violated the sovereignty of another nation since the First World War, upsetting the balance of colonial power and creating uncertainty in the marketplace.[13] The eventual aversion of American business toward fascist Italy was equally determined by shifting attitudes on domestic politics. In March 1936, around the time the New Deal began to appear much more hostile to its interests, fascist Italy introduced the term *autarchy* into its economic policy. From 1922 to 1936, a period covering most of his reign, Mussolini had worked to create an orthodox market economy: he lowered taxes, cut the deficit, favored management over labor, and reduced the percentage of the gross domestic product spent by the government. Fueled by its needs following the Ethiopian invasion, however, Italy embarked on autarchy, that is, economic self-sufficiency guided by the firm hand of the state. As this policy shift was reported across the Atlantic, American business began to read Italy through the lens of its own regimentation at home. In the late 1930s its periodicals depicted Mussolini as a socialist, melding his system with those of Roosevelt, Hitler, and Stalin. Many business writers, however, held out the hope that fascist Italy would come to its senses and return to free markets once again.[14]

The Third Reich enjoyed a shorter honeymoon with the American business community, though its openness to the regime was never uniformly extinguished. Given that Nazi Germany's atrocities were widely known from their inception, the fact that it enjoyed any sympathy at all is astounding. Some have assumed that because American wartime propaganda did not emphasize the persecution of Jews, the American public didn't know the depths of Nazi terror until Signal Corps footage of Buchenwald appeared in movie theaters in 1945. To the contrary, the American public was exposed to Nazi atrocity stories against Jews and leftists throughout the thirties. Reports of brutal concentration camps in Germany circulated widely in the American press soon after Hitler took power; indeed, his regime became associated with the phrase "concentration camps" within its first year, in no small part because of the organizing and agitation of liberal and left-wing organizations, many of them Jewish.[15] In April 1933, two months after Hitler became chancellor, the editors of the *New Republic* wrote, "The Nazi propaganda had for years promised that the Jews would be 'exterminated'; and after the victory no official orders were needed for the undisciplined Storm Troops to begin a spontaneous campaign."[16] The first narratives of concentration camp survivors appeared in the American press that same year, disproportionately in left and liberal publications. These initial stories acknowledged that the majority of internees were socialists and communists, which was true of the early camps, but at times described, in brutal and graphic detail, that Jewish prisoners were subjected to the worst treatment by the guards. An early testimonial in the *New Republic* from 1934 described how *Sturmabteilung* (SA) men at Dachau murdered Jews execution-style at close range, while savagely beating and mutilating others.[17] Those who praised the Hitler government or who took a self-professed balanced view of its record did so while having such information at their fingertips.

Outright adoration of Hitler was rare in the business press, in contrast to the coverage of Mussolini. But for the first two years of the Nazi dictatorship it was not difficult to find sympathetic or at least uncritical portrayals in the pages of *Business Week,* the *Wall Street Journal, Barron's,* and *Time.* Initially, writers at these publications simply transferred their images of fascist Italy to fascist Germany: Hitler was a man who would tame unions and radicals, draw on the talents of the elite establishment, enact necessary economic reforms, and restore a sense of national pride to a worthy people. The *Wall Street Journal* afforded Hitler a forum in which to express his views unchecked by editorial comment, an opportunity the left and liberal presses certainly did not grant.[18] The most consistent sympathies of American business lay with German and Austrian conservatives whose hostility to democracy enabled the rise of Nazism: men like Franz von Papen, Kurt Schleicher, Alfred Hugenberg, Paul von Hindenburg, and Engelbert Dolfuss. In no small measure business writers based their views of Nazism on their perception of its treatment of these elites.

More decisive, however, were business journalists' shifting perceptions of the stability of the Nazi regime: would it work to stabilize European markets? or would it bring turmoil to world trade? For Germany was no Italy: it was a major, worldwide industrial power that possessed enormous military potential, a fact burned into people's recent memory by the First World War. The American business press doubted whether Hitler, the head of this juggernaut, was in control of his own internal affairs. Even after the Röhm purge in 1934, when he assassinated the leaders of the populist SA to appease the German establishment, dramatically removing the socialism from National Socialism, the *Wall Street Journal* continued to doubt whether such a move would resolve the country's economic and political predicament. One of its reporters stated, "Unless some further device, now unforeseeable, should enable the Hitler government to solve its basic problems, another and more serious disturbance to the German state is inevitable."[19] The unevenness in business support for Germany and Italy—disapproving when they threatened U.S. national interests or the predictability of capital flow, yet approving of a fascism that would restore stability and work in tandem with their interests—illustrates that their disapproval of fascism, when it came, was not properly antifascist. Overall, theirs was not a moral critique that read fascism, in any of its guises, as a global malignancy that required all of one's energies to oppose.

A second sector that supported fascism outright was a secular constellation I call, as noted, the law-and-order right. Its most influential representatives were the media mogul William Randolph Hearst, the publisher and entrepreneur Bernarr MacFadden, and the American Legion. The law-and-order right did not cohere into an organized coalition or a political party, though its supporters increasingly found a home with the Republicans; rather, it worked as a bloc, moving in ideologically parallel directions to inject profascist sensibilities into the public sphere. Unlike the business press, the law-and-order right was not attracted to fascism for its supposed pragmatic political economy. It was drawn far more to its punitive, cultural project of national renewal: its anti-Marxism, its willingness to restore the mythic traditions of the nation through violence and military discipline, its project of reestablishing clear hierarchies, and its cult of masculine decisiveness and action, personified in a strong leader. This branch of the right tended to be more emphatic in its support of fascism than business, more frequently embracing the movement as a positive good rather than a necessary evil. As such, its sympathies proved more durable.

The American Legion, the largest veterans' organization in the United States during the interwar period, was the most prestigious segment of the law-and-order right to legitimize fascism. Established in 1919 as a response to the divisive doctrines of class conflict and internationalism, the legion embraced the fascists of Italy as kindred spirits when they appeared on the world stage a few years later. Particularly appealing to American Legionnaires was the visibility of the Blackshirts as a veterans' movement. At the legionnaire convention in San Francisco in 1923, National Commander Alvin Owsley exclaimed, "The American Legion is fighting every element that threatens our democratic government—soviets, anarchists, I.W.W. [Industrial Workers of the World], revolutionary socialists and every other 'red.' . . . Do not forget that the Fascisti are to Italy what the American Legion is to the United States."[20] The legion's amenability to the fascist nexus of anti-Marxism and anti-parliamentarianism was reflected in its founding slogan, "To combat the autocracy of the classes and the masses." During the 1930s the national headquarters of the organization was generally much more circumspect in its fascist sympathies and finally admitted Nazism and Fascism into its pantheon of foreign evils in February 1941. Nonetheless, its magazine, *American Legion Monthly,* brought together the same passions evidenced in its explicitly fascist days: anticommunism, xenophobia, military discipline, hatred of internationalism, and calls for violent repression of the nation's enemies, which it always found among the lower ranks of society. The communist magazine *New Masses* later exposed overlapping memberships between the legion and the Ku Klux Klan at the local level and likewise with the notorious Black Legion in Michigan. Indeed, the legion touted the history of the Klan in its magazine.[21]

In the 1930s those of older generations who had been reared on turn-of-the-century discourses of racial betterment and empire were ripe for fascist appeals. One of these was Bernarr MacFadden, a bodybuilder born in 1868 who earned a national reputation as a promoter of physical culture and parleyed his notoriety into a magazine empire. His MacFadden Publications, founded in 1898, became one of the most lucrative magazine chains in the first half of the twentieth century, comprising such titles as *True Story, True Detective, Photoplay, New York Evening Graphic,* and, from 1931 to 1942, *Liberty* magazine, which had over two million readers.[22] To find a truer expression of American fascist consciousness, one need look no further than the pages of *Liberty* magazine. It was a forum for apologias of Mussolini and Hitler written by the likes of MacFadden, George Bernard Shaw, Crown Prince Wilhelm of Germany, and George Sylvester Viereck, a paid publicist for the German government who was tried as a Nazi agent and imprisoned from 1942 to 1947.[23]

MacFadden met Mussolini personally in 1930 and was awarded the Order of the Crown of Italy by his government. He later trained forty Italian athletes with the intent of building a cultural bridge between Italy and the United States.[24] He initially supported Roosevelt, but his love of enterprise quickly steered him away from the New Deal. Indeed, *Liberty* magazine managed to reconcile the seemingly unreconcilable: free-market capitalism and fascist statism. While defending fascist governments abroad, MacFadden editorialized against any state regulation of market forces at home. Further, he advocated the death penalty for crimes against property and even met efforts to abolish child labor with howls of outrage.[25] He could reconcile fascism with the free market because he saw both as enabling the same basic virtue, competition, a man's game of constant action which elevated the virtuous and culled the weak from the strong.

From his upbringing in the late nineteenth-century age of social Darwinism and the Rough Riders, MacFadden fused class and racial logics, which, to him, best cohered in the figure of the virtuous, muscle-bound, white male body steeled through adventurous contest with lesser races and classes. He read a spirit of adventurous competition in fascism's pageants of male athleticism and in its educational system, which prized willpower-driven physicality over intellect. Echoing *Mein Kampf,* Prince Wilhelm wrote in the pages of *Liberty,* "Every great civilization is built upon sound bodies. The Greeks, like the Romans, were a nation of athletes. The Anglo-Saxon race owes no small part of its world dominion to the physical and character training which it receives by fostering sports and sportsmanship." As late as 1937 MacFadden praised Germany for its "efforts to build up a mighty race of fighting men" and lamented that "in contrast to this we find our government giving billions of relief but not one cent for similar efforts to build a race necessary to maintain the vigor and vitality so badly needed to defend our democracy which has made of us such an amazing record."²⁶ Following this impulse, *Liberty* was replete with war stories. Despite its founder's love of capitalism, the magazine's heroes were generally found on the battlefield, not in the boardroom.

William Randolph Hearst was of MacFadden's generation and was virtually synonymous with American fascism in the left and liberal presses.²⁷ Best remembered as the newspaper magnate responsible for jingoistic yellow journalism at the beginning of the century, his media empire actually reached its peak during first half of the 1930s, when his newspaper chain could claim five to ten million daily readers, the Hearst-Metrotone newsreel, and twelve radio stations across the country.²⁸ His association with fascism was not unfounded. Hearst, an old-line Progressive in the mode of Teddy Roosevelt, turned against his distant cousin Franklin when the latter shifted to the left in the mid-1930s.²⁹ In 1934, the year he began calling for vigilante violence against the American labor movement, he traveled to Nazi Germany and interviewed Hitler. Hearst closed a deal with the German government to supply it with his newsreel service at a cost of one million marks annually and agreed to publish the writings of high Nazi officials in his press. Soon Hearst's American readers would encounter articles written by Herman Goering and Alfred Rosenberg, both later sentenced to death at Nuremberg, without critical introductions or editorial rebuttal.³⁰

In addition to the business press and the law-and-order right, a third influential constellation in the United States openly supported fascism: socially conservative Catholics. The U.S. National Catholic Welfare Conference, which was liberal and pro–New Deal, officially expressed the politics of the American church. But Rome sent a message on global affairs that contradicted Roosevelt. Pope Pius XI, who considered communism to be the greatest threat to Catholicism, regarded fascism as an ally in the battle against Bolshevism and secular liberalism. From the early 1930s on, the papacy tempered its support for Hitler and Mussolini with well-publicized critiques of specific policies, yet these were not broadly antifascist in nature. They generally came when the two regimes broke their promises and violated the independence of Catholic institutions, and in the late 1930s even this ambiguity was undermined by the church's unequivocal support of Franco's forces.³¹ All in all, there were enough profascist signals emanating from the Vatican to enable a measurable degree of fascist sympathy at Catholic colleges and in the Catholic press in the United States.³²

This broader culture of fascist tolerance enabled the rise of the most dangerous protofascist on the American scene in the 1930s: Father Charles Coughlin. Coughlin can rightly be called the founding father of right-wing radio, and his audience dwarfed that of all other fascist sympathizers in the United States: the CBS network estimated that there may have been an audience of up to thirty million people listening to his Sunday addresses. Though the precise composition of his audience is difficult to determine, it appears that it crossed class and denominational lines: many were Protestant and were disproportionately working and lower-middle class. A portion of these listeners were no doubt casual and even critical ones, and most did not subscribe to everything he said. According to one poll, for example, most of Coughlin's audience voted for Roosevelt in 1936, whose presidential campaign the radio priest feverishly devoted himself to derailing.[33] Nonetheless, the acknowledgment that he enjoyed a vast audience of supporters gave his lobbying efforts on issues of domestic and foreign policy real political capital. Liberals and the left called out Coughlin as the face of American fascism more than any other single person before 1945.

In addition to delivering his weekly radio address Coughlin founded a pressure group called the National Union for Social Justice (NUSJ) in 1934, ran a third-party candidate under the banner of the Union Party in 1936, and founded the newspaper *Social Justice* that same year. In 1938 he hailed the formation of an American Christian Front, formed in response to General Franco's call for a Christian Front to combat the left-liberal Popular Front. In the United States the Christian Front became a nationalist, "anti-alien" organization harkening back to the American Revolution and the founding fathers; it billed its rallies with the slogan, "AMERICANS: Keep This a Christian Country!" Its members, mostly Irish and German American young men in urban centers of the Northeast, formed themselves into paramilitary organizations, appeared at rallies with state congressmen, members of the American Legion, and leaders of far-right organizations like the Christian Mobilizers, and were responsible for publicly beating people they identified as Jewish. In the late 1930s Christian Fronters sold *Social Justice* alongside openly Nazi papers like the German American Bund's *Deutsche Weckruf,* and while peddling these wares they often got into street-corner brawls with hawkers of left-wing publications like *Equality* and the *Daily Worker.* The Christian Front was eviscerated in early 1940 after the FBI discovered a terror plot, hatched by its Brooklyn-based members, to destroy Jewish businesses, assassinate members of Congress, and blow up bridges, utilities, and railroad stations in the New York area. Coughlin's fate was linked to those who came to be known as the Brooklyn Boys, and his popularity dwindled to the fringes after he insisted on defending the terrorist group with which he was so closely identified.[34]

Coughlin openly praised Mussolini and Franco, though he was more circumspect with Hitler. His most recent biographer, drawing on surviving archives from the Third Reich, revealed that Coughlin sponsored a trip to Germany in 1939 for Leo Reardon, the publicity coordinator of *Social Justice,* with the aim of coaching Hitler and Joseph Goebbels on how to appeal more effectively to

American Christians (the trip apparently made a short-term impact on Nazi rhetoric).[35] Yet in his radio addresses he disavowed German fascism, at least partly. The radio priest would follow up his denunciations of Nazi persecution with the claim that fascism was "a defense mechanism against communism." To rid the world of fascism, he persistently avowed, one had to first rid the world of communism, which was invariably led by Jews. The Jewish-led Bolshevik revolution, he claimed in his radio sermons, was responsible for a "Holocaust" of twenty to twenty-five million Christians, a disaster the world simply ignored in their obsessive focus on "Jewish persecution." Meanwhile, in the United States prominent Jews sought the "de-Christianization of America."[36] Nazi persecution would stop, he insisted, if Jews acknowledged their past crimes and changed their behavior. In 1940, after Coughlin was forced off the air and the country moved closer to war, the tone of his movement became even more brazenly anti-Semitic as *Social Justice* defended Nazi Germany without even the customary disclaimers.[37]

Coughlin and his movement were unique among the major profascist elements on the American scene for their pronounced advocacy of the common man, an attitude that led Michael Kazin to see the Coughlinites as the first substantive instance of populism on the political right. The bylaws of the NUSJ certainly reflected social democratic views, which upheld the right of private property but also advocated "nationalization of all public necessities."[38] These bylaws, along with Coughlin's early support of Roosevelt, have led some twenty-first-century conservatives to claim that the NUSJ was on the political left, not the right. Yet as Roosevelt tacked left in the second half of the Depression, Coughlin explicitly branded himself a rightist, and for good reason.[39] Coughlin's politics were not of the libertarian sort, but, to use a later term, socially conservative: they emphasized not the dynamism of the lone individual but the moral fortitude of a collectivity with church and family at the center. In economic matters, for instance, he pushed for the corporate state, the model of labor-management cooperation touted by Mussolini and the Vatican. As Coughlin wrote, "A Corporate State is predicated on the principle that society is not composed so much of individuals as it is composed of group units with the family being considered as the atom of the state."[40]

On a more fundamental level, Coughlin was attuned to the deep structure of right-wing thought. He firmly believed in social hierarchy, trumpeted a masculinized nationalism over a feminized internationalism, was obsessed with drawing hard lines between the domestic and the foreign, tended to render domestic elements which did not fit his national narrative as alien (for example, seeing American Jews as "oriental" Communists), and generally directed animosity downward, toward the traditionally marginalized and their organizations, rather than upward. International finance, the only exception to this rule, was singled out among the institutions of great wealth because it was foreign, international, Jewish—in sum, not part of the normative realm of American business. The basis of Coughlin's corporatism was therefore by no means egalitarian. As he explained in *Social Justice,* "All men are not created equal. Nature and nature's God did not so ordain. Some men are born to rule . . . by the natural right of possessing the unusual gifts of leadership, management and judgment."[41] He continued, "The classes, so-called—the leaders and the followers, the capitalist and the laborer, the gifted and the average man—were designed to serve one another, to co-operate with one another." The ideal of corporatism, in Coughlin's view, was to ensure harmonious relations within an unequal but fundamentally just social order. The organic unity of this stratified world was disturbed only by those who promoted "hatred between the classes," an ultimately Semitic and foreign ideology.

In reflecting on fascist sympathies across the board in the 1930s, those of Coughlin and MacFadden, the *Wall Street Journal,* and *Time* magazine and of the Hearst press and the American Legion, it is too simple to claim that they applauded fascism over there but had no real desire to see it over here. Its American sympathizers wanted a government that would elevate the national ideal above all others, preserve established hierarchies, and dramatically increase its punitive powers to crush unruly elements among the marginalized. Yet paradoxically they generally embraced, as a guiding principle, the Constitution of the United States and the liberal freedoms it afforded, even when casting doubt on the desirability of democratic rule. To think through this contradiction, one has to shed the idea that fascism comes to power when people willingly surrender their own freedom, that it arrives because its supporters consciously desire to yield their liberties and submit to the regimentation of an authoritarian state: this narrative is a legacy of wartime propaganda. To the contrary, fascists came to power in Germany, Italy, and Spain by force only after their fortunes at the polls were disappointingly stagnant or in decline. But even fascism's supporters did not necessarily see their desired strongman as taking away their functional freedoms, and for good reason. When the Führer and Il Duce gained command, the German SA man and the Italian Blackshirt suddenly had the power of the law arbitrarily invested in their own hands; they gained the freedom to beat their opponents in the street, to express their opinions uninterrupted by rival views, and to move up the social ladder more easily. It is questionable that these individuals saw fascism as a loss of personal liberty. The fascist rarely sees himself personally shackled by the power of the state he supports—its fury is unleashed on those he despises. He gains certain short-term liberties at the expense of others.

Implicitly, this view was understood by most Americans in the 1930s who excused (or cheered) fascism abroad while desiring its application, whether in whole or in part, to their own country. When MacFadden called for the execution of thieves, he knew he would not fall into that category; when Coughlin called for the violent suppression of the Communist-Jew, he was certain his own followers would not be consumed in the process. And if a clearly undemocratic state came about that otherwise honored their principles, this circumstance could still be defended on liberal grounds. *Social Justice,* for instance, carried articles from Iberian Catholic publications that defended authoritarianism in Portugal and Spain on the ground that these regimes upheld the very liberties that representative government had failed to uphold. As one reprinted Portuguese piece argued, "The liberal democracies have not been able to safeguard the liberties of their people. We today in Portugal are anti-Liberal because we want to save those liberties which the so-called liberal regime deprived us of." Using a similar logic, *Social Justice* reprinted the writings of a Spanish bishop who claimed extralegal violence on the right was necessary in Spain because the political left had come to power through fraudulent elections.[42] Such rhetorical moves are necessary in a culture like that of the United States, in which liberal freedoms are ingrained in the national ideal and indispensable to any nationalist. Yet in the United States, as everywhere, there have always been exemptions to the universality of liberalism. The distinct national hue of the American fascist spirit comes from its attempt to broaden these exemptions in the name of just hierarchy and national renewal. Lacking reflection on the historical contradictions of liberalism, it allows Americans to preserve a degree of faith in liberal freedoms while ultimately pursuing their negation.

It Stops Right Here: The Campaign against Fascism in the United States

Mussolini took power in 1922, yet the American left devoted little attention to the issue of fascism in the twenties. Though many of their countrymen embraced the Italian dictator, his new philosophy of fascism did not seem like a global threat. As John Diggins later observed, "The Left-wing press reacted to the takeover of Rome almost with a yawn." Norman Thomas expressed regret over this reaction, noting that when fascism took Italy, liberals and socialists "explained what had happened in terms of the Latin temperament, the comparative backwardness of the Italian industrial development, the immaturity of its democracy, and popular resentment at the failure of Italy to achieve greater material advantage from the war. That Germany would never go Fascist was an article of faith almost up to the eve of the very election when Hitler managed to get a popular majority."[43] However, the American left did not entirely fail to respond to fascism in the 1920s. The first antifascist opposition emerged soon after the March on Rome, when Italian American and Italian exile leftists launched a campaign to wean their communities from Mussolini's allure. The Italian government actively courted the sympathies of its diasporic émigrés across the Atlantic throughout the 1920s and 1930s, with no small degree of success. As late as 1940 Il Duce was viewed favorably by an estimated 35 percent of Italians living in the United States; to a maligned immigrant community regarded by most Americans as probationarily white at best, he provided an image of affirmative masculinity. In April 1923 the first antifascist organization in the United States, the Anti-Fascist Alliance of North America, was formed by Italian radicals in response to this Stateside popularity. Its 150,000 members were mostly of Italian descent, and many belonged to New York–based labor unions, namely, the International Ladies' Garment Workers' Union, the Amalgamated Clothing Workers Union, and the New York Federation of Labor. Though antifascists remained a minority in Italian neighborhoods, they disrupted fascist rallies, battled Khaki Shirts in the streets, and countered the propaganda of the Italian government over the next two decades.[44]

Only when Hitler became chancellor in early 1933 did most liberals and leftists begin to regard fascism as a global menace and object of frantic concern. When the Nazis imposed a regime on their country modeled along Italian lines, it became obvious that fascism was an exportable phenomenon. With the entire public sphere suddenly attuned to the doctrine of fascism after the National Socialist seizure of power, left-of-center Americans almost immediately feared its establishment in the United States by native reactionaries. Antifascism for the first time became a political rubric through which a broad range of campaigns were conceived and maintained. The writer Upton Sinclair's End Poverty in California campaign is an early example. Launched in 1933, this nearly successful drive for the governor's mansion and the state legislature was based on a wholly domestic agenda of wealth redistribution, yet it was palpably haunted by fascism abroad. Explaining his decision to form a new organization outside the Socialist Party, Sinclair wrote in his manifesto *I, Governor of California,* "I have seen the horror that has come to Germany, and I realize that the American Socialist party wouldn't make one good-sized bite for American Big Business, when it gets to the biting stage. We have only a year or so in which to save ourselves, and save our country"[45] (fig. 2).

From 1933 to 1935 the most widely covered antifascist campaigns in the United States sprang from three organizations: the American Jewish Congress (AJC) (liberal), the JLC (socialist), and the ALAWF (initiated by communists). German atrocities against Jews and other perceived enemies of the Nazi state often appeared in the American press because these organizations staged a

FIGURE 2. Anti-Nazi rally, ca. 1933, New York. Courtesy Daily Worker/Daily World Photographs Collection, Tamiment Library, New York University.

mass demonstration against each new outrage. The AJC and the JLC were key players in a national consumer boycott against German-made goods that ran from March 1933 to October 1941. The economic impact of the boycott was limited, as most American trade with Germany was not in consumer goods but in raw materials like coke, coal, iron, and steel. Yet the rallies and mass meetings held to publicize the boycott, some attended by over 250,000 people and most treated sympathetically in the press, offered constant opportunities to showcase the horrors of the Third Reich and worked to cement it as a brutal regime in the public imagination.[46] The efforts of Baruch C. Vladek and the JLC, representing half a million workers, were critical in establishing the Joint Boycott Council, a joint project with the liberal AJC. Additionally, the JLC enlisted the critical support of William Green and the AFL, which allowed supporters of the boycott to speak and solicit donations at meetings of AFL locals throughout the country. Vladek and other members of the JLC shifted the boycott from a campaign focused squarely on the plight of Jews to one with a broader, antifascist message on discrimination, labor rights, and social democracy.[47]

Broader still in its activities was the ALAWF, perhaps the most successful organization set in motion by the CPUSA. The ALAWF formed the widest antifascist network in the United States and best illustrates the intersectional nature of antifascist politics in the 1930s (its name was changed to the ALPD in 1937, though I refer to it as ALAWF throughout for convenience). The organization, founded in the fall of 1933, was modeled after the putatively nonsectarian Amsterdam–Pleyel movement in France and Holland. Its dues-paying membership was relatively small, reaching approximately twenty thousand at its peak in 1939. Yet it primarily served as a coordinating body and umbrella group that aligned the antifascist activities of its affiliated organizations, including the ACLU, the National Association for the Advancement of Colored People (NAACP), the National Urban League, the American Friends Service Committee, union locals, and hundreds of other organizations. Its national congresses attracted delegates numbering in the thousands, and by 1939 it claimed 1,023 affiliated groups representing well over 7 million people as well as 231 local branches of its own. For its affiliates, the ALAWF served as an information clearinghouse, furnishing its biweekly bulletin *Facts and Figures* and disseminating over 1 million booklets, pamphlets, and newspapers in 1938 alone.[48] Its rallies, congresses, and round tables received wide coverage in print and broadcast media and enjoyed the sponsorship of U.S. congressmen, state governors, and city mayors. Its Fifth Congress, held in Washington in early 1939, received a letter of welcome from Secretary of the Interior Harold Ickes.[49]

But ALAWF did not begin with such official support. During the CPUSA's Third Period (1928–1935) it was quite hostile to the Roosevelt administration, enlisting itself in a broad domestic campaign to sever the roots of fascism in the United States, which it also found in the New Deal. As stated in its manifesto of 1933, its mission was "to oppose all developments leading to Fascism in this country and abroad."[50] The crucial phrase "all developments leading to Fascism" indicated a belief among its activists that the United States was not presently a fascist country but a nation containing oppressive elements that might blossom into an authoritarian state if left unchecked. Thus in the years before Hitler or Mussolini embarked on any major territorial expansions and when Japan appeared sated with its Manchurian conquest, the most pressing task for the antifascists of ALAWF was to organize a cultural campaign against any inequality or authoritarian practice they saw as feeding the demonic energies of political reaction. The notion of developments leading to fascism encompassed a wide range of phenomena: increased military budgets, the use of state violence against trade unionists and picketers, racial oppression, wage inequalities between men and women, and American imperialism in Latin America and East Asia.

Among the diversity of operations waged under the rubric of antifascism, the campaign against martial values in the United States was especially pronounced among explicitly antifascist organizations from 1933 to 1935. Antifascists viewed such values as preparing the cultural ground for a fascist state at home and its inevitable imperial expansion abroad (hence the ALAWF's inextricable linkage of war and fascism). Members of ALAWF and other activists sought to prevent New Deal programs like the Civilian Conservation Corps from degenerating into vehicles of militarization. They waged a lively and largely successful drive on college campuses to end the mandatory enrollment of male students in the Reserve Officers' Training Corps, and they participated in efforts to limit military recruiting and what they called chauvinistic patriotism in primary and secondary schools, eventually by exposing teachers, church representatives, and parents to antiwar pedagogy and curricula.[51] The conflation of fascism, imperialism, and patriotism implicit in some of these efforts represented poor historical analysis. Nevertheless, the campaign to eradicate militarism, given its very real centrality to fascism, was not inappropriate or diversionary to antifascist ends. All the same, the *Chicago Daily Tribune* was correct in detecting a turn from pacifism and a note of bellicosity on the left by 1938. In the second half of the 1930s there was a palpable change in the language and goals of antifascist organizing, one facilitated by the CPUSA's shift to the Popular Front line, rising fascist aggression abroad, and the Roosevelt administration's left turn.

In response to successful initiatives by the French CP a year earlier, the Comintern—that is, the Communist International, the executive body of all the communist parties around the world, directed, in effect, by the CP of the Soviet Union—announced its famous Popular Front line in August 1935. It called on communists in all countries to abandon sectarianism and join a broad unity front with socialists and other potential allies, including the middle class and sections of the bourgeoisie, against the common enemy of fascism. Unlike earlier attempts to create a united front, this shift to coalition building involved real ideological compromises in order to attract noncommunists: it meant abandoning revolutionary language, deemphasizing capitalist imperialism, embracing egalitarian national traditions, organizing the middle class, and, in the United States, adopting a liberal language of equality, democracy, and rights. The CPUSA did not create true unity across the left with this shift in policy. It attracted and worked with liberals, but the majority of socialists and Trotskyists mostly rejected the party's overtures to collaborate within the same organizations.[52] But a movement cannot be deemed a failure simply because it does not generate a single organization uniting all like-minded individuals: by this standard virtually no movement could be judged a success. In *The Cultural Front* (1998), Denning shifted the understanding of the Popular Front by viewing it less as a formal coalition, with constituents working in interlocking organizations and consenting to the same platform, than as a historic bloc as conceived by Gramsci. That is to say, it was a loose constellation of cultural and political forces, aligned in a parallel direction, working to secure ideological leadership within the national arena and to forge a new common sense among the masses.[53]

In the second half of the 1930s, the era of the Popular Front, the numbers of people within the orbit of the antifascist left dramatically increased as the new strategy allowed it to reach into new, broader spheres of influence. Though most Americans were unwilling to see the country intervene in global conflicts, *fascism* became a dirty word in the public imagination. For the first time, an overwhelming majority saw fascism, not communism, as the greatest threat to world security, at a time when the business press, in its newfound aversion to Mussolini, preferred to regard fascism and communism as equivalent dangers at best.[54] The Popular Front, as a broadly conceived movement not reducible to the CPUSA, was able to extend its reach, in part, because international developments and a new domestic political environment drove it much closer to the state.

The second half of the decade was marked by a series of expansionist moves by Germany, Italy, and Japan, raising the fear that fascism might come not only from within but also from without, through military occupation. Expansionism included annexations, proxy wars, and outright invasions in Ethiopia (October 1935), Spain (1936–39), mainland China (July 1937), Austria (March 1938), Czechoslovakia (March 1939), and, finally, the conquest of Poland and the outbreak of the Second World War (September 1939). Around the same time, while the Roosevelt administration failed to lift its embargo on Spain during the civil war, it did, from 1937 on, take steps to instill in the American public the sense that fascism constituted the most immediate menace to world peace and that the country should take action to halt it. Roosevelt, who took office the same month Hitler consolidated his power, was disturbed by the Nazi regime from the beginning of his presidency yet for years remained assured it would internally collapse owing to its huge, economically unproductive outlays on armaments. A speech he gave in Chicago in October 1937 marked a substantive shift in his rhetoric, one that definitively signaled to the communist left that he shared their view of foreign affairs. He distinctly called on Americans to support collaboration with other nations to "quarantine" aggressors. Much of the left initially stood aloof from the Roosevelt administration, denouncing his foreign policy as imperialist, little different in kind from its French, British, and even German counterparts. But at its convention in Pittsburgh a month after Roosevelt's speech, the ALAWF officially revealed a new stance toward the White House, announcing, "The President's Chicago speech marks a turning point in the foreign policy of our country. . . . It gives us the slogans for this conference in the international field. 'Neutrality is not enough. Isolation won't work. Quarantine the aggressor. Concerted effort is necessary.'"[55]

For many on the left these events called for a sharper analytical distinction between the fascist imperialism of Germany, Italy, and Japan and the more conventional imperialism of Britain, France, and the United States.[56] Here, the differences between the black and white Popular Fronts come into focus. Most African American intellectuals in the thirties and forties saw the world more fundamentally in anti-imperialist than in antifascist terms. It was initially difficult for many African Americans to see the regimes of Germany and Italy as hubs of malignancy given their lived experience of racial segregation at home as well as their awareness of the atrocities of British and French imperialism abroad.[57] The fact that Hitler and Mussolini were aligned with imperial Japan, an alignment made official by the Anti-Comintern Pact of 1936, further complicated black attitudes toward fascism. Many African Americans held Japan in high regard ever since its victory over Russia in the Russo-Japanese War of 1904–5, the first time a non-European state had defeated a European power in a major armed conflict. This esteem persisted up to and beyond the bombing of Pearl Harbor.[58]

Mussolini's invasion of Ethiopia was the first event to create a widespread sense among African American publics that fascism was distinctly relevant to their own oppression. What historians subsequently labeled the Second Italo-Abyssinian War (October 1935 to May 1936) was front-page news in the black press for almost a year. Ethiopia held a special place in black American culture not only because of its status as one of the few noncolonized spaces in Africa, but also because of its iconic position within black Christianity. The Italian invasion created more than outrage in black communities across the United States: it led to mobilization. Thousands of black men, organized by the Pan-African Reconstruction Association, volunteered to go to Ethiopia to fight, although the U.S. government prevented this from transpiring. Meanwhile, black Communists in Harlem, aided by the remnants of Marcus Garvey's nationalist movement of the 1920s, formed a Provisional Committee for the Defense of Ethiopia with the aim of creating an antifascist sensibility in black communities and in the nation as a whole. With the support of the ALAWF, it waged a lively "Hands Off Ethiopia" campaign. As Robin D. G. Kelley argues, "The defense of Ethiopia did more than any other event in the 1930s to internationalize the struggles of black people in the United States."[59]

It was not the case, as is often suggested, that the left in this period stopped attacking Western governments for being imperialist; nor did it place them in a separate moral universe from fascist states. Denunciations of British, French, and American exploitation of the global South continued to appear in *Fight!* and the white liberal and communist presses in the late 1930s. Nevertheless, much of the white left stopped offering detailed accounts of human suffering in the colonial domains of France, Britain, Holland, and the United States. They took up a new antifascist emphasis that many people of color in the Popular Front did not fully share. In its Fourth Congress in November 1937, the ALAWF went even further by dropping all references to Western imperialism and colonialism from its platform.[60] While African Americans came to see fascism as a distinct evil after the invasion of Ethiopia, the Popular Front period produced a widening gap between black and white leftists in their assessment of fascism, one which continued to grow during the war.

All in all, developments in the late thirties placed most Britons and Americans aligned with their Popular Fronts in the position of calling on their governments to act tough with a foreign power, a rhetoric traditionally in the province of nationalists. The CPUSA, the ALAWF, the Old Guard of the Socialist Party, and most liberals came to adopt the doctrine of collective security, which argued that Hitler, Mussolini, and imperial Japan could be stopped only if the United States, Britain, France, China, and the Soviet Union formed an alliance to protect their mutual interests. Collective security caused many antifascists to move away from a radical, outsider anti-imperialism, one with a clear North–South alignment that assumed imperialist nations to be unredeemable without a revolution. They pivoted instead toward a position requiring them to argue in support of the national interest, albeit an interest construed as an international partnership with other nations. The ALAWF in its early days tended to organize its rallies on foreign affairs around broad moral positions; the message of one rally in 1933, for example, was "Against the Japanese Invasion of China! Against the Wars in South America"![61] Later, it adopted a less radical, yet more pointed, strategy of lobbying for and against specific bills before Congress and weighing in on mainstream debates over foreign policy. The most consistent lobbying effort was that to amend the various Neutrality Acts, the first of which passed in 1935, in order to distinguish between aggressors and victims so that the United States could boycott the former and allow comprehensive trade with the latter.

While it continued to oppose troop deployments by the U.S. and British governments, the antifascist movement took on a distinctly antipacifist tone, thereby placing outspoken pacifists in a besieged minority position. The Spanish Civil War accelerated this martial dynamic, implicit in collective security. The socialist-pacifist Devere Allen wrote in February 1937, "Inevitably, the rising fascist menace has placed pacifism on the defensive; and the Spanish crisis has brought a growing issue to its climax. . . . Pacifists may legitimately be excused, therefore, when they recoil in confusion and dismay before an onslaught from the Left. The attack has been widespread, unrestrained, and none too well informed."[62] Much has been written on the Spanish Civil War, but, for my purposes here, its importance is that it transformed the global antifascist movement into an actual war effort, one in which friends, family, and fellow activists were in the field of battle. For international advocates across the globe, unsupported by any government outside of the USSR and the Spanish Republic, the war was an all-volunteer effort by civil society that required antifascists to take up roles usually coordinated or sanctioned by the state: raising money to maintain forces in the field, shipping supplies, caring for refugees and the wounded, and, most dramatically, sending soldiers into combat.

The war was almost universally supported by liberals and leftists, including communists, the editorial boards of the *New Republic* and the *Nation,* and a majority of socialists; even Thomas abandoned his militant antiwar stance during the conflict. Much of the enterprise in the United States was coordinated by the ALAWF and its affiliates. The ALAWF was the cofounder and guiding force behind the North American Committee to Aid Spanish Democracy, which organized the shipping of medical supplies, food, and other goods to the Spanish Republic through benefits, mass meetings, and intensive work with trade unions. Famously, around twenty-eight hundred American antifascists served in Spain, mostly in the Abraham Lincoln Brigade, and approximately seven hundred lost their lives. Many of the Lincolns were drawn from the New York area, and garment workers, longshoremen, sailors, and college students were overrepresented in their ranks. As was true of other International Brigades, the Lincoln Battalion was established and coordinated by the national Communist Party, though many of its recruits were not communists (the Socialist Party put out the call for a Eugene V. Debs Column, but this proved to be a fiasco, its handful of volunteers folding into the Lincolns). As Franco's forces gained the upper hand, the New York–based Joint Anti-Fascist Refugee Committee devoted itself to securing asylum for refugees from the fallen republic, providing for their livelihood and medical care while in exile, and lobbying governments to join in their efforts.[63] For loyalist supporters outside Spain, the Civil War was not merely a defensive, military action but also an opportunity to showcase the positive example of an antifascist republic: the Spanish Popular Front government, which secured universal suffrage, medical care, education, basic labor protections, and land reform for a people who had minimally enjoyed these basic human rights.

Though the Spanish Civil War has loomed large in the memory of the antifascist cause, it was far from being the only venture occupying the energies of U.S.-based antifascists. The war in China was also a massive campaign: the ALAWF, for instance, established the China Aid Council, touted as the first secular American medical mission to China during the war.⁶⁴ While fighting for Republican Spain and besieged China, liberals and leftists also devoted their energies to the Austrian and Czechoslovakian crises; the boycott of Italy, Germany, and Japan; the struggle to aid refugees from Nazi Germany; and, at home, the continuing struggle against rightist extremism and for civil rights, free speech, and industrial democracy. The importance of the Spanish Civil War was its visceral nature: antifascists engaged in a shooting war against their archenemy, a war which their sacrifices were palpably impacting. As such, it widened the belief that fascism had to be checked by armed conflict, making it easier for many antifascists to contribute to the official war effort after Pearl Harbor. Moreover, the loss of the Spanish Republic, a direct result of the refusal of Britain, France, and the United States to lift their trade embargoes against all belligerents, drove home the necessity of enlisting liberal capitalist states in the struggle to halt the fascist bloc. In January 1939 Theodor Draper wrote in *New Masses,* "'Appeasement' is now a word of scorn. . . . For most people, the road to peace is no longer one humiliating surrender after another to the aggressors. In its stead has come a deep realization that peace is possible only through the sternest resistance." "The democratic world," he added, now requires "material might and a readiness to use it."⁶⁵

For all such talk, liberals and the left stopped short of calling for U.S. troop deployments to fight fascism. Sending American soldiers abroad to fight any powerful enemy was outside the pale of political debate in the thirties. In a country reeling from the Depression and profoundly disillusioned by the outcome of the First World War, massive military deployments abroad appealed to no one, not the left, the right, or the center. Even Roosevelt was not firmly committed to entering hostilities until the fall of 1941.⁶⁶ Left and liberal interventionism in this period was largely a call for strict economic sanctions against Germany, Italy, and Japan and for amending the Neutrality Acts to allow the shipment of goods and supplies to forces battling fascist aggression abroad, chiefly, those in Ethiopia, China, and Spain. As late as June 1939 the ALAWF could claim its mission was to "keep the United States out of war and help keep war out of the world."⁶⁷ Before the outbreak of world war in September 1939, the majority of liberals, communists, and socialists believed that a firm policy of sanctions against aggressors and of supplying material aid to their victims—lacking under the Neutrality Acts—would render the deployment of U.S. troops unnecessary, and they devoted their energy to this end.⁶⁸

The famous debate pitting isolationists against interventionists in the 1930s was not about sending American troops into combat overseas, an action neither side proposed. It was largely between those who favored picking sides, mainly through trade policy, and those who saw even economic favoritism as a step which could draw their country into war. The latter camp included outright profascists, including Coughlinites, Bundists, and Lindbergh, but its most visible congressional support came from such men as Gerald Nye, Burton Wheeler, and Hamilton Fish, who viewed communism as a greater threat in world affairs than fascism. They advocated building up U.S. military defenses to protect North American coastlines and territory but rejected all foreign military entanglements, including aid to Britain.[69] Liberals and leftists were called warmongers by the likes of McCormick not because they summoned the power of the U.S. Army, Navy, and Marines, but because they demanded economic sanctions against fascists, material aid for their opponents, and a reappraisal of the wisdom of appeasement.

The late 1930s saw increasing collaboration between the antifascist left and the New Deal state on the domestic front. During this period the ALAWF began to cooperate with federal authorities in tracking down right-wing vigilantes of the Black Legion and the Klan. It was also when Mary Elizabeth Pidgeon of the U.S. Department of Labor published in *Fight!* and when Secretary of the Interior Harold Ickes scheduled an address to the ALAWF's Fifth Congress in Washington, canceled only after protestations from Vice President John Nance Garner.[70] But it was not simply the case that radicals became more practical. When the president also moved to the left, particularly on domestic politics, working with him did not seem as great a compromise to their principles. From 1935 to 1939 Roosevelt and his congressional allies adopted a clear antibusiness rhetoric and passed the lion's share of the New Deal's landmark legislation: they put into law the forty-hour workweek, progressive taxation, Social Security, the federal minimum wage, the abolition of child labor, and the legal recognition of union elections and collective bargaining.

With such impressive reforms under way, fueled in no small measure by the political pressure of labor and radical movements, it appeared to some on the left that they were actually part of the nation, provided they accept certain limitations, of course. As Mark Naison wrote of communists in the Popular Front period, "Communists found themselves courted by union leaders and politicians anxious to facilitate New Deal reforms. For people who had been outsiders, and who in some cases had experienced jail and exile, this was heady stuff—but it invariably involved the condition that Communists keep a low profile and push 'utopian' goals to the background."[71] In this environment, left antifascism overwhelmingly took on a liberal language of rights, as the ALAWF and the CPUSA waged new domestic campaigns under the banner of expanding democratic freedoms. In 1936–38, the ALAWF devoted greater energy to building the labor movement by fighting against martial law declarations, anti-picketing legislation, and vigilante activity in industrial centers. It also pursued companies that refused to abide by the Fair Labor Standards Act and aided the auto and steel strikes of 1937. Its activists lobbied for civil rights by pushing anti-lynching bills and measures to abolish restrictions on the franchise.[72] Less well known, it took on a feminist politics to an unprecedented degree. *Fight!* became a forum in which women writers, above all, Dorothy McConnell, demonstrated how the so-called woman question was central to broader democratic struggles. Contributors argued for equal pay for equal work, highlighted the pivotal role of women in the antifascist struggle worldwide, and chastised male comrades for ignoring their oppression.[73]

The signing of the Molotov–Ribbentrop Pact (often referred to as the Hitler–Stalin Pact) in August 1939 severely compromised the left's advance into these broader venues. Scholars of the period have often considered this nonaggression treaty between Germany and the Soviet Union to be a disaster for the left in Western nations. However, the pact in and of itself was not the cause of the calamity. Indeed, the USSR, despite the domestic horrors of its regime in the 1930s, was the last of the great powers to appease Nazi Germany, and it did so only after the Spanish Civil War made it obvious that neither Britain, France, nor the United States was willing to take meaningful steps to halt fascist expansionism. The pact could be seen as a diplomatic attempt by the Soviet state to forestall a similar treaty between Germany and the Western powers at its expense. Such Soviet realpolitik was acknowledged by many American liberal commentators in the months after the treaty was signed; they had long viewed the USSR pragmatically and had come to expect it to engage in the game of diplomatic power politics like any other nation-state. Recalling the Munich agreement, one commentator wrote in the *New Republic,* "Stalin was right that . . . friend and foe might combine against the Kremlin." Like many other liberals, this writer saw the treaty as a temporary expediency and did not expect it to last.[74]

The Hitler–Stalin Pact was a disaster for the CPUSA not simply because its Soviet aspirant had made a deal with the devil, but because the pact required such a rapid turnabout in communist theory and strategy. In foreign affairs the party quickly threw its campaign for collective security and intervention overboard in favor of a quasi-isolationist position that denounced all capitalist powers as imperialist, different only in flavor from their fascist rivals. This rapid shift confirmed liberals' suspicions that CPUSA activists were guided not by universal moral principles, but by an overreliance on a specific and increasingly dubious nation-state. Communists continued to expose American fascists and fight for the rights of labor and people of color, but the party's return to an antiimperial line in August 1939–June 1941 was not marked by the older emphasis on the colonized themselves. They remained but a footnote in denunciations of the French, British, and U.S. governments in the major CP publications. By contrast, writers in the NAACP's the *Crisis* and in the African American dailies adopted an increasingly strident tone against colonialism in these years.

Moreover, the pact was only one of a series of indefensible actions by the Soviet Union that were widely covered in the liberal press, including the Moscow show trials of 1937, the Soviet occupation of western Poland in September 1939, which was secretly allotted to the USSR under the terms of the pact, and, most strikingly, its invasion of Finland two months later. Observers who had been sympathetically inclined to the Soviet Union found it difficult to stomach American communist apologetics for these actions; so did some party members themselves, who resigned their memberships.[75] Robert Sherwood reflected much of the antifascist sentiment of the time in his play on the Russo–Finnish War, *There Shall Be No Night* (1940). Commenting on the Soviet–German alliance, his proxy Dave Corween affirmed the primacy of antifascism while mourning the loss of a crucial ally in that fight. "The cause of revolution all over the world," he asserted, "has been set back incalculably. The Soviet Union has been reduced from the status of a great power to that of a great fraud. And the Nazis have won another bloodless victory."[76]

In 1939–41 the American left in general saw major setbacks: the evisceration of the successful, coalition-building projects of the Popular Front period and a deeper splintering of the divide between liberals, communists, and socialists on how best to deal with fascism abroad. Liberals stuck with Roosevelt and his campaign against neutrality, while communists became vulnerable—and their critical contributions to labor, racial justice, and gender equity imperiled—by their newly adopted opposition to the president's more genuinely antifascist foreign policy, which was quite popular with the AFL and CIO rank and file. The ALAWF, badly split by the defection of communists and the withdrawal of party support, sputtered along until December 1939 before folding. One of its last acts was to call for the U.S. government to boycott the Soviet Union in response to its invasion of Finland.[77] One could argue that the disaster of the Hitler–Stalin Pact resulted from the almost inevitable contradiction of yoking one's politics too strongly to a specific nation-state, in this case, the USSR, a move which had also been partly responsible for CP successes. For one thing, the communists could always claim, something their socialist rivals could not, was that their politics were not strictly utopian. They could point to a concrete place, however far away it was, where their dreams had been actualized. The propaganda value of the living example was immense and conceivably a reason for the appeal of the Soviet Union to noncommunists in a decade in which so many other economies had failed. What led to the CPUSA's success, in other words, was precisely what made it so vulnerable.

This contradiction continued into the war years but on a different basis: while party membership rolls increased and peaked during the war, the party's political behavior, which in many regards differed little from that of the Democratic and even the Republican parties, alienated some of the constituencies drawn to such an avowedly radical organization. Antifascism continued during the war stronger than ever, but its vanguard was nowhere in sight.

Antifascism as State Policy: The United States during the Second World War

By the time the United States entered the Second World War, *Joe Palooka* had become one of the most popular comic strips in the country, syndicated in almost every local newspaper. In the months after Pearl Harbor, millions of readers followed Joe Palooka, the strip's simple, prizefighting protagonist, as he quit the ring to join the army, mirroring the lives of many Americans. In the comic that appeared on October 8, 1942, Joe walks behind enemy lines in the forests of France, accompanied by two comrades-in-arms: the American Jerry Leemy and a French Canadian soldier named Jean Bateese. As they approach the estate of a wealthy French winemaker where they hope to find refuge, Joe asks Bateese in his familiar vernacular style, "Are you sure we kin trust 'im? An awful lot of the rich nobelmun was fer the Nazis. They sold France out! They hated the common people—the majority—like us—so much they'd rather have Hitler, than their own democracy! They only tho't in terms of big money an' Hitler give 'em a line about protectin' *them*. They fell for it—well I don't hafta tell you!" Leemy adds that there were similar, antidemocratic types in his neighborhood back home, whom he called Fronters (a reference to the Christian Front). After a brief stay at the estate, Joe's intuition proved correct: the winemaker, De Polyneaux, was indeed collaborating with the Germans, and the three have to run for their lives after a scuffle in which the villainous gentleman murders his maid.

This artifact illustrates the forgotten left populist nature of American culture during the war. Antifascism, for the first and last time, became an official logic of the state following the bombing of Pearl Harbor. Encouraged by state sponsorship, left and liberal narratives of fascism attained access to wider audiences during the Second World War than ever before. While they had reached broad publics through print media in the 1930s, they were now able to break into the heavily vetted arenas of network radio and Hollywood film with greater regularity. The war also catapulted elaborate expositions of left-liberal antifascism to the top of the nonfiction best-seller list, including William Shirer's *Berlin Diary* (1941), Joseph E. Davies's *Mission to Moscow* (1942), and John Roy Carlson's

Under Cover (1943).⁷⁸ But such narratives of the enemy, which described fascism as a global form of political reaction, had to contend with incompatible wartime visions of Why We Fight. Sometimes produced, paradoxically, by leftists and liberals, these other visions did not entirely contradict the image of European fascists projected by the 1930s left. However, they tended to represent fascism as fully alien to the values of the Allied nations while creating images of the Japanese people dramatically different from those of the left's Boycott Japan and Aid to China campaigns of the previous decade.

One such prominent narrative divided the planet into a free world and a slave world, receiving its most popular expressions in Frank Capra's famous documentary series *Why We Fight* (1942–44), Pearl Buck's novel *Dragon Seed* (1942), and John Steinbeck's novella *The Moon Is Down* (1942). *Dragon Seed* and *The Moon Is Down* topped the best-seller list, and Hollywood adapted Buck's novel to film in 1944. Grounded in the discourse of republicanism, the free world versus slave world narrative shifted focus from Popular Front economic and racial justice to a vision of democracy narrowed to the traditional liberal freedoms: of speech, press, and assembly. Contrary to the radical antifascisms of the 1930s, it hardened the divisions between the peoples of the Allied and Axis nations, affirming the tolerant, democratic essence of the former and the immutable militarism, regimentation, and foreignness of the latter. It offered a People's War of a different sort: a war not between ideas and governments but between peoples possessing unreconcilable cultural, even racial, differences. It took on its most ugly forms in its depictions of the Japanese.

For instance, Capra's *Prelude to War,* the first installment of *Why We Fight*, begins with a quote emblazoned on a title frame that the narrator directly attributes to Henry Wallace: "This is a fight between a slave world and a free world." Required viewing for GIs, the entire film is an exposition of this quote, its visual narrative forming an extended lesson on what makes certain peoples free and others slaves. Free peoples, in short, adhere to democratic principles of free speech and free assembly and are blessed with a culturally ingrained ability to make decisions without direction from political leaders. The slave world, on the other hand, is marked by long-established cultures of militarism and authoritarianism that have created peoples unable to think for themselves, all too willing to surrender their freedom to a strong leader. In Capra's iteration of the free world / slave world narrative, the Japanese, Germans, and Italians are presented in homologous terms: he shows the three current governments to be the product of the same essential militarism, accumulated over centuries. Later installments were more racialized. *Know Your Enemy: Japan* (1944) begins with an image of a Japanese swordsman preparing to decapitate a downed Allied pilot, as cacophonous, alien music plays in the background. A caption appears, in a font designed to look like Asian script, reading "The Sword is Our Steel Bible." The narrator soon reminds viewers that the average Japanese man has "been trained as a soldier almost since birth." Throughout the series, the earlier antifascist critique of militarism, often most urgent when directed at American culture, is displaced onto the enemy, whose belligerence is now an immutably foreign characteristic which no bridge can span.

Given such narratives, scholars have differed on the political import of American wartime propaganda: was it essentially protoconservative, reinforcing extant hierarchies and urging all Americans to set aside claims to social justice in favor of the immediate goal of winning the war? or were more transformative calls lurking beneath the surface of the flag-draped ceremonies and the goads to sacrifice, calls which evoked a nation and world quite distinct from the ones left behind after Pearl Harbor?[79] Much of the language of the official war effort, I contend, aimed to be modestly transformative even while focusing attention on the immediacy of the war's aims. Yet I do not argue here that left-liberal antifascism was dominant during the war: no particular version of Why We Fight attained supremacy. Rather, left-liberal antifascists were able to carve out a viable space for their narratives within the patriotic and often racist barrage of wartime rhetoric, a space sufficiently large and formidable to be easily accessed by those in the first postwar decades who reflected on the war and its outcome.

Forgotten in patriotic commemorations of the twenty-first century is not only the fact that the United States entered the Second World War at a time when the political left was arguably at its highest point of organization and influence in the twentieth century but also that this political power was bringing palpable benefits to the working class. New Deal legislation like the Wagner Act and Fair Labor Standards Act, a largely pro-union War Labor Board that facilitated a vast expansion of union membership, wartime price controls from the Office of Price Administration, and a rank-and-file militancy that took advantage of wartime labor shortages to push for shop floor gains all ensured that the working class benefited disproportionately from the wartime boom. Real wages in manufacturing rose by 27 percent from 1941 to 1944, the poorest paid enjoying the greatest wage increases.[80] Many of the left's constituents, who viewed fascism as a reactionary enemy of the common people, understandably viewed the Allied war effort as extending and solidifying the democratic gains of the New Deal. This view cohered in the narrative of the People's War, ubiquitous in wartime popular culture. This notion defined victory over fascism not simply as the restoration of the status quo but as the undoing of the most reactionary forces at work in the world, a destruction that would bring in its wake a more tolerant, pluralistic, and economically level democracy.

The People's War found a space in the culture partly because key elected officials as well as those who staffed the bodies responsible for defining war aims to the public were palpably impacted by the left-liberal politics of the thirties. Roosevelt's Four Freedoms, the official shorthand for Why We Fight, underscored the left turn of the period. Three of these—Freedom of Speech and Expression, Freedom of Worship, and Freedom from Fear—were standards of Enlightenment liberalism. But FDR's Freedom from Want expanded conventional notions of liberty, adding economic equality to a list of established rights not generally understood to infringe on the rights of property. To use the terms of the French historian George Lefebvre, the fourth freedom added an "equality of means" to a more bourgeois "equality of rights." Moreover, on at least one public occasion the president applied the term *fascism* to the domestic realm in a way fully in line with those of his left-liberal supporters. In his Fireside Chat of January 11, 1944, he warned of "rightist reaction," asserting that "if such reaction should develop—if history were to repeat itself and were to return to the so-called normalcy of the 1920s—then it is certain that even though we shall have conquered our enemies on the battlefields abroad, we shall have yielded to the spirit of Fascism here at home."[81]

Henry Wallace, the vice president from 1940 to 1944, was the public official most associated with the People's War. Though Capra derived his free world / slave world construction from Wallace, the filmmaker used the phrase to create a strikingly different vision. The vice president refused to draw hard lines between domestic and foreign fascism, for he saw racism as its central feature. He explicitly positioned his idea of the war against the publisher Henry Luce's imperial manifesto "The American Century," which imagined a postwar world firmly under American leadership and dominated by its consumer products. In a widely circulated speech titled "The Price of Free World Victory," Wallace asserted, "Some have spoken of the 'American Century.' I say that the century on which we are entering—the century which will come out of this war—can and must be the century of the common man." He then described the American, French, Bolivarian, and Russian revolutions as unfinished struggles which would be complete only with an Allied victory bringing farmers' cooperatives, collective bargaining rights for unions, and universal education worldwide. Wallace's rhetoric was especially important because Roosevelt made fewer and fewer public appearances during the war, leaving to his associates, especially his vice president, the task of defining its aims to the public.[82]

Roosevelt wanted the public to focus primarily on the ideological threat posed by Germany, not on the physical menace of Japan, and in so doing to indict the Nazi leadership rather than the entire German people. Though he was known to play state agencies against one another, this message was consistent across the OWI, the State Department, and other official bodies. An OFF report from mid-1942 defined "those uneducated about the nature of the enemy" as those "inclined to take a shorter view of the war, to think less of the ultimate menace of Hitler and more of settling scores with the Japs in the Pacific." One recent historian has argued that Roosevelt's decision to send troops to North Africa in November 1942 was motivated by his desire to redirect American attention away from the Japanese enemy, a plan that succeeded. Throughout the war he encountered resistance from conservatives, who, fearing that the fight in Europe would leave communists in charge of the continent, intermittently pushed for an Asia-first strategy.[83] The administration's focus on Germany as the central Axis threat as well as its view of the global conflict as a struggle against ideologies rather than peoples was broadly in line with Popular Front antifascism. Though leftists and liberals also participated in the notorious Yellow Peril discourse of the war against Japan, most were far more animated by the war with Germany, as they saw its brand of reaction more closely mirrored in the words and deeds of American rightists.

It was not a coincidence that government agencies disseminated propaganda that sometimes echoed the Popular Front: liberals steeped in the antifascism of the 1930s held key positions in these agencies. Most prominent were Archibald MacLeish, the former editor of the *New Republic,* who was appointed to direct the short-lived OFF; Elmer Davis, head of the OWI, who had also been a member of the American Labor Party; and Robert Sherwood, a key figure in both of these agencies. In addition, the government recruited members of the Frankfurt School to serve as experts on Nazism. Working through the OWI, the Board of Economic Warfare, and the Office of Strategic Services (the precursor of the CIA), Herbert Marcuse, Friedrich Pollock, Franz Neumann, and Otto Kirchheimer contributed to the war effort on a number of fronts: they proposed ways of presenting Nazis to American audiences in the press and in film, devised means of combating German propaganda abroad, crafted de-Nazification policy, and recommended paths to postwar reconstruction in Europe. Neumann's views carried much weight in official circles, which was striking since his major work, *Behemoth: The Structure and Practice of National Socialism* (1942), stridently argued that fascism was a continuation of capitalism and that private property and liberal democracy were incompatible.[84]

Government publications were politically compromised, rarely offering the unvarnished antifascist analysis encountered in the left and liberal presses; yet they contained enough Popular Frontisms to make the OFF and the OWI quite controversial. Replacing the OFF in June 1942, the OWI was to coordinate the federal government's message on the war and its progress, both at home and abroad. It printed literature, directed public relations campaigns (for example, scrap metal, fuel conservation, and Buy War Bonds drives), and produced radio programs and documentaries, sometimes with the help of the culture industry's top talents. The agency was deeply unpopular with congressional conservatives, who perceived it, not incorrectly, as subtly promoting a New Deal vision of the country. Southern Democrats were incensed by one OWI publication, *Negroes at War,* which optimistically held out the hope of racial equality in postwar America. In June 1943, one year after OWI's founding, they teamed up with Republican allies to decimate the agency's budget, prohibiting it from creating materials for domestic consumption. Its Overseas Branch, however, continued to offer political opportunities to those with Popular Front sympathies. Publicly and privately, some OWI personnel stationed abroad worked to undermine what they saw as their government's backsliding on the antifascist goals of the People's War: from its reimposition of French colonial rule in North Africa and its silence on British colonialism in India to its seating of the collaborationist King Victor Emmanuel III on the throne of Italy.[85]

Boosting morale was not strictly an official affair. To this end, Hollywood produced an endless stream of films, network radio offered a barrage of war-related programming, and commercial periodicals, organizational newspapers, and the publishing industry continued to inform and sway vast readerships. The culture industries offered a bill of fare that was overwhelmingly supportive of the war, yet its message often strayed from the OWI guidelines they had promised to uphold. Davis, MacLeish, and officials with the OWI's Bureau of Motion Pictures, for example, complained that Hollywood was offering cheap thrills, gore, and stereotypical portrayals of the enemy rather than serious, sophisticated presentations of war aims. Radio was more cooperative, as stations offered airtime to short commercials and full programs produced by the Domestic Radio Bureau of the OWI and later by the Treasury Department.[86]

Whether or not sanctioned by the government and whether appearing in print, radio, or film, much of the programming designed to bolster wartime morale had an undeniably patriotic tone: praise of the virtues of the American people and the democratic traditions of a free nation were standard fare. Some of the programming was exceptionalist in nature. Speaking on the radio program *What Are We Fighting For?,* a joint project of the War Department and the CBS network, Lee White was in full accord with Luce's American Century when he said, "Consciously or not, we have been an example and a hope for the rest of the world. . . . Pearl Harbor means that America has entered the war, and will win the war, and that America will mold the future of the world."[87] Yet such views were more than matched by other brands of patriotism. In the 1930s the Popular Front had also picked up a nationalist accent, replete with praises of the Constitution, the American people, and national traditions. But Popular Front nationalism was of an aspirational sort: rather than harkening back to national purity best achieved in its founding moments or praising the extant United States as offering the best system in the world, it praised the nation mainly for the promise it held for the future, implicit in its best traditions. The writer Carlos Bulosan best expressed this spirit in his *Saturday Evening Post* piece titled "Freedom from Want," in which he referred to dispossessed workers of America as "the living dream of dead men."[88]

Fearful of alienating global allies, official policy discouraged the message of American world supremacy expressed in Luce's American Century and instead worked in tandem with many in civil society to foment a popular internationalism. This found expression in Wendell Willkie's runaway best-seller *One World* (1943), in which the author, a recent Republican presidential candidate, stressed the need for a world government. Furthermore, nothing would have been more toxic to the administration's political survival at home than to promote the notion, common in twenty-first-century American memory, that the United States fought the war by itself. To dampen continued isolationist grumbling that foreigners were not doing their share, OWI publications and films took pains to highlight the contributions of all Allied nations. Both Roosevelt and Wallace, meanwhile, stressed the reality that the Soviets in particular were doing far more of the fighting and dying than Americans. Thus the nationalism of so much wartime discourse rested not on the claim that the United States was the most superior nation on earth, but on the notion that it was a great and free nation moving forward in tandem with other great, free nations. Corwin's enormously popular radio poem "On a Note of Victory" (1945), for instance, reflected on the meaning of VE Day for all Allied nations when its narrator praised the common soldier of the United Nations, proclaiming, "All the way from Newburyport to Vladivostok, you gave what it took. It seems like free men have done it again!" Corwin followed this proclamation with a sampling of victory songs in Danish, Serbian, Greek, and English, the latter supplied by Woody Guthrie.

In the balance, and notwithstanding its nationalism, wartime programming was far from a negation of 1930s antifascism. Much of the scholarly debate over mainstream propaganda has hinged on the politics of wartime calls to unity; furthermore, the debate has often rested on the assumption that pleas for national unity in wartime were essentially conservative.[89] To the contrary, I would argue that many of the calls to unity during the war were fundamentally left-liberal in nature. On the terrain of national politics, the political left, by definition, is marked by the belief that social divisions are structural and avoidable; it calls attention to social hierarchies in the hope of creating equality and eventual reconciliation. In this vein, what is striking about so much war-related cultural production is the degree to which it acknowledged, sometimes even highlighted, structural divides and prejudices within the United

States. It typically assumed that the nation was divided along the lines of class, race, ethnicity, and sometimes gender: its calls to unity were often aimed at creating a solidarity, one that did not exist before the conflict and that would be realized only through the erasure of established hierarchies. In line with the basic idea of the People's War, a great deal of wartime cultural production imaginatively modeled a nation that would extend the leveling impulses of the New Deal.

Nothing illustrates this dynamic better than "Assignment U.S.A." (1944), aired on the radio program *Words at War*. *Words at War* was a popular show jointly produced by NBC and the National Council on Books in Wartime, an organization established by the publishing industry to support the war by defining its aims. Based on the eponymous book by Selden Menefee (1943) and explicitly dedicated to "the People's War," "Assignment U.S.A." was a guided tour of American prejudice and animosity. Its narrator led listeners through the ethnic caste system of Brattleboro, Vermont; the anti-Semitism driven by the Christian Front in Boston; the Jim Crow racism of the South; the political apathy of the Midwest; and the labor struggles in the shipyards of the West Coast. In almost every region the narrator finds the bigoted and the privileged at fault for cultivating wartime disunity. While in Boston, he talks to an Irish American who has defaced a patriotic poster to make it read "Jew-nited States," and while traveling through Dixie he states, "Large segments of the population are more interested in keeping the Negro in his place than in keeping Hitler and Tojo in their places." The narrator ends on a nationalist note: "Whether or not [reforms] will be done, just as whether or not we're going to drift back after victory to the old head-in-the-sand isolationist ways, depends on the greatest aggregation of free men any reporter has ever surveyed."[90] Far from a nationalism that claimed the United States as a model for emulation, this statement appealed to national pride to get listeners to confront their prejudices and paradoxically questioned their willingness to do so. Further, these upbeat final words do not match the overall tone produced in its coast-to-coast exposure of petty hatreds in the preceding thirty minutes, or its calls for the country to participate in a "world government" after victory. A typical product of the People's War, "Assignment U.S.A." tried to strike a compromise between maintaining wartime morale, mollifying sponsors, and calling for a unity that could come only through structural changes to the prewar status quo. In this instance, the program erred on the side of the latter.

As "Assignment U.S.A." illustrates, the call for a more level democracy was especially marked in the politics of race and ethnicity. As Gary Gerstle has written of the war years, "The contradiction between America's professed commitment to equality and its discriminatory treatment of its black citizens

... received the sort of attention it had not been given since the early days of Reconstruction."[91] American culture in the period of the Second World War was marked by profound crosscurrents. On the one hand, a popular Yellow Perilism fueled the military struggle against Japan. Domestically, there were race riots and so-called hate strikes in industrial cities following African American migration to production centers; the anti-Mexican sentiment of the Zoot Suit riots in Los Angeles; and the infamous internment of Japanese Americans. On the other hand, there was a critical discourse on racial inequality unprecedented in the twentieth century: anthropologists and social scientists who studied racism found themselves with mass audiences hungry for their work; novels and nonfiction works critiquing antiblack racism reached the top of the best-seller lists; the Chinese Exclusion Act was finally repealed in 1943; the federal government made concerted attempts to highlight the contributions of African Americans to the nation; and left and liberal publications continued to expose bigotry and racial violence on the home front and in the military.[92] If war propaganda was forced to acknowledge racial division at home, it was not simply because the public automatically understood Hitler as the epitome of racial hatred and that the war consequently exposed an American hypocrisy requiring redress. Rather, Hitler was legible as racist because of the antifascist cultural work of the 1930s. High-profile agitation by people of color and their allies capitalized on the fight against Hitler to expand and deepen this popular understanding of fascism, forged through a decade of organizing.

The historian Martha Biondi maintains that the Second World War marked the real beginning of the modern civil rights movement, locating its origins in a drive by black Americans to expand the gains of wartime. Their activism impacted the policies of the federal government, which facilitated the expansion of union protections among low-wage workers through the War Labor Board and other agencies. This in turn allowed black wages to rise twice as fast as those of whites and helped to give black workers the biggest bump in their earnings since emancipation.[93] In the struggles of black union activists in the CIO, fights against discrimination in housing and employment, and protests over segregation in the armed forces—all quite intense during the war—a movement took shape. Major black newspapers, most black radicals, and the majority of the black public at large shared an antifascist sensibility that placed the war against fascism in the context of this emerging movement. This sensibility viewed fascism as part of an overlapping, worldwide network of imperialisms.

Most African American writers, journalists, and intellectuals supported the war overall but remained critical of Allied war aims when they deviated, as they often did, from the lofty goals of Wallace's People's Century and the Four Freedoms. This truly global view of Allied wartime aims was fully in line with other antifascisms in that it refused to make strict divisions between the domestic and the foreign. It was the essence of the *Pittsburgh Courier*'s Double V campaign launched in February 1942, which stood for victory overseas *and* victory at home. As part of Double V, the black press consistently praised the bravery of black soldiers serving abroad, whether they were in American uniform or in the uniform of the many other Allied armies.[94] But the campaign's unrelenting attention to discrimination on the home front and in the U.S. military, as well as to the colonial machinations of Britain and France, differed from American patriotic narratives that neatly divided the nations of the earth into a bipolar world of slave peoples (Axis nations) and free peoples (the Allies). Papers like the *Pittsburgh Courier* and the *Chicago Defender* praised the U.S. government when it did the right thing: for example, when it fought workplace discrimination through the Fair Employment Practices Commission (FEPC) and when it used the power of the state to condemn racism. In July 1943 the *Courier* praised a speech by Vice President Wallace, who had asserted, "Those who fan the fires of racial clashes for the purpose of making political capital here at home are taking the first step toward Nazism."[95] But the press quickly critiqued the state when it did not live up to its wartime promises, for instance, when it refused to desegregate the military, failed to give teeth to the FEPC, and facilitated the return of British and French colonial rule to newly liberated territories.[96] The ambivalence of African Americans toward the mission of the Allies revealed an antifascist sensibility that gauged victory in terms broader than the customary military metrics.

The division among liberals and the left during the war pivoted on how one was to address claims for racial and economic justice, manifest in conflicting notions of unity. Most factions supported the Allied war effort, with the notable exception of the small, Trotskyist SWP. The SWP saw an Allied victory as strengthening Western imperialism and creating the precondition for future fascisms; it urged American workers to fight fascism not by supporting the war but by first establishing a revolutionary government at home. (The party leader, James Cannon, spent part of the war in jail for espousing such views.) Outside of such dissident stances there was broad consensus among liberals and the left to support the war on a plan of unity with the following domestic components: acknowledge structural divisions now and agitate against them at the cultural level; prevent conservatives from using the war as a pretext to roll back gains in the areas of labor and civil rights; and curb the influence of violent race-haters and domestic fascists. Within this consensus there was debate as to how aggressively one should fight to expand the gains made during wartime and whether such expansion hurt or helped the cause of unity. Generally speaking, the liberal press, the CPUSA, the leadership of the AFL and CIO, and the New

Deal state tended toward prudence and caution, while the labor leaders John L. Lewis and A. Philip Randolph, the majority of the African American public, socialist militants, and many in the CIO rank and file pursued a more aggressive tack in the areas of civil rights and labor. In the area of labor, the effective difference between the two camps was narrower than imagined by New Left historians. Much has been made of the wartime no-strike pledge that the liberal press and leaders of the AFL, CIO, and CPUSA supported; yet the unions, the Office of Price Administration, and the War Labor Board were able to palpably improve working conditions and organize new unions during the conflict by a variety of other means.[97]

While the differences over the terms of unity were not as vast as some scholars have suggested, they were enough to reshuffle allegiances in some cases. For instance, many African Americans intellectuals who had been supportive of the CPUSA became less so owing to the party's turn from its earlier, principled demands for immediate racial and social justice. The African American novelist Chester Himes, an ardent Double V defender and backer of the CPUSA registered his frustration with shifting party ideas of unity in his novel *If He Hollers Let Him Go.* When his communist union steward ignores his grievance against a white coworker on the grounds of preserving wartime unity, the black proletarian protagonist in the novel responds, "And as for all that gibberish about unity! Get these crackers to unite with me."[98]

Those who stood behind the People's War may have clashed over the terms of unity, but whether they sought to preserve gains or expand them they shared a discourse that was left-liberal in essence and thus in line with the broader world vision of antifascism. The public sphere of the war years contained narrative structures that would later fuel the imaginations of both cold warriors and their critics: but the direction of this anticommunist struggle was not predetermined in the 1940s. Perhaps the greatest accomplishments of American antifascism before 1945 were to keep the darkest currents of American political life from entirely eclipsing the public sphere and to produce memorable analyses that postwar reaction could not extinguish. In one of his weekly radio addresses in January 1939, Coughlin desperately announced, "We on the right today find ourselves on the defensive, because those upon the left have been more successful in winning to their side, either by fair or foul means, great groups of the indifferent—the majority of persons who belong neither to the right nor the left."[99] By means more fair than foul, antifascists kept the Coughlins of America on the defensive, ensuring that a fascist regime in the United States remained a dark fantasy of the cultural imagination.

CHAPTER **3**
Beyond Economics, Without Guarantees
Faschismustheorie in the United States

> [Fascism] certainly shows that men can be coerced or cajoled into accepting pathetically little in a world which might give them abundance, provided the dictator can give them such emotional satisfactions as come from their personal identification with the glory of their nation and the grandeur of their race. What is newest and most significant in Fascism, Italian and German alike, is not its economics . . . rather it is the extent to which it has driven the notion of the sovereignty of the na,tional state exercised under a party dictatorship.
> NORMAN THOMAS, *Fascism or Socialism? The Choice Before Us* (1934)

> The doctrine of economic determinism [is] frequently confused with Marxism. People who say that "it's all a matter of economics" or "fascism is inevitable" are echoing a mechanical fatalism of a theory which pretends to explain all historical events in terms of blind forces over which men have no measure of control.
> SAMUEL SILLEN, *The New Masses* (1939)

A seemingly insignificant back-page story in the *London Times* from September 12, 1933—no doubt digested and quickly forgotten by most readers—illuminates the politics and cultural impact of the early antifascist left. It was a report on a communist mass rally in Paris, organized as a show of solidarity for those accused in the infamous Reichstag fire trial in Germany. After the demonstrators sang "The Internationale," it was reported that "water carafes, chairs, and other convenient missiles from neighborhood cafés were hurled at the police." At a subsequent meeting, those assembled passed a unanimous resolution which the *Times* quoted: "Fifteen thousand citizens assembled at this meeting denounce the parody of justice which is being prepared at Leipzig. . . . They . . . denounce the quadruple crime which is being prepared in the name of *racism and intolerance*."[1]

Sandwiched between other columns buried in the back of the paper, this piece would have been unnoteworthy amid the wash of international media coverage on the trial and its related events, except that it is one of the first appearances of the word *racism* in the English language and is indicative of its early usages. The origins of the term *racism* have gone unexamined in ethnic studies in the United States, which generally notes in passing that it came into general circulation in the 1960s.[2] But long before then it was a recognizable term. That it first emerged in a translation from the French is not coincidental; according to the *Oxford English Dictionary,* the English term likely derived from the French word *racisme,* first recorded in 1902. But in the English-language world people mostly used the word in its early years to make sense of fascism, and it was injected into public discourse by the opponents of fascist regimes. In its sporadic appearances before 1938 the word was synonymous with *Nazism,* functioning as a kind of shorthand for the fusion of nationalism and racial intolerance that marked the German variety of fascism.[3] To be sure, when the antifascist left of the 1930s critiqued the racial politics of its opponents, *racism* was but one word in its arsenal, interposed within an older vocabulary of terms like *race hate, white supremacy, color prejudice,* and *race dominance.*[4] Its usage spiked in 1938, when Italy adopted *razzismo* as a state doctrine and its critics, most notably the pope, were widely quoted as condemning it. The first extended exposition of the word came from the German socialist and pioneering gay activist Magnus Hirschfeld, whose book *Racism* (1938), published for the first time in English, dissected the Nazi ideology of race, demonstrating its etymology in the history of European thought. In May 1939 the first American periodical explicitly devoted to combating "racism," *Equality* magazine, was launched. A quintessential Popular Front journal, it was devoted to curbing fascism in Europe and the United States, particularly the rightist politics of people like Charles Coughlin.[5] By the end of the decade those who employed the term, almost always to criticize fascist regimes, ceased to use quotation marks, signaling its familiarity. In 1939 the *New York Times* opined, "The present era has given us a brand-new word for an old superstition—'racism.'"[6]

Antifascists did not invent what we now call antiracism. Rather, the early articulations of racism often denoted a political force that solidified racial hierarchies precisely because such hierarchies were a function of nationalism, class rule, and authoritarianism. As such, these early usages point to earlier and productive understandings of the term which have since been obscured. Moreover, the first appearances of the word underscore new, influential ways of conceiving the social generated by the antifascist left, the legacy of which has yet to be adequately explored.

I want to look here at the interrogation of fascism by its American opponents in the thirties, namely, what was fascism in the eyes of liberals, socialists, and communists? and what did they view as the broader social forces enabling it? These questions have not been answered in the scholarship to date. Nevertheless, historians of European fascism have made a number of assumptions about the ideologies of its left-wing opponents around the world. A case study of the discourses of American antifascists, heavily informed by European exiles and organizations, should be a call to revisit the theoretical basis of antifascism.

A commonplace assumption among scholars is that Marxist and other left-wing thinkers before the war shared a simplistic reading of their enemy, one that held fascists to be mere puppets in the hands of capitalists. The left, these scholars assert, either misunderstood fascism as an ideological mask behind which lurked monopoly capital, or they narrowly saw it as capitalism in an advanced stage of decay.[7] But this view oversimplifies left-wing analyses of fascism. Often these scholars base their claims strictly on the major statements of Comintern policy or on the assertions of the most prominent international communists, such as Karl Radek and Georgi Dimitrov. However, if one looks beyond the Congresses of the Comintern and into the broader culture of the global antifascist movement of the left at midcentury—even the broader culture of the CPUSA—one finds a more layered class analysis that takes the noneconomic dimensions of fascism much more seriously than has been acknowledged.

It would be problematic to view fascism as a capitalist plot, casting the upper classes as its ultimate beneficiaries and true driving force. As I argued in chapter 1, European fascism was in fact enabled by German, Italian, and Spanish economic elites whose profits from these regimes were quite real. But these beneficiaries were not its primary agents, by and large; this dubious honor went to the dispossessed middle classes, animated by violent visions of national renewal. An analysis of fascism focused exclusively on the machinations of great wealth might be able to inform a counterstrategy capable of redirecting middle-class anger away from people of color, religious minorities, communists, and foreigners. But it would not furnish its opponents with concrete tools for combating the psychological and emotional appeals of nationalism, racism, and militarism so critical to fascism's middle-class base.

Contrary to what many scholars have assumed, fascism's left-wing opponents in the 1930s developed new explanatory models that dispensed with orthodox economic reductionism and discarded teleological notions of their own inevitable victory. Antifascism needed to be able to articulate how ideologies of national supremacy destroy democratic aspirations by appealing to and reinforcing privileges of class, race, gender, and sexuality. Indeed, antifascists rarely met this challenge in its entirety. But with surprising frequency they did make productive connections, even before the birth of the Popular Front in 1935, that scholars would now call intersectional. Indeed, for many antifascists, fascism was less a concrete regime in Germany and Italy than a vehicle to conceive the connectedness of seemingly divergent struggles. Their break with narrow economic reductionism arguably formed the larger movement culture behind Western Marxism, particularly the work of Gramsci and the Frankfurt School. German antifascists and scholars developed a useful term for political interpretations of fascism: *Faschismustheorie.* The word is more than its rough English translation of "fascism theory." It indicates one's definition of fascism and, at the same time, a politicized understanding of it which guides one's strategy and countermoves in the field. The transnational Faschismustheorien animating the various strands of the American left before 1945 are central to any understanding of how antifascism developed in the United States as a political praxis.

There was a surprising degree of intellectual cross-fertilization in the notions of fascism put forth by left-of-center thinkers in the thirties. While communists, socialists, and liberals disagreed on the proper strategy for fighting fascist aggression and while their sectarian fights could be quite harsh, their portraits of the common foe converged in key areas to form a shared framework for understanding their mutual enemy. This framework, which continued to inform left and liberal politics well into the postwar period, was far better equipped to combat Blackshirts, Brownshirts, and their American equivalents than postwar critics have held. If a generic understanding of fascism could be extrapolated from the extended writings on the subject by American liberals and leftists in the 1930s, it would go something like this: fascism is a rightist form of nationalist violence latent in all modern capitalist societies and is fueled by anti-Marxism and established racial hierarchies. Left unchecked, it creates a militaristic, racialist, and repressive society that is forced down its citizens' throats by a one-party state obsessed with atavistic symbolism and that ultimately safeguards private property and furthers imperialism by destroying any space for democratic mobilization.

During the early years of the Nazi regime there were frantic attempts across the public sphere to define this new international force. On the left, influential periodicals that developed the most elaborate sketches of fascism included the *New Republic* and the *Nation* (liberal), the *American Socialist Quarterly* (*ASQ*) and the *New Leader* (socialist), and the *New Masses,* the *Communist,* and *Fight!* (communist-oriented). During the thirties these journals translated the work of European and Asian authors and offered them as privileged commentaries on the situations in their countries. American readers of the left and liberal presses accordingly developed an international perspective on antifascism, one greatly informed by such sources as Henri Barbusse, Chou En-lai, Mao Zedong, Leon Trotsky, Ilya Ehrenburg, Vincenzo Vacirca, Haru Matsui, Otto Bauer, and

John Strachey. In addition, left-of-center American authors Edgar Mowrer, Raymond Gram Swing, and Norman Thomas published books on fascism in the first years of the Nazi regime. As we have seen, the first American novel about the phenomenon, Sinclair Lewis's *It Can't Happen Here,* appeared in 1935.

Aided by commentary from overseas, American leftists and their allies emphasized the class politics of fascism, posing a set of questions that perhaps ring strange to those who came of age after the Holocaust. They debated, for instance, such queries as, what social classes form fascism's primary base of support? can its working-class victims continue to resist? would the cross-class coalitions holding it together fissure or hold? which groups, the middle classes, the capitalists, or declassed adventurers, were really in charge of fascism after it took power? could the Italian and German regimes resolve the economic crises in their countries? what shifts in class composition and the nature of employment made fascism so appealing? Later critics who singled out Marxists for focusing too much on such questions failed to see that an emphasis on the economic dimensions of fascism was ubiquitous in the thirties, not only among liberals but throughout the public sphere. *Business Week, Barron's Financial Weekly, Time, Newsweek, Living Age, Contemporary Review,* and the *Saturday Evening Post* were consumed with these same general questions, particularly in the first half of the decade.[8] Academic writing on the subject, produced by ideologically diverse scholars, also concentrated on the class politics of fascism.[9]

On these economic questions, liberal, communist, and socialist observers of Italy and Germany agreed on the following: (a) fascism could not have come to power without the financial and political support of the upper classes, fearful of Marxist revolution and anxious to preserve their power; (b) before taking power, its main base of support is the middle classes—small business, farmers of modest means, university students, artisans, low-ranking professionals—fearful of losing their social status but unwilling to join the left; (c) while still a political movement, fascism tries to co-opt socialism by addressing the anticapitalist fears of the masses but promptly breaks its populist promises after coming to power; (d) it achieves economic stabilization on the backs of peasants and the urban working class, who endure longer hours, speed ups, reduced wages, and the destruction of their unions; and (e) it will not resolve domestic economic crises to the satisfaction of its people and will eventually need to undertake a war of expansion to avoid political upheaval at home (there was not total consensus on this last point, but it was a ubiquitous view). The first four of these conclusions, it should be noted, have been perennially upheld by postwar historians from a wide range of ideological perspectives, some of whom may draw more from the class frames of the 1930s than they acknowledge.[10] And these observations on the class basis of the Italian and German regimes, particularly the first four, were not much different from those drawn by individuals outside the left and liberal public sphere. A commentator in *Barron's Financial Weekly* in 1933, for example, summarized fascism's class politics in a way that would have been quite at home in the pages of the *New Masses* or the *Nation*:

> [Fascism] is essentially this: the mobilization of the middle classes, of those who have or think they have a small stake in the existing order—the small business man, the professional man, the small farmer—behind big business and big (in Germany feudal) agriculture for the defense of the existing order against a threatened attack by those who have no stake in the existing order. This is necessary and even possible only under conditions of extreme social pressure, when a political and economic crisis reaches such proportions that the existing system cannot afford the ordinary concessions possible under a democratic form of government—the rights of political expression, free speech, free assembly, trade unions, strikes, etc., while at the same time the working classes are driven to press forward more and more sharply their economic and political claims.[11]

Like the rest of the business press, *Barron's* drew rather different moral conclusions about Hitler than the *New Masses*. The "most disturbing element" of Hitler's new government, argued its editorial page, was the cabinet appointment of the industrialist Alfred Hugenberg, who wanted to reduce payments on Germany's external debt.[12] Nevertheless, this example illustrates how detailed class analysis was not a monopoly of the left but the spirit of an age in which economic collapse and an organized workers' movement kept class frames at the center of public debate.

Left and liberal observers of Germany and Italy substantively disagreed, however, on which political groups and class fractions commanded those countries after the fascist state was in place. Were the industrialists and financiers at the helm? were the mostly middle-class fascists an autonomous power in their own right? or, following Marx's writings on Bonapartism, did fascism create a humming capitalist economy without the political supervision of the capitalists, that is, "capitalism without the bourgeoisie"? The left offered its most crude answer to all these questions through what I call the puppet master theory. The puppet master theory posited big business as the true power behind the thrones of Hitler and Mussolini, the capitalist directly or indirectly pulling the strings of the dictators. It was especially common in communist circles during the early thirties, yet was remarkably resilient to the various shifts in the party line. Harry F. Ward, the Methodist minister who chaired the ALAWF, offered this analysis in 1936 when he wrote, "Fascism, both in theory and as a political regime, is a beautiful example of the wolf in sheep's clothing. For the wolf substitute, in your mind's eye, the sleek, crafty, resourceful and utterly ruthless power of finance capital, trapped in the blind-alley of its own contradictions."[13] Such perspectives were common enough among communists but were by no means limited to them. In a speech to steelworkers in 1937, John L. Lewis, the president of the CIO, called fascism "the outright dictatorship of big business," a label also used by the liberal Stuart Chase and the socialist Upton Sinclair earlier in the decade.[14] The puppet master theory often brought with it an inadequate racial analysis that saw racism and anti-Semitism as epiphenomenal smoke screens thrown up by capitalists rather than as deeply rooted hierarchies in which middle- and working-class subjects might have a sincere investment and agency. What was needed here was a theory that could show how racial logics, even when they originate in class structures or function to perpetuate them, can assume a life of their own that spirals beyond the control of capital, constituting a crisis in its own right.

The Enlarged Executive, the central body of the Comintern, was in many ways the origin of the puppet master theory. The Comintern's definition of fascism went through two major incarnations in the 1930s: the period from 1928 to July 1935, when it followed the so-called Third Period analysis, and the summer of 1935 to July 1939, when it pursued its Popular Front policy. In the first phase, the international party leadership described capitalism as entering a third period of development marked by bourgeois dictatorship and increasingly aggressive imperial war. Fascism, one form of bourgeois dictatorship, was the negation of an older bourgeois democracy and was the means sought by a decaying capitalism to continue its rule during a time of crisis. What the Ukrainian Third Period theorist D. Z. Manuilsky called its "extreme nationalism" and "medieval garb" was only its "ideological shell."[15] Its public rituals, spectacles, and racial ideology were only masks to conceal its true face, which was capitalism by other means.

The course of action which followed from this theory was for communists to continue full steam ahead with the struggle to smash capitalism, the origin of fascism, without making serious attempts to cultivate alliances with others who also hated fascism but did not necessarily share this goal, for example, Social Democrats, Jewish organizations, and nonrightists in general. In Weimar Germany the plan of action they deduced from this theory was especially toxic. In February 1932, a year before Hitler's seizure of power, the chair of the German Communist Party (KPD), Ernst Thälmann, argued that since fascism is capitalism in disguise the party must attack it at the root by directing its energies against, of all groups, the Social Democrats, who, as "the moderate wing of fascism," were ultimately the greatest obstacle to revolution.[16] The KPD infamously called Social Democracy "social fascism," and in the early 1930s their American comrades often followed suit by hurling the same epithet at the New Deal.[17] It should be noted that Americans who followed Trotsky to the letter offered a disappointing variant of the puppet master theory in the 1930s. They stressed the petit bourgeois nature of fascism as a movement, but they often implied fascism's firm control by the capitalists once it was established. What they concluded from this theory was the need to combat fascism by directly attacking its capitalist roots, a position the *New Militant* and then the Socialist Workers' Party adopted more stridently as the CP moved away from such rhetoric during the Popular Front. This view did not lead them to probe the nature of its racial nationalism as deeply as they could. American Trotskyists, however, had a much richer debate on the issue of American fascism in the 1950s.[18]

Another common view in the 1930s, inside and outside the left, held that capitalists and traditional elites were beneficiaries and backers of fascism yet were no longer holding the actual reigns after the Duces and Führers took power. Such a position had prominent advocates in the European left. As David Beetham and Dave Renton showed in their respective surveys of European antifascism, communist and Social Democratic orthodoxy was challenged at an early stage by the more productive Faschismustheorien emanating from figures like Gramsci, Klara Zetkin, Gyula Sas, August Thalheimer, and Ignazio Silone. These Marxists concurred that fascism preserved capitalism at a time of crisis, but some also stressed that it possessed a certain autonomy from the capitalist interests with which it was allied.[19] Unsurprisingly, analyses along these lines crossed the Atlantic. Writing in the *ASQ,* for example, the exiled Italian Socialist parliamentarian Vincenzo Vacirca argued that such regimes begin as a class dictatorship supported by the masses, develop into a true oligarchy, and finally become "a personal tyranny which may rule against the will and interests of all classes." Vacirca asserted, "Fascism in Italy now takes towards capitalism the position of certain gangsters, hired by some American manufacturers for strike-breaking purposes, of whom they cannot rid themselves and who blackmail them without mercy." Variations on this "gangster metaphor" of fascism, quite common on the left in the thirties and forties, were given elaborate expression in the modernisms of Bertolt Brecht, Orson Welles, and Dashiell Hammett and were especially common among the so-called Socialist Militants at the *ASQ*.[20] But the gangster narrative began to appear as well in CP publications during the Popular Front period. The *New Masses,* for example, published an exposé on the shakedown of American businessmen in Germany titled "Germany's Al Capone," accompanied by an illustration of the Nazi gun thugs "sticking up" a businessman (fig. 3).[21]

The gangster image served as a digestible metaphor for a generation reared in detective noir, one which crystallized a complex theory of fascist class politics for popular circulation. Behind it was the idea that although traditional

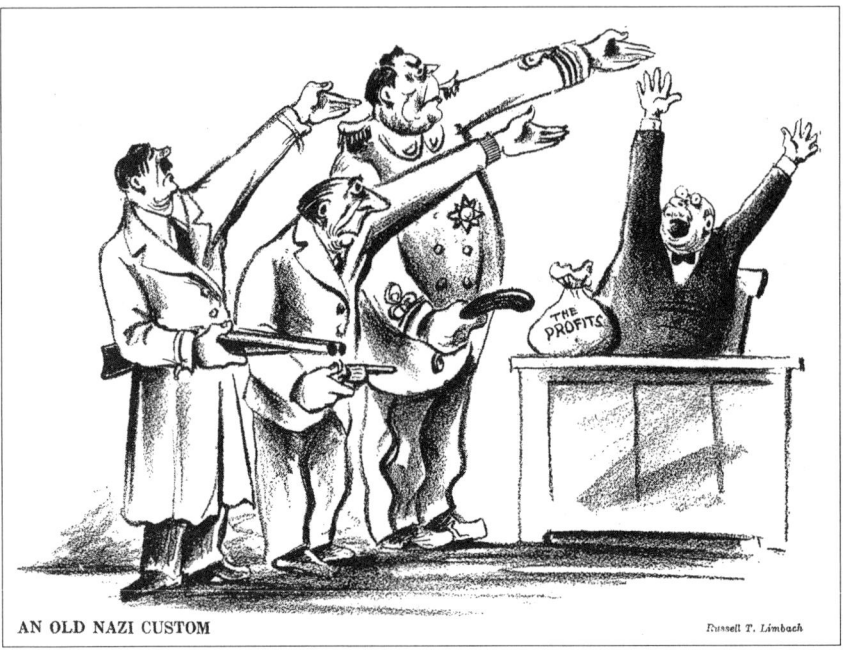

FIGURE 3. The gangster metaphor of fascism in the Communist press. *New Masses*, January 7, 1936.

elites enabled fascism, they could not control its direction once the new authoritarian state was erected, causing real friction within the class coalitions which initially supported the fascist power grab. In some iterations, as in Vacirca's analysis, the gangster metaphor could err in the opposite direction of the puppet master theory, overstating the disempowerment of elites under fascist rule. In accessing the class politics of fascism, the left was at its best and most historically accurate when it posited the notion of fascism as capitalism without the capitalists, a view sometimes expressed through the gangster metaphor. In this interpretation, fascism sustains capitalism but under circumstances in which capitalists are compelled to cede political control. An important group of German and Austrian Marxists, including Otto Bauer and a segment of the exiled Frankfurt School led by Friedrich Pollock, put forth a nuanced variant that viewed the declining control of the capitalist under fascism not as a fundamentally chaotic situation but as part of a concrete phase of capitalist development they called "state capitalism." This theory read fascism as part of a wider trend in political economy which also encompassed Keynesianism. Breaking with laissez-faire and facilitated by monopolistic concentration, state capitalism was a new phase of capitalist development wherein the state, not private capitalists, directs investment within a new synthesis that preserves the system of private property.[22] In the United States the view of fascism as capitalism without the capitalists appeared sporadically across the left and liberal spectrum, for instance, in Lewis's *It Can't Happen Here,* in writings by Thomas and Max Shachtman, in topical reportage in the *Nation,* in the Communist Party Opposition paper *Workers Age,* and in the theoretical journal of the Socialist Party.[23]

Thus the puppet master theory was one idea circulating among others on the left. Even when it was officially promoted by the CPUSA in the early 1930s the idea was not universal, even among communists, for the party never exercised ironclad control over its members to ensure absolute ideological uniformity. (This was a Cold War cliché that has been thoroughly debunked by scholars.)[24] And during the Popular Front period of the second half of the decade, a profound ambiguity within the Comintern's Faschismustheorie took the communist-oriented left further from the puppet master paradigm. Prompted by the French CP, the Comintern itself came to realize that one needed to take the mask of fascist ideology seriously to effectively combat it and formalized this view with the announcement of its Popular Front policy at its Seventh Congress in July–August 1935. The addresses of the Bulgarian communist Georgi Dimitrov to the Congress were widely circulated in pamphlet form around the world, including the United States. In them, he continued to refer to fascist ideology as a mask, but now the true face beneath the mask was not only capitalism but also "unbridled chauvinism and annexationist war" as well as "rabid reaction." Now that its true face included chauvinism, Dimitrov made clear that its nationalism needed to be confronted on its own terms. "Our comrades in Germany," he noted, "for a long time failed to reckon with the wounded national sentiments and indignation of the masses at the Versailles Treaty." Calling for revolution would not be enough to wean people from fascist demagoguery; he urged communists to beat the fascists at their own game, to claim the nation for themselves and refuse to "relinquish to fascist falsifiers all that is valuable in the historical past of the nation."[25]

Dimitrov affirmed the idea that capitalists were the power behind the throne in fascist movements and governments. But, he stressed, fascism should no longer be seen as the intent and end-goal of all capitalists. In an oft-quoted line, he shrank its political base by asserting that fascism, once in power, is "the open terrorist dictatorship of the most reactionary, most chauvinistic and most imperialist elements of finance capital." As such, it serves "the interests of the most reactionary circles of the bourgeoisie," not the class as a whole.[26] Dimitrov thereby opened the door for a coalition with liberals and reformists more inclined to join battle against the common enemy of the hard right than against capitalism in general. As such, the Popular Front inaugurated a sustained attempt to win over the middle classes, fascism's political base. After 1935 the writers of the American magazine *Fight!*, the publication of the ALAWF, followed suit by airing fewer grievances against FDR and the whole capitalist system and more against Henry Ford, J. P. Morgan, U.S. Steel, and Wall Street. And, famously, U.S. communists also took up Dimitrov's call by using icons of the American past, from Thomas Jefferson to Frederick Douglass, to claim the nation for themselves and their project of social leveling rather than leave this terrain to their would-be fascist rivals.

Dimitrov's Popular Front Faschismustheorie was still inadequate, to be sure. From a historical perspective, his assertion that fascism was a machination of finance capital is simply not true: prominent financiers were among its supporters, in Germany in particular, but they were mere coalition partners at best. His focus on the most abstract and universally reviled subdivision of capital makes sense only as a political move to co-opt Nazi anti-Semitism, disassociating finance from Jewishness and internationalism yet feeding the popular anticapitalist animus against the bankers who undergirded it. To maintain the underlying conspiratorial grammar of anti-Semitism, however, was a dangerous move. In all, the Comintern opened the door for a richer analysis of fascism but only partway. Its emphasis on the agency of finance capital helps to explain the continued appearance of the capitalist plot narrative in the American communist press during the Popular Front period and beyond. At the same time, by reducing the cast of capitalist villains to a reactionary core, it facilitated the adoption of the gangster metaphor in periodicals like the *New Masses*. More important, the new emphasis on "wounded national sentiments" promoted a strategy that could address far more than economic exploitation—which is precisely what antifascists did.

What observers of antifascism have typically ignored is the sheer amount of time that American communists as well as their socialist and liberal counterparts devoted to debunking the psychological and institutional specifics of racism, anti-Semitism, patriarchy, militarism, and fascist nationalism, even during the Third Period. *Fight!* committed most of its pages to such issues; indeed, articles in this vein eclipsed those on labor strife and the machinations of the rich. The placement of noneconomic matters in a magazine devoted to combating fascism reveals an assumption that such social phenomena were constitutive of the targeted foe; it also underscores a belief that they needed to be mapped and analyzed in their own right.

During the Popular Front, the review section of the party's cultural journal the *New Masses* praised works which avoided economic determinism in favor of a more multifaceted portrait of fascism's psychological and political appeals to all classes. In 1935, for instance, a *New Masses* review of *Fascism—Make or*

Break?, printed by International Publishers, critiqued its author for "overemphasizing economic factors to the neglect of political and psychological factors." The book *Hitler Is No Fool* (1939) by the German communist exile Karl Billinger, whose birth name was Paul Massing, emphasized the racial nationalism of the Nazi regime and its ideological specifics. When Billinger argued, in this context, that economic determinism was not real Marxism, he was praised for doing so by Samuel Sillen in his review of the book.[27] Another reviewer lauded Ernst Glaeser's novel *The Last Civilian* (1935) for its psychological detail, which he regarded as necessary for meeting the fascist threat. The critic argued that "neither [the industrialist] Thyssen's backing of Hitler nor Goering's perversions suffice to explain the positive note, the almost unreserved enthusiasm with which the middle class and part of the working class hailed Hitlerism."[28] The *New Masses* review section was guided by a long-standing advocacy of realist aesthetics which privileged psychological depth over caricature and a focus on ordinary individuals over an emphasis on villains and heroes. As such, it advocated an antifascist aesthetic capable of probing the nature of fascism's appeal to the average citizen, not one that simply revealed behind-the-scenes machinations of power.

Attention to fascist racial politics was pervasive across the left. The Socialist Party Old Guard was especially disinclined to ignore them: they were intimately tied to the JLC and the German boycott campaign and consequently were in frequent contact with actual refugees. Their journal, the *New Leader,* highlighted anti-Semitism in its discussions of fascism, generally probing its inner workings in greater detail than the avowedly militant *ASQ.* As the decade closed, communist publications became broader forums for exploring the nature of racism and anti-Semitism, and they did so in ways that did not simply reduce racial structures to the status of intentional capitalist smoke screens. The party's campaign against anti-Semitism was part of its broader attempt to attract Jews, wherein its various organizations encouraged the expression of Jewish pride. Such efforts may account for the fact that by 1939, 40 percent of CPUSA members were Jewish Americans.[29] In July 1941 the *New Masses* put out a special issue titled "The Negro in American Life," which its editors framed as a part of the struggle against American fascism by beginning with a reference to "Georgia's Fuehrer Talmadge," that is, Eugene Talmadge, the Jim Crow governor of the state. It featured a piece by Franz Boas, the renowned anthropologist and Austrian Jewish exile, which put forth his famous argument against the idea of race as a biological category, offering in its place the notion of race as a cultural construct.[30] From 1939 on, as Coughlin's audience grew and became more rabidly anti-Semitic, CPUSA pamphlets denouncing fascism in the United States began to focus on the problem of Jew baiting. To this end, the party chair, Earl Browder, coauthored a pamphlet in 1943 titled *Anti-Semitism: What It Means and How to Combat It*.[31] Furthermore, communist publications generally devoted far more space to the issues of racism and anti-Semitism than most of their socialist and white liberal counterparts.

The precise ways in which writers for the communist press linked race, class, and nationalism varied widely; what is important is the sheer amount of energy they expended in exposing the holes in fascist nationalism and its racial theories. If anti-Semitism and nationalism were mere smoke screens, why dissect them in such detail? The communists' constant references to lynching, nativism, anti-Asian violence, the persecution of Jews, and other so-called racial diversions underscore a simple truth: to analyze the mask at length was to take it seriously. It also suggests that a flawed, overly reductionist Faschismustheorie did not always foreclose a more efficacious plan of action. That is, one could hold fascism's racial ideology to be a mask for capitalism but still organize against the mask as such. Within this context, contrary to the claims of a number of later scholars, many leftists during the Third Period and after saw working- and middle-class whites as agents of fascism's racial nationalism, further undermining the notion that the left viewed the fascist movement as a top-down capitalist conspiracy.[32]

Langston Hughes's one-page short story "Conversation," published in *Fight!* in October 1936, exemplifies the kinds of linkages between race and class which were possible in party-affiliated publications during the Popular Front period. Hughes never uses the word *fascism,* but the placement of his story in a magazine devoted to this subject leaves no doubt about its intended context. The narrative is built around a dialogue between two white southerners. The two men run into each other on a street in Washington, D.C., and one brags to the other that he "shot four niggers" on a recent trip back home. They needed to be shot, he says, because the Reds have been organizing African Americans and "settin' their minds against us white folks," instilling in them the belief that they should earn as much pay as whites. The federal government is also at fault for "spoiling" blacks by paying them the same amount of relief as the whites. As the two continue their conversation, the killer adds, "I'm a hundred per cent American! And I reckon I can kill a nigger if I want to." The two then say their goodbyes and return to work.[33]

While the story isn't Hughes's best literary endeavor, it does illustrate a reading of fascism that contradicts assumptions about communist antifascism held by many postwar scholars. "Conversation" does not project anti-Marxism and racial violence as a capitalist plot, but the inverse: it suggests that the southern fascist fear of communists is driven by long-established racial anxieties and a desire to retain relative economic privileges. Further, the man's complaints about outside agitators—both the Reds and the federal government—locate fascism within a broader reactionary worldview, one that sees domestic discord as the result of external interference. The character stops that foreign threat not only through murder but also by announcing his "one hundred per cent" Americanness, restoring national honor and affirming his rightful place in the nation through racial violence. His brutal act is a decidedly fascist move but also a gesture instantly recognizable to American readers as domestic in nature. Though Hughes leaves the class position of the two men indeterminate, the illustrations reveal that disenfranchised whites are also agents of fascist racial violence. Four sketches on the page depict four dialogues occurring: one between two businessmen, one between men of indeterminate social status, and the final two between decrepit farmers or sharecroppers. Visually, the page implies that this protofascist "conversation" is happening among whites of every social class.

"Conversation" is representative of a general pattern of 1930s antifascism in a second sense. As the left argued throughout the decade, hierarchies of class, race, and gender created misery that could be exploited by fascist demagogues who appealed to the masses' desire for relief. Over time, insisted its activists, deep structural inequalities created ingrained modes of thinking among the people, which prevented the lateral unity (often, class unity) necessary to oppose the social degeneration leading toward fascism and war. For example, in describing the divisions among women factory workers in her booklet *Women, War, and Fascism* (1935), the ALAWF activist Dorothy McConnell wrote, "The married women, who have been most discriminated against, are afraid of the young girls replacing them. The young girls are resentful of the married women who hold jobs that might otherwise be theirs. The workers are criss-crossed with deep and bitter antagonisms. The state is thus less threatened." "The tradition at the root of the whole business," she continued, "is that of less wages for women. . . . Woman, as a cheap source of labor, is a danger to man. He resents her as a threat to his economic security." McConnell subsequently stressed that such gendered exploitation was critical to the fascist project of military expansion.[34]

As in Hughes's "Conversation," what becomes clear in McConnell's argument, as with so much antifascist writing in the thirties, is that fascism is almost ancillary to her social critique. McConnell's analysis could work just as well to describe the role of capitalism in perpetuating patriarchy or the role of patriarchy in perpetuating capitalism or imperialism. For McConnell, Hughes, and so many activists on the left, fascism was often less a specific regime in Europe than a way to conceive the relationship between apparently distinct struggles. If socialism was the positive end-goal of efforts to eliminate inequality, fascism designated the nightmarish backsliding of a world in which the suffering generated by interlocked hierarchies was allowed to fester, unredressed. Figures like Dimitrov helped to set general parameters around the use of the term *fascism,* but its meaning was, as always, a structure of feeling refracted through the lived experiences of a diverse range of activists who confronted, in their minds, seemingly every social hierarchy at once.

Liberal Faschismustheorie had much in common with its socialist and communist counterparts. The standard-bearer of most liberals, FDR, adopted an antifascist foreign policy from early 1939 on, though he had regarded fascism as the greatest threat to world peace and stability from the earliest days of his presidency. However, he refused to define the specific traits and features of this menace during the Depression years. Indeed, before December 29, 1940, the president publicly used the word *Nazi* on only five occasions, and very rarely did he name the aggressors to whom he referred.[35] Putting flesh on the monster's bones was a task he left to members of his administration and to allies in civil society: it was they who performed the cultural work necessary to furthering his foreign policy agenda. Prominent in this regard were the magazines the *New Republic* and the *Nation* and the writings and speeches of Raymond Gram Swing, Lewis Mumford, Dorothy Thompson, Edgar Mowrer, William Shirer, Stuart Chase, Waldo Frank, Henry Wallace, Archibald MacLeish, Norman Corwin, Robert Sherwood, Harold Ickes, and Quentin Reynolds.

These individuals largely preserved the socialist and communist emphases on economics and the class struggles over fascism; and like those on the left, they tended to acknowledge the need for a precise examination of its nationalism, racial theories, and psychology in order to effectively counter its existential appeals. In a speech in 1939, then-Secretary of Agriculture Henry Wallace used Boas's work to debunk the idea of Aryan supremacy and, by extension, biological racism. Against the claims of Hitler's government, he argued, "No one can claim with scientific certainty superiority for any race or nation so far as its inborn genetic characteristics are concerned." Wallace saw racialism as a central tenet of fascism; he drew on Boas to describe culture, not innate racial characteristics, as the basis of difference across human societies and refused to order this difference hierarchically. Yet Wallace's image of fascism was not reducible to race. In a piece called "The Dangers of American Fascism," published in the *New York Times* in 1944, Wallace, like most leftists, contended that fascism was widespread in the United States also and said that its most identifiable features were racism, misguided nationalism, and "the lust for money and power."[36]

Yet liberal antifascists betrayed one analytical tendency far more frequently than socialist and communist writers, one that would develop into a distinct strand of wartime propaganda and later prove amenable to Cold War politics. As internationalists, most American leftists rejected the notion that the German and Italian peoples were uniquely depraved and thought the idea that Americans were innately anti-authoritarian was dangerously naïve.[37] Yet some liberal writers placed Germany and Italy outside the pale of Western civilization, and in a few cases elevated American national character as something the fascist menace could scarcely hope to penetrate.

Before Pearl Harbor, the correspondents Shirer and Mowrer, both of whom had been based in Germany for a time, were perhaps most influential in this regard. Mowrer won a Pulitzer Prize for his reporting on the rise of Hitler in 1933, and Shirer's *Berlin Diary* was the number one nonfiction best seller in 1941. Their interpretations of Nazism were remarkably similar, and not by coincidence: they knew one another, since British and American correspondents in Berlin in those days gathered in a tight community centered around a cheap Italian restaurant called Die Taverne.[38] They had virtually the same analysis of the class politics surrounding the Nazi ascent. Their major works assert that it was enabled by conservatives and business leaders who were fearful of Marxism and that the socialist Social Democratic Party was the only force capable of saving the country for democracy. Yet they departed from most radicals by ascribing the failure of the Social Democrats and of the opposition in general to a singular, long-standing deficiency of the German people. Mowrer called this deficiency Prussianism: a penchant for military models of order, leadership, and efficiency combined with a servility to social betters. Thus when the Germans once again deferred to elite rule under Hitler, Mowrer lamented that "Germany had reverted to type." As contributors to what came to be known in academic circles as the Luther to Hitler thesis, Mowrer and Shirer also viewed racial nationalism as singularly rooted in German philosophy, evidenced by the work of J. G. Fichte, G. W. F. Hegel, Richard Wagner, and Friedrich Nietzsche.[39]

The Luther to Hitler thesis was often accompanied by the corollary that Nazism was a phenomenon exterior to the Enlightenment rather than something latent within its unresolved tensions. To Americans this meant it was largely alien to the Anglo-American tradition, a view which sometimes led to an orientalization of fascism. Mowrer wrote, for example, that the absence of liberal republicans in Germany was a sign that "Germany belonged only with about half of its soul . . . to the occidental world."[40] Some liberals used the Luther to Hitler thesis to confidently assert that Americans would be immune to fascist wiles and that fascism needed to be stopped primarily because it was a threat to other peoples. Mumford offered a telling example in his book *Men Must Act* (1939), an adamant call for an interventionist foreign policy. He wrote, "We have a tradition of freedom braced by the long experience of the frontier, with its free land and its sturdy opportunities for the self-reliant man," adding, "The dislike of servility and authoritarianism is deeply engrained in the American character." More radical antifascists, by contrast, would argue that the frontier mentality, grounded in a history of racial extermination, was one factor which made Americans susceptible to fascism.[41] Mumford saw phenomena like racism and class exploitation as ancillary to Western history, not formative, and projected that American institutions like the Constitution would naturally eliminate them over time. This view was stridently espoused by the State Department during the Cold War. Not surprisingly, liberal antifascists like Mumford and Mowrer, who saw the problem of fascism in national terms, easily transitioned to anticommunism after the Second World War.

Black antifascism, whether liberal, socialist, or communist, was distinct for its persistent refusal to extricate the fight against fascism from the struggle against colonialism. Two recurrent themes are visible in the writings of black intellectuals before, during, and immediately after the Second World War: fascism as a belligerent, racialized nationalism that further deforms the class identities of whites; and imperialism as the root cause of fascism and war. The writings of George Padmore are in many ways exemplary. Born in Trinidad, Padmore studied at Fisk and Howard Universities in the 1920s and joined the CPUSA in 1927. For much of the 1930s and 1940s he was based in London, but his work was widely published in the United States as well as in Great Britain, the West Indies, and India.[42] As the London correspondent for the *Pittsburgh Courier* during the war, he shaped the newspaper's coverage of the conflict, and he regularly contributed to the NAACP's magazine, the *Crisis*.

As Alan Wald has argued, influential African American intellectuals were far from dismayed by the Hitler–Stalin Pact: they viewed it as an opportunity to return the colonial question to center stage.[43] After deeming its anticolonialism insufficient, Padmore left the Comintern in 1933, but his writings in the early years of the European war were broadly in line with its positions. Like many black journalists, Padmore initially opposed the participation of non-European troops in the emergent conflict. He wrote in the *Crisis* in December 1939, "Already Africans, Indians, West Indians, and other colored races are being appealed to, and in the French colonies conscripted as cannon fodder."[44] In an earlier piece titled "Hitler, Mussolini, and Africa," he maintained that fascism was essentially a form of imperialism: its main difference from other European varieties was its aggressive use of colonial war as a means to find a home for its "surplus populations." In Italy, for example, it had resolved a domestic crisis triggered by the Johnson Reed Act—which had closed off the safety valve of immigration to the United States—through a racist war in Ethiopia. Striking here, in Padmore's rendering, is fascism's essential similarity to British settler colonialism, which continually sought to resolve the crisis of expropriated, surplus populations within Britain by creating new "homes" for them abroad through colonial violence. To Padmore the disruptions caused by fascism offered a potent world lesson: the root cause of war, fascist or otherwise, lay in the drive to create colonies. "These political events," he wrote, "especially the Abyssinian crisis, have forced public opinion in Europe and America to realize for the first time the close relationship which the colonial question bears to modern wars."[45]

Like many black intellectuals, above all, those on the editorial boards of the *Defender* and the *Courier,* Padmore supported the participation of African and African American troops in the war by the end of 1941. Yet this did not temper his anti-imperial critique of Allied war aims.[46] His prediction that the invasion of Ethiopia would generate a broad reassessment of colonialism among European and white Americans was premature, but his positioning of fascism within a wider continuum of Western imperialism was a theme continually sounded by black intellectuals, one that placed the colonized global majority at the center of history's unfolding.

The antifascisms of the 1930s bequeathed more to postwar generations than an intersectional analysis of reaction, significant though this may be. Another important legacy was the way they decisively shifted the left's very notion of historical time away from assumptions of teleology and automatic progress toward notions of open-ended, historical contingency, wherein progress was fully dependent on political organization. This has certainly been noted of the philosophical tradition of Western Marxism: the Frankfurt School, Gramsci, Louis Althusser, and others; namely, that it broke with the stageism of Social Democratic and Communist historical materialism, which described history as necessarily passing through a prescribed set of stages along a road to progress inevitably ending in socialism. A largely postwar phenomenon, Western Marxism possessed a distinct sense of time that received its highest expression in Max Horkheimer's "negative dialectics." As Selya Benhabib succinctly characterized it, "Negative dialectics . . . denies that there is an immanent logic to the actual that is emancipatory."[47] In other words, contemporary struggles do not necessarily contain latent contradictions that will eventually resolve themselves in a step toward human freedom. A new historical phase like monopoly capitalism, for example, does not automatically possess internal fissures that will lead it to its own destruction and place humanity in a better position as a result. There are contradictions in monopoly capitalism, and it may indeed collapse, or not, but nothing guarantees that its passing from the historical scene will leave the world any closer to socialism.

It is not difficult to see how the encounter with fascism—and the Holocaust in particular—led the Marxist philosophical tradition away from teleology. Using the older sense of temporality, how would one account for the sixty million dead in the Second World War? A bump on the road to progress? The very enormity of the loss and trauma defied the neat closure implicit in the idea of a steadily linear, ever-upward course of human evolution. But what has generally gone unacknowledged is how this move away from teleology was not limited to the philosophers, nor was it a phenomenon that began with the awareness of the extermination camps. Rather, the Lukacses and the Adornos, the Marcuses and the Gramscis were products of a much wider movement culture that drew parallel deductions from its experience in the 1930s. Indeed, there was a broad awareness across the left that the German Social Democratic Party failed to stop Hitler because its strategy was based on a flawed sense of historical time. The mainstream of Social Democratic Faschismustheorie, best represented by the SPD theorist Karl Kautsky, viewed Hitler and Mussolini as aberrations in an otherwise peaceful development of capitalism toward socialism. One deduction from this theory was outright passivity: if fascism proved too popular, one simply needed to wait for it to blow over and allow the normal path of history to resume.[48] The wait-and-see attitude of Social Democratic leaders in regard to the Nazis was universally decried in American left and liberal publications after 1933, fueled by exiles who had barely escaped Europe with their lives.

The very words used by leftists and liberals to describe fascism, especially its German variant, implied a break with teleology. They employed such terms such as *barbaric, medieval,* and *primitive;* fascism's adherents, they said, shrouded themselves in magic, mysticism, and blood ritual. Rhetoric this surely was, but it belied a sense that contemporary events defied an established concept of historical time, confounding the basic assumption that there would be a future. The atavistic revival of ancient Roman Legions and Nordic war gods was simply not what they expected after the collapse of world capitalism, an event they had predicted with no small degree of optimism. As Thomas wrote in 1934, "However complacent Socialists may feel when they consider with what substantial accuracy they foretold the breakdown of the older capitalism, doomed by its own contradictions, they must, if they are candid, admit that they had no distant vision of the Fascist interlude that has come upon the world." The subsequent defeat in the Spanish Civil War, the invasion of mainland China, and, for some, the Hitler–Stalin Pact, further compromised the tattered belief in linear progress. In late 1939 the German Communist exile and concentration camp survivor Paul Massing criticized his comrades in a book highly praised by the *New Masses.* Writing as Billinger, he stressed, "Two of [economic determinism's] favorite cliches are 'inevitable' and 'automatic' and afterward it knows that everything had to happen as it did. It is partial to generalizations such as: Capitalism must inevitably go through the phase of fascism before socialism can be realized; the inner contradictions of the fascist economic system will automatically bring about its collapse."[49]

Massing and many others on the left strove to replace this easy faith in the "inevitable" and "automatic" with a view that ascribed to history a highly contingent course dependent on human agency. As the German exile Ernst Toller wrote in the *New Masses,* "We ourselves create fate."[50] If Western Marxism is to be credited with transforming the Marxist philosophical tradition, its key philosophers should not be seen as isolated individuals deriving their theories sui generis: rather, they should be credited with contributing some of the most elevated expressions of a broader movement culture. Almost immediately after 1945, American antifascists would draw on this sense of historical time, gleaned in the encounter with Nazism, to confront a fresh set of atavisms. Their collisions with the emergent Cold War order would highlight the fragility of the hard-won domestic gains of the war years and call into question even the victory achieved in the war itself.

CHAPTER 4

Resuming the People's War
HUAC, Joe McCarthy, and the Antifascist Challenge of the 1950s

What do Communists call those who criticize them?
"Red baiters," "witch hunters," "Fascists." These are just three out of a tremendous stock of abusive labels Communists attempt to smear on anybody who challenges them....

What is the difference in fact between a Communist and a Fascist?
None worth noticing.

HUAC pamphlet, "100 Things You Should Know about Communism in the U.S.A." (1949)

In American public memory, one moment is evoked above all others to dramatize the downfall of Sen. Joe McCarthy. During the senator's probe of suspected communists in the military he was devastatingly rebuked by Joseph Welch, the head counsel for the U.S. Army. On June 9, 1954, on live television, Welch scolded the notorious inquisitor with words replayed in virtually every documentary on McCarthyism: "You've done enough. Have you no sense of decency, sir?" Less remembered is Sen. Ralph Flanders, who had grabbed national headlines a week earlier and who continued to make headlines throughout the month of June by repeatedly insisting that McCarthy was the face of American fascism. A week before Welch's oft-quoted political epitaph, Flanders, a Republican from Vermont, lambasted McCarthy in a speech on the floor of the Senate. He noted that Jews were universally afraid of the senator from Wisconsin and recalled "the strange tenderness he displayed for the Nazi ruffians" involved in the massacre of GIs at Malmedy during the Second World War. Flanders added, "Perhaps this would not have been enough to perpetuate foreboding, but his anticommunism so completely parallels that of Adolf Hitler as to strike fear into the heart of any defenseless minority."[1] Similarly, on NBC's television program *Meet the Press* on June 14, Flanders warned viewers that McCarthy's autocratic methods and disregard for democratic protocol were "so clearly in the direction of fighting communism with fascism that I am seriously concerned."[2] Flanders emerged as one of the most visible symbols of the anti-McCarthy forces in Congress. On June 11 he called on Congress to strip him of his chairmanships and later that month introduced a resolution of censure. His efforts culminated in the formation of the bipartisan Watkins Committee, which drafted a report on McCarthy's senatorial misconduct and ultimately issued a formal censure in September.

By the time Flanders sounded his warnings in the summer of 1954, McCarthy's reputation was already in deep trouble, and the very politics he embodied were in dispute. The senator did not originate the phenomenon which came to bear his name, McCarthyism, but when he started to fall, the whole edifice of domestic anticommunist repression began to crack. Its postwar incarnation began in earnest with the resumption of the House Committee on Un-American Activities (HUAC) in 1946 and its hearings on the Hollywood Ten in 1947; with Truman's purge of suspected communists from federal agencies and the establishment of a List of Subversive Organizations by his attorney general in 1947; and with the American Business Consultants' publication *Red Channels* in 1950, a reference guide used by radio, television, and film executives to blacklist individuals suspected of communist affiliation. McCarthy, whose plebeian, tough-guy persona made him a seminal figure in the emergence of right-wing populism in the United States, came to personify this wave of political reaction.[3] And as a number of scholars have noted, the wave he rode was not so much one of repression of communism as of any challenge to the Cold War consensus and entrenched power.[4] Over the course of his wild, devastating four years of power, begun in 1950, he used his position as chair of the Senate Internal Security Subcommittee (SISS) to hunt down domestic Communists and in so doing turned a range of social institutions upside down, including the State Department, labor unions, the culture industries, the university system, and the military.

McCarthy had always been a controversial, polarizing figure, one who had more critics than fans.[5] Liberals chafed under his accusations of treason, establishment figures like the U.S. diplomat George Kennan, the publisher Henry Luce, and Dwight Eisenhower eventually saw him as compromising the legitimate fight against communism, and the left justifiably felt that his unchecked power threatened its very existence. His probe of the U.S. Army, an investigation that outraged the military establishment, gave his skeptics and critics the opportunity to go on the offensive. Yet something bolstered the rather diverse resistance to McCarthy that has appeared as mere flourish in the Cold War historiography: the continuing resonance of antifascism in American culture, which furnished his opponents with a language that played a hand in taking him down.

Flanders was not the first to make dark comparisons. In fact, his assertions were only one of the more visible and influential of such analogies. The rhetoric of the Vermont senator illustrates how the associative link between McCarthyism and fascism had fully entered the mainstream by 1954. Ever since HUAC resumed its hearings in 1946, a set of analogies likening its basic impulse to fascism had been gaining traction in American civil society. In the nationally broadcast hearings of both the SISS and of the HUAC, American audiences heard subpoenaed leftists and even liberals denounce their inquisitors as bearers of an incipient fascism, sometimes, as in the case of Arthur Garfield Hays, the general counsel of the ACLU, in eloquent, rhetorically persuasive terms. A number of indicators suggest that the accused were not alone in such sentiments, especially in major metropolitan areas. Following one of McCarthy's televised speeches in 1952, for example, the *New York Times* reported receiving a flood of calls linking the senator to Hitler and his Big Lie technique[6] (fig. 4).

Such perceptions grew in 1953 and 1954 as McCarthy's accusations of communist conspiracy grew ever more outlandish. During this time American newspapers persistently informed their readers that Cold War allies in Western Europe and Japan looked on the senator as an American Führer. More damning, readers learned that a resurgent Nazi movement in West Germany regarded the Wisconsinite as their brother in spirit.[7] Likewise, newspapers and magazines in the United States reported in 1954 that the fight to save the embattled McCarthy brought out a homegrown fascist fringe, among them, most notably, the evangelist Gerald L. K. Smith.[8] Since 1953 public comments by labor leaders and clergy that linked congressional inquests to Nazi Germany were increasingly covered by the press, and in 1954 influential Democratic politicians like Averell Harriman and Franklin Roosevelt Jr. openly and comfortably made the analogy without fear of repercussions.[9]

The fascist analogy was made, often casually, across the political spectrum, but left-wing cultural producers formulated it in the greatest detail. They were joined in this endeavor by liberals whose brands of anticommunism did not entirely eclipse earlier political frames. These writers, activists, and scholars in the late 1940s and early 1950s helped set the tone for reading McCarthy and the whole apparatus of anticommunist repression within the terms of antifascism, and they did so in ways still clearly marked by the Popular Front. In 1944 Henry Wallace had warned Americans, as noted earlier, that the greatest battles against fascism would need to be fought after the war and likely from within the United States. Authoritative figures like Arthur Miller, Paul Robeson, Robert Sherwood, Harry Hay, William Patterson, Elmer Davis, Daniel Bell, Ray Bradbury, Theodor Adorno, John Roy Carlson, and many others took up Wallace's call. Indeed, the fight against anticommunist repression and the shape of

FIGURE 4. McCarthy as a German soldier. Syndicated cartoon by Bill Mauldin, February 25, 1954. Mauldin was a Pulitzer Prize–winning cartoonist famous for his work during the Second World War for *Stars and Stripes,* a newspaper published for military personnel.

the emerging postwar society formed the first major challenge for American antifascism after the Second World War. For liberals like Bell, fascism persisted as an urgent threat despite their support of the Cold War.

Many of the aforementioned figures were veterans of Popular Front struggles, and what reminded them of fascism when they examined state bodies like HUAC and SISS was their rhetoric of xenophobia, conspiracy, and racism along with their very real erosion of civil liberties in the name of anticommunism. They read such repression in the context of a larger, postwar social transformation that bore uncanny similarities to the very regimes they had fought against so recently. They found disturbing echoes in the permanent militarization of society, necessitated by the Cold War; in a growing anti-intellectualism, cultural homogenization, and conformity; in the violent, racial reaction to the nascent civil rights movement; and perhaps most dramatically, in the rehabilitation of Germany, Spain, and Japan as bulwarks against communism coupled with a disturbing silence about their recent victims, most notably the millions who perished during the Holocaust. What linked their readings of fascism to the Popular Front most obviously was an attentiveness to class dynamics and economic interests. To be sure, McCarthyism, unlike later formations such as George Wallace's American Independent Party and the Christian right, was an overdetermined social dynamic that never cohered into an organized, fascistoid social movement or political party; what the left often decried was its potential to become a full-blown, American fascism. But the political and cultural elements it brought together justified a sounding of the alarm.

In making these fears public, postwar antifascists undermined but did not eliminate an official conflation of fascism and communism that was fast becoming a key rhetorical trope of the Cold War. As part of a rapid paradigm shift from antifascism to anticommunism, this dubious coupling rescripted the history of the Second World War as a fight not against fascism but against totalitarianism, an abstract fusion of Stalinism and Nazism, thereby creating a continuity between old and new enemies. To counter what they saw as a collective amnesia regarding the lessons of the conflict, antifascist cultural producers strove to keep in public memory the specifically right-wing nature of the wartime foe. Their efforts kept the discourse of antifascism alive and as a result helped to enable a more thorough and long-delayed public reflection on the nature of fascism and the Second World War in the early 1960s.

In the late forties and the fifties critics often reached for the metaphors of the witch hunt and the inquisition when striking back at McCarthyism, and these analogies continue to be accessed in the public memory of the anticommunist repression.[10] But while the imaginative and historical links between Torquemada, Cotton Mather, and McCarthy have received justifiable attention in both literary and historical studies, the frequent referencing of fascism by the critics of HUAC, McCarthy, and the blacklist has yet to receive serious treatment by scholars.[11] Unlike the allusions to seventeenth-century Salem or early modern Europe, the fascism frame was a way to explore the darkest potentialities of contemporary political reaction. It was to place the erosion of civil liberties wrought by institutions like HUAC and the blacklist in the context of global rightist shifts created by modern dislocations and anxieties, which, moreover, the nation had been mobilized to oppose in recent memory.

When McCarthy lost all effective power in 1954, the whole edifice of repression did not immediately come tumbling down with him, though it was increasingly compromised from then on. (The end is generally dated to 1962, when a jury awarded the blacklisted radio host John Henry Faulk a record $3.5 million in damages for libel, putting blacklisters on notice that they would be the ones to suffer for the practice).[12] And although the fall of McCarthy did not spell the end of anticommunism in the United States, it was a real setback for the American right. Many liberals supported HUAC and the hunt for domestic communists, but the right yoked its political fortunes to McCarthy and the broader repression most visibly and dramatically. With the fall of their icon, whose spiral into alcoholism led to his death in 1957, they were once again on the defensive after years of ascendancy: most notably against charges of fascism. In May 1954, for example, William F. Buckley felt compelled to proclaim, "The coupling of McCarthy with incipient fascism is the greatest red herring of our time." Likewise, in the prologue to Buckley's book *McCarthy and His Enemies* (1954), the conservative William Schamm saw the need to offer a rather elaborate argument that the senator was not an American Hitler. HUAC itself tried to remove the stain of fascism from its image by investigating American Nazism for the first time since the Second World War.[13]

Cultural producers who remembered and made public the earlier antifascist struggles in their fight against McCarthyism played a role in its defeat and maintained the conceptual independence of fascism from its total absorption by the emergent narrative of totalitarianism. In the process they advanced a narrative of betrayal and lost opportunities that countered a variant story of betrayal from the right. Their narratives of lost hope reveal what they found to be fascist about the emerging anticommunist order and contain generative insights for understanding the nature of American political reaction.

Reconversion and the Emergence of the Cold War

The film about the Second World War that resonated most powerfully with the generation that actually lived through it featured no combat sequences. Released in 1946, *The Best Years of Our Lives* was a story of three returning soldiers and their difficult readjustment to civilian life. Directed by William Wyler and written by Robert Sherwood, it was a critical and commercial success, winning seven Academy Awards, including Best Picture. Its three principal characters, Fred Derry, Al Stephenson, and Homer Parish, struggle with restlessness, trauma, alcoholism, estranged marriages, frayed relationships, and, in Homer's case, disability. But readjustment is far more than a personal matter for these three veterans and their families: the social order is also shifting under their feet.

The war had turned the class hierarchy upside down for these men. In the army, the working-class Fred Derry, played by Dana Andrews, was a captain and the well-to-do Al Stephenson was a sergeant, but when they return to their old civilian jobs the earlier pecking order is resumed: Al is a banker and Fred is an unskilled worker at a drug store. Fred gets a hint of this nascent restoration in the first scene of the film. Immediately after his discharge and while still in uniform, he is at a civilian airport trying to book a flight back to his home in Boone City. A businessman pushes him away from the service counter to make room for his enormous golf club bag, then buys the last ticket, foreshadowing what is to come. Once he is back home, his employment becomes even more tenuous than before: the family drug store where he used to work has been bought out by a corporate chain, and his young new boss cares only about the bottom line.

The three characters soon learn that the people back home have seemingly learned no substantive lesson from the war. Their veteran status has meaning only to potential employers, who want to use their service records to sell goods. Homer, for instance, who is struggling with the loss of both his hands, is offered a job in sales by his father's business friend, who tells him that men with disabilities make trustworthy salesmen. More ominous, however, is that the fascism they fought against during the war appears to be gaining the upper hand at home. In a critical scene in the film Homer is relaxing at the drug store counter where Fred works. A middle-class man sitting next to him is reading a paper with the headline "Senator Warns of a New War," and when the man asks Homer how he lost his hands, a heated exchange follows:

> *Man:* Terrible when you see a guy like you who had to sacrifice himself, and for what?
>
> *Homer:* And for what? I don't get you mister.
>
> *Man:* We let ourselves get pushed into war. . . . The Germans and the Japs had nothing against us. They just wanted to fight the Limeys and the Reds. And they woulda whipped 'em too, if we didn't get deceived into it by a bunch of radicals in Washington. . . . We fought the wrong people, that's all. [*Pointing to a newspaper*] Just read the facts, my friend. . . .
>
> *Fred:* You better pay your check, brother, and go home.
>
> *Man:* Who do you think you are? . . . And there's another thing. Every soda jerk in this country's got an idea he's somebody.

Homer angrily buttonholes the man with his hooked hands, demanding, "What are you selling anyway?" He replies, "Plain old-fashioned Americanism." When

Fred steps in and punches the self-proclaimed patriot, he is promptly fired. "I get it," Fred says in resignation. "The customer's always right so I'm fired. But this customer wasn't right."

The stranger's politics evoke the prewar, rightist isolationism of Lindbergh, America First, and Coughlin. Even during the war many of their supporters from the thirties passed along an underground narrative that blamed Jews and communists for plunging the country into a senseless fight.[14] But these politics also reflected an emergent Cold War ideology. The idea that the former Axis enemies were now our true friends and that "we fought the wrong people" would be raised in prominent forums by conservatives like McCarthy, Ayn Rand, and Winston Churchill in the years after the war. In the above scene from *The Best Years of Our Lives,* this viewpoint is shown to have social authority: the old isolationist is an upstanding citizen, and as a patron of the store he has the power to get Fred fired. His anticommunism and his sympathy for old fascist enemies are linked to an "old-fashioned Americanism" that questions working-class power and proletarian claims to national belonging. His indignant statement, "Every soda jerk in this country's got an idea he's somebody" would be reflected in conservatives' attempts to roll back New Deal social legislation in the late forties. As noted in chapter 2, the war had indeed been a great leveler, raising the relative incomes of working people substantially. In the immediate postwar period the rollback manifested itself in a successful drive by Republicans and the National Association of Manufacturers to repeal the popular price controls mandated by the wartime Office of Price Administration, an act which the majority of Americans feared, and rightly so, it turned out, would lead to rampant inflation.[15] But the rollback would achieve its most dramatic expression in the passage of the Taft-Hartley Act of 1947, which allowed states to opt out of New Deal labor legislation and thereby become so-called right-to-work states with minimal union protections.

The Best Years of Our Lives reflected a gnawing fear that the nature of Cold War politics was about to make the sacrifices of the war illegible. Fascism turned out to be "the wrong enemy" in a postwar order that seemed bent on restoring prewar class relations. With no genuine antifascist culture in place, one's veteran status is commodified, useful only for peddling goods in an increasingly corporate culture. Despite its seemingly neat resolution, the picture reflects not only a mourning for the lost idealism of what Wallace called the century of the common man, but even a sense of betrayal at the state of the nation that was emerging from the carnage of the war.

The politics of the film came from Sherwood, who was well positioned to comment on the loss of wartime ideals. He was not only a wounded veteran of the First World War, but also, as the director of the Overseas Branch of the

Office of War Information (OWI) and a speechwriter for Roosevelt, played a central role in formulating those ideals. Under his watch the Overseas Branch of the OWI became a continuation of the New Deal arts programs of the 1930s. He brought into the agency a number of highly talented writers and directors with Popular Front backgrounds.[16] Though Sherwood was never officially blacklisted, both his service at the OWI and the agency itself came under such attack by McCarthy that his loyalty and that of the OWI are still contested by some on the right today.[17] A dedicated antifascist, Sherwood continued to remind Americans of the prewar struggle with isolationism in American life in his voluminous history of diplomacy during the Second World War, *Roosevelt and Hopkins: An Intimate History* (1948). Noting that isolationism was a bipartisan phenomenon supported by the majority of Americans, he stressed that its "chief leadership and essential financing" were conservative and rightist elements like his man in the drug store, including the reactionary Hearst–Patterson–McCormick presses, businessmen who wanted to do business with Hitler, technocrats like Lindbergh who thought fascism represented "the wave of the future," and narrow-minded, chauvinistic politicians.[18] Elmer Davis, who as the director of the OWI was Sherwood's former boss, would later update the nature of the domestic fascist threat in more pointed terms. In magazine articles, public speeches, and his best-selling book *But We Were Born Free* (1954), Davis charged Red-baiters with betraying the wartime ideals his agency put forward. Reviving the gangster metaphor of the thirties, he described McCarthy as a fascistoid leader who could potentially bring about an American Reich and who stood a chance of succeeding because he was backed by wealthy interests who naively thought they could control him.[19]

The popularity and critical acclaim of *The Best Years of Our Lives* are evidence that the rapid official transition from wartime antifascism to Cold War anticommunism was neither seamless nor uncontested. This transition had its critics not only in popular culture but also in Congress. Sen. Claude Pepper of Florida spoke out against "sinister forces" who were bent on supplanting "antifascism with anticommunism."[20] Rep. Wright Patman of Texas commissioned a report titled *Fascism in Action* (1947) that drew on the work of Maxine Sweezy to define fascism as the suppression of free speech in the service of militarism, nationalism, and the defense of private property rights. In the foreword, Patman wrote that fascism represented a far greater danger to the United States than communism.[21] Such sentiments, however, were harder to find in Congress by the end of the decade.

The shift to anticommunism, which the majority of the public embraced by the end of the 1940s, did not happen naturally or inevitably. Under Stalin's leadership, Soviet communism had devolved into a horrific tyranny. But its very real disregard for basic human rights does not in itself explain why American elites focused on the abuses of communism and ignored those of other governments; for instance, the wholly preventable famine in Bengal in 1943, caused by commodity speculation under Churchill's watch, had recently claimed an estimated three million lives.[22] Across the twentieth century the United States allied with and even created a wide range of repressive, antidemocratic governments with little public outcry. So one might ask why continued cooperation with the USSR was politically impossible. Why not retain the wartime alliance with the USSR in order to secure world peace? Gallup polling during the war revealed that the public consistently supported this idea and overwhelmingly thought the Soviet Union could be trusted to cooperate with the United States after the Axis were defeated; even surveys in the late 1940s showed wide faith in cooperation. In April 1945 a wide majority supported a permanent alliance between the two countries in which each would come to the other's aid if attacked.[23] Fueling such sentiments was the knowledge that the Soviet Red Army had done the vast majority of killing and dying against the Axis during the Second World War (current estimates hold that 75 percent of German casualties and equipment losses occurred on the Eastern Front) and that many American lives were saved as a result.[24] Further, the privations of the Depression had cultivated an openness to socialist experimentation among the American public, and the ubiquitous wartime propaganda stressing the essential similarities between the peoples of the Soviet Union and the United States was still in memory. Against this backdrop, Churchill's famous Iron Curtain speech in Fulton, Missouri, in March 1946 elicited a deeply critical reaction from the press.[25]

The transition to anticommunism had to be constructed, from the top down, by an official effort of elite policymakers and the entrenched power they represented. As Joel Kovel has argued, American anticommunism began as an elite project because communism's attack on private property threatened the very basis of elite rule. Soon after the First World War, the privileged few quickly learned that they could interpolate ordinary Americans of the basis of anticommunism, speaking to their religious piety, their xenophobia, and their desire for national belonging. As Kovel writes, "In the ideal case—from the standpoint of the elites, that is—a sufficiently massive fear and hatred of communism can be mobilized effectively to squelch any opposition to their rule, or even serious critical understanding of it. The perfection of anticommunism comes when all America unites in the love of 'free enterprise' and hatred of the dark, red outsider."[26]

The Depression and the war had substantially compromised "the love of 'free enterprise,'" and from the standpoint of elite policymakers, neutralizing the spirit of antifascism was a large part of putting the world back on a proper footing. In their view it would have been difficult to use antifascism to construct a national narrative capable of preserving elite hegemony, especially since it had directed the public to associate the enemy with some of the foundations of conservative rule: a politically repressed workforce and an exclusionary nationalism based on strict social hierarchies. Rhetorically at least, communism professed to be about collective social organization and state power for the underclasses: converting a world force claiming to represent these things into Public Enemy Number One was a project much more amenable to capitalist accumulation and, from the point of view of segregationists, to racial hierarchy. In helping to make a collectivist bloc into the archenemy of the United States, Cold War liberals played a hand in undermining their own domestic agenda over the long term.

Within the governing establishment in Washington, the shift in perspective toward the Soviet Union occurred over the course of one hundred days in the last weeks of 1945 and into the first several months of 1946. Kennan played a major role in bringing about the shift. His so-called Long Telegram, cabled to Washington in February 1946 from the U.S. embassy in Moscow, outlined the doctrine of containment, and in doing so rallied a floundering Washington establishment around a definite course of action regarding the USSR.[27] From there, an official campaign would be under way to re-channel wartime antifascism into anticommunism. Business leaders and the American culture industries would relaunch, on a much more aggressive footing, a corresponding effort in a civil society which had been forced into dormancy by the global war against rightist militarism.

Totalitarianism, Fascist Restoration, and the Politics of Amnesia

In the late 1940s through the 1950s policymakers and ardent anticommunists pursued two overlapping narrative strategies for rescripting the recent past to fit the aims of the Cold War. The first was to rehabilitate former enemies. This entailed a new discourse of the Second World War that minimized the atrocities of Nazism and imperial Japan while downplaying the military role of the USSR and demonizing its intent. The first strategy ensured that public discussions of the Holocaust would be minimal for almost fifteen years after the war and also entailed a policy of alliance with former Nazi war criminals and their East European collaborators. The second, more pervasive tact was to conjoin fascism and communism into a single entity signified by the word *totalitarianism*. Generally speaking, the first strategy was more commonly employed by conservatives and those on the political right, while the second received its fullest articulation from Cold War liberals. Together, these narratives created a cultural environment that made it difficult—but, as it turned out, not impossible—for the public to process the implications of the war and its devastation, which would necessarily involve a self-reflexive examination of the basis and function of fascist nationalism.

Perhaps the single most influential rewriting of the conflict came from one of the principal Allied leaders, Winston Churchill. His voluminous, six-volume history of the Second World War, published over seven years from 1948 to 1953, became a best seller in the United States and was excerpted in the *New York Times* and *Life* magazine.[28] No written history of the war reached a wider audience in the United States during this period than Churchill's master narrative, which earned him the Nobel Prize in Literature in 1953. Since his Iron Curtain speech in early 1946 Churchill was retroactively cast as the true hero of the war by many American conservatives. In their eyes, his unrelenting anticommunism during the conflict made him a more trustworthy authority and truer American patriot than Roosevelt. And his history cemented an account of the struggle that has lingered in American memory ever since: the notion that its purpose was to restore the world order to a hierarchical status quo.

The literary quality of Churchill's magnum opus, from *The Gathering Storm* (1948) to *Triumph and Tragedy* (1953), derives from its largely first-person voice. Churchill focuses on his role in the diplomatic history of the conflict, particularly his relationship with the other Allied commanders. He presents his collaboration with Roosevelt and even Stalin as friendly and cordial, though he does air real disagreements, especially those regarding the fate of territories newly liberated by Allied armies and partisans. Overall, Roosevelt emerges as having played a friendly, supporting, but sometimes dangerously naïve role in the defense of Western civilization.[29] Like the recollections of American postwar conservatives, his account of the European theater is predicated on underestimating the Soviet military contribution. In his forty-seven-hundred-page history he devotes fewer than three pages to the crucial Battle of Stalingrad, and the Red Army's Operation Bagration (the liberation of Belarus), a campaign waged simultaneously with the Battle of Normandy and equal to it in scale, merits no mention at all.[30]

Churchill's defense of the Western world first appears in the way he describes his vigilance over Soviet machinations and crimes. He educates postwar readers on the atrocities committed by the former Soviet ally: the murder of Polish officers in the Katyn forest, the Red Army's refusal to reinforce the Warsaw Underground in 1944, which led to their slaughter, and the countless famine victims of the collectivization drives of the early 1930s.[31] Incredibly, in the thousands of pages on the history of the Second World War, Churchill mentions the Holocaust only once: in a letter he includes in the appendix of the final volume.³² His selective memory of atrocities works to place the USSR in a "separate moral universe" from the West, to use Kovel's formulation of the basis of anticommunism.³³ His politics come into sharper focus as he describes his single-handed restoration of order in the newly liberated zones. Churchill was concerned above all to contain the revolutionary changes set in motion by the war, and he performs this feat narratively by presenting the hierarchical nation-state and its undemocratic colonial appendages as a status quo that had to be maintained to ensure Allied victory. In great detail in *Closing the Ring* and *Triumph and Tragedy* he defends his position on the necessity of restoring the monarchies of Italy, Greece, and Yugoslavia, where, he declared, holding immediate elections would "open the door to communism."³⁴ Similar aversions to democratic participation fueled his attitudes toward Indian decolonization in 1942. Responding to Roosevelt's arguments in favor of Indian independence, he wrote, "Without the integrity of executive military control and the power to govern in the war area, hope and chance alike would perish. This was no time for a constitutional experiment with a 'period of trial and error.'"³⁵

In this broader context of maintaining prewar hierarchies, Mussolini appears as a tragic figure, a misunderstood conservative who sadly wound up on the wrong side of history. Churchill reflected on the Italian dictator as he began his imprisonment in July 1943:

> Thus ended Mussolini's twenty-one years' dictatorship in Italy, during which he had raised the Italian people from the Bolshevism into which they were sinking in 1919 to a position in Europe such as Italy had never held before. A new impulse had been given to the national life. The Italian Empire in North Africa was built. . . . In 1935 the Duce had by his will-power overcome the League of Nations—"Fifty nations led by one"—and was able to complete his conquest of Abyssinia. . . . His fatal mistake was the declaration of war on France and Great Britain following Hitler's victories in June 1940. Had he not done this, he might well have maintained Italy in a balancing position, courted and rewarded by both sides and deriving an unusual wealth and prosperity from the struggles of other countries. Even when the issue of war became certain, Mussolini would have been welcomed by the Allies.³⁶

Churchill recognized in Mussolini a man of his own spirit: a devoted anticommunist who defies the world with his drive to build the nation through imperial conquest (the Italian conquest of Ethiopia claimed as many as 760,000 lives).³⁷ In Churchill's memory the war was not about fascism, ultimately. Its real calamity was its fratricidal nature, which turned brothers in spirit against each other within the madness of a tragically confused era.

Churchill's sentiments toward Mussolini were typical of the views held by the British Conservative Party in the 1930s. The attitudes of most Conservative Party MPs toward fascism in that decade typically ranged from apathy to cautious respect to outright adoration. Many in the party's center and right even thought of Nazism in favorable terms through most of the decade; like Coughlin, they viewed it as having saved Germany from the scourge of communism. By 1938 conservatives began to see Hitler as a threat to British interests, but even then the earlier attitudes informed the policy of appeasement championed by their leader, Neville Chamberlain. Despite the views Churchill expressed toward Mussolini, his position in the party was unique in regard to the Germans. He had the distinction of being one of the few British conservatives who actually pushed for an aggressive line against Nazi Germany in the 1930s. As late as 1939 he was disliked by most of his party for publicly opposing Munich and similar accords.[38] Churchill's status as one of the few Tories untarnished by appeasement gave postwar conservatives on both sides of the Atlantic a powerful icon for a usable past: a stalwart veteran against the enemies of the nation, a man who strove to preserve established order in a world rapidly transformed by the war.

Churchill's narrative persona as a maverick anticommunist—misunderstood because he recognized the true enemy all along—would appeal to McCarthy, a veteran of the Pacific theater nicknamed "the Tailgunner" by his fans. Joe drew liberally from Churchill's history in constructing his own narrative of the war on the floor of the U.S. Senate, yet he was much more brazen in his rehabilitation of fascist nations. In a speech he made in 1951, for instance, he urged Congress "to use those people of the world who are willing to fight with us against international communism. As I say, the four great wells of manpower are anti-Communist China, Spain, Germany, and Japan." Within the broader context of his hunt for domestic subversives, McCarthy scripted a distinct stabbed-in-the-back myth, a narrative genre borrowed from fascism itself, wherein the sacrifices of the brave soldiers on the front are betrayed by communists, spies, and politicians at home (in German, this is known as the *Dolchstoßlegende*). The climax of his narrative was the so-called betrayal at Yalta, where Roosevelt allowed Stalin to dictate the terms of the peace, enabling Stalin to swallow up Eastern Europe. McCarthy's archvillain was Gen. George C. Marshall, famous today for the Marshall Plan, who allegedly created a military situation that allowed the Red Army to freely redraw the map of postwar Europe. He essentially blamed Marshall for losing the war; in a Senate speech in June 1951 he decried "the most significant decision of the war in Europe: the decision by Marshall, which was made against Roosevelt's half-hearted wishes and Churchill's bulldog determination, to concentrate on France and leave the whole of Eastern Europe to the Red armies." Later in the same speech McCarthy opened up the possibility that the general's motive may have been treason.[39] Much like the variants used by his German and Italian predecessors, McCarthy's stabbed-in-the-back-myth arose from the very foundations of right-wing epistemology, rooted in romanticism: that is, the combined willpower of an organically unified nation knows no limits or obstacles, and thus any defeat must be explained merely by an unwavering resolve created by those within the nation who are not truly of the nation.

A more enduring strategy for dispelling the ghost of wartime antifascism was through the discourse of totalitarianism, which united communism and fascism in a single, easily digestible signifier. The term *totalitarian* was coined by Giovanni Amendola, a parliamentary opponent of the fascists in Italy, who used the word *totalitaria* in May 1923 in an article describing fascist efforts to monopolize public office. After Amendola was beaten to death by Blackshirts in 1926, Mussolini positively claimed the term, often boasting of his *totalitarismo*.[40] As a result, many Americans associated the word with the regimes of Mussolini and Hitler during the thirties. Though conflations of communism and fascism appeared in public discourse, there was no consensus during the Depression decade that any essential similarity bound these two forms of government together. Clear human rights abuses by the Soviet government in the late thirties created a link between the two systems in the eyes of many Americans, including liberals, but the war put a freeze on such associations.[41]

However, as part of the decisive anticommunist shift in policy after 1945, U.S. government officials actively encouraged the melding of communism and fascism. J. Edgar Hoover, the director of the FBI, published an influential article in *American Magazine* titled "Red Fascism in the United States Today" (1947) which proclaimed a common identity between the two forms of government. Hoover did not explain the connection, as the earlier enemy held no interest for him: the article was so obsessed with communism that it mentioned fascism only in passing. President Harry Truman officially inaugurated the Cold War by implying a link between communism and the Axis powers in his declaration of the Truman Doctrine that same year and would more readily voice such links later in his term. At a press conference in 1950, for example, he asserted, "There isn't any difference between the totalitarian Russian government and the Hitler government. . . . They are all alike. They are police governments— police state governments."[42] American culture industries did their part to further the identification as well. Meeting at the Waldorf Astoria Hotel in New York City in December 1947, Hollywood studio heads agreed to aid the mission of HUAC by producing anticommunist pictures, and soon thereafter a number of popular films began to depict American communists as former members of the pro-Nazi, German American Bund.[43] In his anticommunist detective novel *One Lonely Night* (1951), Mickey Spillane offered a telling example of how nonsensical the conflation could become in popular usage. His protagonist, Mike Hammer, muses, "One armed Communist was worth twenty capitalists with guns. It was Hitler all over again."[44]

As is the case of many postwar uses of the word *fascism,* the discourse of totalitarianism was an example of what Raymond Williams called a "structure of feeling." That is to say, in the minds of those who used it, totalitarianism was not a well-formulated or consistent concept but a general sense refracted from the broader culture. At its most articulate, it conflated communism and fascism by stressing how both systems blocked free communication, used fear and terror to control their populations, and produced mass conformity through mental and physical regimentation.[45] The most influential intellectual discussions of totalitarianism during the early Cold War, Hannah Arendt's *The Origins of Totalitarianism* (1951) and Arthur Schlesinger's *The Vital Center* (1949), identified the common feature of all totalitarian systems, the thing that makes them total, as their absolute subordination of civil society to the state. Schlesinger wrote, "Old-style dictatorship . . . may be bloody and tyrannical but leaves intact most of the structure of society. Totalitarianism, on the contrary, pulverizes the social structure, grinding all independent groups and diverse loyalties into a single, amorphous mass."[46] Liberalism was the common sense behind the discourse on totalitarianism, presenting fascism and communism as twentieth-century incarnations of an age-old tyranny that outlawed the free association necessary for the full realization of the individual. As such, the two systems were alike in that they eroded the liberal space in which individuals have "the ability to agree to disagree," a space inextricably bound to "the American Way."[47] The discourse of totalitarianism reflected liberal fears of homogenization wrought by the emerging Consumers' Republic of the 1950s.

As a number of scholars have noted, however, the concept of totalitarianism elided the diverse goals, ideologies, and practices of fascism and communism, enabling its users to abstract the methods of the two systems. Ever conscious of the specificity of their object, post–Cold War historians of fascism overwhelmingly reject its conflation with communism.[48] The historian Robert Paxton, for example, discards the comparison because it ignores the specificity of Hitler's and Stalin's ideologies and practices. One regime was grounded in a patriarchal theory of the master race that left the institution of private property intact and thereby enjoyed elite support, while the other destroyed private property on the basis of a theory (not a practice) of universal equality.[49] Consequently, everyday life differed greatly for citizens of Hitler's Germany and Stalin's USSR, particularly for women, farmers, traditional elites, and especially ethno-racial and religious minorities.

But whatever the public rhetoric, communists and fascists were not treated the same according to official policy, which favored the rehabilitation of former Axis enemies proffered by McCarthy and Churchill, not the equal rejection of both totalitarianisms demanded by Schlesinger and Arendt. The most brazen example of this fascist-over-communist policy was the implementation of the Internal Security Act of 1950, a law which, incredibly, contained a provision allowing the use of detention camps for alleged subversives. It ostensibly barred individuals belonging to supposed totalitarian organizations from entering the country, yet in light of nearly ten thousand backlogged visa applications, twelve congressmen protested that *totalitarian* was not meant to apply to former Nazis (in practice, the State Department had already adopted this view). In 1953 it was finally established by the courts that for the purposes of the Internal Security Act, Nazi and Fascist parties did not fall within the definition of totalitarian.[50]

The roots of this policy lie at the very beginning of the Cold War, when policymakers in the United States saw that their recent fascist enemies, whose whole philosophy was predicated on anticommunism, constituted natural allies. Kennan, an architect of the Cold War, played a role in forming this policy as early as 1943, when he served at the U.S. embassy in Germany. That year he wrote a position paper in which he reasoned that most of "the present ruling class in Germany" should be retained for the challenges of postwar reconstruction.[51] In the first months after the German surrender, the main goal of American authorities in Europe was indeed to hunt fugitive Nazis and destroy underground fascist movements, as they were legitimately afraid of their resurgence. The new anti-Soviet turn, however, shifted their focus in Europe from hunting Nazis to hunting communists and their sympathizers. "As the Cold War became an institution," writes Christopher Simpson, "the Nazis were simply turned loose."[52] The Nuremberg Trials, held from November 1945 to October 1946, were aimed at the very top echelons of Nazi leadership. At their conclusion, however, a shadow army of judges, lawyers, scientists, industrialists, military officers, doctors, and civil servants who had been lower-level Nazi Party members—but perpetrators of crimes against humanity all the same—were left at complete liberty. The onset of the Korean War further accelerated the leniency offered to former Nazi war criminals. Because of the unexpected military costs of the Korean conflict, the U.S. military needed to siphon troops away from Europe, necessitating a drastic rearmament of the German military in order to fill the places of the departing American soldiers who had been tasked with guarding the European frontier. A restoration of its former personnel was virtually assured.[53]

In the early days of the Cold War, in other words, the United States provided material support to the immediate postwar survivors of fascism, including individuals who had been directly involved with the Final Solution. As head of the Policy Planning Group in the State Department, Kennan helped convince Truman's National Security Council to approve a series of covert operations in Europe that relied on local anticommunists with highly dubious pasts. To carry out its intelligence operations, the U.S. government began to employ former SS officers and Nazi collaborators in Eastern Europe responsible for some of the most horrific crimes of the Final Solution, including the mass shooting of children.[54] In the late forties and early fifties the CIA instituted programs that brought thousands of anticommunist exiles from Eastern Europe to the United States. These exiles included individuals responsible for grave war crimes under the Nazis. After relocating them, the CIA secretly enlisted these allies to reinforce the urgency of anticommunism within East European immigrant communities. The rightist organizations which emerged from this state-sponsored effort in Latvian, Lithuanian, Ukrainian, Croatian and Belorussian communities maintained ties to fascist organizations in Europe and succeeded in creating new, influential power bases for the far right in the United States.[55]

In sum, the very meaning of the Second World War was almost immediately rescripted through a variety of means. The discourse of totalitarianism abstracted the old enemy of fascism to the point that the new foe of communism could appear as its natural successor, creating the kind of continuity Benjamin identified as "homogenous, empty time." Yet this discourse was employed in bad faith, for it was accompanied by a rehabilitation of former enemies that belied how communism and fascism were *not* the same in the institutional practice of the early Cold War. This political milieu would have long-term effects. Justice for the victims of fascism in Europe would be deferred, in many cases indefinitely. Meanwhile, the idea of totalitarianism became a permanent imprint in American culture, helping to obscure the association between fascism and the political right and thereby speeding the effacement of the Popular Front vision.

The political environment of the early Cold War made it difficult for Americans to remember that former Axis enemies were distinct from present foes, but it did not render such remembrance impossible. To be sure, most Americans had forgotten their wartime goodwill toward the Soviet Union and firmly embraced anticommunism by 1948. However, there was still a definite public space in the late forties and fifties—however besieged, constrained, and at times contradictory—in which many Americans continued to distinguish fascism from communism, revealing that the experiences of the thirties and forties were not so easily forgotten. The contexts in which the term *fascism* appeared in the early postwar period suggest that these Americans drew on their memories to destabilize an ideologically constructed continuum between fascism and communism offered by those in power, maintaining instead an alternative continuity between past and present. And while the repressive culture of the early postwar period imposed real limits on how the lessons of the war could be publicly applied to contemporary politics, by no means did it consistently drive subversive analogies underground. The U.S. government's use of former Nazis and Nazi collaborators had to be kept secret from the public, as popular outrage resulted at every revelation that Nazi war criminals were on American payrolls, and American support of Franco's Spain continued to be highly controversial. Such considerations point to a gap between popular predilections and official policy vis-à-vis fascism.[56]

In the public sphere during this time, connections between American politics and fascism appeared both explicitly and allegorically. Those working in the culture industries, education, and the public sector were under intense scrutiny by governmental agencies, private blacklisting organizations, and popular boycott campaigns. Many careers were ruined; by one recent estimate, only 10 percent of those blacklisted in the film industry successfully returned to their professions.[57] However, more recent studies of the blacklist have called attention to its unevenness, noting the surprising number of critical works that surfaced despite the general environment of censorship.[58] As David Everett has written, "Not only did the blacklist fail to suppress all leftist commentary, it also failed to exclude all blacklistees from the debate."[59] In film, radio, and television—the most scrutinized of the culture industries—producers and moguls simply could not afford to spurn all individuals who had links to subversive organizations, as doing so would eliminate the vast majority of their experienced talent pool. Many individuals, especially those with established careers, were accordingly not blacklisted but "greylisted"; in other words, they were barred from some opportunities but not all.[60] In live theater and book publishing, the blacklist's net was more porous still. Live theater, even Broadway, was an alternative for those shut out from other media. Having independent financing and little need for advertisers, theater was less susceptible to the influence of Red-baiters and did not blacklist directly.[61]

For subversively inclined individuals working in film, radio, television, and theater during the McCarthy era, the most common means of delivering a socio-political message was to couch it in allegorical form, setting it either in a fictionalized past (historical allegory) or a dystopian future (science fiction). Even when the allegorical veil was incredibly thin, this strategy was often enough to avoid censure.[62] But less remembered are other public venues in which social critiques often went completely undisguised. Allegorical subversion may have reigned in narrative film, television, and theater, yet analogies between McCarthyite America and fascism were often quite explicit outside of artistic forums: in speeches by politicians, clergy, and labor leaders, in social science academic work, in congressional reports, in popular nonfiction, and in statements by those accused before HUAC and SISS.

Though the earlier Popular Front analysis of fascism looms large in these iterations of the 1950s, postwar historical shifts caused the emphasis within the Popular Front paradigm to shift. In the 1930s and 1940s, those on the left saw themselves as part of a mass movement, one that opposed a fascism backed by a powerful minority. But in the oppositional productions of the 1950s, the figure of the antifascist becomes an isolated, hunted outsider, and the ways in which fascism operates by mass popular consent receives much more thematic emphasis. Anti-intellectualism, often ascribed to fascism in the 1930s but not central to antifascist critique, becomes one of its key features for social critics in the fifties. This new emphasis was driven not only by the rise of HUAC and similar bodies, but also by a larger transformation in the nature of political reaction within the United States. Conservatives and the political right became populist to an unprecedented degree, using a language that heretofore had been mostly a property of labor and the left. Populism had always envisioned the body politic as a virtuous majority beset by elites out to subvert the founding principles of the nation. When this narrative was used by those on the left, the elites were simply the rich. In the new deployment by the postwar right, the elites were government officials, cosmopolitans, wealthy celebrities, and liberal intellectuals; and communism naturally flourished among all these groups. McCarthy personally embodied this new, rightist populism. Though there is much evidence to suggest he received crucial financial support from wealthy backers, he skillfully played the role of the tough Irishman from rural America, an underdog in a game rigged by a patrician Establishment. His public persona was that of a hard-drinking, poker-loving, average Joe who showed no respect for parliamentary protocol, something he dismissed as a smug restraint thrown in his way by Ivy League snobs who lacked the stomach to do what needed to be done.[63]

Antifascism seemed the perfect language with which to combat the unfolding populist nature of the postwar, American right. After all, the first major American rightist to use populist appeals was Father Coughlin, a defender of fascism.[64] Many Americans saw fascism in Europe as something that had hypnotic appeal to ordinary people, and, as later historians affirmed, it was in fact a movement driven by the middle class, not by the traditional, property-holding elite. Both European fascism and the new American populism were coalitions of the middle and upper ranks, sutured together by a racialized, anticommunist, anti-intellectual nationalism with mass appeal. And now that the American right had redefined intellectuals as elites, thereby excluding them from the people, it is unsurprising that antifascist cultural workers would explore the roots of their symbolic denaturalization through populist anti-intellectualism.

Out in the Open: Explicit Condemnations, Dark Reminders

In the early 1950s the remnants of the besieged, embattled Marxist left did not all agree on the nature of the fascist threat before them, some voices questioning whether it was proper to call it fascist at all. However, reading Marxist periodicals from this period, from the CPUSA's *Masses and Mainstream* and the *Daily Worker,* to the Trotskyist *Labor Action* and the *Militant,* one is struck by how much their writers were still fighting the Spanish Civil War and the Second World War. Like the liberal press, both pro- and anti-Soviet Marxist papers loudly protested the continued backing of the Franco regime by the United States and called attention to the U.S. government's postwar recruitment of Nazi war criminals. *Masses and Mainstream* serialized Steve Nelson's battlefield recollections of Spain, while the *Militant* continued to publish fresh reminders of the Stalinist betrayal of the Spanish Loyalists. Meanwhile, the communist Samuel Sillen lambasted the rehabilitation of Germany by the American culture industries.[65] Indeed, the feature film *Desert Fox: The Story of Rommel* (1951) presented the *Wehrmacht* as a gallant institution, save for its irrational commander in chief, Adolf Hitler.

Within this milieu, what Alan Wald termed "late antifascism," most agreed that the United States was heading in a fascist direction.[66] I concur with Wald that in most cases *Masses and Mainstream* used the F-word far too loosely, rhetorically linking the United States and Nazi Germany without sufficient explanation. However, the Marxist press outside the CPUSA waged a lively debate on the extent to which McCarthyism signaled an American fascism. There was virtual consensus that McCarthy had the soul of a fascist, but the independent socialists grouped around Max Shachtman and the *New International* argued that he lacked an organized, cohesive movement or party, and thus McCarthyism could not be considered fascism. On the contrary, those oriented toward the Trotskyist Socialist Workers' Party argued that McCarthy was uniting middle-class, far-right elements into a force independent of the Democratic and Republican establishments and was thereby already creating a properly fascist politics.[67] Neither side argued that the United States had "gone fascist," and both assumed that the right needed to establish a bona fide fascist party before such a nightmare came to pass.

But if many Americans came to view McCarthyism as a grim echo of prewar Europe, it was not because they read the Marxist press. They encountered this view through much more high-profile, mainstream sources. One popular figure, a first-generation Armenian American named Avedis Derounian, stands out for his explicit and early comparisons of the political right to fascism. Written under his pen name, John Roy Carlson, his book *The Plotters* (1946) hit the best-seller list, and his activist work both in his Armenian American community and among veterans nationwide marked a refusal to let go of wartime antifascism amidst Cold War imperatives to forget it.[68] Like Davis and Sherwood, he derived legitimacy from his participation in the American propaganda effort during the Second World War. The eclectic nature of his research interests during the early Cold War reveal that, for him, the Armenian genocide, the Holocaust, the politics of the American right, and America's unfolding Cold War policy were not separate events but one impending catastrophe.[69] *The Plotters* was written in the sensational mode of the undercover exposé, a kind of nonfiction detective noir he had used with great success three years earlier in *Under Cover,* which in 1943 and 1944 reached number one on the best-seller list in the category of nonfiction. Both *Under Cover* and *The Plotters* were first-person accounts of the author's infiltration of right-wing hate groups, which he claimed were rising in influence. While repeatedly expressing his hostility to American Communists, which did not extend to the Soviets, Carlson nevertheless bucked the emergent Cold War consensus in *The Plotters* by concentrating on the threats to democracy from the right. Writing immediately after the war, he warned readers that "Hitler is by no means dead. Hitler*ism* in our country is a sinister and expanding reality."[70] He stressed that although it appeared to be marginal, it held the potential for growth because it was fertilized by wealthy, influential individuals and mainstream political culture.

Despite the book's sensationalism, evidenced by such chapter titles as "Goons on the Rampage," Carlson proffers a complex albeit unsystematic analysis of fascism, especially in the preface. He understood American fascism to be an organic alliance of nationalists, in which "crackpots" and powerful, respected individuals encourage one another. Driven by privileged social elements who hate the New Deal, mainly because it opened the American Way to people beyond the exclusive domain of Anglo-Saxons, fascism uses anticommunism as a way to subvert democracy and roll back the social democratic gains of the past decade. Its "extreme nationalism" brings together whites of all classes and is directed against blacks, Jews, Puerto Ricans, Filipinos, Nisei, Chinese, and the foreign-born in general. *The Plotters* warns that American fascism will become truly dangerous once it begins to appeal to veterans. If veterans feel betrayed by a postwar reconversion that fails to create full employment, unionized jobs, and a social democratic safety net, Carlson warns that "it can happen here."[71]

Carlson gathered extensive information on veterans' organizations such as the American Legion and the newly formed American Veterans of World War

II. Through his published work and public speaking tours, Carlson and his associates in the Friends of Democracy—a liberal antifascist group founded in 1937 by the Unitarian minister Leon Birkhead—attempted to steer veterans into the left-liberal American Veterans' Committee (AVC). The AVC, an organization with five hundred local chapters, collaborated with Carlson and the Friends of Democracy in exposing nascent fascism across the United States. A statement by the AVC's National Planning Committee in 1946 read, "The military phase of the worldwide war against fascism has long been concluded; the war itself as yet is still unwon." His original title for *The Plotters* underscored his activism among ex-servicemen: it was originally to be called *Veterans, Beware!*[72] By the early fifties the rise of domestic anticommunist repression along with the rearmament of West Germany by the United States shifted his focus away from veterans as the wellspring of an emergent fascism. He was increasingly concerned with a resurgent Fourth Reich in Germany which would take its cues from McCarthy and the American right. At the same time, he sought to expose former Nazi collaborators within the Armenian community and was researching the financial support of exile organizations by the CIA.[73]

Others working in this unconcealed vein commanded much more intellectual prestige than Carlson, though less popular appeal. In the late 1940s and early 1950s antifascism's most intricate, intersectional analysis of power came from a highly influential work within the academic social sciences: *The Authoritarian Personality* (1950), by the sociologist and philosopher Theodor Adorno and the psychologists Else Frenkel-Brunswik, Daniel Levinson, and R. Nevitt Sanford, all three of whom taught at the University of California–Berkeley. Like almost all postwar, left-liberal antifascisms, *The Authoritarian Personality* was premised on the notion that the threat of fascism did not die in 1945 but remained a latent force in all Western societies. A rebuke to Cold War anticommunism, the book argued that fascism was the gravest danger facing the United States and sought to identify the kinds of individuals who were amenable to fascist appeals. The authors originally wanted to call the book *The Potential Fascist* or *The Fascist Character,* but these titles were deemed too risky in the Cold War context.[74] Whatever its methodological flaws, the result was a study which built upon and expanded Marxist antifascism of the 1930s to produce a truly intersectional analysis of the political right.

The Authoritarian Personality was one of the works in the series Studies in Prejudice sponsored by the American Jewish Committee and edited by Max Horkheimer and Samuel Flowerman. Its release came shortly after Horkheimer and Adorno returned to West Germany to reconstitute the Institute of Social Research in Frankfurt.[75] Like many Frankfurt School works of the forties and fifties, it combined European critical theory with empiricist methods culled from American social sciences. The empirical base of the study was an extensive set of interviews, mainly conducted between 1944 and 1946 in California and Washington, D.C., with college students, prisoners, veterans, and men and women from a range of working- and middle-class occupations.[76] The book is most remembered for its development of an F-scale, a quantifiable measure of an individual's amenability to fascism, gleaned from survey questions and interviews. The researchers tried to find the link between fascism and broader social attitudes by correlating the F-scale with other quantified indexes. These related scales underscore the authors' conceptual aggregation of race, class, sexuality, and nationalism. They interlocked the AS-scale for anti-Semitism; the PEC-scale for politico-economic conservatism, largely based on the subjects' class attitudes; and the E-scale for ethnocentrism, which had a number of subscales, including the N-scale for attitudes toward Negroes, an M-scale for minorities in general, and a P-scale for patriotism.

The foundation of the book's argument was that the personality is a "structure," largely formed in childhood, that determines ideological preferences. It is created by a larger, social field which it in turn reproduces and modifies. Prefiguring Raymond Williams's "structure of feeling," the authors wrote that personality is "an agency through which sociological influences upon ideology are mediated."[77] The concept of personality became the central means through which Adorno and his associates connected apparently distinct social phenomena; it was their key to unlocking the mystery of how individuals combined all manner of divergent politics—laissez-faire capitalism, racism, patriarchy, homophobia—into a single worldview. Pivotal here was the subject's view of "ingroups" and "outgroups." Sanford observed that their representative protofascist, named Mack, "talks about the New Deal, the Civil Service, and the OWI in the same way he talks about the Jews . . . [thus] we are faced here not with a particular set of political convictions and a particular set of opinions about a specific ethnic group but with a *way of thinking* about groups and group relations generally." This "way of thinking" about group relations is marked by "rigid categories of unalterable blacks and whites . . . accompanied by imagery of power vs. weakness, moral purity vs. moral lowness, and hierarchical organization." Additionally, they found that the authoritarian personality views all groups as static, stereotypical, and internally homogenous. Thus Mack could speak only of his ingroup, the Irish, in positive terms and saw outgroups as paradoxically weak, corrupt, and domineering in comparison with his own. This personality structure, in which "ethnocentric hostility toward outgroups is highly correlated with ethnocentric idealization of ingroups," views the relationship between nations in the same terms, and thus the study posited a link between ethnocentrism and "blind patriotism."[78]

In *The Authoritarian Personality* and other writings, Adorno was fascinated by a rebellious quality he found in political reaction. Not all conservatives, he argued, possessed an authoritarian personality; rather, he saw this dangerous psychological makeup to be a common trait of a particular kind of conservative—the pseudoconservative. Unlike conservatives proper, who understand how capitalism functions and defend its class structures accordingly, the pseudoconservative, a type Adorno found to be very common on the American right, suffers from a failed identification with established structures and would consequently destroy the very institutions he sought to defend. The pseudoconservative is marked by a rebelliousness that is ultimately subservient to authority. The authors of *The Authoritarian Personality* argued that this quality arose from a veiled resentment toward the patriarch of the family. His or her total inability to critique the patriarch, which develops into an inability to critique any ingroup authorities, leads to a projection of rebellious, resentful impulses onto some outgroup. All repressed, unutterable animosities toward the overbearing father, for example, could be projected onto the Jews or onto the people of another nation, who become an all-powerful, all-controlling force that must be stopped.

Adorno extended the connection between ethnocentrism, patriarchy, and nationalism to capitalism by theorizing the pseudoconservative's rebellious energies vis-à-vis political leadership. To Adorno, pseudoconservatives sense a fundamental truth: employers, not elected leaders, are the authorities in charge of people's everyday lives. They do not articulate this state of affairs as a contradiction within democracy, one to be fixed by improving democratic structures. Instead, writes Adorno, "they want to do away with the form of democracy itself and to bring about the direct control of those whom they deem the most powerful anyway."[79] In this view, movements of the right—from the Goldwater campaign to the Tea Party—are rebellions ultimately submissive to authority because their members know that private-sector employers, not the government, are the real forces in control of daily life. Their left-leaning nemeses thus appear as usurpers of true authority whose constraints on rightful leadership must be abolished. They may rail against the King, in other words, but never the Crown.

Popular Front antifascism of the 1930s clearly informs *The Authoritarian Personality*, though the book also reflects the evolving nature of antifascism in the 1950s. One continuity with the 1930s was its premise that capitalism ultimately determines whether the authoritarian personality will have a chance to violently assert itself. As the authors state in the introduction, if the "most powerful economic interests" decide to pursue an "antidemocratic course" to maintain their hegemony, then and only then does fascism have a chance of becoming a reality.⁸⁰ They built up newer antifascist emphases, however, in the questions they asked their interview subjects to determine the F-scale. Subjects were asked to rank their agreement or disagreement with a series of statements, and their responses would help determine their fascist potential. One statement stressed anti-intellectualism. It asked subjects to agree or disagree with the following statement: "There is too much emphasis in college on intellectual and theoretical topics, not enough emphasis on practical matters and on the homely virtues of living." Other items, however, reflected an expansion of issues that were more marginal in Popular Front readings of fascism. For instance, subjects were asked to affirm or deny the following statement: "Homosexuality is a particularly rotten form of delinquency and ought to be severely punished." Another statement was, "It is only natural and right that women be restricted in certain ways in which men have more freedom."⁸¹

In the two decades following the book's publication, "the authoritarian personality" was a phrase deeply embedded in antifascist vocabulary. The book was also quite well received by reviewers in academic and popular periodicals, its success inspiring a flood of studies on the political right within the academy. This wave culminated in 1955 in the multiauthored collection *The New American Right* (expanded and republished as *The Radical Right* in 1963), in which Daniel Bell, Nathan Glazer, and David Riesman also drew on the experience of fascism as a way of explaining the American right. Their essays managed to attack both communists and fascists without conflating the two, though not all the contributors to the collection were so careful.⁸² *The Radical Right* was followed in 1960 by Seymour Martin Lipset's landmark book *Political Man: The Social Bases of Politics,* which explicitly discussed McCarthy's social base as the American incarnation of Nazism.

Another explicit, high-profile use of the fascist analogy in the early years of the Cold War was the public testimonies of those who stood accused before HUAC. From its early sessions on communist infiltration in Hollywood in 1947, HUAC hearings were elaborate rituals covered in detail by national radio networks, syndicated newspapers, and, later, the new medium of television. As Brenda Murphy has argued, the ritual was a kind of four-act play which audiences came to expect through repeated performance: it involved an opening question about membership in the Communist Party ("Are you now or have you ever been . . ."), an admission of guilt, an expression of repentance, and, finally, proof of repentance through the naming of names.⁸³ Part of this ritual, one could add, was the suspected communist, blinded by klieg lights, denouncing his or her investigators as fascist. As early as December 1946 the Harvard astronomer Harlow Shapley shouted "Fascist!" at Rep. John Rankin during his examination by HUAC. Steve Nelson, to take another example, repeatedly hurled the epithet at the judge and attorney trying him for sedition in Pittsburgh in 1951.[84] As the epigraph to this chapter reveals, Red-hunting examiners had come to expect this charge, and they inoculated themselves accordingly. Additionally, HUAC very openly used a person's earlier participation in antifascist organizations as evidence of communist activity, as if trying to deliberately purge antifascism itself of any positive association.[85]

On the one hand, the cries of fascism from the accused, carefully contained within a state ritual over which they had little control, likely helped to trivialize the term in the public imagination. Shouting about fascism in America, following HUAC's logic, could be seen as just another melodramatic rant from those inclined to treason. On the other hand, as we have seen, many in the anticommunist public shared the view that there was something deeply sinister, even fascist, about HUAC and other investigating bodies, especially as McCarthy fell into near total disrepute. Though impossible to affirm with certainty, the accused may have helped to build an association among the public between the congressional ritual and fascism, unconscious at first, that became more conscious as the Americanism of the investigators themselves was called into question. For example, the writer Irwin Shaw, though blacklisted by *Red Channels,* was outspoken in his anticommunism by 1950. Yet in his anti-HUAC novel *The Troubled Air* (1951), his alter ego, Clement Archer, makes substantive political connections as he grudgingly listens to a communist speech: "There was a protracted comparison between America today and Germany in 1932, with references to artists, Jews and union leaders. . . . Actually, Archer thought, half-listening and resentful, a great deal of what this fellow is saying has elements of truth in it . . . in a way there are disturbing similarities between pre-Hitler Germany and America today; orthodoxy *is* at a premium and deviations from a narrowing and intolerant standard are being savagely punished."[86] Archer, though ultimately put off by the communist's rhetorical delivery, doesn't reject the historical analogy itself.

The significance of the defendant's cries of fascism is not that they were accurate historical comparisons (certainly the America of the fifties was not Nazi Germany). Rather, they were goads to memory, asking the public to recall the lessons of the war, to remember the dark road a society begins to travel when it consents to the removal of basic democratic rights in the hunt for communism. In his defense of the accused in a HUAC hearing presided over by Richard Nixon in 1948, Arthur Garfield Hayes of the ACLU recalled, "I was in Germany in 1933 when it came under Hitler in the days of the Reichstag fire. He had two scapegoats—the Communists and the Jews. The Communists were the most important. He was saving the people from the Reds and they passed a law barring all Communists from the Reichstag and as a result the anti-Communists had the authority and they repealed the German constitution. He did exactly what you are doing here."[87] In his testimony before HUAC in June 1956, Paul Robeson went much further, getting to the very root of the analogy. When asked by Rep. Gordon Scherer why he did not stay in Russia, Robeson replied, "Because my father was a slave, and my people died to build this country, and I am going to stay here, and have a part of it just like you. And no Fascist-minded people will drive me from it. Is that clear?"[88] His reply called attention to the connection between race and citizenship inherent in hard-right nationalism, fascist or not: that is, its racialized attempt to remove citizenship, symbolically and legally, from those who do not fit their national narratives. Appearing before the committee at a time when its influence was decidedly waning, Robeson called on his thespian training to repel the assault to his very right to belong. He took command of the performance, delivering such a powerful rebuke that his cowed inquisitors never called him to the stand again.[89] HUAC's examiners, apparently, were not fully in control of the staging. It had become clear that the ritual could be turned against its masters.

Allegories within Allegories: Antifascism from under the Blacklist

Creative writers in the culture industries who drew upon antifascism to make critiques of American politics in the 1950s rarely produced works with Blackshirts, stormtroopers, or other direct representations of fascism (such works would appear in the early 1960s, however). Those who worked under the shadow of the blacklist in radio, television, and film, where antifascism could be taken as evidence of communist affiliation, were compelled to create allegories within allegories. That is to say, writers would commonly tap their antifascist memories to create historical allegories set not in Nazi Germany or Franco's Spain, but in medieval Europe or seventeenth-century New England.

As Murphy has argued in reference to historical allegories of McCarthyism in the 1950s, writers left it to audiences to make the link between past and present; in asking them to complete the meaning of the narrative, they made their audiences "co-conspirators" in their social critiques.[90] Audiences can be complicit only if they are equipped with the cultural and historical frameworks for making the connections demanded by the allegorical text; one must have at least a general understanding of fascism, for instance, to be able to recognize it in a film about an alien invasion or a play set in seventeenth-century New England. Some of the direct, explicit uses of fascism by scholars, activists, clergy, and politicians may have helped to provide these frames, moving audiences to discern the links between American present and fascist past desired by writers and filmmakers. More likely, however, because of their intricately coded nature, the allegories did not lead readers and viewers to directly apply the frame of fascism to their contemporary culture. This was the cultural work of the more explicit public utterances referenced above. The cultural significance of the antifascist allegory of this period lies in its continuing power as social critique, whether audiences recognized it as antifascist or not. Writers used a submerged antifascism to get audiences to think critically about their emergent postwar culture: for example, about the interlocked injustices of race, class, and nationalism or the link between consumerism, anti-intellectualism, and repression.

A number of B-grade science fiction allegories used the memory of fascism to frame their critiques of the Cold War, for example, the films *Superman and the Mole Men* and *This Island Earth*. The most notable work in science fiction to do so, however, was Ray Bradbury's dystopian novel *Fahrenheit 451* (1953). Well received at the time of its publication and now canonized in American high school classrooms, *Fahrenheit 451* follows the character Guy Montag, a "fireman" whose job it is to burn books in a future society where it is a punishable offense to own them (the title refers to the temperature at which paper ignites).[91] Book burning, the trope around which the novel's title and whole plot revolves, was primarily associated with Nazism, not communism. After Nazi youths created bonfires with the books of banned writers at Humboldt University in Berlin in May 1933, book burning became a focal point for critics of the Nazi regime worldwide, emerging as a symbol of fascist anti-intellectualism and its assaults on basic liberal freedoms.

Professing his lack of interest in anticommunism in a later interview, Bradbury used this iconic symbol of Nazism to structure his critique of the United States.[92] In his dystopian world consumerism erodes the bonds of family and community, creating a passive, one-dimensional citizenry incapable of intellectual depth and critique, who shrug as those who possess knowledge are literally hunted down. A clear commentary on early 1950s America, this consumer culture is enforced by censorship and forced conformity at home and has brought the world to the brink of annihilation through militarism and war abroad. Ultimately, Bradbury uses the trope of book burning, a symbol of fascist anti-intellectualism, to mediate the atrocities of the recent past, the repression of the present, and the impending catastrophes of the future. Though Bradbury's antifascism explicitly draws on the works of the Spanish writer and philosopher José Ortega y Gasset (1883–1955), who is quoted by an intellectual protagonist at the end of the novel, he was in contact with the political left at the time.[93] Above all, *Fahrenheit 451* can be read as a popularized version of the scholarly critiques of consumer culture and mass society in the fifties, found in such works as the seminal *Mass Culture* anthology, in which Irving Howe, Paul Lazarsfeld, and Adorno used the frame of fascism to link consumerism and passivity.[94]

In the area of historical allegory, the influence of the left was undeniable. In the 1950s the plays of Arthur Miller and the television series *The Adventures of Robin Hood* were the most visible allegorical critiques of Red-hunting within an antifascist frame. *The Adventures of Robin Hood* was produced in the United Kingdom by Hannah Weinstein of Sapphire Films and aired from 1955 to 1959 on ATV in the United Kingdom and on CBS in 1955 to 1958 in the United States. The show used the famous medieval legend to present a coded but decidedly Marxist reading of fascism to its audiences. That the series *The Adventures of Robin Hood* would contain a Marxist analysis is not too surprising when one considers that its scripts were written by a roll call of Hollywood blacklistees, including Ring Lardner Jr., Ian McClellan Hunter, Robert Lees, and Adrian Scott.[95] Weinstein was a left-wing antifascist who had been active in the Hollywood Anti-Nazi League, the Hollywood branch of the CPUSA, and the Progressive Citizens of America, an organization which attempted to abolish the HUAC after the war. In 1951 she was sent to London by the ailing Hollywood branch with party funds to set up a production company. Left-wing blacklistees wrote for a wide range of television series set in a swashbuckling medieval past, including *The Adventures of Lancelot* (1956–57 in the United States), *Ivanhoe* (1958), *Sword of Freedom* (1957–58), and *The Buccaneers* (1956–57).[96] But *The Adventures of Robin Hood* was the longest running and most popular. Though many of those involved in the series were in the final stages of their break with the CPUSA, the social analyses they learned from their earlier radicalism apparently did not dissipate as they moved away from the party.

The premise of the show is that Robin of Locksley has returned to England from fighting in the Crusades and finds that in his absence the country has been overrun by pretenders to the throne. The sheriff of Nottingham and other Norman gentry dispossess Robin of his land and brutalize the peasantry, and in response Robin allies with the common folk in a guerilla band that steals from the rich and helps the poor. On one level, *Robin Hood* makes a coded, historical analogy between Robin's band of outlaws and communist partisan resistance movements in occupied territories during the war, for example, Yugoslavia, China, Greece, Italy, and French Indochina. On another level, the metaphor of the veteran who returns home to face counterrevolution and persecution mirrors the blacklisted writers' sense of themselves as having supported the antifascist cause and helped to improve living standards on the domestic front, but who are hunted and exiled, not rewarded, for their efforts. In Hollywood, one also finds this theme in the Western *High Noon,* also a blacklistee product. Overall, *Robin Hood* gives a sense of the Shire as a cruel, authoritarian state which serves the rich, oppresses the poor, and is anti-Semitic to boot.[97]

The episodes foregrounded the class dynamics of fascism, emphasizing the relationship of the authoritarian state to moneyed interests. Its writers suggest that while capitalism and the fascist state do not represent identical interests, they strategically come together at moments of crisis to enforce class rule. A perfect example is the second episode, "The Moneylender," written by Hunter and Lardner (whose brother was killed in the Spanish Civil War).[98] Robin and his band rob a moneylender, who, as it is revealed, oppresses poor farmers by charging an interest rate of 100 percent. With the gold and silver Robin's men steal from him, they win the sympathy of the peasantry through a kind of agrarian reform, providing no-interest loans to the very same farmers he exploited. As the moneylender runs to the sheriff for protection and redress, it becomes apparent that the relationship between the sheriff of Nottingham, the fascist ruler, and the moneylender, the capitalist, is one of shared interest. In a reuse of the gangster metaphor of the 1930s, the sheriff rules over this medieval financier through intimidation and fear, symbolically indicating that while capitalists and fascists have shared interests, the capitalist does not simply pull the strings of the fascist. But the sheriff is also invested in seeing his exploitation of the peasantry proceed smoothly, as he has been taking a cut of the profits. He sets out to recover the moneylender's bullion, brutally retaliating against those he suspects of aiding in the robbery of the moneylender. In a scene that definitively evokes fascism, the sheriff uses terror against a farmer he suspects of assisting Robin's band: on pain of death, he orders the man to burn down his own cottage with two of his comrades still inside. The cold authority and aristocratic poise with which the sheriff orders this brutal act, as well as a close-up shot which reveals his sadistic smirk as the house burns to the ground, visually and gesturally evokes the image of the Nazi officer from Allied wartime propaganda.

The most renowned figure in the world of American theater in this period, the playwright Arthur Miller, was also a closet antifascist. Miller was haunted by the Holocaust and the memory of fascism for his entire life; and like the creators of *The Adventures of Robin Hood* he was deeply influenced by the left of the 1930s. Much has been written about Miller's thematization of the Holocaust, and it is no secret that he was deeply shaken by the rise of Hitler. Indeed, from 1932 to 1939, he remembered "literally having nightmares about the Nazis."[99] But the concrete ways in which antifascism influenced his social critiques have gone largely unnoticed. This hole in the scholarship is particularly striking in regard to his famous play *The Crucible* (1953) because its author openly acknowledged how his fears of fascism animated this tale of witchcraft in Salem, Massachusetts. He was very explicit about this in his essay "Why I Wrote *The Crucible*" (1996), in which he asserted, "'The Crucible' was an act of desperation. Much of my desperation branched out, I suppose, from a typical Depression-era trauma—the blow struck on the mind by the rise of European Fascism and the brutal anti-Semitism it had brought to power."[100]

Two works that appeared shortly after the war, his novella *Focus* (1945) and his short play *You're Next!* (1946), both deal with the survival of fascist movements and forces in the United States. His later plays *Incident at Vichy* (1965) and *Broken Glass* (1994), along with the television screenplay *Playing for Time* (1980), all explore contemporary issues of guilt, injustice and complicity through the lens of Nazi Germany and the Holocaust, a motif he explained in his published commentaries.[101] A second major historical theme in his work was the suppression of free speech by HUAC and McCarthyism, which he dealt with in his plays *You're Next!, An Enemy of the People* (1951), *The Crucible,* and *A View from the Bridge* (1955). These two major themes—Nazism and McCarthyism—crossed paths most clearly in *After the Fall* (1964) and *You're Next!,* which explicitly linked HUAC to fascism. Like Derounian, Miller saw the horrors of nationalist-driven genocide abroad and anticommunist fanaticism at home not as separate events but as the unfolding of a single nightmare: that of twentieth-century political reaction.

Wald recently rehabilitated the formative influence of the CPUSA on Miller's work, an influence denied or downplayed by many liberal critics. The playwright was first attracted to communism in the early 1930s, though he never officially joined the party. He found his voice as a young playwright within the Popular Front of the late 1930s. In 1937 he witnessed police gunning down striking auto workers in Detroit, a pivotal event in his life which he likened to the massacres of the Spanish Civil War. Miller wrote for the communist magazine the *New Masses* in 1945 and 1946 and continued to attend communist party meetings and aligned forums until 1949.[102] He was drawn to the Popular Front because it offered a means to conceptually link and take action against fascist outrages abroad and social injustice at home. Miller broke with the communist party sometime in the early 1950s and publicly spoke out against the Soviet Union during his cross-examination by HUAC in 1956, though he upbraided the committee and refused to name names during his hearing. Although he was a consistent critic of Cold War anticommunism at home and abroad, Miller often used the term *totalitarianism* in his public statements from the late 1950s onward, frequently positioning himself as a defender of human rights against regimes of both the left and the right. Because of such shifts in his thinking and his emphasis on individual moral conscience, critics sometimes try to position Miller beyond the politics of right and left.[103] But his political stances in the postwar years—against McCarthyism, for civil rights, against the Vietnam War—do not reveal a random orientation. Indeed, he regarded McCarthyism, his biggest domestic fear, as a right-wing phenomenon, albeit one enabled by liberal cowardice.[104] And he doggedly refused to follow the underlying logic of the Cold War, wherein communism existed in a "separate moral universe" from the system of the West. As Wald argues, when he broke from his pro-Soviet orientation, he did not break from politics but moved toward "an independent radicalism."[105]

In *You're Next!* (1946), his first play about anticommunist repression, Miller explicitly links domestic Red-hunters to fascism. Its protagonist is a barber who is hounded by "the Rankin Committee" because he collected relief money to support refugees from Franco's Spain and Nazi-occupied Yugoslavia. John E. Rankin, a congressman from Mississippi, was a leading member of HUAC and an outspoken segregationist and anti-Semite. Finding it natural that fascists would dislike antifascist refugee work, the barber asks, "Is this Germany or America?"[106] Miller's anti-HUAC plays of the 1950s did not make such direct accusations, but Popular Front antifascism informed these McCarthy-era works far more than his overtly Nazi-themed plays of the 1960s. *An Enemy of the People* (1951), for instance, revived an earlier work by Henrik Ibsen which allowed Miller to voice a more contemporary radicalism, one in line with his antifascist upbringing. The story is about a courageous rural doctor who is silenced for trying to make public a scientific truth which is inconvenient to those of wealth and power, namely, that a tannery upriver is polluting the water of Kirsen Springs, the economic lifeblood of the town. When the protagonist Dr. Stockmann tries to present his views to the public, he is not allowed to speak. The newspapers refuse to print his perspective—instead, they publish the views of the town elite. When he attempts to speak at a public meeting, everyone in town sides with the spokesmen of the elite and ultimately shout him down. Broadly speaking, the plot is in line with left-liberal antifascism of the 1930s, as it shows how democratic space is crushed by the contradictions of liberalism. The freedom to amass personal wealth, that is, the rights of property, does not naturally coexist with the rights of free speech and the maintenance of a free press. When free speech gets in the way of free enterprise, the former must go, allowing capitalists to pursue their interests by other means.

Miller's two views of fascism at this time—that it arises from the need to protect private property at a moment of crisis and that it is driven by racial hatred—are not synthesized in *An Enemy of the People. The Crucible* begins to approach this synthesis. Miller finished the first draft in the fall of 1952, and he certainly had the Holocaust on his mind when researching the play, as has been noted by Christopher Bigsby.[107] But more than the concentration camps themselves weighed on Miller. The events leading up to such a catastrophe are the real focus of his play, and for this he drew on his antifascist roots. His interest in Salem as a contemporary metaphor was initially inspired by the historian Marion Starkey's *The Devil in Massachusetts* (1949), which also merged the themes of Salem, fascism, and McCarthyism.[108] In *The Crucible*, Massachusetts is an "autocracy by consent," as Miller puts it, and a place where an irrational theocracy crushes all democratic freedoms.[109] Anti-intellectualism, the ubiquitous theme of 1950s antifascism, is present as well: the wife of Giles Corey is condemned merely for reading books. By themselves, however, such factors are too loose to connect the play to antifascism. A more telling way its author draws on his earlier political education lies in the disproportionate responsibility he places on wealth and established power for the frenzy at Salem. It also lies in the brief but significant role he ascribes to race.

In the "Overture to Act One," the narrator describes the witch hunt as "a panic which set in among all classes," and critics have generally taken him at his word.[110] But it is far too easy to leave the matter at that. While all classes in his fictionalized Salem are certainly culpable, individuals of wealth and established authority initially set the tragedy in motion, and it is their social authority which allows a rumor to become a material reality. The dialogue of act 1, which depicts the origins of the witch hunt, is dominated by the Reverend Parris, Thomas Putnam, and Ann Putnam, the symbolic representatives of wealth and authority in town. Parris combines the social authority of the clergy and the bourgeois: he was a wealthy merchant in Barbados before arriving in Salem, where he exploits his parish by demanding ever more goods from them. In the opening scene we learn that the children of these elite characters have fallen ill; their sickness, not cries of witchcraft, provides the initial crisis of the play. The first image on stage is of Parris praying over his sick daughter Betty, and it is later revealed that all of the Putnams' children have died, except for Ruth, who has taken on a strange malady. Though talk of witchcraft is in the air, it is the wealthy Thomas Putnam who most aggressively pushes the wavering Parris, against the rational entreaties of the more humble characters John Proctor and Rebecca Nurse, to accept it as an explanation of the girls' sickness. Moreover, Ann Putnam is the first to make a concrete accusation of witchcraft against an individual when she levels a charge against Abigail. Parris calls on an outside expert on the occult, the Reverend Hale, to ascertain the cause of the crisis. Under the weight of grilling from Putnam, Parris, and Hale, the plebeian characters of Abigail and Tituba finally break, turning against each other and against those who challenge the authority of their inquisitors.

Unlike Bertolt Brecht's staged allegories of Nazism—the plays *The Resistible Rise of Arturo Ui* and *Round Heads and Pointed Heads—The Crucible* makes no representation of Hitler or Nazism. Rather, its antifascism derives from its rendering of democracy's demise. Miller implies that Salem had been a democracy before the witch hysteria, and one that was irksome to the town elite. When the yeoman Proctor corners Parris about his failure to call a town meeting on an important issue, the wealthy Putnam interjects, "I am sick of meetings; cannot a man turn his head without he have a meeting?" In a similar vein, Parris soon adds, "I do not wish to be put out like the cat whenever some majority feels the whim." As in *Enemy of the People,* those with wealth and power destroy democratic space by resorting to extraordinary, repressive means (the hunt for witches) to destroy threats to their authority and resolve an underlying crisis. In this case the crisis is the continuity of elite rule brought about by the death of their children, metaphorically ending the reproduction of their class position. Fully in line with many antifascisms of the thirties and forties, the irrational, antisubversive force set in motion by elites to secure their rule is no longer under their control once unleashed. The role of the wealthy as midwives and enablers to the destruction of democracy is what matters. There is direct evidence that Miller regarded the upper classes as having a special responsibility for the rise of Nazism. In his essay on *The Crucible* titled "It Could Happen Here—and Did," he wrote, "No amount of paranoids walking around has very great political significance unless a partner appears who, naturally, is Interest. Hitler without the support of German big business would have merged with the legions of the mentally lost."[111]

How Miller renders the investment of the lower classes in witch hunting also reveals the influence of antifascism. Almost universally, critics ascribe Abigail's zeal for witch hunting to her infatuation with John Proctor; indeed, accusing Goody Proctor of sorcery allows her to eliminate a romantic rival. While I am not denying the ultimate importance of this motive, the initial train of events which leads this house servant down the path of witch hunting bears scrutiny.

Early in act 1, when Parris expresses his concern that no family will hire Abigail for her service, she angrily responds, "They want slaves, not such as I. Let them send to Barbados for that. I will not black my face for any of them!" Under Hale's examination, Tituba is the first person onto whom Abigail deflects blame; and in doing so she ascribes to her a special black language naturally suited to evoking the devil. When Hale asks, "How did she call him?" Abigail responds, "I know not—she spoke Barbados."[112] Overall, Tituba's religious practices, exoticized and associated with her race, lend credibility to the first accusations of witchcraft, which soon expand and engulf the entirety of Salem.

In the political allegory of the narrative, Abigail holds onto a white racial identity which prevents her from forming a plebeian solidarity with Tituba; this investment in whiteness is the first thing that enables her to merge her interests with those of her social betters. She appeals to a common language of race, and in taking the additional step of associating race and subversion she proves her loyalty to a repressive state and moves up in the social hierarchy. One recalls here that when Hitler and Coughlin willfully conflated communists and racial others, they sought to create an imaginary community among whites and Aryans that crossed class lines, as was noted by their critics in the 1930s. In

The Crucible white underclass complicity with the theocracy is initially based on a racial logic that allows a temporary merger of interests that cuts across class boundaries and comes together in the hunt for subversives.

There is little direct evidence that the antifascism of *The Crucible* was immediately apparent to Miller's contemporaries. Jean-Paul Sartre, for example, found the play's politics so deeply buried that he directed his own film adaptation, *Les Sorcières de Salem* (1957), which made the class divisions of Salem even more sharply visible. But Miller's antifascist roots are more present in these works of the 1950s than in his later, more humanist works like *Incident at Vichy* and *Playing for Time,* which directly render Nazis and anti-Semitism. *The Crucible* in particular was keyed to a more sharply sociological antifascism that sought to rethink race and class as separate analytical categories. It is this, not the overt nature of its representations, that fuels its didactic power as the most widely taught lesson on the perils of McCarthyism in the contemporary American high school classroom.

McCarthyism did great damage to the political and cultural goals of the old Popular Front coalition: it ruined careers, solidified a foreign policy course inimical to its philosophical core, and possibly delayed the civil rights movement for a decade. At the same time, however, McCarthyism did not achieve the full restoration feared by Sherwood in *The Best Years of Our Lives.* In the 1950s and 1960s, policymakers remained committed to Keynesian planning, ensuring that unionization rates remained high and income levels of working-class Americans steadily rose, and the direction of civil rights struggles in the 1960s proved that left-wing thought was far from vanquished in American culture. As I have argued here, antifascism played a role in turning back right-wing anticommunism in the 1950s and in the process bequeathed a number of cultural artifacts which fruitfully examine the complexity of political reaction. The early sixties witnessed an explosion of popular interest in the Third Reich, as the fall of McCarthyism allowed a long-delayed critical discussion of Nazism to resume. The political edge of this discussion, once again, placed the right on the defensive, although, as we shall see, antifascism changed considerably in the sixties as the racial frames created by the civil rights movement moved it away from the Popular Front emphasis on social class so common in the fifties.

CHAPTER 5
Brownshirts in the Twilight Zone
Antifascism in the Liberal Moment
of the Early 1960s

> There exists an obscure and inarticulate groping after reality, which contrasts with the popular mood of a decade ago. The success of [William] Shirer's work [*The Rise and Fall of the Third Reich*] could be a symptom of an attempt to understand and cope with the origins of this century's ills, provided one assumes that Nazism was not a transitory eruption but in some sense a product of modern conditions.
>
> GEORGE K. ROMOSER, *The Christian Century* (1961)

In January 1960 the foreign correspondent Arthur Olsen wrote in the *New York Times,* "Fifteen years after the Allied army stormed into Germany grimly determined to obliterate the Hitler ideology, Nazism and anti-Semitism are again matters of urgent public concern. These hallmarks of Hitlerism survive in part because the attempted purge of German society was in large measure a failure." Olsen went on to observe that, although the very top echelons of Nazi leadership had stood trial and been convicted at Nuremberg, many thousands of individuals deeply implicated in the crimes of the Third Reich still walked free. Some of these figures, he lamented, now held high-level positions in the West German government. "As early as 1948," he wrote, "United States occupation authorities washed their hands of the ambitious effort to pass judgment on the millions of 'little Nazis' not chargeable with specific common crimes."[1] What prompted this commentary on the failure of Nuremberg was an outburst of anti-Semitic vandalism across the world that began in the Rhineland city of Cologne, Germany, on Christmas Eve in 1959, when unemployed youth painted swastikas on the synagogue on Roonstrasse. In the weeks after, similar anti-Semitic acts occurred not only in other German cities but also in every capital of Europe as well as in South America, the United States, and Australia.[2] Hitler's ghost seemed to be alive and well and apparently hailed others around the world from the seat of its original German homeland.

The alarm over the failure of de-Nazification raised by Olsen and echoed by so many other voices that month did not cease once the furor over the swastika painting died down. They reflected a shifting political environment in Cold War America which helped generate a new, vibrant, and highly visible wave of antifascist cultural production. In the early 1950s, as noted earlier, the United States encouraged the rapid rearmament of West Germany so as to enable a transfer of U.S. troops from Europe to Asia during the Korean War. As a military stronghold on the frontier of communism, the former enemy was touted by cold warriors in the United States as an icon of democratic rehabilitation and, under the leadership of Chancellor Konrad Adenauer, a model ally in the war against communism. To note unreconstructed sensibilities in West Germany during much of the fifties was to raise questions about the morality of the Cold War—but by 1960 critics posed such questions with increasing boldness. The discourse surrounding the swastika vandalism set the tone for the kind of antifascist memory that would mark the first half of the sixties and also underscored its political stakes.

In the wake of the vandalism, two distinct poles of debate formed around the issue of German reconstruction that loosely mirrored rival positions on the Cold War. Those who adhered to a more conservative Cold War outlook tended to argue that the defacements of German synagogues were the isolated acts of social misfits within an otherwise healthy and democratic-minded culture and that Adenauer had the situation under control.[3] Sen. Thomas Dodd of Connecticut voiced this position most vocally. On the floor of the Senate on March 15, 1960, Dodd drew on his authority as a former prosecutor at Nuremberg to argue that the West had "lost much of its sense of proportion" in gauging the vandalism in Germany: "After several weeks of swastika headlines and exaggerated reactions, the threat of world communism and the Berlin crisis became items of minor importance in the public mind. If the headlines and the hysteria could be taken as a guide, the real menace confronting the free world was not Communist aggression, but the revival of nazism and anti-Semitism."[4] Dodd's words illustrate how the revival of wartime memories held the potential to destabilize the moral certainties and rigid polarities upon which the Cold War was grounded.

To a larger body of public commentators in the United States, the anti-Semitic wave of 1959–60 raised troubling questions that could not be neatly contained within Cold War logics. While they did not deduce that a Fourth Reich was in the offing, many were forced to acknowledge that the Second World War remained an open wound. And, like Olsen, they called into question whether justice had really been served at Nuremberg. Periodicals in the United States reported on the dismal miseducation of West German youth regarding the Nazi period and the widespread presence of ex-Nazis in politics and professional life in West Germany, extending even to the Adenauer administration. To be sure, Adenauer's government included the controversial figures Theodor Oberländer, who was implicated in war crimes on the Eastern front, and Hans Globke, who drafted official legal clarifications of the Nuremberg Laws. The coverage of the international swastika vandalism died down after the anti-Semitic wave ran its course, but the critical discourse over the unfinished business of the war remained. Popular culture in this period was awash in reminders of the failures of Nuremberg and de-Nazification, which helped to fuel a general sense that fascism was alive and well, both at home and abroad. These years saw the publication of Raul Hilberg's *The Destruction of the European Jews* (1961), the first major historical work on the Holocaust, which directly indicted the West for letting the perpetrators of genocide go free; and of T. H. Tetens's controversial *The Old Nazis and the New Germany* (1961), which chronicled the widespread return of Nazis to public life in West Germany; it witnessed the production in the United States of the German playwright Rolf Hochhuth's *The Deputy* (1963), which called attention to the complicity of the Catholic Church in the Holocaust; and it saw the release of Stanley Kramer's *Judgment at Nuremberg* (1961), an Academy Award–winning film that indicted Cold War politics for thwarting the prosecution of Nazi war criminals.

Millions followed the trial of Adolf Eichmann in Israel in 1961 through its extensive media coverage and commentary, including Hannah Arendt's *Eichmann in Jerusalem* (1963), which rendered the accused Nazi as a familiar, contemporary psychological type. Implicitly, the trial brought attention to the incomplete justice at Nuremberg. Prime Minister David Ben-Gurion of Israel leveled an indirect critique when he called the trial "the Nuremberg of the Jewish people."[5] The early sixties also marked the appearance of William Shirer's *The Rise and Fall of the Third Reich* (1960), often hailed as the best-selling work of history of all time. Shirer ignored Cold War policy imperatives in order to remind readers of the right-wing nature of Nazism. The extent to which this sense of unfinished business permeated American popular culture can be seen in the comic book *Captain America*, the protagonist of which was revived in 1964 by Marvel Comics as the "Living Legend of World War II." In 1965 Captain America battled "The Sleeper," a gargantuan robot that awakens from underneath the soil of Germany to destroy the world, aided by unreconstructed Nazis.

Cultural productions during this period depicted "the sleeper" as awakening not only in Germany but also in all manner of domestic sites. What is striking about the explosion of interest in Nazism in the United States at this time was the way Nazi ideologies and practices were widely discerned in domestic politics and culture. Most cultural commentary read the continuity of fascism not only in the paranoid anticommunism and nuclear brinkmanship of the American hard right but also in the psychology of racism more broadly. And in an echo of the magazine *Fight!* in the 1930s, fascism was once again located in the institutions of patriarchy as well. In the early sixties the political force most consistently legible as the face of American fascism was Sen. Barry Goldwater and a rightist coalition associated with him, including Gen. Edwin Walker, the Reverend Billy James Hargis, and the John Birch Society; at times the American Nazi Party was also explicitly included in this mix. Also in these years influential social scientists like Daniel Bell and Seymour Martin Lipset drew on the memory of fascism to explain what they called "the radical right" and the recent phenomenon of McCarthyism.[6] Additionally, the media widely reported on the obedience experiments of the Yale psychologist Stanley Milgram, who, in uncovering the capacity for genocidal complicity in his New Haven test subjects, overtly recalled the Holocaust. Meanwhile, the feminist Betty Friedan compared the passivity of those in Nazi concentration camps to the enforced docility of American housewives.[7] Edward Lewis Wallant's novel *The Pawnbroker* (1962) and the film and television work of Rod Serling also posited Holocaust echoes within American racism and militarism. Indeed, because of the sheer quantity of high-profile cultural works that used the memory of Nazism to critique Cold War politics and to question hierarchies within the United States, the early 1960s can be considered the postwar high point of antifascism in the American mainstream.

In this wave of antifascist cultural production a number of distinct shifts are visible in the way authors, scholars, and journalists wrote about fascism, shifts that reflect the changing scope of the political. From the early 1960s on, the mass murder of European Jews and Nazi racial ideology became key markers of fascism, and even retroactively became the reason Why We Fought the Second World War. For the first time, American antifascism consistently emphasized race and the genocide of the European Jews in its memory of Nazism, and it did so in a way that brazenly critiqued Cold War foreign policy and the larger domestic American culture it produced. Deemphasizing social class yet retaining its critical edge, antifascism began to move away from the earlier Popular Front narrative that guided it through much of the fifties. In what might seem striking in hindsight, Jews for the first time were distinctly legible as the primary, but by no means the exclusive, victims of Nazism.

Another important shift in this period is the psychologizing of fascism, a trend inspired in part by the coverage of the Eichmann trial. That is to say, cultural producers employed the figure of the Nazi more frequently as a site to explore the psychology of evil and the capacity of ordinary individuals in contemporary Western societies to commit unspeakable acts.[8] The authors of *The Authoritarian Personality* blazed this trail in 1950, but the psychologizing motif became much more widespread in the early 1960s. Mainstream coverage of the Eichmann proceedings presented the accused Nazi not as a diabolical villain or fanatical bigot but as an ordinary career man, one who blandly obeyed orders and moved up the ranks with no concern for the moral implications of his work.[9] Arendt gave this image the most elaborate articulation in *Eichmann in Jerusalem,* a book which popularized the phrase "the banality of evil." The judges at his trial, she wrote, initially thought that Eichmann's contradictory, nonsensical statements were a means of deception and self-protection, but they came to realize they were no mere mask. As Arendt wrote, "He was genuinely incapable of uttering a single sentence that was not a cliché."[10]

The emphasis on psychology might suggest a depoliticizing of antifascism, signaling a trend that removed its fascist target from sociopolitical contexts so as to universalize it as part of the human condition or reduce it to an individual pathology. But the psychologizing motif often maintained the social and political edge of earlier antifascisms. Arendt's "banality of evil," for instance, spoke to anxieties of a corporate, mass society taking hold in postwar America. In doing so, it entered a cultural ground prepared by David Riesman's, Nathan Glazer's, and Reuel Denney's *The Lonely Crowd* (1950) and Sloan Wilson's *The Man in the Gray Flannel Suit* (1955), which critiqued the empty "organization man," anchorless and adrift in an increasingly bureaucratic society. As Marianna Torgovnick writes, Eichmann was "the man in the gray flannel suit gone over to Big Brother," and she summed up the lesson of the trial for its contemporaries as "There is a little Eichmann in all of us."[11] Torgovnick rightly notes the ethical dangers of such a lesson: that is, if we are all guilty, no one is really guilty. The statement "there is a little Eichmann in all of us," one could add, depoliticizes antifascism by its very universality. Yet the psychology of (Nazi) evil was applied to rather specific kinds of individuals in the 1960s, and only one of them was the organization man in the mold of Eichmann. Those who psychologized fascism in the 1960s were, almost without exception, politically left or liberal. They were interested in the psychology of fascism—the minds of its perpetrators, bystanders, and victims—because that seemed to hold the key to explaining the roots of social injustice and political reaction.[12]

To writers and cultural critics in the early 1960s, antifascism was a deft tool for exploring the psychology of anticommunism. With the experience of McCarthyism still raw in memory, fascism continued to be read as an excessive anticommunist nationalism. The domestic fascist subject was one who overidentified with the dominant discourses of the Cold War and American nationhood and whose patriotism was used as a form of domestic repression against

Jews, people of color, liberals, and intellectuals. Thus writers and cultural critics often used a psychologized antifascism to explore what Joel Kovel called the moral black hole of anticommunism, wherein fear of communists becomes so acute that one resorts to assaults on reason and atrocities against physical bodies in the attempt to thwart it.[13]

But why was there so much open discussion of fascism in the early 1960s as well as such a readiness to apply the concept to American life? And what was behind the shift of emphasis to Nazi racial ideology in recalling the war in Europe and the Third Reich? The Eichmann trial is commonly seen as a central moment in Americans' consciousness of the Holocaust. It has been held up as the one event that broke the relative silence on the genocide that had reigned in the 1950s, the episode that transformed its piles of corpses from anonymous "victims of Hitler" to specifically Jewish bodies central to the meaning of the Second World War.[14] But as the discourse over the swastika vandalism illustrates, this shift in perception had begun before the Eichmann trial in the spring of 1961 and even prior to his capture by Israeli agents in May 1960. When Dodd spoke of "the revival of nazism and anti-Semitism" in March 1960, he echoed a wider discourse in which "nazism" and "anti-Semitism" were becoming inextricable.

Scholars have credited the civil rights movement and the ethnic nationalisms of the late 1960s for enabling Jewish Americans to highlight the Nazi genocide as a crime specifically perpetrated against Jews. The word *Holocaust,* connoting the six million Jews murdered by the Third Reich, came into common usage after the 1960s. These movements authorized expressions of ethnic identity, group rights, and the particularity of group experience which had formerly been seen as distasteful or even un-American.[15] But the civil rights movements at home and anticolonial movements abroad arguably impacted the memory of the Second World War even before the late 1960s. Before the Eichmann trial, the global revolutions and movements opposing white supremacy had, by the early 1960s, helped the public to see race and racism as causal factors driving historical events. In so doing, they fundamentally prepared audiences to be receptive to the Eichmann trial by making the Nazi genocide legible as a racial event and anti-Semitism a retroactive reason for Why We Fought. In this context, what is remarkable about public discourse in this period is the use the word *racism* to refer to the murder of European Jews and the frequency with which commentators, while fully acknowledging the anti-Semitic nature of the Nazi genocide, described it as a crime against a *minority.*

Additionally, the liberal culture of the late fifties and early sixties enabled this representational shift. As a number of scholars have argued, the suppression of progressive activists during the McCarthy period delayed the emergence of civil rights as a national mass movement by a decade.[16] The same dynamic applies to other progressive politics in the public sphere. The anticommunist repression embodied by McCarthy interrupted an open, public discussion on the nature of fascism and the sociopolitical implications of the Second World War. In the wake of his downfall, liberal politicians won important gains in Congress in 1958 and won the White House in 1960 and 1964, marginalizing the political right. Even for cold warriors the successful Sputnik launch, the rising civil rights movement, and the implosion of McCarthyism seemed to necessitate a new course. American leaders began to see domestic reform, not a rigidly policed ideological conformity, as the most effective means of winning the Cold War. As Kirsten Fermaglich has argued, this liberal milieu not only lent visibility to the Holocaust but also enabled scholars and cultural producers, particularly Jewish American ones, to make comparisons between American society and Nazi Germany with few repercussions.[17] Now that the obstacles to antifascist dialogue were removed, in other words, a more thorough processing of the war and its aftermath could resume. The swastika vandalism was merely a catalyst, opening the door to a repressed conversation that had been waiting to erupt.

The shift in Cold War strategy from forced conformity to more open dialogue, a shift enabled by the downfall of McCarthy, opened a real space for antifascist cultural production. Although not all antifascisms of this period were critical of the Cold War, they should not be simply read as a new means of waging the war on communism, one that furthered the goal of anticommunist containment through liberal, pluralistic dialogue rather than through Red Squads and the blacklist. Calling attention to the deep roots of fascism and its potential reemergence within Western culture was not exactly convenient for those pursuing U.S. foreign policy goals. By and large, the antifascisms covered in this chapter ruptured the amnesia necessary to the American Cold War project of elevating a key Western ally as a beacon of freedom and of placing the West in a separate moral universe from communism. In so doing they further undermined the paradigm of totalitarianism, that is, the officially sanctioned conflation of communism and fascism prevalent in the 1950s, while not eliminating it from the cultural vocabulary.

The cultural work of four individuals provides highly productive sites at which to examine the shape and impact of antifascism in the early 1960s: the popular historian William Shirer and his best-selling history *The Rise and Fall of the Third Reich* (1960); Stanley Kramer and his film *Judgment at Nuremberg* (1961); the work of the television and film writer Rod Serling; and Betty Friedan and her famous *The Feminine Mystique* (1963). These productions reveal the centrality of Holocaust frames, the continuity of Cold War critique, and the psychological emphasis constitutive of this wave of antifascism. Just as important, they were among the most widely discussed cultural works of these years.

The Unfinished Business of Nuremberg and the Politics of the Cold War

After four years of military occupation by the Western allies, the Federal Republic of Germany (FRG, commonly known in the English-speaking world as West Germany) held its first elections in August 1949. Konrad Adenauer was elected as the republic's first chancellor, a role he served in from 1949 to 1963. Representing the conservative Christian Democratic Union, Adenauer was somewhat of a rarity in German public life: an old conservative untainted by complicity in the Nazi regime. He had been mayor of Cologne before 1933 and had been imprisoned for a time during the Third Reich. Through most of the 1950s relations between the Eisenhower and Adenauer administrations were excellent: they shared the same hard line against the Soviet Union and the Eastern bloc. The FRG refused to diplomatically recognize the German Democratic Republic (GDR, or East Germany) and pushed for reunification, which meant the absorption of East Germany into itself and the Western alliance. As a result of this cordial, public relationship and because of the strong anticommunist sensibilities which had hardened across the Atlantic, a hagiography of Adenauer developed in the American media in the 1950s that lingered into the next decade. In what the German exile and former political prisoner of the Third Reich T. H. Tetens criticized as "the Adenauer image," Americans often portrayed him as an ideal combination of firmness and moderation, a leader who came to embody a people who had strikingly reentered the pantheon of free, democratic nations. In 1954 in its issue naming him Man of the Year, *Time* magazine reported, "West German voters swept all their Communists and Nazis out of national office and overwhelmingly put their faith in the dedicated, firm-handed democrat, Konrad Adenauer."[18]

The reality of German reconstruction was more complex, however. Both East and West Germany were officially founded on an opposition to fascism, albeit different notions of fascism. In the East, a complex, contradictory daily life emerged, marked, on the one hand, by a repressive state apparatus antithetical to the emancipatory dreams of the former resistance and, on the other, by a unique culture that in certain respects was genuinely antifascist.[19] The Soviet Red Army routinely shot captured SS men in the field during the war, yet, after the smoke cleared, the GDR, like the FRG, took a "pragmatic" approach to de-Nazification, which allowed former Nazis to enter positions of authority.[20] In the West the discourse of totalitarianism was etched into a new constitution that conceived fascism and communism as equivalent threats to democratic order. But despite the state's official opposition to totalitarianism, the status of memory in West German culture during the Adenauer era remained problematic. The vast majority in the FRG felt that Germany should never again wage war and had no desire for another Hitler to appear, yet there emerged a sense that the Germans were the real victims of the war, a sense that the blunders of the Allied reconstruction arguably facilitated.[21] In 1951 the U.S. High Commission for Germany conducted an opinion survey of the citizens of the FRG, asking them which groups had the greatest claim to public assistance. The most common answer was war widows and orphans, followed by victims of Allied bombing raids, ethnic Germans expelled from the East, the resistance fighters of July 20, 1944, and, after all of these, the Jews.[22] In an essay published in Germany shortly before the desecration of the Cologne synagogue in 1959, Adorno critiqued such disturbing notions of victimhood and perpetration in West Germany, writing, "Irrational too [is] the widespread settling of accounts about guilt, as if Dresden made up for Auschwitz."[23] More unsettling still, by 1948 there were widespread public calls for full amnesty for convicted Nazi war criminals. This campaign was fueled by an effective, professionalized lobbying apparatus to secure their release that politicians could not afford to ignore.[24]

By the late fifties, however, powerful countercurrents in the FRG led to the resumption of war criminal investigations and prosecutions by West German authorities. The relationship between the Adenauer and the U.S. governments had become frayed by this time and during the Kennedy years grew more fractious still. The root issue was a German feeling of abandonment as the Eisenhower administration backed away from the policy of anticommunist liberation and its push for German reunification, a shift brought about by a strategic need to focus on contested spaces outside Europe.[25] At the same time, a sudden resurgence of antifascist memory across the Atlantic added fuel to the fire.

In the early sixties, Shirer's *The Rise and Fall of the Third Reich* and Kramer's *Judgment at Nuremberg* were the two most widely circulated American cultural works to raise critical awareness of the unfinished business of the war. In highly influential forums, both works called attention to an unreconstructed German people and did so in ways that ignored or even indicted established Cold War frames for reading international politics. This is not to say that other, less well-received works were without significance or that Shirer and Kramer were the most far-reaching in their social critiques. Tetens published *The New Germany and the Old Nazis* in 1961, a scathing attack on the failure of reconstruction which highlighted the return of former Nazis to almost all areas of public life in the FRG. Although his book was published by a major trade press, Random

House, it was panned by critics as a one-sided, inflammatory work, some accusing him of harboring an irrational hatred of Germany.[26] Hilberg, regarded as the founding father of Holocaust historiography, struggled to find a publisher for his seminal *The Destruction of the European Jews* (1961). After being rejected by Princeton University Press, his work finally found a home under the relatively obscure imprint of Quadrangle Books and generated modest levels of public discussion in its early years.[27] Like Tetens, Hilberg directly indicted the Adenauer government, Allied occupation authorities, and the German public for enabling genocidal perpetrators to elude justice. His book included a list of individually named war criminals spanning eleven pages; in the vast majority of entries, each name cross-referenced the mild or nonexistent punishment each perpetrator received. Hilberg concluded, "By the law they had not lived. By the law they did not die."[28]

Shirer and Kramer, while also critical of Cold War politics, enjoyed a far different reception. *The Rise and Fall of the Third Reich* did especially well, selling millions of copies since its publication in 1960, winning the National Book Award in 1961, and remaining in print today. Despite the hefty price tag of its first run as a clothbound book, over one million readers bought a copy in its first year, jump-starting its reputation as the best-selling work of history in modern times.[29] In addition, excerpts of the book were serialized in *Reader's Digest*, which had a circulation of twelve million readers per month, the *Boston Globe*, and *Look* magazine.[30] Indeed, more Americans have learned the history of the Second World War through Shirer's work than through any other written narrative, including Churchill's popular five-volume history published a decade earlier. Newspaper and magazine reviewers warmly embraced the book, although academic reviews at the time were mixed; his critics generally took Shirer to task for failing to read the Third Reich through the now-discredited frame of totalitarianism. Nevertheless, the book is now regarded as a respectable, albeit dated, work of history. Its rampant success was a stunning reversal for Shirer, who had spent the 1950s in obscurity after being blacklisted by *Red Channels* and dropped from CBS news in 1947.[31]

While Shirer, Kramer, Tetens, and Hilberg all criticized the Cold War for derailing justice at Nuremberg and undermining the resolution of the war, the variations in their reception nonetheless illustrate the limits of what was utterable in the public sphere of the early 1960s. To be sure, Shirer and Kramer both skillfully employed popular storytelling modes, whereas Hilberg's magnum opus, by contrast, was a professional academic history that methodically laid out its case. More critical was that Shirer and Kramer, unlike the virtually unknown Tetens and Hilberg, enjoyed established reputations. Shirer had earned fame among the war generation for his *Berlin Diary: The Journal of a*

Foreign Correspondent, 1934–1941, the number one best seller in 1941. Kramer was a familiar figure as well. He was the producer and director of star-driven "message films," including *High Noon* (1952), *The Caine Mutiny* (1954), *The Defiant Ones* (1958), and, later, *Guess Who's Coming to Dinner* (1967). Thus in the early sixties, absent a mass anti-imperial movement, one still had to be of known, professional stature to take on the foreign policy paradigm and get away with it.

Though popular and decidedly liberal (not radical), their antifascist politics were clear. Shirer and Kramer both accessed wartime frames, still active in memory, which fifteen years of Cold War had not erased. Their renderings of fascism as a fanatically anticommunist, broadly racist force enabled by established authority resonated with pre-1945 discussions of the term, yet they accrued new meaning in the aftermath of HUAC. To draw from Raymond Williams, their reception speaks to the ways in which antifascism formed a "residual culture" in postwar years. That is, antifascism was a cultural mode formed in the past but still active in the present, one wherein values and meanings which could not be expressed in terms of the dominant culture lived on as residue, forming a reservoir of disruptive energies.

Shirer sporadically used the term *totalitarianism* in his famous work, but the concept does not shape its structure. *Rise and Fall* departed from Cold War constructions in a number of ways: by conveying the essentially right-wing nature of Nazism; by effectively avoiding the conflation of the USSR and Hitler's Germany; and by refusing to single out the former Soviet ally as uniquely cynical in its prewar diplomacy. Moreover, the fundamental premise of the book, that German culture was inherently militaristic and threatening, conflicted with the underlying Cold War consensus that communism presented the greatest danger to the world. Unlike Churchill's epic history of the war, which was told entirely from the view of Allied diplomacy, Shirer's account reconstructed the conflict as it unfolded inside Germany. Fluent in German, he based his narrative on official documents of the Third Reich and the diaries of its military and political leaders captured at the end of the war. This perspective enabled him to present a portrait of the conflict that implicitly contradicted the former British leader. To Churchill the war was a threat to established order, but to Shirer it stemmed from antidemocratic tendencies produced by prewar hierarchies and inequalities. On the most basic level, Shirer departed from his predecessor by reminding readers of the real enemy in the war: not world communism but fascist Germany.

Shirer reproduces the antifascism of the Popular Front generation by placing Nazism firmly on the political right. He explicitly refers to Hitler as a "politician of the Right," and to the NSDAP in its early days as "one of several right-wing movements in Bavaria." More arresting is his long account of how conservatives and the propertied classes enabled Hitler's rise, a facet of the book that resonated with reviewers.[32] In what Brecht had earlier allegorized as "a resistible rise," Shirer relates how aristocrats, capitalists, professionals, and a rightist military establishment—all fearful of a leftward swing, contemptuous of democracy, and desirous of maintaining their power—reversed the political fortunes of Hitler and his middle-class movement by placing him at the head of a rightist coalition government. Much like Lewis's character Buzz Windrip, Shirer's Hitler privately assures industrialists that he is for "free enterprise and competition," however much he rails against accumulated wealth in public. Echoing a class analysis of the Third Reich postulated by his predecessors Lewis, Elmer Davis, and later historians like Robert Paxton, Shirer writes, "In the former Austrian vagabond the conservative classes thought they had found a man who, while remaining their prisoner, would help them attain their goals. . . . What they then wanted was an authoritarian Germany which at home would put an end to democratic 'nonsense' and the power of the trade unions and in foreign affairs undo the verdict of 1918. . . . These were Hitler's aims too. And though he brought what the conservatives had lacked, a mass following, the Right was sure that he would remain in its pocket."[33]

Like other interpreters of the Third Reich from the Popular Front generation, Shirer pays close attention to the class relationships undergirding its rise but does not simply reduce the Nazi state to its economic motives. Although a capitalist desire to restore class hierarchies enabled the ascent of Hitler, it was not the Führer's driving passion once in power, according to the author. Here, a distinct difference from earlier narratives is visible in *Rise and Fall*, one reflective of a cultural milieu transformed by civil rights. While the antifascists of the 1930s also called attention to Nazi Aryanism, Shirer describes the racialist philosophies and policies of the Nazi government, as well as their origins in nineteenth-century European philosophy, with a minuteness of detail that was rare before 1945. The Holocaust, hardly mentioned in Churchill's history, receives a meticulous, even graphic treatment in *Rise and Fall*, and its author makes clear the specificity of its Jewish victims from the outset. Reading Shirer, many readers learned for the first time what are now familiar aspects of Holocaust memory: the mass shootings by the *Einsatzgruppen*, the gas vans, the planning of the Final Solution at Wannsee, the introduction of the poison Zyklon B and its administration in "showers," the participation of German industry in the extermination, ghastly medical experiments, the Warsaw Ghetto uprising, and the use of human skin as lampshades.[34]

But the Holocaust as told by Shirer is not bracketed off as a distinct event, separate from the overall war or from the totality of Nazism; neither are the victims of the genocide exclusively Jewish. In *Rise and Fall* the destruction of the Jews formed a major part of a wider, murderous "New Order" that included the mass extermination of Slavic and particularly Soviet peoples, slave labor, economic imperialism, and brutal reprisals against civilians.[35] Shirer emphasizes that Soviet citizens, in addition to Jews, formed a considerable number of Germany's victims: indeed, recent estimates hold that twenty-seven million people in the USSR, overwhelmingly civilians, died during the conflict.[36] He covers the genocidal treatment of Soviet prisoners of war, especially those deemed to be Asiatic, and also the purposeful mass starvation of people in occupied territories of the Soviet Union, which was intended to facilitate German colonization and the extraction of resources for the use of the Reich.[37] In chronicling the atrocities endured by Soviet peoples in great detail, Shirer emphasized a facet of the war displaced by Cold War amnesia and increasingly forgotten today.

In a patent rebuke to the Cold War history of Churchill, *Rise and Fall* reminds its audience not only of the victim status of its former Soviet ally, but also of its full military contribution. In stark contrast even to most twenty-first-century narratives of the war, Shirer devotes more space to the battle of Stalingrad than to the invasion of Normandy and resurrects the spirit of 1940s wartime journalism to describe the heroic efforts of ordinary Soviet soldiers.[38] Furthermore, the work complicates the standard postwar explanation for the stiff resistance of the Red Army. In place of the popular, oversimplified story that they fought for the motherland, not for communism, he introduces a narrative of Soviet development in which its soldiers fought to preserve the recent economic progress of the socialist nation.[39] Finally, Shirer revises Churchill's history of prewar diplomacy in meaningful ways. Churchill emphasized the Hitler–Stalin Pact of August 1939 in his work and advanced it as evidence of the singular depravity and hypocrisy of the Soviet state. To Shirer, however, this treaty was only one of a long series of diplomatic appeasements. Far more avoidable and hence reprehensible were the appeasements orchestrated by Chamberlain and the French in the months and years preceding August 1939. Indeed, he blames an earlier "bankruptcy of Anglo-French diplomacy" for making the pact with Hitler a rational choice for Stalin.[40]

The last facet of *Rise and Fall* to contradict Cold War politics was its view of the German people. A theme running throughout the book is the failure of the Germans to resist, a failure stemming from deeply rooted militarist and racialist strains within German culture. A great deal of Shirer's narrative is focused on the various plots by German military officers to assassinate Hitler, most of which faltered owing to an insufficient resolve on the part of the plotters at every stage of the regime. After surveying critical figures in German statesmanship and intellectual history, including Martin Luther, G. W. F. Hegel, Friedrich Nietzsche, Otto von Bismarck, and Richard Wagner, Shirer concludes, "The mind and the passion of Hitler—all the aberrations that possessed his feverish brain—had roots that lay deep in German experience and thought. Nazism and the Third Reich, in fact, were but a logical continuation of German history."[41] This notion of continuity, known among historians of Nazism as the Luther to Hitler thesis, was common in American scholarship during the 1930s and 1940s and was a constant theme in American propaganda during the war.[42] In short, it was a pervasive narrative during Shirer's formative years, one which he advanced in his wartime *Berlin Diary* and later reproduced, almost intact, in *Rise and Fall*.

Among the various aspects of *Rise and Fall,* its notion of a congenital German failure to resist Nazism posed the most salient problem for Cold War geopolitics. As Gavriel Rosenfeld writes, "With the German people, rather than Hitler, to blame for the nazi disaster, Shirer was implicitly arguing that post-war West Germany—composed largely of the same populace as the Third Reich—was not to be trusted."[43] After the publication of the German translation of *Rise and Fall* in October 1961, it came under relentless attack by West German scholars, journalists, and politicians. German reviewers took Shirer to task for failing to reconfirm the totalitarianism thesis (also dominant in West German historiography in the fifties and sixties) and for having a long-standing hatred of the country. One German detractor claimed even that he approached his subject "with the soul of a Nuremberg prosecutor." As critics on both sides of the Atlantic argued, *Rise and Fall* threatened to undermine the North Atlantic Treaty Organization (NATO) alliance at a highly sensitive moment.[44] The same month the German translation appeared, American and Soviet tanks squared off against one another in Berlin, where the construction of the Berlin Wall had begun two months prior. Adenauer personally attacked Shirer as "a German hater," and, in a desperate public relations effort, the Bonn government put together a twenty-four-page pamphlet containing negative reviews of the book and then distributed it to American book critics and newspaper editors.[45]

Shirer's reception forcefully illustrates Williams's notion of residual culture. A discourse like the Luther to Hitler thesis, which served a regressive function in 1941, when redeployed virtually intact by a stubbornly persistent memory twenty years later can play a very different and subversive role in its new political context. Interestingly, Shirer accomplished his critique of contemporary politics with scarcely any explicit reference to postwar developments. His book does not fault the outcome of the Nuremberg tribunals—with which he was well acquainted, its trial proceedings being one of his source materials—and he does not point to specific postwar examples of the failure of de-Nazification. In this regard, Kramer's contemporaneous film *Judgment at Nuremberg* picks up where *Rise and Fall* leaves off.

The release of the big-budget *Judgment at Nuremberg* in December 1961 was a major cultural event in North American and Europe. Produced and directed by Kramer, an established creator of liberal Hollywood message films, it was regarded as his most ambitious effort to date. The screenplay was by Abby Mann, primarily a writer of television anthology dramas. Mann based his script on his earlier one of the same title written for the television program *Playhouse 90* in 1959. The film's huge all-star cast of Spencer Tracy, Burt Lancaster, Marlene Dietrich, Montgomery Clift, Maximilian Schell, Richard Widmark, and Judy Garland helped to make it a box office draw. Kramer had a history of generating publicity for his films by staging their world premieres in controversial locales. In 1959 he riled officials at the State Department by opening his film *On the Beach*, which depicted life after a nuclear apocalypse, simultaneously in eighteen cities around the world, including Tokyo and Moscow.[46] Following his earlier modus operandi, Kramer premiered *Judgment at Nuremberg* in West Berlin's Kongress Halle, on December 14, 1961, right next to the recently completed Berlin Wall.

The date of the premiere coincided with the reading of Eichmann's verdict in Jerusalem. It also came at a moment when Soviet and American forces faced each other in Berlin during a tense crisis in the city over which Nikita Khrushchev and President John Kennedy had both threatened nuclear war the previous summer.[47] In attendance at the televised premiere were NATO military commanders, including Kennedy's personal representative, Gen. Lucius Clay, Soviet bloc correspondents from East Berlin, German professional leaders, members of the city government, and journalists from around the world. The screening and subsequent party were sponsored by Willy Brandt, the Social Democratic major of Berlin, later known for his politics of reconciliation with the East, which he enacted on becoming chancellor in 1969.[48] Despite Brandt's advocacy of the film, the responses of his countrymen were mixed, and after an initial burst of enthusiasm it played to largely empty theaters in Germany. In the United States, where it sparked heated debate among critics, often along political lines, reviews were generally positive, and it earned Kramer his first Oscar.[49]

One should not regard the film's high visibility as an intrinsic sign of its political limitations, as a number of its contemporary and later critics have done.[50] At the time of its release, many people, including Eleanor Roosevelt, praised Kramer for his courage and bravery in raising controversial issues in the film, but the point is not the director's personal bravery or lack thereof.[51] Certainly, controversy invites publicity, and just as surely Kramer could have garnered fame by producing nonpolitical work, as many others in the movie business did. Rather, the creators of the film could proffer the message they did precisely because they inhabited a historical conjuncture in which alternative narratives of the war had not yet been effaced from public memory. For my purposes, the significance of *Judgment at Nuremberg* is that it reveals the fissures in the public's acceptance of the totalitarianism thesis, a Cold War logic countered by the whole premise of the film. Like Shirer, Kramer accesses official wartime discourses from the 1940s, discourses which, in certain ways work at cross-purposes with the progressive politics of his film. But overall the film facilitates a self-reflexive politics of memory which critiques the retreat of U.S. policy from antifascism abroad while subtly evoking the dangers of a resurgent fascism within the United States. It performs these tasks by hinting at the existence of a continuity between the fascist states of the past and the Cold War culture of the present.

The setting of the film is Nuremberg, Germany, in 1948, during the second wave of Nazi war criminal prosecutions. Historically, the first Nuremberg trials took place from November 1945 to October 1946 under the auspices of the International Military Tribunal (IMT), led by judges and prosecutors from the United States, France, Great Britain, and the Soviet Union. Twenty-four of the men deemed to be the most prominent Nazi leaders were tried by the IMT in this first round, and twelve received the death penalty. In addition, individual nations held tribunals for crimes perpetrated within their territories, and from December 1946 to April 1949, the U.S. Nuremberg Military Tribunals (NMT) held a second round of trials at Nuremberg for 185 lesser Nazi perpetrators. The difference between the IMT and the NMT trials is that the latter took place when the Cold War was firmly underway. They were thus more controversial in American foreign policy circles because of the danger they posed to the U.S.–West German alliance against the Soviet Union. The trials of the NMT are the focus of *Judgment at Nuremberg,* particularly the so-called Judges' Trial, wherein prominent judges of the Third Reich themselves stood accused of enforcing the brutal laws of the regime.

Like Shirer's *Rise and Fall, Judgment at Nuremberg* reintroduced a popular and officially sanctioned narrative of the 1940s, this time by pitting a virtuous American protagonist against a debased German populace. Both its writer and director grew up with this black-and-white narrative: Kramer served in the army during war, while Mann, who was born in 1927, was not drafted into the service on account of his age.[52] Frank Capra's film series Why We Fight and John Steinbeck's best-selling *The Moon Is Down,* as we have seen, constructed the Germans and the Japanese as *slave peoples* defined by a deeply rooted militaristic, anti-individual culture. They were opposed, in this schema, by Allied *free peoples* marked by an equally rooted commitment to the democratic process. Kramer did not draw this line so sharply in his film, but the structure of the plot makes it fairly easy for audiences to make such deductions. The protagonist and central character of the film is Judge Dan Haywood, played by Tracy, an amiable, tolerant, fair-minded American whose ultimate decision to convict the accused in the face of enormous anticommunist political pressure contrasts his moral integrity with that of the German judges he condemns. By contrast, there are no clear-cut examples of German independence or morality in the film: its German characters generally fall into the roles of pitiable victims, immoral bystanders, or crass perpetrators. Its central German character, Mrs. Bertolt (played by Dietrich), evinces a self-serving amnesia.

Such a dichotomy, if left unchallenged, would take the history of the Third Reich out of the realm of left/right politics and place it firmly within a narrative of American exceptionalism. Fortunately, there are strong crosscurrents in the film. Most dramatically, the ending undercuts the idea that Haywood's righteousness is characteristically American. In the final shot, as he walks out of the prison between rows of stern military police, an image suggestive of his isolation, a title announces, "The Nuremberg Trials held in the American Zone ended July 14, 1949. There were ninety-nine defendants sentenced to prison terms. Not one is still serving his sentence." While Haywood's actions give the audience a point of identification, the conclusion reveals that the larger American system in which he operates is not guided by his sense of justice. The American side is rocked by moral divisions throughout the film, with memory and amnesia falling into specific political patterns. Haywood describes himself as "a rock-ribbed Republican who thought that Franklin Roosevelt was a great man" and is thereby positioned outside the realm of partisanship. But the political affiliations of the other American characters are clear. The lead American prosecutor and most uncompromising anti-Nazi of the film, Col. Tad Lawson, is revealed to be a former New Dealer; his prosecution is his means of extending the People's War. By contrast, the American character who most emphatically urges a forgetting of the past is Haywood's colleague Judge Curtiss Ives, explicitly identified as a conservative. Ives ultimately dissents with Haywood's decision to convict the accused and thus becomes the personification of the system that morally failed; he chides his colleague on the bench for his insufficient conservatism and complains that the problem with the prosecution is that "it is filled with young radicals like Lawson."

This plot trope elides the formative role of the Truman administration in abandoning de-Nazification. Yet the political specificity of memory in the film is meaningful because it works to undercut a clear division between the German and American systems, providing a tangibly didactic basis for its narrative of historical continuity between Nazi past and Cold War present. In a forum on *Judgment at Nuremberg* published in *Commentary* magazine in January 1962, Jason Epstein, the vice president of Random House, defended the film against its critics, who had accused its creators of drawing unfair parallels between Nazi Germany and Cold War America. Epstein wrote, "In fact he is not suggesting a parallel at all, but a continuum. That is, he sees the history of the past thirty years as a single unit held together by the presence of a tendency in the modern world toward mass violence, particularly when national interests are threatened." He gleaned from Mann's screenplay that "not Germany itself but our civilization as a whole was represented by the Nazi episode, and that the cold war is a further, more virulent, symptom of the same disorder."[53] The sense of continuity, more than an exceptionalist narrative of American virtue over German degradation, came across to a number of contemporary reviewers of the film. The narrative of Nazism that emerges in the courtroom scenes enabled reviewers to see a continuum. The film audience, positioned as jurors, was to see Nazism as a kind of demonic nationalism fueled by a fear of communism and racial difference, one that made citizens gradually consent to the loss of their rights. This anticommunist sense of national crisis, furthermore, served as a pretext for a nationalist violence resulting in mass murder (the new Cold War mass murder, concluded Epstein in 1962, would be one not of racial extermination but of nuclear annihilation). Ernst Janning (Burt Lancaster), the face of the respectable, prewar German establishment, gives the following account on the witness stand:

> We had a democracy, yes, but it was torn by elements within. Above all, there was fear. . . . Only when you understand that, can you understand what Hitler meant to us. Because he said to us, "Lift up your heads! Be proud to be German! There are devils among us! Communists! Liberals! Jews! Gypsies! Once these devils are destroyed, your misery will be destroyed. . . ." Why did we take part? Because we loved our country. What difference does it make if a few political extremists lose their rights? What difference does it make if a few racial minorities lose their rights? It is only a passing phase. . . . Hitler himself will be discarded. . . . The country is in danger! We will march forward!

Janning's testimony reflects two now-familiar facets of Nazism which the film put back into public memory: its anticommunism and its genocidal racism. And in large measure the film succeeded in this respect. Few reviewers failed to note its connections between 1930s Germany and 1950s McCarthyite America or its allusion to the unfolding civil rights struggle. Janning's use of the phrase "racial minorities" is telling, as it had no commonly used German equivalent in Weimar discourse. Mann viscerally produces continuity by putting the arguments of the Cold War establishment into the mouth of the convicted Nazi judge Emil Hahn, who says in his closing statements, "We were a bulwark against Bolshevism. We were a pillar of Western culture. A bulwark and a pillar the West may have wished to retain."

Kramer's broad application of the lesson of the Second World War has been viewed more critically with the passage of time. A number of later scholars in Holocaust studies have criticized Kramer and Mann for supposedly universalizing the Holocaust. In this reading, the film deemphasizes the specificity of the Jewish victims in favor of an unproductive, ecumenical interpretation of the genocide that applies its meaning too widely. Judith Doneson writes, "*Judgment* makes the Jew a victim among victims, universalizing becomes shared history; the Holocaust is not a uniquely Jewish event."[54] A crucial point of contention here is the lengthy film within a film. In a shocking scene remarked on by almost every reviewer, the prosecutor Lawson presents to the court a graphic documentary newsreel shot by Allied forces at the liberation of Buchenwald and Bergen Belsen. The newsreel is composed of actual footage shown in movie theaters across the United States for a brief moment in 1945, then quickly taken out of public circulation. In 1961 audiences were shown—some as reminders, most for the first time—documentary images of heaps of bodies bulldozed into mass graves, charred skeletons in ovens, heaps of gold taken from tooth fillings, objects made from human skin, and the shrunken heads of Polish laborers. During the courtroom presentation, when Lawson states that even children were hung, the camera cuts momentarily to the disturbed face of an African American guard in the courtroom, a clear evocation of southern lynching which came through loud and clear to contemporaries.[55]

The focal point of later critical controversy among Holocaust scholars is Lawson's analysis of the newsreel, in which he states, "Who were the bodies? Members of every occupied country of Europe. Two-thirds of the Jews of Europe. Exterminated." Alan Mintz sees this statement as indicative of a larger failing by Kramer. He writes, "The Jews are mentioned among others, and that is the solitary reference."[56] I concur that the bodies of the victims need to be granted a specific identity, and I share the critique that the film includes no Jewish characters. However, it is not true that *Judgment at Nuremberg* presents the Jews as only one victim among many. Jews are mentioned more frequently than any other category of victim: for example, in the discussion of the anti-Semitic Nuremberg Laws in the film's fictionalized Feldenstein case, in the German house servant's statement, "The Jews and the rest, we knew nothing about that," in Janning's testimony, and even in Lawson's commentary, which identifies Jews but not any other specific group. More to the point, to say that Nazi genocide claimed the lives of millions of non-Jews is not to universalize but to speak with historical precision. It is accurate to state that the bodies discovered at Buchenwald and Bergen Belsen came from "every occupied country of Europe," for in these camps the Nazis murdered a large number of Soviet POWs, political prisoners, homosexuals, Roma, and Jews.

In sum, *Judgment at Nuremberg* presents the Jews as the preponderant, but not the sole, victims of Hitler's Germany. While it says nothing about homosexual victims, and its portrait of the communist victims is deeply problematic, the film could be considered part of a unique moment in Holocaust consciousness.[57] Like Shirer's *Rise and Fall,* it occupies a historical space between the dominant 1950s view, which often failed to recognize the singular place of the Jews or any specific group in the genocide, and the present, when the identities of the millions of non-Jewish victims are infrequently acknowledged in popular narratives. In the main, the film is a productive, ethical guide for viewing the history of the Nazi period, one which neither universalizes its meaning too broadly nor consigns its carnage to the madness of a distant time and place. The German defense attorney Hans Rolfe (Schell) initially argued that Hitler represented a disease facilitated by the whole world, and hence his defendants could not be found uniquely guilty. Rolfe reasoned that all the Allies, together with the Vatican, made various pacts with Germany which facilitated Hitler's rise. Moreover, he argued, the American legal scholar Oliver Wendell Holmes supported forced sterilizations much like the Nazis, and one could also show shocking images of thousands of corpses at Hiroshima and Nagasaki.

Yet by the end of the film the audience is led to fully identify with Judge Haywood as he makes the decision to avoid such relativism and to convict the accused. The various parallels between Nazi Germany and the Cold War in the United States that are drawn in *Judgment at Nuremberg* do not ask one to conflate Nazism and the Cold War but to acknowledge that fascism's underlying logics do in fact reside in a broader Western culture beyond the frontiers of Germany. As Rolfe argues, this shared culture contributed to the making of the Third Reich. But this observation is only a starting point. What is up to the film's audience—who occupy the terrain of moral and political action—is whether the various rudiments of fascism, present in all modern cultures and most manifest in political reaction, crystallize and converge to form an authoritarian, even genocidal state. In keeping with the most progressive traditions of antifascism, one is led to see fascism not as a property of some nations and not others but as a form of political reaction *within* nations. One must refuse to be morally paralyzed by its ubiquity so as to condemn it at home and abroad, taking decisive action to prevent its full manifestation.

The Eichmann Next Door: Rod Serling and the New American Right

In the early 1960s the revival of public interest in unvanquished fascism abroad had its counterpart in a discussion of an emergent homegrown American variant. The political force that was most often read as fascist in this period was a new radical right that eventually coalesced around the presidential candidacy of Barry Goldwater. All but the most explicitly conservative periodicals, namely, the Luce press, viewed this new rightist coalition with varying degrees of either condescension or alarm. As identified by most mainstream publications, the new right included the ultraconservative John Birch Society, established in 1958, Protestant evangelicals like the Reverend Billy James Hargis, the Minutemen paramilitary organization, Gen. Edwin A. Walker, assorted McCarthyite leftovers from the 1950s, and, often mentioned in the same context, the American Nazi Party under George Lincoln Rockwell. Other archconservatives were regarded as more mainstream, nonfascist expressions of the movement, but only nominally so. These included William Buckley, who founded the *National Review* in 1955, Phyllis Schlafly, the future founder of the Eagle Forum, and Goldwater himself. No other political constellation in the American scene during this period was consistently discussed as fascist. The political right, in a self-defensive attempt to neutralize the charge, occasionally hurled the epithet back at the left, but not persistently. As in the fifties, conservatives devoted more time to defending themselves against the ubiquitous label.[58]

What made this new right fascist, according to its mainstream detractors, was the toxic combination it brought into play: a rank and file evidencing a visceral racism and anti-Semitism; an anticommunism so intense that it threatened democratic freedom; and, most consistently, a white, antipluralist, extreme nationalism which, if allowed to crystallize under a Goldwater presidency, would potentially lead to mass annihilation, this time in the form of nuclear war.[59] In addition, leading social scientists of the day such as Lipset and Bell characterized the contemporary right and the recent McCarthyites as fascist because of their middle-class nature. Deploying a sociological reading of conservatism common in the early sixties, they argued that an important link between the American radical right and its prewar European antecedents was middle-class "status anxiety"; that is, right-wing extremism, past and present, appealed to middle-class individuals fearful of losing their social status amidst the constantly shifting terrain of modernity.[60] Lipset noted further that populism, while originally a liberal movement to protect the small farmer and urban merchant, had now taken a fascist turn in the United States.[61]

News journalists working in major media generally refrained from directly tarring Goldwater and his followers as fascist, likely because the use of such language would compromise the neutral tone demanded by the standards of journalistic objectivity. But they made the association in thinly coded ways, namely, by informing audiences that Goldwater was adored by undisputed fascists in Europe and Asia. CBS News aroused the fury of the candidate's supporters by reporting in July 1964 that he was planning a postconvention trip to Berchtesgaden in Bavaria, the site of Hitler's famous mountain retreat, to form a common cause with "right-wing elements" in Germany.[62] Other pieces reported that his admirers included monarchists in Spain, far-rightists in Germany, the fascist press in Italy, and the Kuomintang in Taiwan, all of which were directly or implicitly associated with fascism.[63] An editorial in *Newsweek*, for example, noted the populism of the Goldwaterites as the basis of the transatlantic connection:

> Its leaders use a special political vocabulary—to proclaim their cause "a movement" or "a revolution," rallying against an enemy darkly defined as "The Establishment" or "the power structure," and brandishing such sophomoric slogans as "extremism in defense of liberty is no vice." This is not the plain speech of a Taft. This is an accent quite alien: the stale jargon of ultra-rightist movements in Europe over the last quarter century. And so it is no coincidence that it has there evoked some approving response in only two regions: conservative Bavaria and totalitarian Spain.[64]

Other journalists identified the American Nazi Party as part of the new right-wing coalition and reported that clergy and politicians such as Gov. Jerry Brown of California and James Deprete Jr., a Republican, used the fascist label to describe Goldwater.[65]

What these journalists, scholars, politicians, and clergy read as fascist was the distillation of a new kind of conservatism, one that was marginal and denigrated in the liberal early sixties but would become formidable with the rise of Ronald Reagan. Emerging out of new centers of growth in the West, particularly southern California, the phenomenon found its novelty in a fusion of economic libertarianism, white anxiety, and a backward-looking social conservatism expressed in a populist language that its supporters wielded against a liberal establishment and the federal government. Its activists campaigned to grant authorities the legal power to restore law and order, to desecularize public schools, to withdraw from the United Nations, and to support private property rights while simultaneously opposing civil rights. Its glue was a brand of anticommunism broadly directed against collectivism in all its guises, and hence, unlike liberal anticommunism, it tended to be directed against enemies on the domestic front. The primary difference between this incarnation of conservatism and the early twenty-first-century right was that the former was generally aware of its marginal status as a political minority, albeit one in line with American traditions. Accordingly, they often exhibited profound doubts about the desirability of democracy, the best-known example of which was the slogan repeated by Goldwater and the John Birch Society, "This is a Republic, not a Democracy."[66] That the heirs of this political movement, once considered extremist and even fascist, are now treated as a legitimate, respectable force by the mainstream press speaks to the fundamental transformations occurring in American political life in the past fifty years.

The antifascist cultural producer who traced the new right in the most influential forums was the television and film writer Rod Serling. A stern, cigarette-smoking man, Serling is known mostly for his appearance on the television series *The Twilight Zone* (1959–64), but his career reached far beyond this program. He began writing for radio in the late 1940s, producing scripts for critically esteemed drama anthology series throughout the 1950s, including *Playhouse 90, Studio One,* and *Kraft Television Theatre.* Indeed, Serling won three Emmy Awards for his "prestige programming" during the so-called Golden Age of television before he began work on *The Twilight Zone.* In addition, he periodically wrote screenplays for Hollywood films, including *Requiem for a Heavyweight* (1962) and *Seven Days in May* (1964). Outside of his most famous program, little of his work was in the genre of science fiction; most of his oeuvre before *The Twilight Zone* was in the vein of realist drama.

Fascism, especially its American incarnations, was a running theme throughout his work, a fact that has gone unrecognized in cultural studies scholarship on early television. The theme appears in his anthology teleplays "To Wake at Midnight" (*Climax,* 1955), a story about neo-Nazis; in his Holocaust drama about the Warsaw Ghetto titled "In the Presence of Mine Enemies" (*Playhouse 90,* 1960); in "Grady Everett for the People" (*Stars Over Hollywood,* 1950); and also in his later script on neo-Nazi violence "Hate" (*Insight,* 1966). Fascism was a motif informing his earliest radio work as well, which was deeply influenced by the blacklisted Popular Front celebrity Norman Corwin. But in ways both direct and oblique the theme also carried over into his writing for *The Twilight Zone,* appearing in the episodes "Monsters Are Due on Maple Street" (1960), "The Obsolete Man" (1961), "Deaths-Head Revisited" (1961), "Four O'Clock" (1962), and "He's Alive" (1963). In his script for *Seven Days in May,* which depicts an attempted coup d'etat by antidemocratic elements within the U.S. armed forces, fascism is a salient motif.

In these scripts as well as in his private correspondence Serling unmistakably imagined the new American rightists in terms homologous to the ways he envisioned Nazis and vice versa: as hysterically anticommunist, racist, anti-Semitic nationalists who render their domestic enemies as foreign and who are hell-bent on wreaking apocalyptic violence. Much in the spirit of the time, he explores the psychology of the fascist perpetrator and in doing so emphasizes his anti-Semitic and racist brutality. Although Serling came to see unrestrained property rights as antithetical to human rights, class considerations are largely muted in his antifascism. While it is tempting to conclude that the politics of earlier decades had vanished from the historical stage by Serling's time, a survey of his work reveals that he initially gleaned his sense of fascism as a set of politics intimately connected with race from the left of the 1930s.

Like that of many others, Serling's relationship to fascism stemmed from his personal history. Born into a Jewish family in 1924, he was raised in a Jewish community in Binghamton, New York, and later converted to Unitarianism. His family experienced economic insecurity when his father's small grocery store closed in the Depression. During the Second World War he served in a parachute regiment in the Philippines, where he took part in horrific battles to liberate Manila and was wounded a number of times. The young GI was initially disappointed to be shipped to the Pacific because he wanted to fight Nazis; one of his fellow soldiers remembered him as being visibly upset over the unfolding news of the Holocaust. By the end of the war 70 percent of the regimental cohort who had shipped off with him in April 1944 was dead.[67] Returning to civilian life, he enrolled in Antioch College on the GI Bill in 1946. This campus environment, a radical outpost where Paul Robeson and Henry Wallace were regarded as heroes in the late 1940s, cemented the course of his left-liberal politics.[68] At Antioch, Serling began his career by writing plays for the campus radio station; these early works were highly derivative of Corwin and Orson Welles, Popular Front antifascists who had helped to legitimize radio drama and were the idols of his youth. Transitioning to television in 1949 after a hardscrabble existence as a radio writer, he quickly became established as a leading talent in this new frontier, which, at least until the mid-fifties, was widely regarded as a respectable medium with the potential to elevate the public taste. But by the end of the decade the increasing commercialization of television left little room for the acclaimed drama anthologies.[69] Rather than forsake television for other venues, as many of his contemporaries did, Serling compromised by using science fiction as a vehicle to address the serious themes he had earlier explored through more realist genres.

These serious themes included civil rights, to which he was particularly drawn, the moral bankruptcy of corporate culture, the Holocaust, the mourning of the dead, and McCarthyism, to name a few. In the early days of television he was able to explore such topics because of the liberal politics of early network executives and their commitment to high-quality programming; equally important, he had never been a member of the radical organizations that typically invited the scrutiny of blacklisters.[70] However, despite his obvious left-liberal profile, he appears to have internalized some of the basic assumptions of American Cold War policy abroad, at least initially. In the early 1960s he participated in cultural exchanges with Asia sponsored by the State Department. In early 1965 he defended his country against charges of imperialism while on one such mission in the Philippines and was dismayed that no one in the villages there received him as eagerly as they did when he was a soldier.[71] The next year, owing to his grave doubts about American incursions into Vietnam, he refused to go on any more tours. He informed his contact at the State Department that he would complete one last tour in South Korea and Taiwan. "I'm one of those who really don't know what the hell we *are* doing anyplace on the map!" he wrote in a letter.[72] His public speeches against the Vietnam War in the second half of the 1960s reveal a more fundamental critique of U.S. foreign policy and hence a harder tack to the left.[73]

In Serling's files there is a script for a radio play titled "Nightmare at Noon" which illustrates his Popular Front inheritance.[74] It was derived from a poem of the same title written by Stephen Vincent Benét and published in 1940; the verse was originally read on the air during the war by Frederic March for *Treasury Star Parade,* a program created by the Treasury Department to sell war bonds. It is not clear whether Serling suggested it for use by *Hollywood Radio Theatre* or whether he simply retained it for inspiration. Written in a style both epic and accessible, bombastic and colloquial—what one of Philip Roth's narrators called "the high demotic poetry that was the liturgy of World War II"—the original poem imagines how the United States would be transformed in the event of a fascist invasion.[75]

The poem suggests that one of the biggest changes wrought by a fascist occupation would be the end of whatever ethnic and racial pluralism exists. While Benét acknowledges lynching and economic inequality in the United States, he writes that in America one can at least see a man reading a paper in Yiddish, adding,

> *You can be a Finn or a Dane and an American.*
> *You can be German or French and an American*
> *Jew, Bohunk, Nigger, Mick—all the dirty names*
> *We call each other—and yet*
> *American. We've stuck to that quite a while*
> *Go into Joe's Diner and try to tell the truckers*
> *You belong to a Master Race and you'll get a laugh.*

These lines, repeated verbatim in Serling's radio adaptation, reflect the style Serling employed in his early radio work and foreshadows his lifelong emphasis on racial democracy. Moreover, it reveals that while postwar decades transformed his voice and his politics, the thirties and forties provided a kind of political foundation wherein fascism was intimately connected to the issue of race.

Serling's engagement with fascism and his recurrent return to the war were fueled as well by other factors, and it is in this respect that trauma studies prove highly illuminating. In short, the war was a trauma for Serling, both as a Jewish American deeply disturbed by the Holocaust and as a combat veteran who personally experienced incredible violence. The trauma theorist Jenny Edkins posits that those who have experienced trauma possess a unique sense of time. In Western cultures, she argues, the past is assumed to come before the present, and human agency is predicated on the notion that the two realms are precisely demarcated from one another. But for the traumatized subject, the past lives in the time of the now, and temporal registers uncontrollably blend together. For instance, the past may recur in nightmares or flashbacks in which an event replays itself, or the traumatic event remains "stored in the eyes" without being consciously acknowledged by the subject. In what Edkins calls "trauma time," the past trauma is experienced simultaneously with the survivor's current life.[76]

This temporality informs the structure of Serling work, mostly notably in *The Twilight Zone,* a universe in which characters continuously go backward and forward in time, in a number of cases jolted out of their present context and dropped into the battles of the Second World War, Nazi rallies, or German concentration camps. The pilot episode of the series, titled "The Time Element" (*Westinghouse Desilu Playhouse,* 1958), is about a man named Peter Jenson who experiences a recurring dream in which he is ripped from the present moment in 1958 and transported back to Honolulu, Hawaii, on December 6, 1941. "In my dream it's always the same," he tells his psychiatrist in 1958. "It's real. I'm going back in time." Every time he returns he is ostracized for attempting to warn people of the impending attack on Pearl Harbor and is ultimately powerless to stop it. Jenson, in constantly returning to a crucial site of the war, living the past in the present, and feeling socially dislocated because of his persistent memory, is arguably Serling's figuration of his own "trauma time."

The production which best illustrates the author's trauma-informed antifascism is an episode of *The Twilight Zone* titled "He's Alive" (1963). The show depicts the rise and fall of a young American neo-Nazi named Peter Vollmer, played by Dennis Hopper. As it begins, Vollmer delivers a soapbox speech to a small crowd on a street corner in an unnamed urban area. The narrow iron fire escapes and front stoops suggest New York City, the site of Bundist and Christian Front agitation in the 1930s. With an American flag and torches hanging behind him, Vollmer says to crowd, "Examine the phenomenon of foreign control . . . you will find the lines lead directly to Palestine. They lead directly to Africa. They lead directly to the Vatican! There's the conspiracy. . . . A conspiracy personified by the yellow man, by the black man, and by foreigners who come in and infiltrate our economic structure." As Vollmer shouts the words "Africa," "Palestine," and "the Vatican," the camera cuts to closeups of three different faces, one African American and the other two presumably Jewish and Catholic. Shot at eye level or from slightly below, the faces evoke the exaltation of the people in the multiethnic photographic tableaus of the OWI and Wallace's Century of the Common Man. In a symbolic restaging of the Second World War, the diverse, heckling crowd then turns violent and beats up Vollmer and his fascist band. Had the episode ended here, the message would be in line with the Cold War consensus: that is, unlike totalitarian states, multiethnic America has no place for intolerance.

In *Twilight Zone* fashion, however, a supernatural element intervenes to help Vollmer increase his power: a shadowy stranger with a German accent, undoubtedly Hitler, appears on the scene and teaches him to perfect his rhetoric. This enables Vollmer to pack lecture halls with whites of all classes, who come to hear him speak on the threat posed to "a free white America" by "minorities" that are "stabbing us in the back" and hobbling the country in its struggle against the Soviet Union. All the while Vollmer has a tortured relationship with an old Jewish concentration camp survivor named Ernst Ganz, who, it is revealed, has been a kind of surrogate father to Vollmer. Ganz had taken Vollmer into his home when he was a scared working-class boy from a broken home, and the elder man's example establishes an antithetical metaphor of inclusiveness within the episode. Vollmer's rise is finally checked by the bravery and resolve of Ganz, who refuses, as he says, to "let it all happen again." Ganz interrupts Vollmer's speech at the podium, making him appear before the crowd as a scared little boy. Soon after, following an order from Hitler's ghost, Vollmer shoots Ganz to prove his will to his new father and ultimately is hunted down and killed by the police for committing an earlier murder.

To make the connection between Nazism and American racism abundantly clear, Serling ends the episode with an unusually intrusive narrator who comments on Hitler's ghost while the Führer's shadow, slowly pacing, is projected against a brick wall:

> Where will he go next, this phantom from another time, this resurrected ghost of a previous nightmare. Chicago, Los Angeles, Miami, Florida, Vincenes, Indiana, Syracuse, New York: any place, every place. Any place where there's hate, where there's prejudice, where there's bigotry, he's alive. He's alive so long as these evils exist. Remember that when he comes to your town. Remember it when you hear his voice speaking out through others. Remember it when you hear a name called, a minority attacked, any blind, unreasoning assault—on a people or a human being. He's alive because through these things, we keep him alive.

A number of intriguing differences separate Vollmer and his organization from the recurrent representation of fascism in the fifties and also from the contemporaneous depiction of Eichmann available to American audiences.

First, unlike Eichmann, Vollmer is not a professional man but working class. And unlike Miller's Thomas Putnam from the previous decade, he lacks any ties to capital and the state (on the contrary, the state hunts him down and destroys him). An inversion of the sheriff of Nottingham in Hannah Weinstein's *The Adventures of Robin Hood,* Vollmer is not an elite who cynically manipulates race to enforce class power; rather he is a disadvantaged type who uses race, in part, to mobilize class resentment. His marginal status, furthermore, is crucial to Serling's psychoanalysis of his character. Like other television dramas of the Holocaust in the sixties and seventies, the shows Serling wrote were concerned with the intricate details of the psychology of evil. His narration roots the psychology of fascism in a general human lust for power and prestige and implies that Vollmer's marginalized class position has left him vulnerable to such appeals.[77]

This psychological reading of American fascism, with its emphasis on the ideology's appeal to the marginalized, was present in the decades of the recent past as well, most notably in the literature of the Chicago school of proletarian writers: Richard Wright, Nelson Algren, and James T. Farrell above all. Popular Front forays into psychology were connected to a critique of capital, yet Serling's "He's Alive" severs any substantive link between capitalism and fascism. Indeed, though Vollmer blames the breakup of his initial speech on communists, his rhetorical linkage of moneymaking with Jewishness, which he expresses twice in the episode, evokes the socialism of National Socialism, when the Brownshirts (the SA) dominated and an antifinance rhetoric pervaded. Whereas the series *The Adventures of Robin Hood* (1955–59) evoked the post-1934 period of Nazism, when Hitler had won the support of much of the German business class, Vollmer's uniform visually evokes this earlier period. Serling was of a generation who came of age when capitalism was no longer at the center of public debate, and his reading of fascism and the Second World War reflects this. On the other hand, his repeated conceptual linkage of fascism and racism, while present in the Popular Front culture that was Serling's early inspiration, acquired much greater salience in the era of civil rights.

Serling's use of the term *minorities* in the script links fascism not only to the backlash against civil rights but also to the nationalism of the American right in the early 1960s. Vollmer's early speech offers a recurrent observation of right-wing nationalism within antifascist cultural production. That is, one is prompted to see its nationalism as a means of denaturalizing domestic subjects and rendering them as foreign, since, as Vollmer argues, the "phenomenon of foreign control" is ultimately "personified by the yellow man, by the black man, and by foreigners." A more specific linguistic trope links Vollmer to the right wing of the early 1960s, however. Hitler's shadow teaches the American soapbox speaker to reach a broader audience by inverting the term *minority*. In Vollmer's next speech, in which he addresses a different audience of white citizens, one that takes him quite seriously, he shouts, "Minorities? We are the minorities! Because patriotism is the minority. Because love of country is the minority. Because to live in a free white America seems to be of a minority opinion. We had the atom bomb, and suddenly the Russians had it. We wanted to send men into space, but it was the Russians that got there first. . . . Who gave them the bombs? Who sold us out? Who stabbed us in the back?" As we have seen, the new right, sensing its political weakness, often spoke of itself as a virtuous minority. Writing in *Commentary* only months before the scripting of "He's Alive," David Danzig spoke of the "radical right" as "a minority" whose adherents "feel that they, as well as the nation as a whole, has been losing power," adding, "Their program of 'Americanism' becomes a way of explaining the national loss of supremacy and autonomy."[78]

Serling's play with conspiratorial political rhetoric, anchored in the term *minority* (the German equivalent of which, *Minderheit,* was not a staple of Nazi rhetoric), ultimately links Vollmer to the John Birch right, and Nazism to the populist turn in American conservatism. Rightists correctly saw themselves as the targets of *The Twilight Zone* and wrote angry letters to its author. In 1966 one outraged correspondent reacted to the episode "Four O'Clock" by writing, "The message of this story appears to say that Anti-Communists are bigots, fanatics, psychotics, and are *really* the 'bad guys'" and then enclosed right-wing literature for Serling to read. Serling responded to him by writing, "The 'national patriots' whose writings you adjure me to take of are a species of anti-Semitic, anti-Catholic, and anti-Negro demagogues."[79] Vollmer's imagined conspiracy, as noted, originated in Palestine, the Vatican, and Africa. "He's Alive" generated four thousand letters of protest, making it, according to one source, the most controversial episode of *The Twilight Zone* ever shown.[80]

Serling's resolution, wherein a committed antifascist derails the American Führer with the help of the state, offers an optimistic reading of the course of U.S. history, one appropriate to his liberal milieu, in which the nascent right-wing movement was commonly dismissed as an assortment of "extremists" and "crackpots."[81] But there is certainly a call for vigilance. The Holocaust survivor Ernst Ganz recalls the German past to a friend, remembering how they once dismissed the Nazis as well: "We ignored them. Or we laughed at them. Because we couldn't believe that there were enough insane people to walk alongside of them."

Though his representation was informed by Popular Front antifascism, the Brownshirt antihero in "He's Alive" was framed more immediately by the liberal culture of the late fifties and early sixties. The episode illustrates how the civil rights movement in particular created the conditions for antiracism to be retroactively read in the sphere of mass culture as one of the primary reasons the United States fought Nazi Germany. To be sure, the institutional context of television constrained the author's representational choices. Serling was an outspoken critic of commercial censorship, lamenting in a speech he gave at Ithaca College in 1967 how television had become "a display case for a box of Wheaties." Yet he made few political alterations to the script of "He's Alive."[82] By that time he was a veteran of the industry and well aware of what was permissible, likely self-censoring his ideas in early drafts before committing them to print. The fact that he was able to make such critiques on network television speaks to the mainstreaming of antifascism, which created a political environment wherein even television executives were willing to weather the fallout from associating the American right with Nazism.

Using different media, the writer Betty Friedan also employed the memory of fascism to lodge influential critiques of American society in the early 1960s. She had more in common with Serling than one might expect: both were middle-class Jewish Americans of roughly the same age, haunted by the Holocaust, and stamped by the politics of the Popular Front in their youths. Their memories, both personal and historical, created a productive tension between themselves and Keynesian America, one generative of novel political interventions. Friedan's most famous work was *The Feminine Mystique* (1963), regarded by historians as the trigger of modern feminism; its narrative of emotionally dead housewives with thwarted ambitions framed feminist politics for a generation of white middle-class women.[83] Yet less remembered today are its repeated evocations of Nazism and the Holocaust.

Early in the book, for instance, Friedan recalls a sexist conversation among her male coworkers at a magazine publishing house, writing, "As I listened to them, a German phrase echoed in my mind—'*Kinder, Küche, Kirche*' [Children, Kitchen, Church], the slogan by which the Nazis decreed that women must once again be confined to their biological role. But this was not Nazi Germany." More prominently, she devoted an entire chapter, titled "Progressive Dehumanization: The Comfortable Concentration Camp," to comparing the plight of suburban housewives with that of concentration camp prisoners. Her comparison was a psychological one that paralleled the mental degeneration, in both instances, resulting from a condition of confinement. In the camps, she wrote, "the prisoners literally became 'walking corpses.' Those who 'adjusted' to the conditions of the camps surrendered their human identity and went almost indifferently to their deaths." Like housewives, the prisoners "were forced to adopt childlike behavior, forced to give up their individuality and merge themselves into an amorphous mass."[84]

Friedan's analogy between housewives and concentration camp prisoners certainly marks one of the more hyperbolic left-wing namings of fascism. It was recognized as such by the author herself, who later retracted it. The significance of the Nazi evocations in *The Feminine Mystique* lies not in their historical accuracy, but in what they revealed about antifascism in American culture, namely, the disparate political connections it facilitated and the mainstream position of such connections in the public sphere. As Kirsten Fermaglich has shown, Friedan's Holocaust analogies were much less controversial in their own day than ours: most newspaper and magazine critics reviewed the book positively and hardly objected to the parallels she drew as they praised her work. Not even Holocaust survivors who wrote to Friedan questioned the comparison, although one of them hated the book on other grounds.[85] In retrospect, the metaphor of the comfortable concentration camp was not only a feminist move to make women legible through Holocaust frames. It was also an attempt to make the Holocaust legible to the American public, writing from an identity otherwise suppressed in the book: the identity of a Jewish American struggling to find a space to process the enormity of the loss. As a telling passage in the book reveals, she associated postwar reconversion with a broad-based amnesia dangerous to women, Jews, and the public as a whole. After 1945, she wrote, "women went home again just as men shrugged off the bomb, forgot the concentration camps, condoned corruption, and fell into helpless conformity."[86]

In *The Feminine Mystique* Friedan looked to the thirties as a time before "helpless conformity" had set in, a time when women were on the rise. Studying magazine heroines from 1939, she observed, "They were New Women, creating with a gay determined spirit a new identity for women—a life of their own. There was an aura about them of becoming, of moving into a future that was going to be different from the past." Friedan no doubt read herself into these magazine heroines, as she was an aspiring freshman at Smith College in 1939. Named Bettye Goldstein then, she was on the cusp of her own political "becoming," one fundamentally guided by the Popular Front. As was true of other women surveyed in Kate Weigand's *Red Feminism*, her radicalism began as a Popular Front mixture of class-consciousness, racial awareness, and feminist critique that laid a crucial foundation for the second wave of the women's movement in the sixties and seventies. What brought these disparate politics together was the discourse of antifascism, first imparted to the young Goldstein by the faculty at Smith, some of them European exiles. As Daniel Horowitz describes her sophomore year at Smith in 1940, "As she shifted to more public expressions of anti-Semitism, anti-fascism was becoming the bridge to her commitment to labor unions that would in turn flower into a passion for women's issues."[87] One person who had a great influence on her was her professor James Gibson, who compared anti-Semitisms across the Atlantic and taught the quintessential Popular Front lesson that labor unions were the key to preventing the spread of fascism. From another left-wing faculty member, Dorothy Wolff Johnson, she learned of the plight of women under fascism and the phrase Kinder, Küche, Kirche, the proper spheres for women in Nazi ideology.[88]

Goldstein was editor of the student newspaper at Smith for one year, beginning in March 1941. In her time at *Smith College Associated News,* or *SCAN,* she and her coeditors left behind an editorial archive that illustrates how antifascism was a means through which she and her cohort conceptually organized the various struggles unfolding around them, including free speech, women's education, union organizing, civil rights, decolonization, world peace, and the defense of the Jews.[89] She and her compatriots first used the phrase Kinder, Küche, Kirche in an editorial in January 1942, her first published piece on the ties between Nazi ideology and American forms of patriarchy. In the editorial she lamented the treatment of women under fascism and saw similar attitudes governing women's education in the United States.[90] When she began her term as editor, Goldstein was opposed to all forms of U.S. military intervention abroad and its attendant "patriotic indoctrination" at home; in the second half of her tenure, however, she supported military intervention but aimed to make sure it stayed true the goals of an antifascist People's War, an ideological and material struggle to level all forms of social hierarchy.

The status of antifascism as a broad analytic continued in *The Feminine Mystique.* Friedan's chapter on the concentration camps, read alongside an earlier chapter called "The Sexual Sell," offered a kind of popularized Frankfurt School analysis of American mass culture, one that held the psychological devastation of housewives as crucial to the reproduction of an alienated consumer society. She wrote, "It is not an exaggeration to call the stagnating state of millions of American housewives a sickness, a disease in the shape of a progressively weaker core of human self that is being handed down to their sons and daughters at a time when the dehumanizing aspects of modern mass culture make it necessary for men and women to have a strong core of self." As the reader later learns, consumer capitalism is the force behind "modern mass culture," and central to its smooth functioning is the commodification of women's desires and the sublimation of their aspirations.[91] Friedan's metaphor of the comfortable concentration camp is a flawed means of synthesizing the operations of patriarchy, consumer capitalism, and their homogenizing impulses. It inappropriately fixates on the material site of the camp, not the patriarchal discourses of fascism that were in fact part of a broad, historical continuum in the West.

Yet her contrast between the optimistic women of 1939 and the degraded housewives of the sixties reveals the politically generative nature of antifascism long after the Second World War. She returned to antifascism because of its ability to register the tragic sense of history in reverse, its capacity to harness the anxiety brought about when events that are contrary to the expected forward motion of history unfold. "To live according to the feminine mystique," she wrote, "depends on a reversal of history, a devaluation of human progress."[92] For Friedan, as for Goldstein, antifascism was a way to confront atavism through a language capable of enunciating parallel struggles: but the terms she used to speak its intersectionality changed dramatically. In the 1940s she connected distinct political sites with words and phrases such as "war and fascism," "democracy," and "the inequality of social, economic, and political power." In 1963 the urgency of connectivity remained, but she now met the challenge with expressions like "mass culture," "conformity," "de-humanization," "internalized oppression," and "self-realization." Friedan, in sum, bridged an earlier antifascism, grounded in the Marxist-inflected populism of the thirties, to a newer variant guided by a psychoanalytic social critique and an emergent identity politics.

In the early 1960s antifascism was proving its adaptability to new social movements and the changing political modalities of Keynesian America. As they confronted new and frightening social forces, activists and cultural producers shaped by the emergent racial and feminist politics of the era were finding the discourse flexible enough to suit their ends. In the late 1960s young radicals with no direct memories of the Second World War absorbed the antifascist work of an older generation—sometimes quite consciously—and added to its insights as they confronted a new form of political backlash with uncanny echoes of an old yet persistent danger.

CHAPTER 6
United Front against Genocide
African American Antifascism, the Black Panthers, and the Multiracial Coalitions of the Late 1960s

> The fate of Jews, and the world's indifference to [the Holocaust], frightened me very much. I could not but feel, in those sorrowful years, that this human indifference, concerning which I knew so much already, would be my portion on the day that the United States decided to murder its Negroes systematically instead of little and catch-as-catch-can.... When a white man faces a black man, especially if the black man is helpless, terrible things are revealed. I know.
>
> JAMES BALDWIN, *The Fire Next Time* (1962)

> Other peoples ... besides the direct victims of the Axis aggression also have a genuine awareness of the democratic significance of the present conflict. Their awareness is born of their yearning for freedom from an oppression which has pre-dated Fascism.
>
> PAUL ROBESON, "American Negroes in the War" (1943)

In July 1969 the Japanese American activist Penny Nakatsu rose to speak at a conference in Oakland, California, organized by the Black Panther Party (BPP). Called against a backdrop of intense FBI and police repression leveled against Black Power and its allies, the event was intended to bring together a wide array of left-wing organizations and individuals to form a United Front against Fascism (UFAF). The fascism they sensed in the air in the late 1960s was a growing white backlash in the United States against people of color movements. Increasingly, whites saw the demands of black and brown people for social justice as excessive, disorderly, and criminal; as the decade closed, there were loud calls for them to be tamed, not through the adoption of social democratic reform but through a restoration of law and order. In her speech, Nakatsu, a founder of the Asian-American Political Alliance (AAPA) at San Francisco State University, boldly claimed authority on the subject of fascism. She stated from the podium, "I come from a generation of children born in concentration camps. Many of these places you will find no longer exist on the map. We were born in places with names like Manzanar, Tule Lake, Topaz." After excavating a buried history of the Japanese American internment for her audience, she concluded with words greeted by a standing ovation: "The lesson that I hope we can learn from 1942 is not to wait, not to wait until we have positive irrevocable proof of the racism, and [of] the all-encompassing determination of our monopolistic capitalistic system to suppress all movements, all people who will work for social change . . . who will work for the defeat of fascism and imperialism."[1]

Much like activists in the 1930s, those present at the UFAF conference in 1969 used fascism to mediate a seemingly diffuse range of issues. The Chicano activists Rodolfo Martinez and Oscar Rios, for example, spoke of the arrest of Los Siete de la Raza, seven young Latino men framed for the murder of a police officer in San Francisco, as a sign of an incipient American fascism; Father Earl Neil railed against the complicity of certain churches in "Fascism in South Africa."[2] Yet for all the variety of examples, there was a consistent, general sense of the term. In his keynote speech, the BPP leader Bobby Seale put forth an understanding of the concept that was common among the Black Panthers and shared much with definitions from the thirties: fascism, in his view, was the racially driven state repression of a mobilized, militant left, one which ultimately restores full political control to capitalists.[3] The connection to the antifascisms of the past was not just discursive: Herbert Aptheker, a prominent white communist who joined the CPUSA in 1939, was also in attendance. In his speech he sounded very much like the younger radicals when he stressed the U.S. government's growing anxiety in the face of black radical movements and when he claimed that fascism "enhance[s] the power and the plunder of the top monopolists and it does this by repressing . . . all popular and all democratic and all radical expressions."[4]

The Panthers' use of the concept fascism was not limited solely to the UFAF conference in July 1969. In fact, the BPP, an organization founded two decades after the end of the Second World War, used the term more frequently than any African American organization in the 1930s. More to the point, the Panthers evoked fascism more often than any postwar political organization in the United States as a whole. Particularly from 1969 to mid-1971, it is difficult to find an article in its publication the *Black Panther* that does not use the word (fig. 5). At this time antifascism was a central concept of Panther ideology, and it animated a range of party activities. To be sure, the term *fascist* (often followed by *pig*) was an epithet in casual usage within Black Panther circles and can be considered part of the self-conscious, radical performance or style for which they were known. But it should not be treated merely as a form of radical posturing or a strategic act of hyperbole. And contrary to the only study that has seriously examined African Americans' uses of the term, the Panthers' application of fascism to the United States was not so historically inaccurate and misapplied as to be politically immobilizing.[5]

The question remains as to why the Panthers were drawn to fascism as a chief marker of their enemy and not to other frames of reference. In this regard, the prevalence of Latinos, whites, and Asian Americans at a conference organized by the BPP comes into sharp focus. The Panthers' use of the word was often bound to a self-conscious historical awareness of the coalition-building possibilities of antifascism that explicitly drew on the memory of the Popular Front. The BPP did not single-handedly add fascism to the lexicon of radicals in the late 1960s, but, as a result of their efforts, antifascism became a more conscious political mode among other politically emergent groups, particularly Latinos, Asian Americans, and white student radicals. Antifascist politics were not as central to the movements of the late sixties and early seventies as anticolonialism or anti-imperialism, which have received a great deal of scholarly attention. But antifascism was ubiquitous, and its allure to movements of people of color has not been mapped in studies of the left during the Vietnam War period. In this chapter I concentrate on the BPP and the National Committees to Combat Fascism (NCCF), a nationwide network of organizations that had its beginning at the UFAF conference. I want to show how antifascism became more central to the politics of radical activists of color in the United States in the late 1960s and early 1970s than ever before or since. The late sixties was not the first time people of color had organized around the concept of fascism, but it did mark the first moment that the concept had become a focal point within a multiracial coalition in which whites played an auxiliary role at best. More important, this chapter identifies the unique contributions to the discourse that emerged from this political work, demonstrating, in the process, a cognizance of the Popular Front and Old Left antifascism that has not been sufficiently acknowledged. To this end, I outline here the postwar development of an older black antifascism.

The widespread appeal of antifascism as an organizing mode for people of color in the late sixties had much to do with the revised memory of Nazism earlier in the decade, in which the left and earlier civil rights activism also played a hand. Namely, it was enabled by the popular diffusion, in the early sixties, of the idea that at the heart of fascism lay the monstrous desire for a racial Holocaust. Because of the rise of Holocaust consciousness at this time, such terms as *concentration camps* and *genocide* became key tropes in antifascist activism and cultural production. As a result, many non-Jews, including Chicanos, Puerto Ricans, African Americans, Asian Americans, and, later, gays and lesbians, also

THE BLACK PANTHER, SATURDAY, DECEMBER 6, 1969 PAGE 7

JAKE WINTERS MURDERED BY FASCIST PIGS

"When they killed Jake, they took the best that humanity possessed."

Spurgeon "Jake" Winters, 19, member of the Illinois Chapter of the Black Panther Party, paid the most that one can pay towards the liberation of oppressed people- his life. At 3:30 a.m. November 13, Jake was murdered in a shoot-

SPURGEON "JAKE" WINTERS

out in Chicago where three pigs were killed and seven were wounded.

The shoot-out was precipitated by an ambush made by the Standing Army of Chicago (Chicago Police Department) on an abandoned building at 5801 S. Calumet. Arriving on the scene with the armaments and men (more than 1000 policemen equipped with .12 gauge shotguns, M-1 carbines, .357 magnums, billy clubs, mace, tear gas, paddy wagons, helicopters and canine units) for domestic warfare against the people in the Black colony, these fanatical pigs started their attack by opening fire on the brother in the building. Party comrade, Lance Bell, 20 was wounded by the pigs as they shot wildly in that area.

With these seemingly insurmountable odds, Jake defended himself as any person should do. In essence, he had no choice; it was kill or be killed. And realizing such, Jake tried to enact a basic premise of war: preservation of self and destruction of the enemy. But although Jake was equipped only with a shotgun and was murdered, the results attest to the fact that the people with their intense desire for freedom can combat the greatest forces of aggression.

A June 1969 honor graduate of Englewood High School, Jake worked in the Breakfast for Children Program and for the Free Health Clinic; he was a member of the Education Cadre. In essence, he was a Servant of the people.

America's tradition of oppression compounded with brutality and murder is strengthening and stabilizing, although it is directly contradictory to the people's desire for peace and freedom and is in violation of the universal laws of human decency. But the tradition is one that will continue, just as the observance of the mockery, "Independance Day" until the people eradicate it. And eradication means resisting as Jake did...resisting, if necessary, until the last breath. There can be no compromise with the forces of oppression or the forces of fascism. The enemy must be wiped out thoroughly, completely, and resolutely. And we say, "Right on, Jake."

Jake, a dedicated brother, will never be forgotten and not primarily for the things named. But primarily because he lessened the forces of aggression and because he said as Alprentice "Bunchy" Carter, John Huggins, Sylvester Bell, Lil Bobby Hutton, and Larry Roberson said:

"WHEREVER DEATH MAY SURPRISE US, IT WILL BE WELCOME PROVIDED THAT THIS, OUR BATTLE CRY, REACH SOME RECEPTIVE EAR, THAT ANOTHER HAND STRETCH OUT TO TAKE UP WEAPONS AND THAT OTHER MEN COME FORWARD TO INTONE OUR FUNERAL DIRGE WITH THE STACCATO OF MACHINE GUNS AND NEW CRIES OF BATTLE AND VICTORY."

Long Live The Revolutionary Spirit Of Jake Winters

ALL POWER TO THE PEOPLE
Illinois Chapter
Black Panther Party

LONG LIVE THE SPIRIT OF JAKE WINTERS

"The Racist Dog Policeman Must Withdraw Immediately From Our Communities, Cease Their Wanton Murder And Brutality And Torture Of Black People, Or Face The Wrath Of The Armed People." Huey P. Newton, Minister of Defense, Black Panther Party.

Point No. 7 of our Ten Point Platform and Program says, "We want an immediate end to police brutality and murder of Black people."

On November 13, 1969, brother Jake Winters was felled by those dirty treacherous creatures called pigs. The brother was a profound revolutionary. He worked seven days a week for the people. He participated in the Black Panther Party Free Breakfast for Children Program, and was helping contract the people's Free Medical Care Clinic.

November 13, brother Jake was killed in the line of duty, serving the masses and defending the Black community from the aggression of those murderous pigs who make mass interventions into our communities under the disguise of law and order. The pigs who on their weekly search and destroy mission to spread terror and murder and brutality throughout the Black community, departed with their pants down and their a--es showing.

Brother Jake immediately began to defend the Black community against these Nazi storm troopers of Nixon's fascist regime. He put his life on the line and dealt the pigs the biggest loss they have received since their defeat at the Henry Horner housing projects. The people who were on the scene then began to defend their lives and property. There was a battle in which Jake and the people destroyed three of the enemy soldiers and sent eight to the hospital. In the ensuing battle brother Jake was killed.

It is proven fact and a reality that Daley's task force makes daily and weekly raids on the Black community. They murdered little John Soto who was sixteen years old, Micheal Soto who was 20 years old and shot viley and unconcerned into every window of the Henry Horner projects, injuring scores of children. They murdered Jimmy Tucker, they murdered Wayne Black, Linda Anderson and untold others.

Brother Jake a true revolutionary and a member of the Black Panther Party was a public servant and a guardian of the liberties of the people. He showed the responsibility and the dedication of the Black Panther Party to the interests of the people in the oppressed communities. Like the masses at Henry Horner, brother Jake moved like a true Panther to destroy the aggression of the pigs and rid the community of that unwanted scurvey.

With the spirit of the highest personification of the Black Panther Party as illustrated by the actions of Jake Winters we intend to move forward to serve the masses and hold ourselves responsible to the people. We intend to carry on Jake's work to defend the Black community from the most inhumane, vile, wicked government the world has ever seen.

By lifting their hands against Jake Winters they lifted their hands against the best that humanity had to offer. We are determined to liberate our communities. LONG LIVE THE SPIRIT OF JAKE WINTERS!

Lawrence Bell

Brother Lawrence Bell, who was on the scene with Jake Winters when Daley's private army came into the Black community to brutalize and murder our people, is being held for two counts of murder. We know he didn't do it. The pigs know he didn't do it. Witnesses on the scene, Thursday, November 13, say he didn't do it. The pigs are holding him because brother Jake sent three of their slimy partners to cold storage and put eight on the wounded list. The pigs don't like it when they lose. They are used to killing our people and getting away with it. Justifiable homicide. But this time they were caught. The masses were on the scene. Brother Lawrence was an eye witness and they want to kill him. They don't like for the people to see them committ crimes against Black people. These reactionary monsters think we are going to let them send Lawrence Bell to the electric chair. They are wrong, dead wrong. If they try to kill Lawrence Bell we will release the armed wrath of a thousand Jake Winters. We will set up a thousand Henry Horners and set thousands of angry Black proletarians on them. The pigs don't like our people to be in a position to defend themselves. We don't give a f--k what they like. We intend to defend ourselves and we don't care how many pigs are killed. We want them all killed.

If you kill Lawrence Bell you have to face the wrath of a thousand Jake Winters.

ALL POWER TO THE PEOPLE
"REVOLUTION IN OUR LIFETIME"
Illinois Chapter
Black Panther Party

FASCIST TACTICS

On Tuesday, November 11, at approximately 6: 30 p.m. Claude Artist and myself were putting up posters about the two Free Breakfast Programs in New Haven, when a pig drove up. After he got off the radio he got out of the car and asked what we were doing. I told him very plainly that we were putting up posters about the Free Breakfast Program. He told us to stay where we were. We inquired if we were under arrest and the pig said "no", so I said that we were leaving, and we didn't have to listen to him. The pig then said I was under arrest. He got back on the raido and within 15 seconds 12 cars of pigs were on the set.

People from the community came out of their houses to see what the pigs were doing in their community. The pigs tore the posters down and stepped on them. I pointed out to the people the low-natured and foolish actions of the pigs, and that these actions would not stop the Free Breakfast Program. The pigs didn't like this and started waving clubs in my face, telling the people to go home or face arrest. I told the people to go home because they couldn't possibly deal with those armed pigs. I yelled "ALL POWER TO THE PEOPLE", as the pigs escorted me to a pig wagon. I heard people cussing at the pigs outside the wagon. I yelled out again, "ALL POWER TO THE PEOPLE, and for them to go home.

Then a sister said, "Why did you arrest her?" The pigs grabbed the sister Regina Burruss who lives at 280 West Portsea St. and beat her in the legs and stomach with their clubs. What could a 5' 4" sister 5 months pregnant possibly do to 45 armed pigs? A miscarrage may result from the atrocious, unwarranted, unjust, inhumane actions of these pigs against sister Regina. (Pig-a low natured animal with no concern for human life). Eugene Burruss, Regina's brother asked the pigs why she was arrested and why such actions had to be taken against her, he was thrown into a truck. Two other brothers and a sister were also arrested and beat by these fascist pigs. Several others were also beaten and brutalized but managed to escape.

We can clearly see that these pigs who occupy our communities are not there to protect the people or defend the peoples' interests, but are only there to keep us poor and oppressed. Point #7 of the Black Panther Party Platform states: "We want an immediate end to police brutality and murder of Black people." A feasible solution to this problem is community control of the police. The police would have to come from or reside in the community in which they are working. The people of each community would deal with the police through their elected councils. If the pigs refuse to implement this plan, we can end police brutality in our Black community by organizing Black self-defense groups that are dedicated to defending our Black community from racist police oppression and brutality. The Second Amendment to the Constitution of the United States gives a right to bear arms. We therefore believe that all Black people should arm themselves for self-defense.

ALL POWER TO THE PEOPLE
POW'S FOR PANTHERS

Elise
New Haven, Chapter
Black Panther Party

FASCIST PIGS VAMP ON ALBANY BLACK PANTHER OFFICE

On Monday, Nov. 10, the Albany Branch of the Black Panther Party opened their office in order to begin to meet the needs and desires of the people of their community.

On Thursday, Nov 20, early in the morning the paper tigers (who seem to come alive every now and then) left their scar, right in front of the office. Two big bricks had been thrown in the windows and bullets had shattered and penetrated through the glass. The bricks were found inside the office but no sign of any bullets could be traced.

It took these dirty, slimy, motherf--kers 10 days to try and stop us from serving the people. did it work? Hell no! This morning, Thursday, Nov. 20, we held our 4th day for the Free Breakfast Program. The pigs saw just how much progress was being made in the community. Liberation school, Free Breakfast Program, new Panthers in Training damn near every day, and large attendance for our P.E. classes held every day, plus moral and financial support from the community. What more could scare a pig, a preventer of progress. (Or one who tries to prevent).

This, we know is not the end, but the spirit of the people is greater than the man's technology. We are the advocates of the abolition of war, we do not want war, but war can only be abolished through war, and in order to get rid of the gun it is necessary to take up the gun, so we say; BLOOD TO THE PORKCHOPS ASS, AND WOE TO THOSE WHO CANNOT COOK, so there has to be some barbecue.

INTENSIFY THE STRUGGLE!
Branch Secretary
Jackee Harper

FIGURE 5. From the *Black Panther*, the Black Panther Party's newspaper, December 6, 1969.

began to voice the notion that genocide was something their group had experienced or was soon to experience. Public recollections and warnings of genocide thereby became a basis of collective identity and group solidarity. But the rise of Holocaust consciousness presented a problem that cultural producers have faced ever since: they have had to recall the memory of fascism within a larger, dominant culture that increasingly reduced fascism to the Jewish Holocaust and to a limited, Americanized narrative of that event which too neatly extricated it from the broader currents of Western history. As images of watchtowers, barbed wire, crematoria, and gas chambers became a cultural lingua franca, Americans would struggle to recall other facets of fascism necessary for a full understanding of it; among these were the political history of its enablement, its fundamentally anticommunist nature, the politics of its opponents, its middle-class agency, the nature of its nationalism, its multitiered hierarchies (racial and otherwise), its forms of repression outside of outright extermination—all of which are critical to recognizing the continuity of fascist modes after 1945. These aspects were sometimes eclipsed in the historical memories of gay and nonwhite activists as well, who also struggled to maintain an antifascist usable past fully pertinent to their own histories.

Fortunately, the inheritance of black radicalism helped the Panthers avoid some of the pitfalls of what has been termed "the Americanization of the Holocaust."[6] When African American activists and intellectuals linked fascism, a political mode which attained power only in Europe, to class and racial structures in the United States, they joined a continuum of black radicalism which had for many years connected black suffering in the United States to larger, deeply rooted Western patterns. As Robert Self has argued, black radicalism has "long interpreted the color line in the United States as extending outward in an unbroken arc across both the Atlantic and the Pacific, where it joins the racial imperialisms of the European powers. Rather than seeing the United States as a fundamental break with European patterns of racial ideology and domination, radicals have characterized the U.S. as representing their logical extension."[7] In this instance, a history of black anticolonialism and anti-imperialism helped prepare the ground out of which a black antifascism could grow, thereby establishing a political tradition habituated to placing racial oppression within a wider, transnational context. Like the broader left, African American antifascism thus tended to see its jackbooted foes as arising from the contradictions of liberalism. But unlike many other constituents of the left, black intellectuals from the 1930s to the 1970s emphasized fascism as a nightmare rooted in specific facets of liberalism that characterized their lived experience in putatively democratic states: namely, white supremacy, racialized social death, and legal nonpersonhood. Thus genocide emerged as a core concept in postwar African

American antifascism to name the dark *telos* of a fascist development nourished by liberalism's racial structures that threatened to engulf the whole world in flames. African Americans and people of color on the left during this period resorted to antifascism not only to mediate their particular group experiences but also to strategically place their experiences in the service of a universal politics, one that would benefit humanity as a whole.

Spatial Metaphors and the Origins of African American Antifascism

Nakatsu's claim to have actually experienced fascism reveals the existential terms through which many intellectuals and activists of color approached this dark political mode. Following Carl Schmitt, the contemporary scholar Nikhil Singh argues that liberal capitalist societies have tended to produce a dual system of political subjects. They create, on the one hand, a democratic order that affords liberal rights of property, free association, and the franchise to citizens. But, at the same time, the right of property continually necessitates zones of political exclusion, for example, the plantation, the reservation, the colony, the ghetto, wherein human beings exist as what the Italian philosopher Giorgio Agamben called *homines sacri,* or "bare lives": nonsubjects stripped of every right and living under a palpable threat of death. Agamben sees Nazi Germany as the most highly developed system for reproducing human beings as *homines sacri*—but he intimates that so long as liberalism continues to generate *homo sacer* alongside the free citizen, fascism will always be with us. Singh proffers a more pointed "afterlife" of fascism when he suggests that the zones of exclusion, required by private property, can operate for the *homines sacri* consigned to them as a functional equivalent of fascism.[8] One should not infer from Singh that those inhabiting such zones as the colonial shantytown or the black neighborhoods of the Jim Crow South live in circumstances equivalent to those vegetating in a concentration camp; rather, they live under a condition of rightlessness not far removed from that of an ordinary Christian citizen of Nazi Germany, fascist Italy, or occupied Czechoslovakia. That is to say, they live in a state wherein they could be subjected at any time to violence or imprisonment for the smallest infractions.

Extrapolating further from Singh, if one can say that liberalism, under capitalism, is necessarily marked by a dual system of political subjects—one set enjoying a degree of liberal freedoms and the other marked for an existence outside of this—then one can also assert that a full fascist state or authoritarian regime is marked by a condition in which all subjects live with the fear once reserved for those excluded under liberalism; that is, the fear that they too could be subject at any moment to the violence of an oppressive state.[9] Under fascism, the space of existential dread, reserved only for some in the liberal state, grows to the point of encompassing the social whole, at the same time that those marginalized in the old regime may face extinction altogether. Looked at in this way, fascism, which violently intensifies the dual system rather than eliminating it, is more closely aligned to liberalism than Stalinism, which, in the main, did not oppress on the basis of liberalism's established hierarchies.

The notion of fascism as a widening circle within a liberal state—what I call the spatial metaphor—is found throughout the activist writings of people of color since the 1930s, but it becomes especially salient after the Second World War. It begins to explain how Nakatsu, a former internee, could say she literally endured fascism in California, and it illuminates Langston Hughes's declaration in 1936 that "fascism is a new name for that kind of terror the Negro has always faced in America.... This kind of terrorism is extending more and more to groups of peoples whose skins are not black."[10] Such statements affirmed that while the United States has not been a generalized fascist state for all, it has been *experienced* as something uncannily similar by people of color living outside of its system of rights. They reveal an existential perspective on fascism, one that acknowledges that for those consigned to the status of *homo sacer* the line between fascism, right-wing authoritarianism, Jim Crow, and colonialism can sometimes be murky at the level of lived experience. The Panthers refined their spatial metaphors through their engagement with anticolonial movements and theories and, like their African American antifascist predecessors, used them as the foundation of a universal appeal that crossed the color line.

Early Black Antifascism from the 1930s through the Early 1960s

The Panthers' understanding of fascism at the UFAF conference and beyond was informed not only by Giorgi Dimitrov and Aptheker, but also by an earlier black antifascist discourse stamped by such intellectuals as W. E. B. Du Bois, William Patterson, Paul Robeson, George Padmore, Claudia Jones, Robert Williams, Frantz Fanon, and Aimé Césaire. In some cases, this influence was direct. For example, Patterson, a communist since the 1920s and the leader of the postwar Civil Rights Congress (CRC), contributed to the BPP's weekly newspaper the *Black Panther* and was on the steering committee of the UFAF conference. Likewise, Williams, a Second World War veteran and founder of the Revolutionary Action Movement (RAM), one of the political currents that led to the formation of the Panthers, was haunted by Nazism and spoke on the subject at Panther events.[11] In this sense, antifascism should be considered another site of what scholars have referred to as the long civil rights movement. That is to say, it adds to a more recent historiography of black freedom struggles in the mid-twentieth century that has emphasized a continuity within black activism from the 1930s through the 1960s, abandoning a neat timeline in which an early, reformist, southern-based struggle preceded a later nationalist radicalism based in the North and West.[12]

As I argued in chapter 3, most African American intellectuals in the 1930s and 1940s were drawn more fundamentally to anti-imperialism than to antifascism, yet they used this orientation to insightfully theorize fascism, placing it within a broader history of Western colonialism and racial formation. In 1945, for instance, Du Bois argued in *Color and Democracy* that the failure to recognize the seamlessness between fascism and the colonial question spelled the "certain promise of future war" and thus threatened the destruction of all peoples, whites included.[13] After the war, the black Caribbean writers Fanon and Césaire developed this idea further, mapping the broad historical dynamics identified by Du Bois onto individual, white psychology. These writers, especially Fanon, are important to the development of African American antifascism because of their crucial position in the formation of Black Panther ideology. For both of these Martiniquan intellectuals, the war was a formative experience. Césaire was profoundly disturbed by the racist conduct of French soldiers trapped in Martinique for the duration of the conflict. Fanon served in the Free French Army and received a Croix de Guerre medal for bravery following an action in which he was seriously wounded, yet he was transformed by the racism he experienced in the military.[14] To Césaire and Fanon alike, as to Du Bois and Padmore before them, fascism was a species of colonialism. But for the later writers, fascism represented the colonization of Europe itself. "Not long ago," Fanon wrote in *The Wretched of the Earth* (1961), "Nazism transformed the whole of Europe into a veritable colony."[15]

Césaire discussed fascism in far more detail than Fanon, so much so that Fanon, rather than develop his own views of Nazism, cited those of Césaire in his famous work *Black Skin, White Masks* (1952).[16] Césaire's statements on Hitler in his *Discourse on Colonialism* (1950) are crucial to understanding the spatial metaphor of fascism:

> Yes, it would be worthwhile to study clinically, in detail, the steps taken by Hitler and Hitlerism and to reveal to the very distinguished, very humanistic bourgeois of the twentieth century that without his being aware of it, he has a Hitler inside him, that Hitler *inhabits* him, that Hitler is his *demon*, that if he rails against him, he is being inconsistent and that, at bottom, what he cannot forgive Hitler for is not *the crime in itself, the crime against man,* it is not *the humiliation of man as such,* it is the crime against the white man, the humiliation of the white man, and the fact that he applied to Europe colonialist procedures which until then had been reserved exclusively for the Arabs of Algeria, the "coolies" of India, and the "niggers" of Africa.

I have talked a good deal about Hitler. Because he deserves it: he makes it possible to see things on a large scale and to grasp the fact that capitalist society, at its present stage, is incapable of establishing a concept of the rights of all men.... Whether one likes it or not, at the end of the blind alley that is Europe, I mean the Europe of Adenauer, Schuman, Bidault, and a few others, there is Hitler. At the end of capitalism, which is eager to outlive its day, there is Hitler. At the end of formal humanism and philosophic renunciation, there is Hitler.[17]

Nazism, here, is not part of a universal human condition: it is the culmination of European culture in the age of colonialism. As such, it represents the abject failure of the Enlightenment, the impossibility of maintaining the freedom even of Europeans within a dual system of rights it cannot transcend. For in creating a system of liberal rights for some and a state of racial abjection for others, a "demon" grows within the white soul that threatens to become so overpowering as to swallow Europe itself. The space that Euro-American capitalism "reserved exclusively" for the bare life of the colonial subject, in other words, will grow and expand to encompass the social whole.

Césaire was certainly not alone in holding such views. Arendt developed a similar point in her concurrently published book *The Origins of Totalitarianism* (1951), which posited Nazism as a domestic blowback from Europe's colonial projects abroad. The Nazis, she argued, used the logic of colonialism to turn European nations into colonies, and colonial racism in Africa facilitated the development of modern anti-Semitism in Europe.[18] The sense of Hitler as a nascent demon lying within every white person first found popular expression in African American communities through the Nation of Islam. Founded in 1930, the Nation of Islam had developed into a significant force in black, urban neighborhoods nationwide by the late fifties; by 1960 its publication *Muhammad Speaks* enjoyed the highest circulation of any African American newspaper.[19] The paper not only commonly used the words *Nazi-minded* and *Nazi* to describe racial violence in the United States, but also frequently covered the public appearances of the American Nazi Party and its leader George Lincoln Rockwell. The inference of this coverage was that Rockwell's American Nazis represented the truth of white consciousness: they un-hypocritically spoke what other whites thought but would not openly express.[20]

Césaire's logic—that Nazism was but the most demonic expression of Western racial thinking—was actually put to legal use in one dramatic instance. In 1951 the CRC, an organization closely linked to the CPUSA, submitted a lengthy document to the United Nations in Geneva titled *We Charge Genocide*. Signed by a veritable Who's Who of the African American left, including Benjamin Davis Jr., Du Bois, Harry Haywood, Robeson, Claudia Jones, Patterson, and many others. In short, it charged that the United States practiced genocide against black people living within its borders as well as those it battled in Korea. And the country did so, moreover, through a legal system that exhibited the general racial logic of Nazism. The CRC based its legal argument on a broad definition of genocide set forth in article II of the UN "Convention on the Prevention and Punishment of the Crime of Genocide" (1948), which defined genocide as the "intent to destroy, in whole or in part, a national, ethnical, racial or religious group." According to the UN convention, this took the form not only of "killing members of the group," but also of "deliberately inflicting on the group conditions of life calculated to bring about its physical destruction in whole or in part."[21] According to the CRC, the genocidal crimes for which the United States was culpable included extralegal killings on the basis of race, men beaten to death on chain gangs, the chartering of the Ku Klux Klan as the "semi-official arm of government" by several states, and an "economic genocide" that reduced the lives of blacks by an average of eight years as compared with the life span of the general population. The authors of *We Charge Genocide* also noted that the Nazis openly credited the U.S. legal system with supplying models for their own racist legislation, namely, the penalties against miscegenation in southern states, the spatial segregation of "proscribed minorities," and the denial of legal protections to racialized subjects.[22]

To be sure, the racial hierarchies of the United States up to 1951 were distinct from those of Nazi Germany. Unlike Nazi policies toward Jews and the Roma, the United States never aimed at the total extermination of the black population; its violence toward the part was intended to discipline the whole, whose superexploited labor was required for its mode of capitalist accumulation. But the legal argument of *We Charge Genocide* was not baseless. The United States refused to sign the Convention on Genocide in 1948 because of a fear that doing so would allow the UN to prosecute southern lynchers who had been acquitted in U.S. courts, the very thing the CRC was now attempting to get the UN to do.[23]

We Charge Genocide mobilized a pervasive black reading of fascism in a way that palpably intervened in Cold War politics. Like Padmore, Du Bois, and Césaire, its authors viewed fascism as a form of racial thinking, which, because it is immanent in all of Western culture, remains a living force that threatens to consume the world in war and violence. With the war in Korea in mind, its authors wrote, "We cannot forget Hitler's demonstration that genocide at home can become wider massacre abroad, that domestic genocide develops into the larger genocide that is predatory war."[24] Applying this logic to the Cold War, they wrote, "The genocidal doctrines and actions of the American white supremacists have already been exported to the colored peoples of Asia. We solemnly warn that a nation which practices genocide against its own nationals may not be long deterred, if it has the power, from genocide elsewhere. White supremacy at home makes colored massacres abroad. Both reveal contempt for human life in a colored skin. Jellied gasoline in Korea and the lynchers' faggot at home are connected in more ways than that both result in death by fire."[25] *We Charge Genocide* channeled a 1930s discourse linking war and fascism but gave it an even sharper racial edge, blurring the line between the foreign and the domestic by arguing that racial policies at home could not be separated from practices outside national borders. As charged in *Color and Democracy,* the racialization of blacks at home begets suppressions of democracy abroad, in this iteration a spiral of global violence that could possibly end in nuclear annihilation. The petition furthered a line of thinking among black intellectuals that viewed the Cold War as an unhealed wound of the Second World War, for when a society creates a space of abjection for its racial others—a space capitalism requires—the space to which they have been consigned threatens to expand like a cancer, engulfing all in the *telos* of fascist genocide.

When Patterson personally delivered this document to the UN Committee on Human Rights in Geneva, *We Charge Genocide* and, by extension, black antifascism visibly contested Cold War geopolitics. The UN ultimately took no action on the petition, as it met resistance from seemingly all quarters. This resistance came not only from the U.S. government, which prevented Patterson and Robeson from traveling overseas to present the petition, but also from those who might be expected to support it, including the NAACP, the African American press, and the Soviet bloc.[26] Its submission to the UN was extensively covered abroad, however, especially by leftist presses in India, and the booklet continued to circulate overseas. In this unofficial capacity the petition momentarily offered a stinging rebuke to the NAACP's civil rights strategy of cooperation with American Cold War projects abroad in exchange for the possibility of civil rights reform at home.[27]

The CRC's antifascist petition had long-term effects as well. After 1951 the phrase "We Charge Genocide" recurrently appeared in black radical activism and reportage; these words, repeated time and again, became a means by which African Americans and other racialized groups used the memory of fascism to articulate their own oppression. In 1962, for example, writers for *Muhammad Speaks* revived the phrase as they denounced the killing of black youth by the Los Angeles police, condemning it as only the latest episode in a long-standing global campaign of violence against blacks as a race. The anonymous Muslim writer praised the *We Charge Genocide* petition from 1951 and called the CRC "the only so-called Negro organization at that time with guts and brains enough to label these fantastic, day-end [*sic*] and day-out murders for exactly what they are."[28] *Muhammad Speaks* perennially used the term *genocide,* with the Nazi instance clearly in mind, to refer to crimes against black people across the world, particularly in southwest Africa.[29] The words "We Charge Genocide" were passed on to revolutionary black nationalist organizations like RAM and the Black Panthers, who used it with increasing frequency as the sixties came to a close. Indeed, the phrase was the headline of a special newspaper the Panthers produced for the UFAF conference in which they also quoted the language of the original CRC petition at length.[30]

George Wallace, the Southern Strategy, and the Politics of Repression

When Black Panthers and their allies warned of fascism on the American scene in the late 1960s and early 1970s, their charges frequently missed the mark, but they were far from groundless. A violent racial backlash arising from seemingly fringe elements like the Ku Klux Klan and George Wallace's American Independent Party was sanctioned by the state and eventually incorporated into mainstream politics. The Klan, with its cultish reverence for atavistic symbols and ritual, its nationalist violence aimed at supposed communists, Jews, and nonwhites, its language of racial purity (which, after the war, openly praised Hitler's SS and its discourse of the Aryan), and its antidemocratic, populist drive to restore national tradition, certainly qualifies as an American-style fascist organization.[31] Though it had terrorized blacks since the Reconstruction and peaked in national influence in the 1920s, the Klan was still a force to be reckoned with in American society during the era of civil rights. More disturbing, some of its activities were subsidized by the state.

The chilling overlap of local police forces and the Klan was widely known in the fifties and sixties. As early as 1951 the CRC charged that the Klan was "chartered by several states as a semi-official arm of government" and used this fact to link the genocide of the Negro people to the U.S. state.[32] Post-Watergate congressional hearings in 1975 further revealed that the Klan's violence against the left-wing movements of the sixties had been either tolerated or directly funded by the FBI.[33] The director of the FBI, J. Edgar Hoover, was well known for his desire to crush civil rights agitation, and he devoted far more resources to repressing African American social justice movements than to the suppression of what the FBI called "white hate groups." His campaign against the Klan from 1964 to 1971, unlike his campaigns against black activists and the left generally, was the result of outside pressure from Attorney General Robert Kennedy, the White House, and the civil rights movement itself.[34] Yet Hoover turned the FBI campaign against the Klan to his advantage, using it as yet another opportunity to go after his real enemies. The fine line between an alleged FBI informant in the Klan and an ordinary Klan member provided legal cover for the bureau's repressive activities. From the mid-1960s on, Hoover had to defend the whole organization for the practices of some of its recruits, who beat civil rights activists and publicly called for their murder while receiving federal money. An FBI informant was even in the car with the murderers of the civil rights worker Viola Liuzzo in Selma in 1965. To be sure, some of the FBI's operatives in the Black Power movement were also responsible for violent acts; but, in common with the activities of its Klan informants, these acts were perpetrated mainly against black activists. The continued violence against civil rights workers by federal informants takes on added meaning when one considers that at one point in 1967 individuals on the FBI payroll formed 20 per cent of overall Klan and white hate group membership. Charles Morgan Jr., who founded the ACLU's first southern office, underscored the federal complicity in vigilante violence when he stated, "Years before those miserable, ignorant white men killed Mrs. Liuzzo, FBI agents surreptitiously peddled the lies which those killers believed."[35]

More immediately alarming to urban-based activists in the movements of the late sixties were the broader politics of racial backlash. It confronted them most immediately in the form of local, state, and federal police repression, but was fueled nationally by mainstream political figures like Wallace, Lyndon Johnson, and Richard Nixon. The third-party presidential candidacies of Wallace, the governor of Alabama, in 1968 and 1972 are instructive. Like the Klan, Wallace espoused the functional equivalent of an American fascist politics, and they were acknowledged as such by contemporary mainstream columnists like Joseph Alsop, Rowland Evans, Robert Novak, and even William F. Buckley.[36] Throughout his presidential campaign in 1968 Wallace confronted student demonstrators all the way from El Paso, Texas, to Bridgeport, Connecticut, who regularly heckled him with the chant, "*Sieg Heil*, y'all!"[37]

Wallace's political rhetoric and the public statements of his American Independent Party merited an antifascist response for a number of reasons. He and his supporters brought together enough telltale fascist traits to merit the Blackshirt label: a right-wing populism appealing to the lower middle class, one that claimed to mediate the demands of capitalists and workers; a visceral willingness to intensify state violence against racial others and the left in the effort to restore a mythic national tradition; a sharp, anticommunist narrative of national betrayal and treason in the midst of war; anti-intellectualism; and a hypermasculine, ex-military brawler persona at the center of it all. Wallace's violent oratory fueled even more violent behavior among his supporters, as illustrated by the Wallace rally of October 1968 in New York City. In Madison Square Garden, Wallace addressed a packed audience of 17,500 people which included members of two organizations that were no strangers at Wallace events: the Klan and the American Nazi Party (members of the latter appeared in uniform). As 3,500 New York police battled around 1,000 counterprotestors on the streets outside, fights broke out inside as well. Anti-Wallace protestors, many of whom were African American, disrupted the speech with the familiar chant of "Sieg Heil!" In a speech vacillating between eroticism and violence, Wallace snarled, "We don't have riots in Alabama.... They start a riot down there, first one of 'em to pick up a brick gets a bullet in the brain, that' all. And then you walk over to the next one and say, 'All right, pick up a brick. We just want to see you pick up one of them bricks, now!'" His supporters went berserk with joy. A group of white college students charged black protestors, screaming, "Get the niggers out! Kill 'em. White power." Fistfights erupted in the auditorium, and by the end injuries were reported among both Wallace opponents and supporters.[38]

Wallace publicly disavowed fascism. As a veteran of the Second World War (he flew B-29 missions over Japan), he was fond of answering sieg-heiling hecklers with the retort, "I was fighting the Nazi before you fellows were born."[39] But as the Madison Square Garden rally illustrates, he was never far from darker elements. His speechwriter through much of the sixties was Asa Carter, the editor of the *Southerner,* one of the country's most racist magazines in the fifties. Carter, who helped write Wallace's infamous "Segregation Now ... Segregation Forever" speech of January 1963, was a virulent anti-Semite and secret admirer of Hitler. He was the leader of a vicious Klan Klavern responsible for the public beating of Nat "King" Cole in Birmingham in 1956 and for the castration of a black civil rights activist. Carter even shot two Klansmen who questioned his leadership.[40] Despite his association with such extremists, including his running mate, Curtis LeMay, who had the bad habit of claiming that Americans were irrationally afraid of nuclear weapons, Wallace performed surprisingly well on election day in 1968. He was the choice of one out of eight voters, including 8–15 percent of those outside the South, and carried five states.[41]

The Wallace campaign as well as the postwar Klan and the American Nazi Party all had one major difference from their European antecedents, a distinction that reveals much about the American face of fascism. That is, the Klan, the American Nazi Party, and the American Independent Party advertised themselves as upholders of the U.S. Constitution and as advocates of its liberal rights, including free speech, free press, representative government, and the right of private property.[42] By contrast, although Nazis participated in the electoral process in the late twenties and early thirties, both Hitler and Mussolini were openly hostile to the very idea of democracy and representative government. Does this mean, then, that Americans are so infused with the air of Enlightenment liberalism that even the likes of Wallace and Carter are incapable of practicing true fascism? On the contrary, it is necessary to recall the historian Robert Paxton's injunction that "the language and symbols of an authentic American fascism would, of course, have little to do with the original European models."⁴³ If one looks to the examples of Wallace, the postwar Klan, and the American Nazi Party for clues as to the shape of fascism in the United States after 1945, one finds that American fascism has a different relationship to liberalism than its German and Italian antecedents. Like its American forerunners in the thirties, it would pair its language of rights with accompanying rhetoric and actions that would be empty of democratic content.

The Wallace movement's punitive calls for law and order were often accompanied by a language of inalienable rights. For example, a flyer circulated during Wallace's presidential campaign of 1968 reminded its readers, "We learned in school that the 'government is best that governs least.'" But a few sentences later its anonymous author complains, "We can't stop crippling strikes because of pressure from labor unions or election-scared politicians. We can't curb massive street demonstrations, or club looting rioters, for fear of election reprisals from civil rights groups."⁴⁴ Thus at one moment the author calls for less government and a smaller state, and at the next calls for strong statist action, even violence, against the democratic demands of workers and people of color. This contradiction is apparent throughout the flyer, which in one breath calls for "Government by the People" and in the next asks, "Shall We Have Government by Organized Mobs?" Such slogans were meant by Wallace and his party to flatter the egos of his followers. It assured them that they were "the People" and that their functional freedoms would not be touched by the violent power of the state he was primed to dramatically unleash on those they despised. Though this move was necessarily couched in the language of freedom in the American context, the underlying gesture would have been familiar in prewar Europe. If we return to the idea that liberal capitalism has always relied on a dual system—one space reserved for citizens enjoying liberal rights as well as a zone of abjection for *homo sacer*—what the Wallace campaign called for is an act that lies at the heart of authoritarianism. It urged a dramatic widening of the space of social death that nonetheless maintained a hierarchy of subjects with differential claims to citizenship, in a process which would make legal personhood more tenuous for all (whether everyone recognizes it or not). Such talk, when voiced in the service of a broader right-wing populist call for national renewal, takes on an uncannily fascist hue.

Wallace's defeat in 1968 and his abortive campaign in 1972 might have made him a historical footnote but for his long-term impact on American politics. A strategy he crafted would become a standard feature of the mainstream Republican Party. Legitimately fearful that Wallace was drawing away too many conservative votes, the Nixon campaign of 1968 began to co-opt his message, appealing to the racial anxieties of white voters in what came to be known as the southern strategy. In his role as the governor of Alabama, Wallace had pioneered a racist politics that, while violent, usually avoided the mention of race. Above all, he couched his anti–civil rights positions as a defense of states' rights, thus allowing whites to think of segregation not as a racial issue but as an abstract constitutional one.[45] The Nixon campaign took up Wallace's strategy, realizing that it skillfully tapped into a widespread sense among white voters in the late 1960s that civil rights demands had gone too far. Many whites outside the South felt threatened by urban riots, "forced busing," neighborhood integration, and supposedly profligate black and Latino welfare dependents. As Nixon's aide John Ehrlichman self-consciously described their Wallace-inspired strategy, the trick was to present positions on crime, public housing, and education in such a way that a prospective voter could "avoid admitting to himself that he was attracted by a racist appeal."[46]

This aversive racist strategy would later be visible in Reagan's narrative of welfare queens, George H. W. Bush's famous use of the black convict Willy Horton in negative campaign ads, and Newt Gingrich's high-profile linkage of welfare and excessive taxation in the 1990s. Institutionally, the strategy would manifest itself in a new policy toward working-class people of color, a shift from lifting their burdens through civil rights and social democratic legislation to a new strategy of ghetto containment using the iron fist of mass incarceration. As the southern strategy, begun under Nixon, decisively became national policy with the further turn to law and order in the 1980s, the United States now has one of the highest incarceration rates in the world; in 2010 one in three black men was under the control of the criminal justice system. The long-term denial of voting rights instituted for former felons in many states and legalized employment discrimination against ex-convicts nationally have widened the zone of rightlessness since Wallace's day. The strategy has not left unscathed the working-class whites interpolated as free citizens by rightist rhetoric, whose life expectancy actually fell by four years between 1990 and 2012 as deindustrialization and neoliberal restructuring devastated their neighborhoods as well.[47]

Contemporary American society, while by no means fascist, was able to create its current hierarchies by incorporating strategies arising from the darkest corners of twentieth-century politics. Activists in the era of Black Power had every reason to be fearful of the impact of fascism in American life.

The UFAF, the Black Panthers, and the NCCF

In confronting the increasing surveillance and criminalization of people of color, the Black Panthers recognized the strategic importance of antifascism. As they set up NCCFs across the country, they moved from the black antifascism of Césaire, Du Bois, and the writers of *Muhammad Speaks,* for whom fascism was an existential weight, to a new modality which resurrected antifascism as a key form of political organizing on the ground. Unlike the campaign surrounding *We Charge Genocide,* the NCCFs constituted a national movement, one that answered a pressing need.

Black politics had taken a more visibly radical turn when mainstream civil rights leaders came out against the war in Vietnam in 1967. In response, President Johnson gave Hoover carte blanche to operate against black activists and authorized the FBI to target African Americans through a series of community surveillance programs. Such efforts intensified under Nixon, who combined them with a rollback of Great Society programs, thus beginning the southern strategy in earnest.[48] The year 1969 saw a ferocious barrage of violence against the BPP by state, local, and federal authorities, one which culminated in the murder by Chicago police of Fred Hampton, the BPP chairman of Illinois, in his sleep.[49]

In response, the Panthers moved antifascist politics to center stage with the UFAF conference in 1969. It was neither their first coalition nor would it be their last. Arguably, the goal of the UFAF was to transform the alliances the BPP had forged during the Free Huey campaign of 1968 into a concerted national effort centered not on the defense of one man but on the shielding of an entire movement (Newton had been convicted of killing a police officer, but a higher court overturned his conviction in 1970). Like prewar leftists, they recognized that the rising wave of repression, along with the reactionary sentiment fueling it, marked a threat to their very existence. It required the support of a wide array of similarly threatened allies and hence a united effort to end sectarianism. In their call to activists in the weeks preceding the conference, the BPP stated, "We are asking all progressive elements of this society to forget our ideological differences and pose a UNITED FRONT against the racist police force in this country."[50]

What has gone unnoted in scholarly accounts of the UFAF conference is that it marked a self-conscious attempt by the Black Panthers to revive the Popular Front of the thirties. In calling the conference, the BPP leader Eldridge Cleaver explicitly cited Dimitrov, while other Panthers resurrected the old Popular Front definition of fascism as stated in 1935, albeit with a slight twist. Reviving Dimitrov's words, they announced, "Fascism is the open terrorist dictatorship of the most reactionary, most chauvinistic (racist) and most imperialist elements of finance capital."[51] The twist was clarifying the meaning of chauvinist as racist. By 1969 the CPUSA was a symbol of the so-called Old Left, known for its struggles against historical fascism in the thirties and forties. It was also an organization Cleaver had publicly rebuked in 1967.[52] The Panthers' quite visible turn to the CPUSA for support in planning the conference in 1969 revealed, in a sense, the sincerity of their belief that what they were fighting was indeed a new incarnation of an old enemy.

But in contrast to the Popular Front, the Panthers had a modest domestic legislative goal in mind when they assembled the UFAF: decentralized policing, wherein black and white neighborhoods would self-manage the police in their respective communities. In fact, a legally drawn petition for a referendum on community policing in the city of Oakland was already in place at the time of the conference.[53] Though their call for community policing predated the UFAF, the centrality of this nonrevolutionary goal illustrates the larger organizational context out of which the antifascist turn emerged. At the beginning of 1969, under the leadership of Seale and David Hilliard, the BPP began to shift its emphasis from paramilitary tactics to a community service orientation. Swelling with new recruits following the Free Huey campaign of 1968, Seale and Hilliard devised an organizational structure more suited to a disciplined national party than to a small, loose, Oakland-based group. This involved community programs, a greater emphasis on coalition building, and the purging of approximately one thousand members deemed unsuitable for party work (that is, those more drawn to crime and Panther fashion than to methodical political activity). In November 1969, a few months after the UFAF conference, Seale announced the formation of two nationwide Programs for the People: the free breakfast for schoolchildren program and the establishment of free health clinics in black communities.[54]

In shifting to a less revolutionary politics in the name of antifascist coalition building, the BPP followed the path of the CPUSA during the Popular Front. But what followed its initial call for a United Front was no mere repetition of the thirties. Panther activists expressed their respect for the CPUSA at the time of the UFAF, as when Seale stated in an interview with the *Berkeley Barb* that the party was far more helpful than other organizations in putting the conference together. But the Panthers also made it quite clear that this time around, unity would be formed on black terms. Shortly after the event, an interviewer from a white New Left paper asked Hilliard, "There was rumors around that the Communist Party was dominating the conference. . . . What's your relationship with C.P.?" Hilliard responded, "We dominated the conference. C.P. didn't dominate no conference."[55] His statement reflects the reality that in the late 1960s people of color were more palpably visible as central players in the left-wing mass movements of the era than they had been in earlier decades; white radicals now looked to them for leadership, even though their constancy as followers was dubious at best.

The UFAF differed from the Popular Front in other important respects. In a sign of the times, those attending the event in 1969 quite vocally expressed their awareness that broad unity fronts could marginalize the concerns of their constituent groups. The Black Panther Roberta Alexander, for example, supported the idea behind the UFAF when she stated at the conference, "Huey P. Newton says . . . we have to limit our bickering as much as possible between the movement and make our concentration upon the enemy. This is correct." But, she added, unity did not mean that the fight against patriarchy would disappear; quite the opposite. "One of the most destructive aspects of male supremacy," she continued, "is how it divides people who should be united. This is a very important concept to understand. When we struggle against male supremacy, we struggle because we want unity." Also, like other Panthers of the period, Alexander projected her model of unity onto a specific geographic location, one with different coordinates than the site offered by the earlier Popular Front. She concluded her speech by saying, "I hope the sisters in the rest of the United Front against fascism follow the example of the Vietnamese women."[56] Thus, in keeping with a longer arc of black radicalism, anticolonial movements, not the Soviet Union or the American past, would be the model for antifascist unity.

If, in its conception, the UFAF conference was no mere historical repetition, what happened beyond the speakers' podiums was also no return to the thirties. The Popular Front never achieved organizational cohesion on the left: but when Alexander exhorted her audience to follow the example of Vietnamese women, she did so in order to repair a unity that was unraveling before it had even begun. A group of mostly white feminists was threatening to walk out of the conference because of what they saw as its inadequate attention to women's issues; in raising the model of the Vietnamese sisters, Alexander was telling other feminists, in effect, that the best way to fight patriarchy was within a broader struggle, not outside of it. Representatives of the white New Left were dismayed by the presence of old Communists at the conference, embodied most visibly by Aptheker. The Boston paper *Old Mole* reported that "Apthekar [sic] droned on for an hour, irritating many who were worried that communist party influence might swing the political line of the United Front to the right." Members of the Progressive Labor / Worker-Student Alliance, a Maoist splinter group that had been expelled from the primary white New Left organization, Students for a Democratic Society (SDS), were physically attacked during the proceedings for passing out leaflets calling for a boycott of the event.[57]

After the conference many white radicals voiced their agreement with the Panthers' view that fascism was a palpable danger in the United States. Stanley Aronowitz, for instance, published a pamphlet on the history of antifascism in which he averred, "The call for a United Front Against Fascism by the Black Panthers is an appropriate slogan for this period."[58] Further, white feminists revived Wilhelm Reich's *The Mass Psychology of Fascism* (1933), which had a major reissue in 1970. Reich viewed the patriarchal family as the root of authoritarianism, a belief many feminists advanced in their own social critiques. But the various factions of the SDS refused to support the central, concrete political goal of the UFAF. The Panthers' practical aim in organizing the UFAF was, as noted, to push for decentralized policing. As David Barber has rightly noted, SDS's rejection of the call for decentralized policing marked a refusal to heed, in practice, an established Black Power strategy earlier articulated by Stokely Carmichael in his role as leader of the Student Nonviolent Coordinating Committee (SNCC); that is, blacks should autonomously organize against racism in black neighborhoods while whites organized against racism in white neighborhoods.[59] After the conference, many whites in the New Left, while continuing to voice support for the Panthers as a vanguard, increasingly refused to accept their leadership and even viewed their new shift as "reformist."[60] In an uncanny repeat of radical critiques of the Popular Front, a reporter from *Old Mole* rebuked Seale at the UFAF conference for using the terms *policemen* and *cops* rather than *pigs* and for speaking of "progressive forces" rather than of revolution or socialism.[61]

The NCCFs were the Panthers' attempt to institutionalize the demands of the UFAF conference, but they did not become multiracial organizations in practice, nor did they serve their intended legislative function. The Panthers succeeded in establishing NCCF branches all over the United States and in cities not typically associated with the postwar radical left: these included New Bedford, Massachusetts; Winston-Salem, North Carolina; Omaha, Nebraska; Bridgeport, Connecticut; Dallas; New Orleans; Flint, Michigan; and Lima, Ohio. Officially, they were open to all races, but their membership remained almost exclusively African American. The immediate legislative goal of the UFAF was more of a disappointment. In 1970 the BPP's petitions for community policing circulated only in a few cities where the Panthers or their affiliates were active. It appears that the UFAF mandate for police reform was seriously pursued only within range of the party's headquarters in the San Francisco Bay Area. There, in early 1971, the multiracial Berkeley NCCF obtained the fifteen thousand signatures necessary to get a measure on the ballot calling for three local police departments, one for the white community, another for the black community, and a third for students and the counterculture. But even in Berkeley, a hub of sixties radicalism, the measured failed by a 2 to 1 margin when voted on that April.[62]

However, the NCCFs served the purposes of a multiracial, largely working-class front in another sense. Latino and Asian American organizations took up the language of antifascism in the wake of the UFAF conference, using it as a focalizing concept to animate a range of activities. And while the NCCFs may not have served their intended political purpose, they did further a major structural goal within the BPP reorganization: they aided Seale's and Hilliard's goal of establishing a small, disciplined core of BPP members surrounded by a larger mass base in black communities. In practice, an NCCF branch would often function as a provisional Black Panther chapter in which members proved themselves worthy of full Panther status through their activist work in the community. In many cities NCCF branches administered the popular Free Breakfast for Children Programs and free health clinics. They also held political education classes, sold the *Black Panther* newspaper, subjected themselves to party discipline, and pushed its political line like regular chapters. Some NCCFs thereby graduated into regular party chapters, while others had their statuses revoked. In one dramatic instance, central headquarters charged the Dallas NCCF with embezzling money intended for the breakfast program and liberation school and for collaborating with the FBI. It disbanded the branch and barred its core activists from ever joining the party.[63]

The Winston-Salem NCCF, founded in early 1970 and elevated to a full Panther branch in April 1971, illustrates a more successful and almost seamless relationship to the national organization. But it also reveals the precarious nature of this antifascist work. A disturbingly comprehensive FBI file for the Winston-Salem NCCF allows one to piece together its day-to-day operations in detail. It rented an office in a building that also served as a community center in a poor African American neighborhood. Its funding came from BPP headquarters (which paid the salaries of a few full-time organizers), from donations by local businesses, but mostly from the sale of the *Black Panther*. Half of the funds from newspaper sales were remitted to Panther headquarters in California. FBI informants, incidentally, did not report any skimming by NCCF members in Winston-Salem.[64] The branch did its best to administer the Programs for the People. At political education classes held two nights a week and attended by five to thirty people from the community, they discussed and analyzed articles in the *Black Panther* along with local developments. Every weekday the members would administer the Free Breakfast for Children Program for around thirty children, then eat breakfast themselves, hold a political training session (often based on the BPP newspaper), and go out into the neighborhood to sell the paper, clearing up to twenty-five hundred copies per week. A number of members enrolled in first aid classes so as to eventually provide health services to the community. Other NCCF branches had access to trained medical personnel. The Seattle office, for example, was able to enlist the services of four doctors, a nurse, and a medical secretary.[65]

The solidarity work of the Winston-Salem branch was concentrated mostly within the black community of the city. The branch organized a May Day rally in 1970, which, according to FBI estimates, drew a crowd of three hundred and included some whites. The leaders of the branch, Robert Greer and Larry Little, spoke at area campuses such as the University of North Carolina–Chapel Hill and Winston-Salem State University. One of the local organization's most dramatic actions was its armed defense of a Winston-Salem woman who faced eviction. In March 1970 Polly Graham sought help from the NCCF after sheriff's deputies kicked down her door and moved her belongings into the street. Activists moved her things back into her home, which was situated in one of the most impoverished neighborhoods in the city, then posted guards with rifles outside her door. The police soon withdrew when a local antipoverty agency paid Graham's rent. The NCCF took this action because the police initially told Graham's neighbors they would soon return to carry out more evictions. No such evictions took place after their armed intervention, however.[66]

The Winston-Salem NCCF worked under very tenuous circumstances. Like other Panther groups across the nation, it drew its members from among the poorest segments of the African American population, or the lumpenproletariat, as the Panthers called themselves.[67] FBI files on the group report severe financial difficulties and even hunger among its activists. One member was forced to drop out of the branch and return home because, as was reported by an FBI informant, "he was hungry and his clothes were ragged."[68] NCCF members were well aware of being extensively surveilled by the federal government and expected a police attack to come at any moment. Their office in Winston-Salem was heavily fortified, with sandbags stacked "armpit high" and 2½ feet thick around the perimeter of the first floor. Activists had further plans to install bulletproof sheet metal on the doors. In addition, they stocked a dozen rifles and shotguns at this location which they ended up using against the police a number of times. When local police tried to evict them from their fortified office in February 1971 a gunfight erupted that left one officer and one activist wounded.[69] That same year, in what later congressional investigations revealed to be an FBI setup, local police arrived at the NCCF office on the pretext of investigating a stolen meat truck. Soon after a gun battle broke out, raging for forty-five minutes, although no one was injured.[70] This state of war between NCCF branches and the police reflected national trends and marks yet another similarity between these auxiliaries and regular Panther chapters. In New Bedford, Omaha, Detroit, New Orleans, and Hartford, shootouts and other forms of violence erupted between the NCCF and law enforcement, often during a raid on an NCCF office.[71]

One should not discount the word *fascism* in the name of the NCCFs as merely a term of strategic convenience or a ploy used by an organization that otherwise engaged in many of the same activities as a regular Panther chapter. For a critical two years in the BPP's history, its affiliates waged their struggles, from eviction protests and May Day rallies to gun battles and community service, under the banner of a fight against fascism. The California-based party newspaper, from which NCCF activists in Winston-Salem got their daily political education, instructed its southern comrades to view all their local efforts as part of a larger, national resistance movement, not against the government or, primarily, imperialism but against perceived fascist forces in the United States. In earning their revenues from sales of the *Black Panther,* the North Carolinians materially funded their operations on words recalling a repression evocative of the thirties, one seemingly bent on genocide. But what notions and theories of fascism did the Panther newspaper offer?

The Panthers were much more adept at outlining antifascism as a political strategy than they were in formulating fascism as a specific mode of oppression. As in the case of *Fight!,* the magazine of the ALAWF, the Panther newspaper can be faulted for not putting forth a consistent definition or theory of fascism. As a concept, it was less developed than other terms the paper regularly employed, like *Marxist Leninism,* the North Korean organizing concept of *juche,* and Newton's later idea of "intercommunalism." Nor did the Panthers employ *fascism* with the same ideological consistency they applied to other concepts, like colonialism. George Jackson's *Blood in My Eye* (1972) contained the most elaborate exposition of the concept from BPP circles. Unfortunately, Jackson revived some of the worst Third Period analysis of the CPUSA, stressing the direct control of fascism by the ruling class, minimizing its racial nationalism, and defining its essence as the attempt to crush revolutionary parties by reforming capitalism. "If one were forced for the sake of clarity to define [fascism] in a word simple enough for all to understand," he reasoned, "that word would be 'reform.'" Before the war this line of thinking had led communists to direct their energies against their would-be allies, the moderate socialists, whom they called social fascists. Jackson entered this self-defeating tradition by arguing that the United States is currently a fascist state and that it was first established as such by Roosevelt's New Deal.[72] Jackson's definition appeared as the NCCFs were winding down and fortunately did not take hold.

As in the days of the Popular Front, no single theory of fascism definitively stuck in the late 1960s and early 1970s among either BPP activists or their coalition partners. Some of those involved in Panther circles understandably expressed confusion about its definition. A woman involved in BPP political education classes in Denton, Texas, for instance, wrote to Newton, "I've been reading a lot of material on Fascism. Mainly, I would like for you to send me your interpretation as to 'what fascism is'?"[73] While there was no consensual definition, the persistent situations to which Panthers across the country applied the word reveal a consistent "structure of feeling" around its meaning. For leaders and rank-and-file activists, fascism was intensified, racially driven state repression, first, of dissidents in communities of color and then, as it spreads outward in an ever-widening spiral of violence, of people at large. Its chief perpetrators were local and state police, Hoover and the FBI, and the Nixon administration. Left unchecked, its logical result is the actual genocide of people of color. If this notion of fascism differed from earlier iterations by white leftists, the difference lies in its emphasis on selective violence, conceived in spatial terms, and its stress on law enforcement as the index of fascism's rise.

In the pages of the *Black Panther,* in interviews, and at the UFAF conference, Panther leaders like Seale and Eldridge and Kathleen Cleaver helped to create this broader structure of feeling as they tried to bring some order and consistency to the organization's usage of the term. Roughly a year before the UFAF conference, Kathleen Cleaver stressed how those in the black ghetto are fascism's first targets, but only its first. "The advent of fascism in the United States," she argued, "is most clearly visible in the suppression of the black liberation struggle, in the nationwide political imprisonment and assassination of black leaders coupled with the concentration of massive police power in the ghettos of the black community across the country." Yet she qualified her statement as follows: "Black people have always been subjected to [a] police state and have moved to organize against it, but the structure is now moving to encompass the entire country."[74] Eldridge Cleaver, holding a position similar to that of his wife, saw fascism as something unevenly applied within a liberal state. He extended this idea by positing the idea of fascism as a general institutional force with localized intensity. Drawing from Dimitrov's position on its class nature, the Panther leader stated, "In this country the state apparatus for fascism already exists. Economic, military, and political power are already concentrated into the hands of a small, unified ruling class." But to Cleaver, the incorporation of fascism by the state apparatus does not mean that all citizens experience fascism:

> Besides fascism being legal, it can also be directed. It does not have to be "indiscriminate." For example, the black colony can come under attack, as has happened all over the country, while the white neighborhoods are not necessarily affected. But terror will come down in broad, indiscriminate forms in those places where the movement in the mother country has developed into a serious threat, as in Berkeley.... Fascism in America recently has been isolated to specific revolutionary and potentially revolutionary targets; this is especially true of terror used against the black and brown nations, which only rarely has spilled over into the white population."[75]

Both Eldridge and Kathleen Cleaver suggest a spatial theory of fascism, in which fascism deepens the contradictions of the liberal state's dual system of rights. That is to say, in a fascist state the violence exacted among the traditionally ghettoized by the former liberal state is dramatically intensified, while, at the same time, it widens its circle of terror, however unevenly, to enclose formerly privileged sectors as well (in Eldridge's example, the white student movement).

Kathleen Cleaver's evocation of "the black ghetto" and Eldridge Cleaver's reference to "the black colony" begin to explain the spatial emphasis of African American antifascism. Such rhetoric was informed by a lived history of residential segregation mediated by a twentieth-century global discourse of anticolonialism. Seale more dramatically underscored how anticolonial politics informed the spatial idea of fascism. Unlike the antifascists of Dimitrov's era, he urged others to see fascism as "domestic imperialism," to be distinguished from "imperialism abroad," as exemplified by the war in Vietnam. Seale outlined this view in a letter written from a San Francisco jail and printed in the *Black Panther* in January 1970: "Domestic imperialism at home is in fact fascism. But what in essence is it? I think Black people if we go over the concrete experiences that we've had in America and what's going on now against us we can understand exactly what it is—to be corralled in wretched ghettos in America and look up one day and see numerous policemen occupying our community, and brutalizing us, killing brother Linthcomb, murdering young Bobby Hutton."[76] The notion of the police as an "occupying" army in the black community relies, again, on a colonial metaphor of race and class common in Panther circles, a metaphor wherein urban ghettoes were imagined as colonies that needed to declare independence from a foreign power. But more than this, Seale's protest against the state-sanctioned murder of those "corralled in wretched ghettoes" implies there is a fine line between fascism and the liberal state at the level of lived experience, that is, for those relegated to social death by both systems. Like the Cleavers, Seale spoke against a violence that was necessarily uneven in application but that always held the potential of exceeding its own thresholds.

In this vein, the idea of a contemporary genocide was quite pervasive among black radical activists and their allies in the late sixties and early seventies. Genocide, a charge first issued in a civil rights context by the CRC in 1951, was fundamental to the Panthers' sense of reparative justice. The word was highlighted in their Ten Point Party Platform and Program, adopted in 1966. In their demand in the party platform for "forty acres and two mules" they reasoned, "The Germans are now aiding the Jews in Israel for the genocide of the Jewish people. The Germans murdered 6,000,000 Jews. The American racist has taken part in the slaughter of over 50,000,000 black people, therefore, we feel that this is a modest demand that we make."[77] Indeed, talk of genocide was never far from talk of fascism in the pages of the *Black Panther*. Its writers frequently applied the word to instances of what Michel Foucault would term the biopolitics of the state, from official efforts at population control to police murder. For example, one contributor used the phrase "black genocide" in reference to a measure in the Tennessee legislature that would involuntarily sterilize mothers who received welfare. In another instance Charlotte O'Neal of the Kansas City BPP described the lethal lack of health care for the poor of the city as "a 'Mass Genocidal Plan' to exterminate all poor, oppressed people in general and Black people in particular."[78] Black radicals of the older Second World War generation like Williams and Patterson encouraged such Holocaust frames among younger activists.[79] Also, while some contemporary Holocaust scholars viscerally reject the application of this historical catastrophe to the predicament of non-Jews, an earlier generation of Jewish American antifascists actively invited ethical comparisons between the plight of the Jews in Germany and the circumstances of black people in the United States. But the genocide trope does raise a critical issue: what does it mean to read one's oppression in the United States not merely in terms of fascism but in terms of the specifically Jewish experience of the Holocaust?

I have argued here that the application of *fascism* to American politics by African American radical writers and activists is a charge to be taken very seriously as a historical claim, and, furthermore, that it is not a politically immobilizing act in and of itself. But to charge genocide raises another set of complications. First, racial violence in the United States has generally been a means of disciplining a subordinate group within a particular class configuration. To exterminate nonwhites altogether would leave the system without the most exploited segments of its laboring class, whose sizable presence is necessary to maintain the class structure overall. In the 1920s, for example, eugenicist efforts to maintain the purity of "American racial stock" by halting all Mexican immigration were decisively curbed by western ranchers, farmers, and railroad men, who required low-paid workers.[80] Fascism has certainly been a force in American life, but the institutionalization of a genocidal variant aimed at the total extermination of people of color within its borders is almost inconceivable. To denounce local acts of racist police brutality as genocide can be immobilizing, for it is to perpetuate a politics without a proper historical ground.

Moreover, the evocation of twentieth-century Nazi genocide, in which fascism and genocide were repeatedly paired, deflects one from the historical, racially driven mass murders of the liberal state more germane to mapping the place of people of color within it: for instance, the millions dead from the slave trade and Middle Passage, the five to ten million dead in the Belgian Congo, the preventable famines of European imperialism in India, Brazil, China, and North Africa. Mike Davis has called attention to the thirty to fifty million deaths in three global mass famines wrought by the European imperialism of the late nineteenth century, and there are many more such famines in its longer history.[81] Precise figures for colonial genocides were not available in the late 1960s, when there was little historical work on the nature and extent of mass murder perpetrated by European empires; even today, the work that now exists has yet to enter American popular consciousness.

Nevertheless, the charge of genocide by activists of color in the late sixties should not be dismissed. Black radical uses of the Holocaust in the 1950s and 1960s reveal a general sense, correct in essence, that white supremacist institutions had committed unnamable crimes, the full details of which, still to be unearthed, hovered as an absent presence. Furthermore, given the often mysterious assassinations of so many Black Power and civil rights activists and the overwhelming federal pressure brought to bear against the movement, it is quite understandable that the political stakes might be raised to apocalyptic levels. But however one evaluates this move, the sense that one needed to have a genocide in one's cultural past to authorize claims of reparative racial justice reveals the depth to which antifascism framed black radical consciousness in this period.

A United Front against Fascism? Asian American and Latino Antifascism in the Late 1960s and Early 1970s

Recent scholarship on civil rights and the late 1960s has charted how African American demands for social justice sparked similar struggles among other marginalized groups in the United States. In this period radical organizations in nonblack communities sprang up, sometimes modeled closely on the Black Panthers, including the Chicano Brown Berets, the Puerto Rican Young Lords, the Chinese American I Wor Yuen and Red Berets, and the urban, white Appalachian Young Patriots. These groups tended to mirror the Panthers in their cultivation of a distinctive clothing style or look and in their urban, working-class composition. They also echoed the Panthers in their political language: a synthesis of Marxism, nationalism, and Third World anti-imperialism which sought community self-determination from a colonial, white capitalist culture. The Black Panthers maintained contact with these groups and collaborated with them on projects of mutual interest.[82] But the grammar of Black Power could be found in a wide range of organizations in Latino and Asian American communities, well beyond the bereted and uniformed youth movements.

Antifascism was a ubiquitous part of this grammar. This discourse was certainly present in Asian and Latino politics in the United States before the late sixties. In the Second World War era, for example, it figured quite actively in the work of the Filipino writer Carlos Bulosan and the Chinese American writer H. T. Tsiang, and it featured prominently in the San Francisco–based,

Spanish language communist paper *Lucha Obrera*.[83] It could be found as well in nonwhite, left-wing newspapers, often in connection with police abuse, even before the UFAF conference in 1969. But appearances of the word *fascism* in the radical Asian American, Chicano, and Puerto Rican presses picked up noticeably after the conference, the exception being the American Indian Movement, which turned to its constituents' own direct history of genocide in the New World.[84] While the NCCFs did not recruit many members outside of African American neighborhoods, the Panthers' organizational shift intensified the use of antifascist language throughout the wider activist milieu of the time, where it became a central component of radical Asian American and Latino political discourse. However, even given this increased intensity, Latino and Asian American radical publications charged fascism less frequently than the *Black Panther*. Radical writers in other communities of color did not simply mimic the Panthers' antifascism: instead, they adapted the discourse to their own particular histories and experiences, both in the United States and abroad.

In the Chicano movement, the Panther-styled Brown Berets were not the only ones to charge fascism and genocide. Such language is commonly found in the periodicals and public statements of the Movimiento Estudiantil Chicano de Aztlán, El Partido Revolucionario Chicano, the La Raza Legal Defense Committee, the New Mexico–based Alianza Federal de Mercedes, Los Siete de la Raza (the organization), La Causa Legal Defense Fund of El Paso, Texas, and in the newspaper *La Raza*.[85] Talk of fascism and genocide was notably persistent in *Basta Ya!* (Enough!), a weekly paper subsidized by the BPP and distributed twice a month along with the *Black Panther* (fig. 6).[86] *Basta Ya!* was the only explicitly antifascist vehicle subsidized by the Panthers outside their own community. Beginning its circulation shortly after the UFAF, the paper relentlessly called for community police to stem the tide of fascism in the barrio. Its formal independence from the BPP illustrates the organizational forms antifascism would need to take within the nationalist turn of the late 1960s: that is, the supposed unity front would be housed not in a single multiracial organization, but inside a set of separate, interlocking bodies working toward a parallel set of political and cultural goals.

Showing a direct influence of the Panthers, the word *fascism* commonly appeared in the Chicano press in reference to police abuse and to repression at the hands of the criminal justice system. In 1970 and 1971 it was not infrequently linked to the Panther call for community policing. For instance, Daniel Gorostiza of La Raza Legal Defense Committee wrote, "It is the people in the community who must control the police if the police are to serve the people. Anything short of this is fascism."[87] Likewise, when the Brown Berets revised their Ten-Point Program of 1968 into a new Thirteen-Point Program in 1970,

FIGURE 6. Cover of the newspaper *Basta Ya!*, part of the Black Panther Party's antifascist coalition, August 16, 1969.

their new plan of action contained references to fascism and genocide. The demand for community policing was present in their original manifesto, but point 2 of the new document expressed it in much starker terms: "We demand the immediate end to the occupation of our community by the fascist police. We realize that the police occupy our communities just as the US imperialist armies occupy foreign countries. Only by organizing and arming ourselves can we ever hope to stop the police brutality and genocide in our communities."[88] Like the Panthers, the Brown Berets used a rhetoric of fascism and genocide to push back against internal colonialism. The more mainstream La Raza Unida Party also adopted "Chicano community control of law enforcement agencies" as one of its national priorities at its first national convention in El Paso in September 1972.[89]

The term *fascism* appeared even more frequently in the Chicano press in late 1970 and 1971, and, as was the case with the BPP, its enhanced use was the result of heightened brutality against the Chicano movement. The FBI had declared the Brown Berets a national security threat in early 1968 and by the end of the decade was conducting surveillance operations against every major Chicano organization. Though the Brown Berets never engaged in Panther-style shoot-outs with law enforcement, violence between police and Chicano activists became severe in 1970, especially in Los Angeles.[90] Los Angeles was a center of Chicano movement activity; this birthplace of the first Brown Beret organization had the largest concentration of Mexican Americans in the United States during the 1960s. The chief of police in Los Angeles, Thomas Reddin, authorized aggressive action against the movement, prompting shows of force at its demonstrations along with infiltration and surveillance behind the scenes. In dealing with urban riots, he once instructed his officers to use "overkill—kill the butterfly with a sledgehammer." The results of this mandate were predictable. A massive Mexican American antiwar rally in August 1970, the largest of the Chicano movement, ended in violence as police clubbed and tear-gassed demonstrators, leaving three dead. One of the dead was the outspoken journalist and community leader Rubén Salazar, killed by the police in what appeared to be a political assassination.[91]

Within this increasingly repressive atmosphere, Chicano antifascism would often connect local police violence to the national political culture. A full-page montage in the December 1970 issue of *La Causa*, for example, contained head-shots of Johnson, Wallace, and Nixon, the latter, at top-center, being the most visually prominent. Spliced between these national political figures were images of police violence at home and soldiers in Southeast Asia. In the center of the montage, which was titled "Law and Order," was a quote from Hitler that was ubiquitous in activist circles in the late 1960s: "The streets of our country are in turmoil. The universities are filled with students rebelling and rioting.

Communists are seeking to destroy our country. Russia is threatening us with her might and the Republic is in danger. Yes, danger from within and without. We need law and order. Yet without law and order our nation cannot survive. Elect us and we shall restore law and order."[92] The message implicit in "Law and Order" is one that even Popular Fronters of the 1930s would have appreciated, namely, that fascism is a political force arising from within a liberal state and manifests itself in the call for a paranoid spiral of state violence at home and anticommunist militarism abroad. The montage also signals that some activists in the late 1960s continued to draw on the memory of fascist politics without directly evoking the tragedy of the Holocaust.

This was not always the case, however. Injunctions against genocide also proliferated in the Chicano movement press. Unlike the Panthers, who tended to use the term in reference to American biopolitics, Chicano activists often employed it to describe the mass slaughter of Mexican American soldiers in Vietnam. In the late sixties, antiwar protests were more central to the Chicano movement than to Black Power, largely owing to Mexican Americans' closer relationship to the military, a relationship activists tried to sever. Because Mexican Americans, unlike African Americans, were not assigned to segregated units in either world war, military service, to them, had come to function as a marker of whiteness. The Chicano press carried stories of disproportionately high casualty rates among Mexican Americans in Southeast Asia, a contention later confirmed by historians.[93] It was commonplace during the antiwar Chicano Moratorium marches in 1970 to reference this fact as an instance of genocide against people of Mexican descent in the United States. During the rallies that year *La Raza* printed statistics of the high casualty rates among Mexican Americans and juxtaposed them to photographs of demonstrators in Denver carrying signs that read, "Stop Chicano Genocide."[94]

As noted, the word *genocide* entered common usage in English as a result of rising Holocaust awareness in the 1960s, and the Jewish Holocaust has tended to serve as the referent for all genocides. However, the use of the term by Chicano activists signaled a slight shift from its usual European frame of reference. Apart from the high number of deaths among Chicano soldiers overseas, the other genocide they often decried was that of the people of Southeast Asia. The term and concept thus served as a basis of identification with the Vietnamese, a fellow colonized people fighting back against mass death at the hands of the U.S. military. As *La Causa* polemicized, "The Vietnam War is the ultimate weapon of genocide of non-white peoples by a sick decadent *puto* [male prostitute] western culture . . . The random genocide in the barrio, *campos* and ghettos is escalated to a calculated cold-blooded policy to enslave the Vietnamese people and rape their land of its resources."[95] *Genocide* is used here to form a lateral relationship among nonwhite peoples, indicating an effort to make the term take on a life of its own, not reducible to the ever-present Holocaust template.

Chicano antifascism served the movement's transnational politics in another sense. Ignoring Seale's injunction to use fascism in reference to politics at home and imperialism to situations abroad, Chicano activists evoked the term to refer to right-wing authoritarian governments in Latin America. They brandished the label against the dictator Augusto Pinochet in Chile with particular venom, and in this instance the Chicano movement was inspired by its compatriots across the border. When Hortencia Bussi de Allende, the widow of the deposed president of Chile, Salvador Allende, came to speak at the Los Angeles Convention Center in December 1973, *La Raza* covered her speech in full, both in Spanish and in English. Titled "No to Fascism!" (¡No al Fascismo!), the speech enjoined the audience to "fight fascism in Chile," which Allende described as the violent taking of power by an elitist right. No longer able to achieve its will through the ballot box and aided by American imperialists abroad, she said, it destroyed workers' living standards and whatever freedoms the liberal state offered.[96] In using antifascism to link American imperialism with undemocratic regimes in their region of origin, Chicano activists shared a conceptual frame with Filipino leftists in the United States. Throughout the seventies, the San Francisco–based Filipino newspaper *Kalayaan International* (later *Ang Katipunan*) consistently used Nazi imagery to delegitimize the regime of Ferdinand Marcos in the Philippines. Like the Chicano movement, this paper sometimes used *genocide* in ways that de-centered it from Jewish Holocaust rubrics, as when it compared the genocide of the native Muslim population of Mindanao, "the frontier of the Philippines," to that of Native Americans.[97]

While some instances of Asian American antifascism in this period hued closely to the models provided by the Black Panthers, Asian American militants, much like their Chicano counterparts, adapted the discourse to their own historical experiences in the United States. Panther-style groups in Chinese American communities like the Red Guard in San Francisco and I Wor Kuen in New York could not use the same tactics as the Panthers because of their comparative isolation within their neighborhoods, filled as they were with anticommunist exiles. When I Wor Kuen's newspaper reported that "fascist white goons" almost burned down their office, it noted with dismay that other Chinatown papers "applauded the act of arson righteously."[98] Its bilingual paper *Getting Together* tried to use the perceived fascism of Hoover and Nixon to rally New York's Chinatown behind a unified banner, arguing that distinctions drawn within the community between assimilated and unassimilated, communist and anticommunist, immigrant and naturalized ultimately did not matter to the FBI.[99]

A pervasive anxiety was deeply rooted in the memory of Asian American radicals, one almost always evoked by their brand of antifascism: the Japanese American internment. Unlike African American and Latino cultural politics, Yellow Power did not require metaphors grounded in European Jewish history when imagining concentration camps in the United States. Some in the movement, such as Penny Nakatsu and Yuri Kochiyama, had been interned as children; but one did not have to have been interned or even be of Japanese descent to be haunted by the camps. Chinese American militants also speculated that a life behind barbed wire would be their fate if full-scale war broke out between communist China and the United States.[100] The internment camp thereby functioned as a usable past which worked to create a pan-Asian solidarity. However, references to Nazism were still salient when Asian American radicals recalled the internment. For example, the first issue of I Wor Kuen's *Getting Together* contained a two-page collage juxtaposing images of Nixon, a swastika-emblazoned ghost labeled "Hoover," barbed wire enclosures, watchtowers with captions like "Concentration Camps U.S.A." and "a call for law and order" as well as the text of Hitler's own call for "law and order" against communist unrest (see above).[101]

The association between Nazism, anticommunism, and American calls for law and order was common across the left during the Vietnam War era. But Asian American activists added a legal reality to this association that made the specter of "Concentration Camps U.S.A." much more concrete: the Internal Security Act of 1950. Sometimes called the McCarran Act, this legislation allowed for the denaturalization of subversives for a period of five years, and, more ominously, its title II authorized the emergency detention of those deemed an internal security threat (pursuant to this act, detention camps were erected but never used). The memory of the Japanese American internment made the mere existence of this law chilling to Asian American activists, especially when, as recently as 1968, the chairman of HUAC, Edwin Willis, suggested that antiwar protestors and black militants be placed in McCarran Act detention centers. As an anonymous writer for *Getting Together* warned in reference to HUAC's threat, "We can't say it can't happen here because it already has."[102] Activists in the Asian-American Political Alliance (AAPA), including Nakatsu, drew on the memory of the internment to highlight the dangers of the McCarran Act's state of exception, even in latent form. One of the AAPA's position papers from 1968 argued as follows:

> The key issue is not whether or not Title II of the McCarran Act can be invoked or not. It is rather the very existence of the Act itself which provides for detention centers and which therefore permits some one like Willis to suggest their usage.... We of the Asian-American Political Alliance believe, as long as it is in effect, that it

can be, and for that matter will be, invoked against Black militants as well as white radicals. Moreover, given the current assumptions of American foreign policy, we see the clear possibility of a major war with Communist China; and if such should come to pass, then we do not preclude the possibility of Chinese-Americans being placed into detention camps in the same way Japanese-Americans were during World War II."[103]

In common with the largely Jewish American protests against the McCarran Act on its original passage in 1950, the members of the AAPA strategically mobilized their own histories to remind others that all citizenship is made contingent by legislation targeting a particular community. Once again, group experience, animated in part by the language of antifascism, became a way to push for universal freedoms.

Antifascism ceased to be a central organizing logic of the BPP after Newton returned to operational leadership of the party following his release from prison in August 1970. While he polemicized against fascism like other Panthers, he did not share with Seale the same faith in the concept's ability to cement a broad unity front. The NCCFs quickly fizzled out, and Newton's concept of intercommunalism became the new theory of coalition building. Antifascism gains coherence by projecting an oppressive nation-state, yet intercommunalism held the very concept of the nation to be outmoded because of an increasingly globalized capitalism. It called for a new coalition between local "communities" across the world, united in opposition to American imperialism.[104] Antifascism, in its brief but explosive resurgence in the late 1960s and early 1970s, did not have the same political impact on the dominant culture as its earlier incarnations, even in the short term. In contrast to its antecedents in the 1940s, Panther antifascism did not significantly help to define a war effort; unlike the antifascisms of the 1950s, it did not aid in bringing down a mode of political reaction; and as opposed to the antifascist interventions of the early 1960s, it did not raise a broad awareness of the brutal expediencies of U.S. foreign policy. And unlike these earlier instances, its immediate target—in this case, police repression as the state's response to civil rights demands—not only survived institutionally but thrived, becoming common sense for the white majority. Though aiming for this target was highly pragmatic, striking it would have compromised the very foundations of white supremacy, and thus the goal of community policing was far more challenging to actualize than its reformist nature suggests.

Yet the didactic value of black, Latino, and Asian American antifascism is singularly immense: its spatial understanding of fascism productively revises the concept, alerting one to the universal danger to the social whole implicit in violence and repression unleashed against the part. The Holocaust frames set in motion in the 1960s would continue to make antifascism relevant in the age of identity politics, as genocide spoke to political identities informed by racial understandings of group experience. In the 1980s the gay and lesbian movement took up the discourse in pronounced ways; like radical movements by people of color in the late 1960s, it would turn to antifascism at a moment of intense political reaction. In so doing, it would also properly identify a tenacious and uncanny threat.

CHAPTER 7
Queer Antifascism
Pink Triangle Politics and the Christian Right

> Our emblem's significance depends on foreknowledge of the use of the pink triangle as the marker of gay men in Nazi concentration camps, its appropriation by the gay movement to remember a suppressed history of our oppression, and, now an inversion of its positioning. . . . The power of this equation under a triangle is the compression of its connotation into a logo, a logo so striking that you ultimately have to ask, if you don't already know, "What does that mean?"
>
> Douglas Crimp, ed., *AIDS DemoGraphics* (1990)

> I read the histories of Germany. I read the Book of Revelations. I read the *Times*. I sense parallels. Just call me paranoid.
>
> The character Zillah, in Tony Kushner's play *A Bright Room Called Day* (1985)

When the Nazis imprisoned gay men in concentration camps, they infamously forced them to wear a pink triangle on their striped uniforms to signify their homosexuality. Four decades later, in 1986, an American art collective known as the Silence = Death Project repurposed this Holocaust symbol to create its hallmark image. In the context of the AIDS crisis, its shameful neglect by most all authorities, and a vicious public backlash against gays and lesbians, their graphic inverted the orientation of the triangle (men in the camps wore it facing down, the new symbol pointed up) and placed it over the words "Silence = Death." The Silence = Death image greatly expanded public awareness that Nazism was not only anti-Semitic but also homophobic at its core, thereby positioning contemporary antigay politics within a longer and palpably barbarous tradition. While not denying the status of the Jews as central targets of the Nazi regime, the graphic worked to defamiliarize a growing popular sense of the Third Reich as a historical event carrying a semantic valence reducible to the mass murder of European Jews. When the AIDS Coalition to Unleash Power (ACT UP) adopted the Silence = Death image a year later, the inverted pink triangle rapidly became a ubiquitous symbol in gay and lesbian communities across the country. The gay and lesbian movement thereby became the only major American postwar movement to evoke the memory of fascism in one of its signature icons.

In 1987, in the front window of the New Museum of Contemporary Art in New York City, an art installation became the most elaborate visual expression of the concept behind the pink triangle and its accompanying caption, "Silence = Death." Titled *Let the Record Show . . .* , the installation conveyed a message that could be discerned primarily from the juxtaposition of its background and foreground elements (fig. 7). In the foreground appeared a rogue's gallery of six individuals: from left to right, Jesse Helms, Cory SerVaas of the Presidential AIDS Commission, an anonymous surgeon, Jerry Falwell, William F. Buckley, and Ronald Reagan. The viewer, positioned simultaneously as prosecutor, judge, and jury, was invited to draw a connection between the series of individuals immediately before them and a number of infamous historical figures appearing in a black-and-white photomural in the background: Nazi defendants, seated in a row, at the Nuremberg trials. What made the analogy between American conservatives and the Nuremberg defendants easy to draw was that the Americans were made to appear as if they were seated before a tribunal, their life-size photographic cutouts, also in black and white, cropped to display only their heads and shoulders, each framed in separate boxes. Also inviting the analogy was what the writer Douglas Crimp called "the foreknowledge of the use of the pink triangle as the marker of gay men in Nazi concentration camps." An increasingly familiar symbol of AIDS activism by 1987, the pink triangle and its accompanying logo, "Silence = Death," appeared in neon colors above the accused figures. It was as if the visual juxtaposition of the two sets of criminals was intended to explain the logo and to answer the nagging question, by means of yet another direct action, "What does that mean?"

Let the Record Show . . . did not stake its claims through visuals alone. The various captions associated with each American figure invited the viewer to think more closely about the link between the European past and the American present. Affixed below the image of each of the six Americans was a stone tablet on which was etched words they had spoken, words for which they now stood accused:

> Jesse Helms, U.S. Senator—"The logical outcome of testing is a quarantine of those infected."
>
> Cory SerVaas, Presidential AIDS Commission—"It is patriotic to have the AIDS test and be negative."
>
> Anonymous surgeon—"We used to hate faggots on an emotional basis. Now we have a good reason."

Jerry Falwell, televangelist—"AIDS is God's judgment of a society that does not live by His rules."

William F. Buckley, columnist—"Everyone detected with AIDS should be tattooed in the upper forearm, to protect common needle users, and on the buttocks to prevent the victimization of other homosexuals."[1]

Reagan did not even mention the word *AIDS* in public until June 1, 1987, after he had been in office for six years. Thus his tablet was blank, signifying his years of public silence on the AIDS epidemic and his complicity as a bystander. The stone etchings gave the words of these six people a kind of permanence as documentary evidence, affixing them as an eternal part of their record which they could not unmake.

But if the juxtaposed images invited a visceral comparison between past and present, the tablets asked the viewer, in far more specific ways, to reflect on the meaning of fascism and how it might appear in an American context. Moreover, they revealed something vital about the artists who created the piece, namely, that their understanding of fascism was informed by a half century of struggle on the left. The call for the quarantine of an unpopular minority and the desire to see them "tattooed in the upper forearm" built on an understanding of the Jewish Holocaust, introduced to the public vocabulary in part by earlier antifascist interventions. The corresponding view that fascist crimes have their roots in the hatred of a traditionally marginalized group, a view which was not common sense before civil rights, appears in the words of the surgeon, who speaks of a rational basis "to hate faggots." SerVaas's sentence, "It is patriotic to have the AIDS test and be negative," links all of these views to nationalism; coupled with Falwell's proclamation, it suggests, as a marker of fascism, the physical disposability of those who do not conform to the national ideal. The presence of Falwell reveals a new emphasis within American antifascism introduced by the gay and lesbian movement: the idea that the American incarnation of fascism may very well have an evangelical Christian face. But as many antifascist writers and artists did before them, the creators of *Let the Record Show . . .* exhibited the catastrophe of the 1940s as an unredeemed struggle, one which they, like Walter Benjamin's historical materialist, would "blast" out of the homogeneous empty time of the dead, dominant history and make "citable" and living in the present.

Let the Record Show . . . was not created by artists who were merely sympathetic to those fighting the AIDS crisis; rather, it emerged organically out of movement activism. It was created by an ad hoc committee which had been invited to create a work for the New Museum by the curator, Bill Olander, a member of ACT UP and a person with AIDS. Some of those involved in this committee had been a part of the Silence = Death Project. Out of the collabora-

FIGURE 7. Street view of *Let the Record Show . . .* , New Museum of Contemporary Art, New York City, 1987. Courtesy New Museum Digital Archive, New York.

tion that produced *Let the Record Show* ... a new artists' collective, Gran Fury, formed and went on to produce numerous graphics for ACT UP.[2] But neither *Let the Record Show* ... nor the Silence = Death image originated what can be termed queer antifascism. Indeed, by the late 1970s the gay and lesbian movement was the primary bearer of antifascist politics in the United States. The close of that decade, a time when the antigay activism of the Christian right first made itself unmistakably known, witnessed the emergence of gay and lesbian activist work, cultural production, and archive building that explored the fate of homosexuals within the Third Reich. The pink triangle was already a familiar symbol in many American gay and lesbian communities by that time. With increasing frequency in the mid- and late 1980s gay men in particular drew on the new archives of "the gay Holocaust," opened up by post-Stonewall historiography, and deployed the memory of the Nazi persecution of homosexuals as they confronted the AIDS crisis and the Christian right. Through documentaries, reportage, popular history, theater, literature, and graphic art that recalled the German past and warned of its parallels in an emerging fundamentalist America, many gay cultural producers turned their own "grief and anger" (to quote the famous Silence = Death poster) into personal and political action. In the process they injected into the liberal public sphere a notion of the Christian right as a new face of fascism, transforming antifascist politics in a way that impacted the broader culture of the United States.

The discursive turn to genocide by the Black Panthers and their allies has not been widely examined within ethnic studies. But the same is not true for the gay and lesbian movement's use of the Third Reich, which has been subjected to a great deal of scrutiny in lesbian, gay, bisexual, and transgender (LGBT) studies.[3] German historians of Nazi persecution, moreover, publicly intervened in the discussion during the 1980s in the gay and lesbian press.[4] The heightened commentary on this issue among LGBT scholars perhaps arises from the relatively controversial nature of the pink triangle in the movement itself during the 1980s and 1990s. While the symbol found widespread acceptance within the movement when adopted by ACT UP in 1986, it was not without its detractors, particularly in the following decade. In comparison, there were few public critiques of the Panthers' use of fascism within the left, and there was certainly no debate about the appropriateness of its usage in the party's newspaper itself.

Scholars have taken a range of positions on the appropriateness of gay and lesbian evocations of Nazism. Their positions range from the full support of observers like Gregory Woods to the outright rejection of R. Amy Elman and Les Wright. A more common stance lies somewhere in between, as in the views held by Erik Jensen, Deborah Gould, Kai Hammermeister, and Dorthe Seifert. Most of these scholars are critical of the way many in the gay community evoked a gay Holocaust, but at the same time they recognize the continued relevance of Nazi persecution and advocate a more precise and productive historical understanding of homosexuals in the Third Reich. One criticism lodged in this latter scholarship is quite germane here: that is, Jensen and Seifert have identified a counterproductive tendency in gay and lesbian communities to couch homosexual persecution under the Nazis in terms of the Jewish Holocaust experience.[5] Informed by the work of German historians of the Hitler regime, these scholars correctly argue that National Socialist discourses on homosexuality were not identical to those which decimated its racial others and that the fates of most gays and lesbians in the Reich did not lead to the concentration camp.[6] Hence an overt conflation of gay and Jewish experiences of the Nazi regime is indeed problematic. Setting aside the long-debated issue of victim identity, such a conjoining perpetuates a dominant American understanding of the Third Reich that, by the seventies, understood Jews as the sole victims while reducing the meaning of the regime to a limited, Americanized understanding of the Jewish Holocaust. While American gay activists often compared the treatment of gays and Jews in the Nazi regime, their counterparts in the German movement commonly made parallels between the Nazi persecution of gay men and political radicals.[7]

However, this scholarship has tended to focus disproportionately on American works of gay Holocaust literature, namely, Martin Sherman's *Bent* (1979), Lannon Reed's *Behold a Pale Horse* (1985), and Robert Reinhart's *Walk the Night* (1994), works which do in fact contain a number of problematic historical representations. This focus stems from a broader critical tendency—not only in LGBT studies but also in American cultural studies more broadly—of only seeing representations of the Holocaust and not noticing when the writers and activists being analyzed and discussed are really speaking of fascism in much broader contexts. Some gay cultural productions in the seventies and eighties did rely heavily on Jewish Holocaust rubrics to mediate the memory of Nazi Germany, but many others, before and after, did not. Most English-language works by cultural producers who referenced fascism, including the art of the Silence = Death Project and Gran Fury, the drama of Tony Kushner, the writings of the activists Harry Hay and Larry Kramer, the documentary work of Stuart Marshall, the popular history of Richard Plant, and even some of the gay potboilers of such writers as Marty Rubin and Paul O. Welles, did not enact simple conflations of Jewish and gay experience. Nor did they suggest anything so crude as a simple equation between AIDS policy and Auschwitz. Rather, they posed questions, to both gay publics and the population at large, about the possible connections between the Nazi past and the American present. And they did so by calling on the memory of German fascism in its broader sociopolitical manifestations and legacies rather than by focusing exclusively on the site of the concentration camp.

Some cultural producers in this vein have been quite conscious of the limitations of the genocide frame. As the British documentarian Stuart Marshall wrote,

> What PWAs [people with AIDS] have in common with homosexuals at the time of the Third Reich is not the status of the concentration camp victim. Rather it is being a recruit within a complex and contradictory regime concerning the state's regulation of desire by means of moral, legal, and ideological manipulation of a society's anxieties about sex and deviancy. The parallel is to be found in the positive and negative pressures to conform to a politically defined imaginary moral norm and the construction of the hierarchy of susceptibilities, vulnerabilities, predilections, and fear of reprisal used by Nazism to construct different levels of disposability within a population."[8]

Marshall's parallels are unique, but the self-conscious, historically informed, and critical sensibility he expresses here is by no means rare within gay and lesbian antifascism. This complexity becomes more comprehensible when one considers a facet of such cultural work which deserves far more scholarly examination. That is, in order to see the efforts of these artists and writers as forming a coherent body of cultural work and to fully appreciate its political contribution, one must examine their engagement with left-wing antifascism, both in the United States and Europe. To a much greater degree than other postwar antifascist mobilizations in the United States, their queer antifascism was transnational in scope, materially informed by gay, left-wing antifascist writing and scholarship in Germany (East and West) as well as in the United States. I call it queer antifascism because it eschews an assimilationist model of political activism, one marked by a call for inclusion within a heteronormative culture, in favor of an approach that seeks to transform the dominant culture itself.

Another factor has been sidestepped by scholars who have evaluated the applicability of the German past to American gay and lesbian politics: the very real fascist tendencies within the Christian right in the United States. I advance the admittedly controversial thesis that the Christian right, up to the present day, is guided by ideas and organizations that do in fact constitute a functional equivalent of American fascism. Although many of its explicit politics have shifted over time, the Christian right has never strayed far from the ideological deep structure exhibited by three of its primary forebears, Gerald Winrod, Gerald L. K. Smith, and Charles Coughlin, all of whom looked to European fascism as they waged their campaigns to create a "Christian Nation" in the thirties. To consider the aptness of the parallels drawn by queer antifascism in the United States, which often targeted pastors and televangelists like Jerry

Falwell and Pat Robertson as well as political organizations such as the Moral Majority—the well-financed, Christian right political operation that quite successfully mobilized religious voters in the eighties—one must take into consideration not only the fidelity of such comparisons to the Nazi past, but also their historicity within the postwar American political landscape. In this regard, I take issue here with scholars who label the evocation of Nazi Germany by gay writers and activists "paranoid" and instead argue that they, like other activists before them, have effectively used antifascism to highlight the very real historical dangers—dangers to everyone—of right-wing social movements that strive to create national purity and cultural homogeneity.[9]

The National Socialist Past and the Early Years of Queer Antifascism in the United States

Gay men have had a different relationship to historical fascism than heterosexual people of color who spoke of fascism in the late 1960s. Unlike peoples of African, Latin American, and Asian descent, gay men were categorically singled out for persecution in the historical Third Reich. Such persecution, like the more frequently cited Jewish Holocaust, reveals a longer history of oppressive structures which neither began nor ended with the Hitler regime. The Nazis punished gay men by strengthening an existing nineteenth-century law, not by creating a new one out of thin air. Paragraph 175 of the German Penal Code, adopted upon German unification in 1871, criminalized homosexual acts between men. The Nazis used §175 as the legal basis for their campaign against gays, widening its definition of homosexuality, dramatically hardening its punitive measures, and enforcing it to an unprecedented degree. Yet the Nazis' assault on homosexuality came at a time when the gay and lesbian movement in prewar Germany was at its peak of mobilization, a fact that American activists in the 1970s and 1980s often noted. Indeed, in the decades preceding Hitler's rise to power Germany had the most visible homosexual emancipation movement on the globe and was home to the world's first organization devoted to homosexual rights: Magnus Hirschfeld's Wissenschaftlich-humanitäre Komitee (WHK, Scientific Humanitarian Committee), founded in 1897.[10] In the 1920s the growing movement helped to create a vibrant gay public sphere and succeeded in placing homosexuality in the realm of political debate. The Social Democratic Party (SPD) and the Communist Party of Germany (KPD) acted, to a point, as the gay community's parliamentary allies during the Weimar era.

By contrast, though the Nazi Party contained a few gay members within its ranks, most famously, the SA leader Ernst Röhm, its violent rejection of homosexuality was visible even before it took power in 1933. As Günter Grau has written, the Nazis saw gay men as "an immediate threat to the growth of the nation." In NSDAP discourse, both before and after it took power, male homosexuality undermined the martial virtues necessary for national greatness. At the same time, it threatened the health of the nation because gay men presumably lowered the birth rate of the Aryan race and were seen as vectors of disease. The Nazis inherited such ideas from the "medicalization of homosexuality" before 1933, which also taught them that their victims' sexuality was a threat to children, a danger to public morality, and an "epidemic" menacing the health of the national community.[11] Female homosexuality, on the other hand, was not viewed in such threatening terms. Gay women were not penalized under §175 during the Kaiserreich, an d after the Nazis came to power following a lengthy internal debate, they retained this legal exemption. Because the leaders of the Third Reich assumed women to be passive and naturally dependent on men, they did not see female homosexuality as capable of threatening their fully remasculinized nation. Thus for lesbians the broader NSDAP policy on women was of more crucial importance in restricting their lives.[12]

There were critical divergences between Nazi policies toward Jews and toward homosexuals. The experiences of gay men and women in the German Reich from 1933 to 1945 were multiple, and most did not wind up in concentration camps. In his landmark study, Richard Plant concluded that a substantial number, possibly the majority, survived the period undetected. The religion and ethnicity of Jews and Romani were listed on their birth certificates, and Communists and Socialists could be discovered through confiscated party membership lists, but homosexuals were much more difficult for authorities to identify. Still, the undetected lived in constant fear of discovery and witnessed the complete destruction of the public gay and lesbian culture many had begun to enjoy. It was not uncommon for gay men to marry lesbian friends to avoid suspicion; others volunteered for the Wehrmacht, navy, or air force to elude the murderous jurisdiction of the SS, seeing brutal combat as a result.[13] But for those who were discovered by the authorities the situation was dire. From 1933 to 1945 between fifty thousand and sixty-three thousand men and six women were convicted of homosexuality in German courts, the most dramatic wave of repression falling in the period 1936–39.[14] Those convicted could face imprisonment, torture, castration, and the horrors of the concentration camp, which included medical experimentation. Those branded with the pink triangle in places like Dachau, Buchenwald, Auschwitz, Sachsenhausen, and Flossenbürg generally occupied the lowest tiers in the camp hierarchy and had among the smallest survival rates of the various prisoner groups. In all, between five thousand and fifteen thousand homosexuals died in the camps.[15]

The Nazi regime did not consistently view homosexuality as a biological condition, a vital factor in the comparison of homosexual and Jewish persecution. Those who engaged in homosexual acts were not always seen as belonging to an inferior race. To be sure, the Nazis combated both Jewishness and homosexuality on eugenicist grounds, as diseases injurious to the biological health of the nation. The eugenic foundation of the campaign against homosexuality became manifest with the establishment in 1936 of the Reich Office for Combating Homosexuality and Abortion, which aimed to eliminate a dual hindrance to the bountiful, Aryan family. But the doctors, jurists, and administrators of the Nazi regime, like the earlier medical experts whose work they consulted, did not agree on whether homosexuality constituted an inborn, biological condition or if it was a vice that could be corrected. Policy therefore proceeded from both viewpoints: police and the courts tended to distinguish between so-called incorrigible homosexuals, who were naturally inclined to their behavior, and people who merely engaged in homosexual acts, often through seduction by the incorrigibles (hence children were seen as being at risk). Grau concludes that an overall logic of extermination did not apply to homosexuals as it did to Jews, for whom, in the eyes of the authorities, the observance or nonobservance of the Jewish religion was irrelevant.[16] An influential strand of National Socialist thinking held out the possibility that even the incorrigibles could be cured of their sexuality; to this end, prisoners in the camps endured compulsory visits to brothels, experimental hormone treatments, and grueling labor assignments designed to turn them into real men. To be certain, most all of those whom the regime sought to "cure" by these methods died in the process.

The history of homosexual persecution outlined here came to light as a direct result of the gay and lesbian movements of the 1960s and 1970s. Before the uprisings in Europe in 1968 and the Stonewall riot in the United States, only vague contours of this past were known to those who did not witness it firsthand. A central idea put forward by this movement, that gays and lesbians constituted a people, required the creation of a shared history that could serve as a firm basis for identity and political expression. Chronicling the Nazi terrors was part of a much larger project of creating a gay archive to bolster this emergent sense of peoplehood. Most of the historians who documented and interpreted the experiences of homosexuals in the Third Reich were born in Germany and worked in East Germany, West Germany, or as exiles in the United States. From the mid-1970s to the 1990s such scholars as Grau, Rüdiger Lautmann, Klaus Müller, Claudia Schoppmann, Richard Plant, Hans-Georg Stümke, and the American James Steakley researched the long-neglected record of Nazi sexual politics, and much of their published work was translated into English and accessible to readers in the United States. In 1980, moreover, the first survivor narrative of the gay genocide became available to Americans. The autobiography of the pseudonymous Heinz Heger, a former pink triangle prisoner from Austria interned at Sachsenhausen and Flossenbürg, initially appeared in German as *Die Männer mit dem rosa Winkel* (1972) and then in English as *The Men with the Pink Triangle* (1980).

Much of the postwar silence about the gay persecution has been attributed to the direct continuity of Nazi sexual politics in the legal system of West Germany in the decades after the war, for which the Western allies were also culpable. Tragically, §175 remained on the books after 1945 and in the form augmented by the Hitler regime. As a result, some liberated concentration camp survivors were imprisoned a second time to complete the sentences imposed on them by Nazi courts, a cruelty enforced by the British and American occupation governments. Still a criminalized group and often rejected by their families after they returned home, gay survivors could not come forward to tell their stories, let alone claim reparations. Unsurprisingly, the postwar mortality rates of pink triangle survivors were higher than those of other groups persecuted by the Nazis. Plant blamed "the climate of the Cold War and the conservative moralism of the Adenauer administration" for this state of affairs, which did not end until East Germany abolished its penalties against homosexuality in 1968 and the Bonn government in the West followed suit in 1969.[17]

The pink triangle found its way to the United States by way of the German gay and lesbian movement of the seventies. Indeed, what I have called queer antifascism should be viewed as the result of a decades-long transnational relationship between the German and American movements. On both sides of the Atlantic these movements had been part of wider left coalitions from their very beginnings. In Germany the collaboration between gay organizations and workers' parties went back to the earliest days of the twentieth century. The SPD actively campaigned in the Reichstag for the abolition of §175, particularly from 1898 to 1914. But it retreated from this stance during the Weimar years, a period in which the KPD maintained a closer relationship to Hirschfeld's WHK than any other political party. Hirschfeld himself was a socialist who enjoyed a congenial correspondence with Friedrich Ebert, the head of the SPD and chancellor of Germany for much of the Weimar period. And key figures in the WHK, including Felix Halle and Richard Linsert, were also communists. The relationship of the workers' parties to the gay movement was often deeply problematic. But before the Second World War many gay activists in Germany were drawn to the left not only because of its relative willingness to take up their causes but also because of the persistent demonization of homosexuality by rightist, clerically oriented, and conservative parties. The fact that the Soviet Union initially adopted the most liberal sexual legislation of any nation in the world at that time (although later annulled by Stalin in 1934), also made communism appealing to some.[18]

In the United States a formative relationship to Marxism also existed at the foundation of the modern gay movement. The founders of the Mattachine Society in Los Angeles, the country's first modern gay emancipation organization, established in 1950, were mostly CPUSA members or fellow travelers. The intellectual contributions of Harry Hay, a principal founder of the society, are still cited as the basis of gay and lesbian identity in the United States. According to Will Roscoe, Hay's "cultural minority thesis," which he reworked from communist theory, "is the implicit mode of self-understanding and community organization of Lesbian/Gay communities wherever they exist."[19] As the scholars Aaron Lecklider and Daniel Hurewitz have argued, the convergence of bohemianism and radical politics in the culture of the left afforded a space for some gays and lesbians to find one another and to express nonnormative sexualities even in the 1930s, before the emergence of a bona fide gay political movement.[20]

Scholars who have studied Hay have discussed the singular import of racial frames, gleaned, above all, from CP theory, on the formation of a gay political identity in the United States. But an attentiveness to the role of antifascism in shaping this oppositional discursive convergence of race and sexuality in the forties enriches one's understanding of the terms on which the modern gay and lesbian movement formed. It also leads to a deeper understanding of the connections between this movement and the military mobilizations of the Second World War itself, which, as the historian Allan Bérubé has shown, was a watershed moment in the history of sexuality in the United States.[21] Hay's cultural and historical work, especially his lecture notes from the Marxist education classes he gave in the late 1940s, underscores the meaning of antifascism to gay liberation long before the reclamation of the pink triangle.

Hay drafted a prospectus for the Mattachine Society in July 1950, which he originally intended to name Bachelors Anonymous. A striking feature of this document, which Roscoe called "the prospectus that launched the modern Gay liberation movement," is its evocation of fascism in the very first sentence. Under the heading "Statement of Aims and Purposes," it states,

> With full realization that encroaching American Fascism, like unto previous impacts of International Fascism, seeks to bend unorganized and unpopular minorities into isolated fragments of social and emotional instability;
>
> With full realization that this socially censured Androgynous Minority was suborned, blackmailed, cozened, and stampeded into serving as hoodlums, stool pigeons, volunteer informers, concentration camp trustees, torturers, and hangmen, before it, as a minority, was ruthlessly exterminated....[22]

Hay's knowledge of the Nazi campaign against homosexuals was directly informed by his partner and Mattachine cofounder Rudi Gernreich, an exile from Vienna who fled Austria in 1938. Gernreich educated Hay on the fate of

Hirschfeld's Institute of Sexual Research and on the presence of gays in the death camps; in transmitting this history, he also taught the lesson of caution, which informed the secretive structure of the early organization.[23]

While a few gay men and women were pushed to become "concentration camp trustees, torturers, and hangmen" in the Third Reich, the fact that Hay felt compelled to introduce the subject of homosexual victimization with this mea culpa speaks to a challenge that gays and lesbians were forced to confront *within* antifascism. As early as the 1930s gays and lesbians faced a persistent notion, manifested across the political spectrum in Europe and North America, that Nazism was somehow innately homosexual. In what Gordon Wood called "the myth of Fascistic homosexuality," Nazi behavior and ideology were seen to derive from sexual deviance. This myth was largely based on the widely publicized sexuality of Röhm and his inner circle, who were murdered by the SS in 1934 (partly because of this publicity), and a corresponding amnesia in regard to the regime's systematic torture, internment, and murder of gay men. Despite their strategic alliances with the WHK, the prewar German left also perpetuated this notion when it polemicized against Nazis by associating them with homosexuality. For many leftists in Germany and beyond, homosexuality was a form of bourgeois decadence, a view that persisted in Soviet, French, and Cuban communist writings long after the war.[24] Among American antifascists the myth of fascistic homosexuality can be seen as late as Shirer's *The Rise and Fall of the Third Reich* (1960), which fixated on the "notorious homosexual perverts" within the ranks of the SA. In one of his typical formulations, Shirer wrote, "A conglomeration of pimps, murderers, homosexuals, alcoholics and blackmailers flocked to the [Nazi] party as if to a natural haven."[25] Hay was well aware of this antifascist narrative of gay perpetration, for he literally performed it. As an actor in Los Angeles during the Depression he played the role of Adolph, a homosexual Nazi villain in Clifford Odets's play *Till the Day I Die* (1935).[26] Partly because of the ground cleared by Mattachine, gay writers after Stonewall would not feel so compelled to respond to the myth of gay perpetration in their discussions of fascism, past or present.

As a Marxist teacher in the 1940s Hay was not at liberty to fully discuss the sexual logics of racism and capitalism with his students. But his lecture notes from this period reveal that antifascism was a fundamental means by which he developed the intersectional theory of race he would later apply to "the Androgynous Minority." In his classes at the People's Education Center in Los Angeles immediately after the war Hay elaborated the concept of white chauvinism. His lecture notes are unfortunately blank beneath the question, "What is chauvinism?" Presumably, he had the answer committed to memory. But in his usage, it appears as a kind of racial nationalism, one that facilitates capitalist reproduction by creating spaces of superexploitation and politically segmenting the working class. Because fascism builds on established structures of white chauvinism, which is constitutive of capitalism, and because it dramatically intensifies the violence of those structures, Hay asserted that groups at the bottom of the racial hierarchy feel the shift to fascism most immediately. But, he taught, subaltern minorities are not just victims—they are also the key to resistance. In his lecture notes he writes,

> *What position do the negro people hold in [the] present period?*
>
> (a) the first targets of fascist reaction
>
> (b) in face of which they are fighting back, and in so doing are strengthening and broadening their advance toward nationhood
>
> (c) without their alliance, there can be no successful struggle against fascism in the U.S.[27]

Three elements here would be transferred to Hay's later theory of the Androgynous Minority as articulated in Mattachine's founding documents. First, those most marginalized under the old order are "the first targets" of fascism and thus are most likely to resist. Second, the struggle of "the negro people" is not theirs alone but has universalist implications, for it is essential to the fight against a broader wave of reaction that impacts everyone. Third, it is, at the same time, *their* struggle and must be respected as such in order for it to contribute to the whole. In many of his points Hay grafts antifascism onto the CPUSA's "black belt thesis" of the thirties, which stressed that African Americans' organizing on the basis of race to achieve their own "nationhood" was fully compatible with proletarian revolution. But in doing so he borrows equally from Dimitrov's iteration of the Popular Front line. Later in the same lesson, he stressed to his students that white chauvinism should not be conceived as an epiphenomenal part of the superstructure but must be fought on its own terms. Like Dimitrov, he argued that white chauvinism continued to exist in communist ranks precisely because earlier party thinking viewed it as merely "a political phenomenon," from which followed the destructive practice that "the conducting of a struggle against it in general is obviously no struggle at all."[28] In other words, to assume that racism will be negated by focusing one's attention solely on its capitalist roots is to effectively ignore race and thus to leave the door open for fascism.

Hay later worked these ideas into his writings on Les Mattachine, originally a dance in which gay men in medieval France led the folk in a struggle against political reaction. The implication behind the usable past of Les Mattachine was that gay men, like the African Americans he referred to in his earlier lectures, were key targets of the state and also essential to the struggle of the people as a whole. And in keeping with the anti-assimilationist logic implicit in his earlier writings on white chauvinism, they could fulfill their critical role in a fight against "encroaching fascism" only if they were able to maintain their own cultures and not be subsumed within a homogenous proletariat.[29] Overall, antifascism functioned for Hay as a kind of grammar through which he mapped the relationship of minorities to one another and to their individual and collective struggles against capital and the state. It was, in short, a broader analytic which framed his thinking just as much as the black belt thesis and communist theories of culture. Since the 1930s antifascism had been an intersectional critique used to simultaneously articulate class and racial formation, but it was fluid enough, in the hands of Hay and others, to be extended to hierarchies of sexuality and to help construct the political ground from which the emergent gay selfhood advocated by the early Mattachine could arise. Its usage was not merely strategic for Hay; it was not just a self-conscious attempt to build coalitions, forge alliances, and make gay men and women legible to the broader left. Rather, in using antifascism to chart the relationship between heteropatriarchy, racism, and capitalist accumulation, he revealed that he was genuinely incapable of ignoring any of these modes of oppression in his struggle for human emancipation.

In 1953 Hay and his cofounders lost control of the Mattachine Society, as it was transformed by new leaders with less radical pasts from a secret society to a larger, more public organization, albeit one that eschewed leftist modes of organizing and rhetoric. However, still legible in the revamped organization's main publication, the *Mattachine Review* (*MR*), were the various ways in which Hay had used antifascism to situate gay men and women. These included not only the racial frame of gays as a persecuted minority (now, in need of civil rights) and the notion that homosexuals possessed a distinct, valuable culture, but also the idea that their subjection worked to enslave society as a whole. For example, one contributor to *MR*, Carl Harding, drew on *The Authoritarian Personality* by Adorno et al. to argue that the psychological drive to impose a "rigid conformity" that subjugates homosexuals is the basic impulse behind all manner of destructive social phenomena, from sexual repression to the Nazi murder of the Jews. Harding concluded, "The power of authoritarian personality is well to be feared as a dangerous threat to personal peace and to democratic civilization."[30]

But while elements of the founders' worldview continued to appear in *MR*, the journal's authors, with a few exceptions, ceased to use explicitly antifascist tropes to position themselves and their community. In fact, fascism ceased to be a pervasive frame of reference for the gay and lesbian movement, even in its constructions of gay history, until the late seventies. When *MR* evoked

Germany, it was typically the Germany of Hirschfeld, police tolerance, and movement building, not the Germany of pink triangles and barbed wire. Many works on its list of suggested readings were written by German psychologists, including Hirschfeld, Sigmund Freud, and Wilhelm Reich, further cementing the association between Germany and sexual tolerance.[31] In attempting to create a gay archive, *MR* tended to look for an affirmative, usable past. Ancient Greece and Rome served this purpose much better than the horrors of recent history.

Some of the early Mattachine radicals regrouped under the auspices of ONE, Inc., a new homophile organization in Los Angeles founded in November 1952, yet this organization offers a similar story.[32] In its early days *ONE* magazine showed a distinct awareness of Nazi homophobia, praising the work of homophile movements fighting its remnants in West Germany. Yet by the late fifties, when *ONE* magazine evoked fascism to describe the right-wing drift of American society and its repression of homosexuals, it used the term in the same way other left-oriented publications at the time did, its authors seemingly unaware that the historical Nazi regime actively targeted homosexuals.[33] In 1954 ONE Inc. established an education division which offered lectures, research opportunities, and courses on topics "pertaining to homosexuality," much of it through its Institute of Homophile Studies, founded two years later. The aim was to go beyond the "narrowly limited medical or psychological approach" to the study of homosexuality, a move which opened up inquiries into a more broadly conceived gay history.[34] While the amount of knowledge it produced on homosexuality is astounding, very little of this early archive building at the institute focused on the recent gay persecution in Europe. The course descriptions of its few offerings on history, most notably its two-part seminar titled "Homosexuality in History," concentrated almost entirely on ancient societies around the world; it introduced "Modern European History" almost as an afterthought. Even the institute's course "Homosexuality in Modern German History" seemed to focus more on that country's emancipatory influence. Its overview of the Third Reich stressed the homosexuality of the Nazis themselves rather than the nightmares they visited upon gay men and women. Part of its description read, "How German sex mores have influenced other societies, especially the U.S. The complex homosexual intrigues of many of Germany's rulers. The stranger story of the Nazi Party."[35]

In the blossoming gay press of the late 1960s and early 1970s—the years of the Stonewall riots in New York City, gay liberation, and the overall explosion of the gay and lesbian movement—references to fascism and the persecution of homosexuals in the Third Reich were even less frequent than they had been in homophile publications such as *ONE*, the *Ladder,* and *MR*. This is striking given the pervasive antifascist rhetoric among other left-wing movements of the period, especially the race-based organizations from which gay liberation borrowed much of its political philosophy. Gay, mostly student groups and publications which sprung up in this period often used a colonial paradigm that situated gays and lesbians in the context of an oppressed nation in need of independence from a colonizing dominant culture. As late as 1976 a writer for the journal *Magnus* argued that "homophobia is a product of cultural imperialism, and consequently gay people are *culturally* colonized people." He noted a traumatic past in which homosexuals were "slaughtered by Hitler" but did not afford the Nazi regime any special weight in a list of perpetrators that included Stalin and the Roman Catholic Church.[36] While gay liberation borrowed its anticapitalist, colonial paradigm most immediately from the Black Panthers, it did not, by and large, position the fascist as the external enemy of its anticolonial nation building, as Seale and Eldridge Cleaver had. Neither did the myriad gay liberation organizations use antifascism, as Hay did, to structure their spatially conceived push for self-determination. This despite the fact that Hay was still very much active in the Stonewall era and was one of the founding members of the Gay Liberation Front, Los Angeles, in 1969.[37]

Explicit antifascist language did not catch on within homophile organizations or among gay liberationists, but for different reasons. For the later Mattachine, ONE Inc., and the lesbian homophile organization Daughters of Bilitis, the dramatic and even apocalyptic nature of this language would have chafed against their attempts to show a respectable, upstanding, scientifically informed public face. And for gay liberation of the late sixties and early seventies, harkening back to the darkness of fascism would have struck a discordant note with the forward-looking, optimistic spirit of emancipation in the years after Stonewall, a time when explorations of gay history were not as pronounced as in earlier or later stages of the movement. The striking absence of references to a Second World War–era gay genocide in both homophile and gay liberation literature also implies that to many activists entering the movement in the fifties and sixties this disturbing recent chapter in the history of sexuality had slipped from consciousness. In the United States early knowledge of the Nazi repression was largely passed on by word of mouth within a largely closeted gay community. In the virtual absence of public interest in the Nazi's homophobic atrocities and the rejection of overt antifascism by the homophile movement, there would have been little to sustain this memory.

Gay Liberation in Germany and the Emergence of the Pink Triangle

In the mid- to late 1970s the American gay and lesbian press began to show greater awareness that homosexuals had been targets and victims of the Nazi regime.

At that time, the pink triangle began to surface as gay activists reappropriated it as a symbol and began showing greater willingness to render their opponents, particularly those in the Christian right, as fascist. This change was evident in the push against Anita Bryant's "Save Our Children" campaign to repeal the gay rights ordinance of Dade County, Florida, in 1977.[38] By the middle of the next decade direct references to fascism were almost ubiquitous in gay activism, cultural production, and reportage. The resurgent appeal of antifascism by gay and lesbian publics can be explained by three main factors: the transatlantic reach of the heavily Marxist German gay movement and its politics of memory; the rise of the Christian right, a movement pledged to rid the nation of homosexuality; and, in the 1980s, the catastrophe of AIDS and the apparent willingness of the heterosexual public to let the disease physically eliminate gay men.

The pink triangle was first used as a symbol of gay liberation not in the United States but in West Germany, where it arose from the radical Marxist wing of the country's gay and lesbian movement. In German-speaking Europe, the stalled, century-long campaign for gay liberation was dramatically reignited by the uprisings of 1968 and the Stonewall rebellion in the United States. Homosexuelle Aktion Westberlin (HAW) was at the forefront of the German movement in its early days. Marxist in outlook, with many of its members cross-affiliated with other socialist and communist organizations, it argued that true homosexual emancipation was impossible under capitalism. The HAW played a pivotal role in bringing gay liberation groups together in a nationwide coalition when it organized a series of national conferences in the first half of the decade. Initially, the new German movement, steeped in the language of liberation, paid little attention to the Nazi repression of homosexuals, but this changed with the publication of Heger's survivor narrative. The first known call to wear the triangle came in 1973 from a feminist faction of HAW, and the organization as a whole made more concerted calls to wear the symbol in 1975, when the members first used it in a street action in the posh Kurfürstendamm district of West Berlin. That same year a handful of HAW members formed the first gay press in postwar Germany, which they named Verlag Rosa Winkel (Pink Triangle Press), an indicator of how central the icon was becoming to the organization's identity.[39] Despite the anticapitalism of the emerging movement, the major socialist and communist organizations of the student left still relegated homosexuality to the status of a *Nebenwiderspruch* (side contradiction) to be resolved after the revolution. They were often quite hostile to the idea of gays and lesbians fighting for socialism through their own separate organizations. Despite this attempt to marginalize them, the HAW and similar gay liberation groups participated in joint actions of the left, such as May 1 marches and demonstrations against the Vietnam War, and its members simultaneously fought for the legibility of gay and lesbian concerns within unions, progressive parties, and other socialist groups.[40]

From its inception, the repurposed symbol of the pink triangle—converted from fascist to antifascist ends yet still facing downward at this point—was designed to display the living nature of the fascist past in the present context. In its first official call to wear the pink triangle in March 1975, the HAW's magazine *Info* proclaimed, "Show What Happened to Gays under Fascism! The Discrimination Continues! Wear the Pink Triangle!" Its writers pointed to the quite literal survival of the Nazi past in the contemporary West German legal code, which, as noted, upheld a modified version of the Nazi's §175 at that time. In light of the recent publication of Heger's book, the writers of *Info* stated that their Pink Triangle Action was intended "to make *present* the original function of the pink triangle and the connected situation of gays in the concentration camps." As part of this impulse to make fascism "present," the authors took pains to illustrate the position of interned gays in relation to other prisoner categories, a common move in political iterations of the pink triangle since that first call. They laid out the various color-coded triangles (red for politicals, brown for Roma, green for criminals, and so forth) and argued that the pink triangle was "an expression of the hierarchy among the prisoners," one that, in part, gave other captives the means to project the violence of their own oppression onto those lower than themselves in the chain.[41] This badge-mapping impulse among recollections of the pink triangle was a reminder that in the space of the camp established social hierarchies are carved into stone. Moreover, the various groups cast out of the national body, rarely united outside the camp, are placed at war with one another on the inside, and in a way that fully insulates those who set the system in motion. As such, the system is the fullest, most brutal, and even utopian expression of hard-right nationalism. That oppression does not take a monolithic form and that the oppressed thereby reproduce the violence of the system on each other is a persistent refrain in queer antifascism.

The scholar, writer, and cultural critic Richard Plant served as a bridge between the German and American gay liberation movements and was essential in shaping the historical memories attached to the pink triangle in the United States. Plant was born to a Jewish socialist family in Frankfurt in 1910. As a Jew and a homosexual, he was forced to flee Germany for Switzerland in 1933; he was exiled there for five years before emigrating to New York, where he remained for the rest of his life. Though he eluded the Nazi's grasp, many of his homosexual friends did not, and it was their stories he imparted to his English-speaking readers in the 1970s and beyond. By no means was Plant the kind of radical who would have felt at home in a group like the HAW (he was far past its average member's age, in any case), and I am not suggesting that he personally introduced the pink triangle icon to the United States. Plant did, however, closely collaborate with German historians and activists whose work was stamped by the radical *Aktionsgruppen* of the early 1970s, and he melded insights from this work into his own as he helped to shape the meaning of the pink triangle among gay and lesbian publics in North America.

Plant is best known for his book *The Pink Triangle: The Nazi War against Homosexuals* (1986), the most frequently cited nonfictional account of its subject in the American gay and lesbian press. In the years after its publication, a number of its readers wrote the author to thank him for introducing them to the Nazi's antigay persecution for the first time.[42] But in the decade before the book appeared, Plant educated the public on this grim historical episode in periodicals like *Gay Tide,* published in Vancouver, the nationally circulated magazine *Christopher Street,* and, later, the *New York Times*.[43] Plant served as the historical adviser for Sherman's play *Bent* (1979), the first dramatic representation of gay men in concentration camps. The East End Gay Organization for Human Rights gave his book *The Pink Triangle* to the United States Holocaust Memorial Museum as part of their lobbying efforts for an exhibit on the gay and lesbian persecution, to which the institution ultimately consented.[44]

Plant conducted research for his book for more than a decade, traveling between New York and West Germany and devoting a great deal of time to locating and interviewing pink triangle survivors. In the process he corresponded with a range of individuals, including the academic historians Steakley, Grau, and Lautmann, as well as others who helped his research in various ways, like Erich Henschel and Egmont Fassbinder, a key member of the HAW. In the mid-1970s he frequently corresponded with Fassbinder, who helped put him in contact with survivors.[45] Plant also had extensive correspondence with Lautmann, whose analysis of the sexual politics of fascism and capitalism drew from the same radical milieu as the HAW. Lautmann, for instance, wrote that National Socialist racial theory was simultaneously a sexual theory, one the Nazis culled from established reactionary institutions and put to instrumental use in order to control a range of social groups. The HAW, in its founding document, also focused on the instrumental use and function of normative sexual politics, though mostly by the ruling class.[46]

Plant's politics, though of a nonpartisan sort, had long been to the left. In 1949 he published the well-received English-language novel *The Dragon in the Forest.* Loosely based on his youth in prewar Germany, it highlighted the left-wing politics of Hitler's opponents and the conservative status of the Nazis' enablers. Its narrator's sympathies are unmistakably aligned with the opposition, though he is frustrated with its established parties: he bemoans the fanaticism of the KPD and the passivity of the SPD. Plant alludes to his narrator's sexuality only in coded ways in this early work, but *The Pink Triangle,* which appeared at a very different moment in the history of sexuality, allowed him to place sexual politics at the center of his antifascism. What emerges in *The Pink Triangle* is a desire, shared with his more radical colleagues, to wean the public from reading the persecution of homosexuals through the prism of the Jewish Holocaust and an impulse to link Nazi antigay politics to wider patterns of political reaction. Like Lautmann's work, Plant's popular history stresses how the Nazi repression of homosexuals facilitated the oppression of almost everyone, from racial inferiors to women to workers. The eugenicist logic behind antigay measures, he revealed, removed the rights of women as well, while the Nazis killed the homosexual Röhm to appease industrialists and aristocrats, allowing them to cement their alliance at the expense of workers. Like other left antifascisms, that of *The Pink Triangle* emphasizes the reliance of Nazi policy on established reactionary discourses and institutions, including anti-Semitism, anticommunism, patriarchy, homophobia, and rightist conceptions of the nation, which had long rendered homosexuals as a morally corrosive force on the national body, unfit to produce new subjects of the state.[47]

The Pink Triangle frustrates attempts to conflate gay and Jewish relationships to the Nazi regime and to reduce all gay experiences of the period to the site of the concentration camp. Plant argues, for instance, that many, perhaps most, gays and lesbians lived out the war undetected; that some gay men avoided the scrutiny of the SS by volunteering for military service or enlisting the support of well-connected friends; and that gay men and lesbians faced a range of different terrors under the regime. His book contains only one chapter on the camps, and even there he highlights the specificity of gay prisoners' experiences in relation to those of other interned groups.[48] Such historical representations were fueled by Plant's belief in the necessity of placing the concentration camp in a much wider, structural context of political reaction, a belief he shared with his radical correspondents. In a letter to Plant in 1976 Fassbender outlined his HAW colleagues' efforts, writing, "We had to study the antigay foundations of German fascism more precisely—this is not done merely by describing the terrors of those affected."[49] Similarly, Plant saw the wholly limited state of Holocaust memory in the United States as an immediate problem that he intended his work to counter. Shortly after the broadcast of the TV series *Holocaust* in 1978 he wrote to his German friend Henschel, "The *Holocaust* series was so full of inaccuracies that you can only shake your head. A woman visits her husband in Buchenwald! And all Jews fought bravely in the ghetto, and the better-looking ones emigrated to Israel. . . . A friend of mine counted some 122 factual errors. And then: only Jews died. No resistance fighters, leftists, liberals,

Catholics, priests, Poles, Hungarians, Russians, Gypsies, gays, etc. . . . That is so unbalanced."[50]

The Uncanny Echoes of the Christian Right

As the work of Plant and other German historians circulated in the United States, a political force that would lessen the distance between the two countries for many American gays and lesbians took shape, giving this research a frightening topicality: that force was the Christian right. As the liberal state and cosmopolitan mass culture increasingly penetrated peripheral regions in the 1960s and 1970s, a right-wing populist movement rooted in Christianity arose, seeking to reclaim the nation from what it saw as the values of the cosmopolitan center. By the late seventies the Christian right was a conspicuous political presence, and by the nineties it had developed into one of the most dynamic social forces in the country. Since the courting of its leaders by the Reagan campaign in 1980 and 1984, it has become a permanent formation within the American right, reaching the height of its political influence during the administration of George W. Bush, when its activists entered the federal government at almost every level. Gay and lesbian publics viewed the rise of this movement with great alarm, for by the 1980s antigay politics were at the center of its vision of national renewal. Its component organizations, including, most prominently, Focus on the Family, the Moral Majority, the Family Research Council, and the Christian Coalition, devoted themselves to rolling back the social and cultural gains the LGBT movement had achieved since Stonewall and in doing so gained some degree of success.[51]

Over the past thirty years the Christian right has become one of the prime manifestations of American fascism in the eyes of liberals and the left. In 2006 the journalists Chris Hedges and Michelle Goldberg each wrote a best-selling book—respectively titled *American Fascists: The Christian Right and the War on America* and *Kingdom Coming: The Rise of Christian Nationalism*—that placed it squarely within the pantheon of historical fascist movements. Conducting their research shortly after the election in 2004, a time when the movement appeared to be at the peak of its political influence, Hedges and Goldberg delineate the most elaborate connections between the Christian right and fascism of any authors on the American scene. (That these works had to appear outside the academy speaks to the decline of antifascism as an academic discourse. To recall, leading social scientists like Seymour Martin Lipset, Daniel Bell, Daniel Levinson, Stanley Milgram, and T. W. Adorno published highly respected work on the fascistic qualities of the American right well into the sixties.) A number of canonical modern authors also gave this view literary expression in dystopian novels about authoritarian Christian states, most notably Philip Roth in *The Plot Against America* (2004) and, more famously, Margaret Atwood in *The Handmaid's Tale* (1985). However, gay and lesbian writers and activists were the first to put forward groups like the Moral Majority as a fascist constellation, and it is difficult to imagine how these non-LGBT authors could have drawn such connections without the relentless cultural work of queer antifascism.

I want to briefly consider the veracity of the claim that the Christian right constitutes a fascist or quasi-fascist movement, for it highlights the political significance of the post-Stonewall cultural production I explore here. To revisit the working definition of fascism outlined earlier in this book, fascism is a right-wing political movement animated not primarily by economics but by a symbol-laden drive for national renewal based on anti-Marxism, militarism, a masculine cult of action, and a violent reimposition of social hierarchy. Following Robert Paxton, I also argued that a postwar American fascism need not exactly replicate the historical precedents of Italy and Germany but would instead draw from its own national context to constitute functional equivalents of these earlier movements. With this in mind, Goldberg and Hedges perhaps overstate the ubiquity of violence in the Christian right as a whole, for, unlike the dictates of George Wallace and his supporters, blood does not drip from their every utterance. But there are enough fascistic strands congealing under the umbrella of the Christian right to make it of serious concern, and Hedges and Goldberg have correctly identified many of these.

Most broadly, what begins to bring the movement into the family tree of fascism is the way it is animated by an explicitly antipluralist vision of national renewal—an idea of a spiritual awakening that would restore an order threatened by movements for social equality—and a visceral willingness to condone violence in achieving this goal. This dynamic can be seen in Hal Lindsey's *The Late Great Planet Earth* (1970), a foundational Christian right text which has sold tens of millions of copies and was avidly read by Reagan. In this openly racist book, featuring a chapter titled "The Yellow Peril," Lindsey predicts the following: "Internal political chaos caused by student rebellions and Communist subversion will begin to erode the economy of our nation. Lack of moral principle by citizens and leaders will so weaken law and order that a state of anarchy will finally result. The military capability of the U.S., though it is at present the most powerful in the world, has already been neutralized because no one has the courage to use it decisively. . . . The only chance of slowing up this decline in America is a widespread spiritual awakening."[52] Typical of the movement's rhetoric, "spiritual awakening" is here synonymous with national resurgence, the "courage" to use military force, and the restoration of traditional political authority unsettled by the left. Alarmingly, the Christian right has become ensconced in the officer corps of the U.S. military and its mercenary contractors over the past few decades; many of these evangelicals in uniform pursue the wars in the Middle East as a crusade against Islam and as a means to help set in motion the apocalypse outlined in Lindsey's book.[53] Unlike that of most fascist movements, the nationalism of the Christian right is generally conceived as a means to bring about a post-nationalist end, namely, the reign of Christ's Kingdom on Earth. But if one follows its rhetoric, the nation is central to its operative, day-to-day social vision.

Overt fascism in the United States has long carried a deeply Christian strain, and religion is arguably a distinctive marker of its American incarnation. In the 1930s Gerald L. K. Smith, Charles Coughlin, and Gerald Winrod, those pioneers who first combined right-wing populist nationalism with Christian missionary zeal, all actively sympathized with Hitler, Franco, and Mussolini. Likewise, during the Cold War American fascists in the Ku Klux Klan and the American Nazi Party bluntly called for "a Christian Nation."[54] Yet the most immediate link between the modern Christian right and certain fascism is the work of Rousas John Rushdoony (1916–2002). As the father of Christian Reconstructionism, Rushdoony was crucial to the development of modern evangelical politics and a pioneer of the homeschooling movement. His postmillennialist philosophy argued, in essence, that Jesus would return only after Christians built his kingdom on earth. It exerted a formative influence on conservative evangelical heavyweights such as Tim and Beverly LaHaye, George Grant, Gary North, William Dannemeyer, Paul Weyrich, Robert Dugan, Donald Wildmon, and D. James Kennedy. In the 1990s Rushdoony's reconstructionism also profoundly impacted Pentecostal churches, the congregations out of which Sarah Palin, the former governor of Alaska and the Republican vice presidential nominee in 2008, emerged.[55]

Rushdoony's most famous work, *The Institutes of Biblical Law* (1973), is without exaggeration the closest thing to an American *Mein Kampf* to appear on the postwar American scene. It advocates an antidemocratic theocracy which quite violently uses its power to cement existing hierarchies, punish those already marginalized by the liberal state, and enforce cultural and religious homogeneity. The author wants such a theocracy to curb the leveling influences of democratic movements, which threaten the hierarchies of men over women, father over family, property owner over unions, heterosexual over homosexual, and white over nonwhite. His hostility to democracy is explicit; his social model is colonial New England, where only a select few, the morally elect, enjoyed voting rights, in a time before "the heresy of democracy . . . worked toward reducing society to anarchy." Much like the fascist subject of *The Authoritarian Personality*, Rushdoony is incapable of imagining a world of pluralistic leveling.

He sees the attempt of subalterns to win social equality as a drive to dominate and enslave currently privileged groups. On civil rights, for example, he writes, "[Blacks'] goal is not equality but power. The background of Negro culture is African and magic, and the purposes of magic are control and power over God, man, nature, and society."[56]

More disturbing is that *The Institutes of Biblical Law* prescribes that this voodoo-driven will to power, like all similar impulses, must be met by state violence. In discussing this remedy, Rushdoony is fond of the word *cleansing*. He writes, for example, "The godly exercise of capital punishment cleanses the land of evil and protects the righteous." In this context, his penalty for homosexuality should come as no surprise. He writes that homosexual culture "works to undercut the family and small-town culture." Thus "deliberate and mature warfare against God marks the homosexual. God's penalty is death, and a godly order will enforce it." Capital punishment and spatial segregation are Rushdoony's consistent answers to the spread of spiritual disease, for, as he writes, "the risk of moral contagion must be avoided. . . . God identifies Himself as the God who separates His people from other peoples: this is a basic part of salvation." In keeping with the continuum of twentieth-century fascist thought, Rushdoony's ideal state is tasked with a dual function: to limit liberal rights for all and to take those groups traditionally marginalized by liberalism and make their status as *homo sacer* abundantly clear, partly as a means of inducing fear in the more privileged citizenry. It is no wonder that Rushdoony acknowledged a kinship with historical fascists like Vidkun Quisling and Pierre Laval, whom he termed "patriots in their own way," and felt the need to insist that only 1.2 million Jews were killed by the Nazis.[57]

To be sure, evangelical activists now commonly disavow reconstructionism. However, even Rushdoony's Christian right detractors, among them Pat Robertson, positively acknowledge his contributions (Robertson repeatedly invited him to appear on his TV show, *The 700 Club*). Further, the scholar Didi Herman argues that reconstructionism's basic tenets are arguably more central to right-wing evangelical political activism than to the premillenialist theology it more consciously embraces.[58] In addition, there was extensive cross-fertilization between reconstructionists and other Christian right activists, notably through the Coalition on Revival, which brought Rushdoony together with Randall Terry, the founder of Operation Rescue, a Christian anti-abortion organization.[59] One could add that while the broader Christian right has rejected the most overt aspects of Rushdoony's racism and might recoil, at moments, from his bluntness, the elements he brought together have tended to animate the movement as a whole: the rejection of democratic pluralism, the restoration of social hierarchies through a combination of force and spiritual renewal, and the eagerness to imagine the violent death of one's enemies, not to mention a shared list of foes that encompasses gays, intellectuals, feminists, secularists, liberals, and non-Christian religionists. The Moral Majority aligned itself with one of Rushdoony's most outlandish prescriptions when, in its early days, it pursued a campaign to have the death penalty instituted as a standard punishment for homosexuals.[60]

A final trait that places the Christian right in the continuum of fascism is the structure of its othering. In *The Authoritarian Personality* R. Nevitt Sanford argued that the object of fascist animus was transferrable; the key to understanding the authoritarian personality was not its view of Jews per se, but its "*way of thinking* about groups and group relations generally." In this spirit Herman and Goldberg noted that gay men occupied a space in Christian right narratives comparable to that of Jews in anti-Semitic ones. In other words, old hatreds were transferred to new objects but were maintained within the same general, ideological structure: to Herman, a rhetoric of disease and contagion as well as the ascription of elite, conspiratorial power to both Jews and homosexuals.[61] The analogies drawn by Goldberg and Herman are compelling. But if one is to look for the bellwethers of fascism in the structure of rightist demonization, what would happen if one looked not to anti-Semitism but to Nazi discourses on homosexuality? As a number of queer antifascist cultural producers have contended, the relevance of the Third Reich to contemporary homophobia should not be sought solely in the context of the Jewish Holocaust. Rather, it can be illuminated by examining Nazism's complex biopolitical discourse of sexuality, which was certainly linked, though not reducible, to its racial theories. Shifting focus in this way, one would not need to find a contemporary ascription of immutable biological traits to homosexuals in order to identify echoes of fascism. To reiterate, National Socialist policy differentiated between so-called incorrigible homosexuals and those who merely engaged in homosexual acts: thus to the Nazis homosexuality did not consistently form an essence like race. It is precisely this vacillation between seeing homosexuality as an essence, with the attendant themes of disease, contagion, and seduction, and as a vice, that is, an act of will carrying the possibility of rehabilitation, as well as the constant tendency for these boundaries to collapse into one another, that mirrors the antigay attitudes of the Christian right. On the one hand, conservative evangelical literature recognized the gay and lesbian movement's long-established strategy of positioning homosexuals as a racial group and complained that this move cast its righteous opponents as bigots aligned against legitimate claimants of group rights. The Christian right sought to combat this strategy by deracializing homosexuality, positioning it as a sin rather than an immutable condition. At the same time, their view of homosexuality as an act of free will fit uneasily with their simultaneous representation of homosexuals as a malign force.[62]

Enrique Rueda's and Michael Schwartz's *Gays, AIDS, and You* (1987), widely circulated among conservative evangelicals, illustrates this sliding. On the one hand, Rueda and Schwartz argue that "biologically and genetically, homosexuals seem to be the same as everyone else" and that "it is possible for homosexuals to resist [their] desires. They, like everyone else, are endowed with free will." But their descriptions of the gay and lesbian movement imply that it is composed of individuals who have no desire to exercise their agency, who combine into a collective force bent on spreading physical disease and corrosive moral values to "the general population." In this context, Rueda and Schwartz made the incredible claim that the gay and lesbian movement was working to thwart federal attempts to halt the spread of AIDS. They continued, "Some studies suggest that over 90% of active homosexuals have had hepatitis B or other chronic or recurrent viral infections, including genital herpes and cytomegalovirus. Also prevalent among homosexuals are a variety of intestinal parasites, known collectively as the 'gay bowel syndrome,' and hepatitis A, which is spread through ingestion of fecal matter." No wonder, they add, that "AIDS progresses more rapidly among homosexuals than among healthier people." There is a fine line here between gay men as diseased and gay men as disease incarnate, between a sinner and a biohazard. Either way, Rueda and Schwartz urged that gay men be contained before their physical and moral contagion spreads to "healthier people."[63]

Unlike historical fascisms before 1945, the Christian right has not operated in a cultural field in which biological racism is acceptable within mainstream discourse. For this reason Nazi discourses on homosexuality are perhaps a more chilling antecedent to present forms of hatred than its positioning of racial others. These older discourses worked to carve out a space of abjection within the national body for a category of persons whom it contradictorily rendered as both salvageable and irredeemably corrosive; these persons were not quite a race with immutable characteristics yet they required quarantine and elimination all the same. If one is to look for precedents of eliminationist violence that are distinctly relevant to a post–civil rights age, it is to such spaces one must return.

The Rebirth of Queer Antifascism

In 1979, a moment marked by a growing, dynamic gay public sphere and a corresponding backlash from the Christian right, the first major cultural work on the gay Holocaust appeared: Martin Sherman's play *Bent*. The plot follows the main character Max, an out gay man who enjoys the nightlife of Berlin but whose life quickly descends into a nightmare when he is arrested by the Nazis and sent to Dachau. In the play Sherman vividly dramatizes his vision of "bare life" for gay men: the destruction of homosexual culture, a complete atomization that comes from constant surveillance, and the brutalization of any public expression of sexuality. *Bent* was a major production on both sides of the Atlantic. The premiere in London starred Ian McKellen, and its debut on Broadway the next year with Richard Gere in the leading role drew large crowds. It has been perennially restaged ever since, both in small productions on college campuses and in a major Broadway revival in 1989–90; it was also adapted to film in 1997 with Clive Owen playing the role of Max. Aided by Plant's consultation on historical points, Sherman's play introduced many people in its audiences to a history they had little or no knowledge of. Jonathan Ned Katz of the *Advocate,* writing nine years after the play's first production, stressed that it "played the most influential role in notifying the world that homosexuals were among those groups systematically persecuted by the Nazis."[64] *Bent* was followed by a number of gay Holocaust novels by American writers with no direct experience of the event it referenced, including Lannon Reed's *Behold a Pale Horse* (1985) and Robert Reinhart's *Walk the Night* (1994).

Sherman's play appeared in the United States shortly after the broadcast of the television miniseries *Holocaust: The Story of the Family Weiss* (1978). Viewed by an estimated 130 million people but panned by critics, the series is recognized by scholars as a landmark moment in Holocaust consciousness in the United States, one that burned now-familiar tropes of the Jewish Holocaust narrative into the public imagination.[65] Like its novelistic successors, *Bent* relied on this popular awareness, yet, by introducing nonassimilated gay men into the narrative, it disrupted the heteronormative, middle-class family construct around which the television series revolved. At the same time, the play, as a first, was compelled to perform another historical task in order to reframe how its audiences accessed the memory of homosexuality in the Third Reich: it still had to debunk the lingering myth of the gay Nazi. Following Heger's nonfictional narrative, Sherman elected to portray a sexually abusive camp commandant but he offsets this representation by beginning act 1 on the night of the Röhm putsch in 1934. The SS break into Max's apartment and murder a Brownshirt he brought home with him the night before. Plant's collaboration played a decisive educational function here, as his knowledge of the historical facts allowed Sherman to show that although individual homosexuals were present in the ranks of the Nazis, the regime was nonetheless systemically devoted to the elimination of homosexuality.

Bent provided a vital foundation for later cultural work by introducing a historically significant and dimly remembered persecution to the public, reminding audiences that Jews were not the only despised group hunted by the Nazis. Nonetheless, it inscribed gay men into the basic structure of the popularized Jewish Holocaust frame on a number of levels. In both the *Holocaust* series and Sherman's play the concentration camp is the primary and ultimate space defining the subject's relationship to the fascist regime. The ideological and structural forces leading to internment are deemphasized; instead, there is a universal psychologizing of the perpetrator and a thematic emphasis on the individual struggle to survive against powerful odds. Finally, the play avoids anticommunist themes and multi-tiered structures of oppression in favor of a thematic focus of the singularly horrifying oppression of one group. On this later point, *Bent* was criticized for showing gays as occupying a lower position in the camp hierarchy than Jews, a dubious historical claim. Max "earns" a yellow star en route to Dachau by having sex with a dead Jewish girl to prove he is not "bent"; his yellow star allows him to avoid the worst manual labor assignments and abuse, saving his life for a time. Sherman, who is Jewish, mainly intended to make visible a long-neglected aspect of the Nazi regime. But as a critic for *Theater Journal* wrote, this plotline had the unfortunate effect of making audiences "choose sides" between gays and Jews.[66]

The tendency to inscribe gay men into popularized constructions of the Jewish Holocaust is even more pronounced in later, American writers in the gay Holocaust genre. For instance, Reed's novel *Behold a Pale Horse* follows two gay characters, Franz Richter and Van Bertolds, who are thrown into the hell of Dachau, where they mount a heroic effort to survive. Like *Bent*, Reed's book decenters Jews from its account of the camps while retaining the major tropes of the popular Americanized Jewish Holocaust narrative, particularly the avoidance of multilayered oppression in favor of an emphasis on the singularly bad treatment of one group. Reed's main character, Van, is a Jew, and his sexual identity is as suppressed by his coreligionists as it is by the Nazis. Like Max, he tries to avoid wearing the pink triangle in camp and thinks himself fortunate to have been assigned a yellow star. But when other Jewish prisoners discover his homosexuality, they form a mob and beat him mercilessly, rip the star off his uniform, and place a wooden pink triangle around his neck that they created especially for him. Banished from the Jewish community and reduced to a singular identity, Van finds that his newfound, clarified essence is at open war with all other groups. Thus it comes as no surprise when Van's partner Fritz later murders a vicious Jewish inmate who threatens to rape him. Historically, pink triangle prisoners were maligned by others interned in the camps and could by no means count on their solidarity. But the problem here, once again, is the failure to adequately explore the complexities of fascism as a right-wing discourse. Such an analysis would take into account the established structures of oppression fascism relied on to place homosexuals, Jews, and other "contragenics," to borrow Plant's term, outside the nation and inside the realm of *homo sacer*. As a result, *Behold a Pale Horse* is characterized by a liberal multiculturalism that reads the root of Nazism as the rejection of difference and analyzes its horrors through a pop psychology of bigotry, intolerance, and scapegoating. Reed writes that in Nazi Germany "being different was the unforgivable sin" and describes the concentration camp as "Germany's newly found solution to difference, diversity, and uniqueness."[67]

Bent created an enlarged archive through which broader publics could educate themselves about the Nazi persecution of homosexuals at around the same time that the gay and lesbian movement had begun to use antifascist frames against the Christian right. But not until the mid-1980s did the appeal of antifascism truly explode in the movement. AIDS was first reported in the United States in 1981, and over the next few years the federal government's failure to respond to the epidemic was apparent. The Reagan administration neglected its duty to inform a hysterical population about the disease, to adequately fund AIDS research, to provide services for those impacted by HIV, and to include community organizations fighting the epidemic in policymaking decisions. It even went so far as to refuse to spend money allocated by Congress for AIDS research.[68] It did not require uncanny powers of perception to link this neglect to the fact that those disproportionately impacted by the disease were from groups deemed undesirable: gay men, people of color, and intravenous drug users. Robert McFarlane, an executive director of the Gay Men's Health Crisis in its early days, recalled that "for a white man with a graduate degree and a good job who can pass, [discrimination was] not an issue. Never was. Until AIDS really got down to it and you realized they want you to die."[69]

Influential sectors of the public responded to the AIDS crisis not only with negligence, but also with the active demonization of homosexuals, now viewed as vectors of disease. In a syndicated column in March 1986 Buckley proposed, "Everyone detected with AIDS should be tatooed [sic] in the upper forearm, to protect common-needle users, and on the buttocks, to prevent the victimization of other homosexuals." Amidst calls for quarantining and tattooing, the Supreme Court in *Bowers v. Hardwick* (1986) upheld a Georgia sodomy law criminalizing anal and oral sex between consenting adults. In his written opinion Chief Justice Warren Burger stated that homosexuality was "an offense of deeper malignancy" than rape, "the very mention of which is a disgrace to human nature." The *Hardwick* decision confirmed the homophobic attitudes fueling public apathy toward a disease disproportionately affecting gay men and pushed many in the gay and lesbian community over the edge into militant political action. Within months of the decision, direct-action AIDS groups appeared across the country, the most famous of which was ACT UP, formed in March 1987.[70] A year later ACT UP's founder, Larry Kramer, would write, "I have come reluctantly to believe that genocide is occurring: that we are witnessing—or *not* witnessing—the systematic, planned annihilation of some by others with the avowed purpose of eradicating an undesirable portion of the population."[71]

Out of this context emerged the Silence = Death Project, an art collective formed in 1985 that drew on the memory of fascism to fight what its members rightly viewed as unnecessary mass death. It began as group of six gay artists and activists in New York, all personally impacted by AIDS, who came together for support in gatherings held on the feminist consciousness-raising model.[72] The original six members—Avram Finklestein, Charles Kreloff, Brian Howard, Chris Lione, Oliver Johnston, and Jorge Socarras—soon developed into an art and design collective that would furnish ACT UP with some of its most famous graphics, mostly notably the Silence = Death poster, which, as noted, became the logo of that organization. At the center of the poster, set against a black background, stood a pink triangle with the words "SILENCE = DEATH" emblazoned in a large font toward the bottom. A caption underneath this read, "Why is Reagan silent about AIDS? What is really going on at the Center for Disease Control, the Federal Drug Administration, and the Vatican? Gays and lesbians are not expendable . . . Use your power . . . Vote . . . Boycott . . . Defend Yourselves . . . Turn anger, fear, grief into action." The SILENCE = DEATH poster was a reversal of the earlier strategy of "de-gaying AIDS," in which advocates for AIDS services and research courted support by emphasizing the impact of the disease on all populations. This graphic, with the pink triangle at center and the explicit mention of gays and lesbians beneath, boldly identified one of the groups most affected by the disease.

The artists of the Silence = Death Project, who began working on the poster in late 1985 and finished it in early 1986, wanted a powerful symbol that would speak to people both inside and outside lesbian and gay communities. In the process, they rejected both the lambda icon as too class based and the rainbow flag because they felt it intoned victimhood. They decided on the pink triangle because it was a familiar symbol within the community which, to use Finkelstein's phrasing, would "reconfigure the codes" by which it was read when inverted and properly captioned. At the same time, they felt the pink triangle could serve as a powerful means to educate those outside the community. When asked about the response to Silence = Death by gays and lesbians in New York, Finkelstein remembers that although the poster was not without controversy, he was surprised by its generally positive reception and by the willingness of ACT UP to fully embrace the analogies it proposed. Buckley's call for the tattooing of people with AIDS, he recalls, lent the graphic an immediate topicality. The Silence = Death Project gave the image to ACT UP when it formed in 1987, then folded its own activities into the new organization. ACT UP then distributed the graphic on stickers and buttons, placing it on its press releases, information sheets, and calls to action. The pink triangle was thereby firmly established as one of the signature symbols of gay and lesbian pride.[73]

If the Silence = Death poster eschewed assimilationist strategies by placing the spiral of neglect and criminalization visited on people with AIDS in the context of homophobia, it also educated its audience that homophobia and its consequent rendering of gays and lesbians expendable were silenced facets of the history of Nazism. Members of the Silence = Death Project were quite sensitive to the complexities of accessing Nazism and the Holocaust in the context of the AIDS crisis. "In truth," recalled Finkelstein, "we discussed it often." Finkelstein and Kreloff in particular approached this history not only as gay men but also as Jewish Americans, an identity which also informed their selection of the symbol. To be Jewish, asserted Finkelstein, means that to be silent about an injustice is to be complicit in it. Thus the "Silence" in the graphic's equation was not only a call to action among those facing "Death," but also an indictment of the crime of the indifferent bystander, whose passivity is lethal. Finkelstein affirmed that the collective never attempted to equalize or conflate Hitler and Reagan, Auschwitz and AIDS. Rather, he stressed, the graphic was intended to pose a question about the prevailing response to AIDS, namely, Is this genocide? "As Jews," he stressed, "we should be cued into the subtext of political and social interactions." And the subtext of the discourses on AIDS and homosexuality in the 1980s—the calls for quarantine and tattooing, the apathy to the mass death of gay men, the blunt hatred of the *Hardwick* decision—still invite, in Finkelstein's view, parallels to the history of fascism. Kreloff likewise still fully stands behind the logo and its dark evocations. Referring to the U.S. government of the 1980s, he asserted, "They weren't putting people into camps, but by not doing anything they were letting another Holocaust happen."

Finkelstein and Kreloff were able to discern fascism as a subtext of contemporary social interactions because of their family histories, which connected them directly to the antifascist left of midcentury. Kreloff's mother was a second-generation Russian Jew who went to meetings of the Young Communist League in 1938 and was very aware of the events unfolding in Nazi Germany. Like many leftists of her generation, she adopted a stance against fascism that was so fundamental to her politics that she abandoned communist circles after the signing of the Hitler–Stalin Pact in 1939. She came out as a lesbian in the 1960s and from then on was deeply involved in the women's movement. Because of his mother's early departure from party circles Kreloff jokingly referred to himself as less of a red diaper baby than a "pink diaper baby." Finkelstein, however, does describe himself as a red diaper baby. When pointedly asked about antifascism, he said the term needed no explanation. "I was marinated in it," he replied. Both of his parents were immersed in the world of the midcentury left in New York, and he recalled spending summers at radical camps outside the city. He went on left-wing retreats with this father, who knew Ethel Rosenberg and counted many of the artists in the Works Progress Administration among his friends. His parents and older sister were among those attacked in 1949 in the Peekskill Riots, in which anticommunist, anti-Semitic mobs in Westchester County, New York, descended on those who came to hear Robeson in concert.[74] Kreloff's and Finkelstein's life histories illustrate that as late as the 1980s, and beyond, some cultural producers gleaned antifascism not merely from its residual traces in popular culture but also from personal family histories which gave the political struggles of the Depression and the Second World War a palpable immediacy.

The acceptance of the pink triangle observed by Finkelstein was reflected in the gay and lesbian press across the country. From the mid-1980s through the early 1990s it is not difficult to find warnings of rising American fascism alongside reminders of Nazi persecution in major LGBT periodicals, including the *New York Native, Windy City Times,* and even the *Advocate* (Los Angeles). At this time a number of novels by gay authors appeared offering what-if scenarios in which Christian fundamentalists take over the United States, including Marty Rubin's *The Boiled Frog Syndrome* (1987) and Geoff Martin's *Gentle Warriors* (1989). These novels were direct literary heirs of Lewis's *It Can't Happen Here*. Rubin's despotic Reverend President Wickerly is an updated Buzz Windrip, his call for a "Christian Nation" guided as much by Cold War anticommunism as by homophobia.

These novels and articles recurrently posited two interrelated social phenomena as signs of incipient fascism: the public response to the AIDS crisis and the rise of the Christian right.[75] While much of this cultural work indicted the complicity of the heterosexual public in general, it identified the political right generally and the Christian right in particular as the fountainhead of antigay fascism. Comparisons between the social positions of gays and Jews were legion in this public sphere, and not all instances partook of the critical antifascist strand I have identified. But in locating fascism on the political right, the majority of these writers, like Hay a generation before, not only lent the concept a degree of political specificity but also used it to situate homophobia within a wider range of social injustices. Many writers in the *New York Native*, for instance, identified a particular brand of nationalism as the key feature of the protofascist right and conceived of nationalism as a way to map the right's various exclusions within a coherent conceptual scheme. Miles Michael, for example, wrote in 1986, "The word 'fascism' comes from the Latin *fascis*, meaning bundle—and a belligerent ethnocentrism which manifests as super-patriotism is probably the hallmark of this social disease." Such ethnocentric patriotism, he continued, is premised on a "denial of basic human equality" which "leads directly to a belief in an elite." Using this notion of right-wing nationalism as his guide, Michael could begin to chart why the same rightists who targeted people with AIDS supported the apartheid policies of the Pieter Botha regime in South Africa and asserted the supremacy of men over women. Michael's views were directly in line with those of the Italian political scientist Norberto Bobbio, who argued that right-wing epistemology is premised on "a vertical or inegalitarian perception of society."[76]

In announcing that "the Religious Right is spearheading the rise of American fascism," Michael echoed much of the antifascist reportage, which was devoted to exposing the far-right organizations and individuals responsible for directing antigay initiatives and stoking violent homophobic sentiments. Most dramatic was a cover story in the relatively mainstream magazine the *Advocate* titled "The Rise of Fascism in America," published in 1992. The magazine's cover displayed a giant swastika set against a black background. The author, John Gallagher, detailed a ballot initiative proposed by the Oregon Citizens Alliance (OCA) which would amend the state constitution to declare homosexuality abnormal and explicitly forbid lawmakers to protect gays and lesbians from discrimination. The author charged the OCA, "a right-wing group" that "receives much of its support from fundamentalist and evangelical churches," with fueling a general climate of hatred and fear leading to a statewide increase in antigay violence, including murder. Gallagher reported that gays and lesbians in Oregon "have heard their sexual orientation linked to pedophilia, bestiality, and necrophilia," adding that "this kind of talk has now moved from the fringe to mainstream political debate."[77] Gallagher's comment on the fringe and the mainstream underscores an analytic tendency within this coverage. In exposing the rhetoric and actions of far-right groups like the OCA, it did not generally depict violent antigay sentiment as being marginal or "un-American" phenomena. Rather, it showed how the fascist organizations and individuals behind homophobia's most dangerous manifestations were helping to produce mainstream discourse and how they, in turn, were produced by it.

The most insightful literary instance of pink triangle antifascism, however, is Tony Kushner's first drama, *A Bright Room Called Day* (1985). Its self-reflexive commentary on the entire antifascist tradition serves as a fitting conclusion to this book. Overlooked by scholars, panned by many critics, yet popular with audiences, the play depicts the precarious lives of seven left-wing artists in Berlin from the final days of the Weimar Republic into the first year of the Nazi regime. Their stories are broken by a series of present-day "Interruptions" in which a young Jewish American woman, Zillah Katz, comments on dark trends in contemporary American politics, fully aware that her warnings of a reemergent fascism sound paranoid to others. The play's juxtaposition of German past and American present works to create its self-conscious reflection on the history of antifascism, didactically highlighting the complex humanity of those opposed to Hitler while arguing for the continued relevance of antifascist frames. Its form is a nod to this political tradition as well. Kushner, a Marxist, modeled his drama after Brecht's *Fear and Misery of the Third Reich* (1938). Like Brecht's, Kushner's action is broken into a series of short vignettes, its staging is a rejection of realist set design, and its didacticism is direct. Slides projected at the end of each scene, for instance, educated the audience on the historical contexts behind the dialogue. Kushner's play was first presented in a workshop production by Heat and Light Co., Inc., in New York in 1985 and premiered in San Francisco at the Eureka Theater in October 1987. Its production coincided with the creation of the Silence = Death poster, the exhibition of *Let the Record Show . . .*, the publication of Plant's *The Men with the Pink Triangle,* and the formation of ACT UP. This simultaneity speaks not only to the appeal of queer antifascism in the second half of the 1980s but also to the need for a cultural work which could dramaturgically elaborate its vitality.

A Bright Room Called Day gleans much of its political power from being set in 1932–33, before the concentration camps, which enables Kushner to fully explore the politics of complicity, enablement, and resistance. Almost all of its characters are antifascist artists and activists; they are Jewish and Gentile, gay and nongay, working class and middle class, all tied in some way or another to the political left. In Kushner's Berlin plot most of the activist characters are involved with the KPD, but one of them, Baz, is a gay man who works with Hirschfeld's WHK.

The playwright avoids melodramatic characterization: none of his creations come to embody virtue or moral failing, insight or myopia. For instance, the communist Annabella Gotchling endorses the exclusions of the KPD when she tells the homosexual Baz, "You are the victim of a mental illness that deflects admirable energy into bad romantic posturing." Yet her proletarian indefatigability later in the play approaches the heroic, as she continues, at great mortal risk to herself, to agitate against the Nazi regime amidst the paralyzing fear of the other characters. Baz, meanwhile, rightly criticizes the inadequacy of economic rubrics in gauging the appeal of fascism and correctly predicts that the Nazis will become popular with the German masses after they take power. Moreover, his all-too-human mixture of mortal terror, gallows humor, and laudable endurance when faced with possible internment make him ripe for audience identification. One comes to suspect, however, that there is some merit to the other characters' rejection of his psychoanalytic interpretations of current events. And he too succumbs to the notions of historical inevitability characteristic of the Social Democrats and rejected by Kushner: he calls for a "Meteorology of History" that would allow one to predict the cycles of history and become active or silent in the appropriate "season." Such complexly drawn characters highlight the political and strategic failings of the German antifascist coalitions of the Weimar period, while at the same time avoiding antiradical cliques that sketch political activists as rigid and undynamic, the more genuine of them inevitably passing from zeal to disillusionment. Much as in Brecht's "alienation effect," Kushner's characters engender a degree of critical distance in audiences but possess enough humanity to trigger a real investment in their struggles.[78]

The Interruptions of the contemporary character Zillah work to make the play a meta-commentary on the history of antifascism. Zillah is connected to the Berlin characters through her research, which uncovers an old photograph of a crowd at a Nazi rally in which only one woman has not raised her arm in salute (we later discover that this is the character Agnes). The photograph becomes the means through which Zillah acts like Walter Benjamin's historical materialist, seizing an image at a moment of danger and blasting it out of the lifeless past of bourgeois historiography into the time of the now. Kushner read and was heavily influenced by Benjamin, and one sees this influence in his rendering of Zillah, the bearer of "messianic" time in the play. In Kushner's prologue for the New York Shakespeare production of *A Bright Room Called Day,* she looks at the old photograph of Agnes, imaginatively conjuring the dead: "Time now to remember, to re-call: / dismantle the memorial, disinter / the dead: / To call into the Now / other people, not my own; / an other city, not my own, an other people, not mine. / History. As I Conjure it / From out of too many nights spent / reading and dreaming / . . . I find / one lonely / familiar / other face . . . / Now."[79] Zillah feels the urgency of "conjur[ing]" this history because of what she sees unfolding in the United States: the conservative shift to Reaganism, the preventable mass deaths of the AIDS crisis, and the rise of the Christian right.

Perhaps the most instructive part of the play is Zillah's cognizance of the "paranoia" implicit in "crying fascism." Kushner uses this aspect of her character to comment on the contemporary status of the antifascist tradition in the United States. She is well aware that antifascism has a paranoid streak and that it verges at all times on hyperbole, but she urges its use all the same. In the Third Interruption, titled "German Lessons," she states,

> Overstatement is your friend: use it. Take Evil: The problem is that we have this event—Germany, Hitler, the Holocaust—which we have made into THE standard of absolute Evil—well and good, as standards of Evil go, it's not bad—but then everyone gets frantic as soon as you try to use the standard, *nothing* compares, *nothing* resembles—and the standard becomes unusable and *nothing* qualifies as Evil with a capital E. I mean how much of a Nazi do you have to be to qualify for membership? Is a twenty-five-percent Nazi a Nazi or not? . . . I mean just because a certain ex-actor-turned-President who shall go nameless sat *idly* by and watched tens of thousands die of a plague and he couldn't even bother to say he felt *bad* about it, much less try to *help,* does this mean he merits comparison to a certain fascist-dictator anti-Semitic mass murdering psychopath who shall also remain nameless? Of COURSE NOT! I mean I ask you—how come the only people who ever say 'Evil' anymore are southern cracker televangelists with radioactive blue eyeshadow? None of these bastards *look* like Hitler, they never will, not exactly, but I say as long as they look like they're playing in Mr. Hitler's Neighborhood we got no reason to relax.[80]

Like the Berlin characters, Zillah is flawed. She has a tendency to become mired in the tangential, as in the Sixth Interruption, when she observes that the names Ronald Reagan and Adolph Hitler share the same number of letters. But this flaw makes her character's didactic function even stronger. In his published commentary on the play Kushner embraced the analogy between the Reagan revolution and the ascendancy of the Nazis and, like his proxy Zillah, was fully aware that critics labeled such parallels paranoid or immature. But he defended the "f"-word in a way that acknowledged its tendency toward semantic inflation, stating, "I am sometimes embarrassed by Left hyperbolism, even if I recognize the fundamental truth behind it." He added, "The differences between progressive and reactionary politics are differences of life and death. When faced with a choice between the two, one must respond decisively, with passion. Better to be a Zillah than an Agnes."[81]

Thus through the character Zillah, Kushner implies that cultural producers and ordinary individuals who call fascism are never without their analytical flaws and rhetorical excesses. Yet their excesses can be productive, partly because there is often a core of truth in the parallels they draw, a truth which they sense but cannot always fully articulate. The very openness to admitting the possibility of such darkness—manifest in the present—gives one the moral agency that is a prerequisite of taking effective political action. Kushner suggests, moreover, that this has always been the case, for the analytical caution of fascism's opponents in the 1930s obscured the mortal danger presented by the Nazis themselves. Within the main, Berlin plot, for example, the devil appears in the form of Herr Swetts, a "distinguished" Aryan who states that the very inability to recognize evil is a distinctly twentieth-century phenomenon, one that allows it to flourish: "And in this century, still new, / when questions of form / are so hotly contested, / my new form seems to be / no form at all. / I am simply unbelievable. Nonobjective. / Nonexistent. Displaced. / Stateless. A refugee. / . . . I have at last attained / invisibility."[82]

For Kushner, as for other antifascists dating back to the 1930s, dispelling the devil's formlessness and giving him concrete shape required abandoning the belief in teleology, that is, the passive notion that progress automatically unfolds with the passage of time toward a utopian end of history. While Kushner draws on Brecht's dramaturgical means of presenting history—philosophical dialogue among representative historical agents, overt didacticism through slides and placards, the alienation effect—Benjamin's anti-teleological sense of time informs the message of the play. The rise of Hitler challenges all the characters' belief in progress, and the one figure who maintains this belief uncritically is shown to be delusional. Only Traum, whose name means "dream" in German, holds fast to his view of stagism and historical necessity: unable to incorporate fascism's reversion to barbarism into his temporal scheme, he effectively ignores it. Kushner, like Benjamin and other critics of the SPD in the 1930s, thereby presents the faith in automatic progress as enabling a passivity verging on fetishism, for one does not have to act when assured that history will ultimately right itself, nor can one recognize evil when guided by a sense of ever-forward movement. Teleology, moreover, engenders a kind of second death for those who have been lost, for it carries the assumption that their tragedies have all been spent in the forward march of history. In place of this temporality, the play makes overt allusions to Benjamin to present the history of antifascism as a living, unredeemed presence holding great emancipatory force for those attentive enough to unlock it (Finkelstein also expressed the need for an alertness to the living presence of history when he asserted, "We should be cued into the subtexts of social and political interactions").

Yet for the playwright, the void created by the abandonment of teleology can create a political and existential paralysis as great as a naïve faith in progress. The character Husz is a cautionary tale here: he abandons all faith in the future, leading him to defeatism and politically immobility. This dread is given fuller poetic expression in the words of Agnes, who refused to flee the country and has forsaken political action. She takes on the voice of Benjamin's "Angel of History" when she laments, "I fear the wind / Will make me stray / Much farther than / I want to stray / Far from home / Bright room called day." Kushner, who believes that history has progressed in some respects, uses the tragic beauty of the Angel of History while critiquing the stance it embodies, as it leaves one with an immobilizing, even maudlin, view of history. For him, it is not *the* dialectical image.

So what is the way out? As in his masterwork *Angels in America,* in which the character Prior rejects the dreary words of the Angel at the end, Kushner reveals his belief that history can and does bring gains. The playwright is aware of the dangers of Enlightenment teleology but wants to maintain a concept of progress independent of its contours—one that can accommodate unnecessary human loss and suffering, is contingent on the motor of collective human agency, recognizes how this agency has left humankind in a better place, and can actively seize upon the sense of danger offered by a notion of time which holds no guarantees for the future. Such temporality would combine the hardened optimism of the tireless character Goschling, who avers, "We progress. But at great cost," with Zillah's militant alertness, grounded in the urgency that comes from seeing history as an unredeemed ruin.[83] *A Bright Room Called Day* hints, moreover, that the historical lessons of antifascism can impart this enabling temporality precisely because it has survived, and even emerged victorious, in encounters with the devil himself.

As the twenty-first-century examples of Chris Hedges, Philip Roth, and Michelle Goldberg illustrate, American cultural producers have perennially returned to antifascism to alert others to the uncanny subtexts beneath the surface of American politics and culture. And some of those in the 1980s who tried, like Benjamin, to seize images of the past at a moment of danger still find the present moment perilous. When Charles Kreloff was asked in 2012 whether he still saw fascism as a trend in American life, he replied, "This history of fascism, I think we're still living in it." In the spirit of the 1930s he added that capitalism always carries the danger of fascism: "That's where it wants to go, as far as I can see."[84] But the queer antifascisms of the 1980s and early 1990s marked the last point in American history in which this discourse was used in a sustained, concentrated manner by a left-oriented social movement. The fading of the Depression and the Second World War from living memory have made the cues of that era ever more abstract, even as they are obsessively referenced. But one would do well to remember the assertion of the Oxford University historian Roger Griffin, who wrote, "As a *political ideology* capable of spawning new movements [fascism] should be treated as a permanent feature of modern political culture."[85] Following Kushner, one might say that the devil which is displaced, formless, nonexistent, and invisible is the most dangerous of all.

EPILOGUE
Antifascism in Strip Mall America

In April 2009 the U.S. Department of Homeland Security released a report titled *Rightwing Extremism: Current Economic and Political Climate Fueling Resurgence in Radicalization and Recruitment.* Though it did not use the word *fascism*, it unwittingly drew from eighty years of transnational antifascist cultural work to describe a pressing terrorist threat within the United States. Like so many individuals covered in the preceding chapters, its authors identified a dangerous domestic "right-wing extremism" that was fueled by high unemployment, hounded by a feeling of national humiliation, and held together by an admixture of militarism, racism, and xenophobia. Homeland Security consulted German expertise in dealing with right-wing extremism, citing a recent German study that linked the long-term unemployment of parents to the creation of "xenophobia and antidemocratic ideals" in their children. The most pressing threat highlighted by the Homeland Security report was the recruitment of military veterans by extremists, as they possessed highly valued combat and weapons training. It concluded that the current social environment is similar to that of the 1990s, when there was a rise in "domestic rightwing terrorist and extremist groups and an increase in violent acts targeting government facilities, law enforcement officers, banks, and infrastructure sectors."[1] Though its assessment of domestic terrorism was essentially correct, the report generated immediate outrage from the political right, which saw it as a slander against veterans and a pretext for government surveillance of their activities. Homeland Security Secretary Janet Napolitano was compelled to apologize to veterans and personally met with the American Legion commander, David Rehbein, who, in a letter to Napolitano, had protested the department's use of Timothy McVeigh, the bomber of a federal building in Oklahoma City in 1995, "as an example of the stereotypical disgruntled military veteran."[2]

The Homeland Security report underscored a real and palpable danger. According to data available from the Southern Poverty Law Center (SPLC), right-wing extremists have perpetrated a major crime somewhere in the United States persistently since 1995, including plots to bomb government buildings, schemes to assassinate political leaders, and the murder or beating of police officers, people of color, and gay men and women. Kathleen Belew's recent work provides empirical evidence that alienated and marginalized combat veterans have tragically proven ripe recruits for rightist militias and hate groups.[3] Avedis Derounian attempted to warn the public of this fact as early as 1946. In the parts of Europe where an explicitly antifascist movement is still visible, there is at least a public discussion on the street-level violence carried out by politicized skinheads and hooligans. But the furor over the Homeland Security report reveals that in the United States, with its increasingly mainstream far right and no mass movement on the left, the pressing subject of domestic political violence cannot cohere into a national debate. When Napolitano apologized to the American Legion, there was no one there to note that the venerable organization began quite literally as a fascist group, one deeply implicated in vigilante violence for the first two decades of its existence.

As an analytic and as a political movement, antifascism is as necessary now as it has ever been. In 2011 the SPLC identified 1,018 hate groups and 1,274 extremist patriot groups across the United States, an alarming rise that it partially credited to the election of the first African American president.[4] There is little danger that the militias, Christian Identity groups, neo-Confederates, and neo-Nazis tracked by the SPLC will establish a dictatorial regime in the United States. But there are far too few organizations like the SPLC, which was founded against the backdrop of anti–civil rights violence, to chart the symbiotic relationship between rightist hate groups and mainstream politics: how the former are generated by established hierarchies, and how the latter sometimes incorporate discourses originating on the fringes. In recent memory, after all, the Republican southern strategy began as a co-optation of the fascism of George Wallace, and the Christian Right's drive for national renewal, fueled by distinctly neofascist elements, was something the Republicans could not afford to ignore.

In the 2010s the Tea Party as a whole is not a fascist movement per se, as it explicitly focuses on economic questions and is sincerely wedded to liberalism's dual system of rights. Yet it does need to explain why actual neofascists are attracted to its coalition—and merely saying that they are opportunistic will not suffice. White nationalists and neo-Nazis like Billy Roper were certainly opportunistic when they helped organize Tea Party events in Arkansas, yet they were not opportunistically drawn to the Democratic Party, Occupy Wall Street, or the American Friends Service Committee. Neither was the Tea Partier Rich Iott, whose bid for the U.S. House of Representatives on the Republican Party ticket was derailed after photos emerged of him reenacting the Second World War dressed as a member of the SS Viking Division.[5] Outright neofascists are attracted by the Tea Party's brand of exclusionary nationalism and share many of its possessive investments; they know that if conditions change, the movement could be a home for politics more fully in line with their ideals.

In the twenty-first century, one factor obscuring the legibility of antifascism in the United States is the widespread adoption of the term *fascism* by the political right. Members of the Tea Party are not the first rightists to use the word, but they are the first to use it as more than a passing smear and to elaborate a history so radically revised as to actually identify fascism as a fundamentally left-wing, even liberal, movement. Conservative cold warriors who conflated fascism and communism generally argued that the programs of the two systems were different but that their methods were the same. On the right, the novelty of Jonah Goldberg's *Liberal Fascism* (2008) is the unprecedented detail with which it develops its central premise that American liberals, not just communists, are fascist to the very core. "Before the war," he writes, "fascism was widely viewed as a progressive social movement with many liberal and left-wing adherents in Europe and the United States."[6] Goldberg's 487-page screed is filled with factual errors and misrepresents its primary and secondary sources, particularly John Diggins, almost to the point of lying.[7] It presents a rather imaginative history in which liberals and leftists never opposed fascism but furthered it in spirit, word, and deed. Goldberg argues that Woodrow Wilson, Franklin Roosevelt, John Kennedy, and Hillary Clinton are fascists by postulating a conveniently broad definition of fascism (in his view, it is more or less any use of the state) and the highly dubious premise that modern liberals and leftists directly descended from turn-of-the-century progressives. In the first years of the Obama administration, Goldberg elaborated his theories on Glenn Beck's television program and right-wing radio, both of which informed Tea Party conflations of the sitting president and Hitler.

Ironically, twenty-first-century rightist uses of fascism draw on analyses popularized by liberals and the left in the twentieth. Goldberg, for instance, sees Nazism as a combination of militarism, nationalism, autocracy, and racial hatred, though his sporadic use of footnotes makes it difficult to pinpoint where he gleaned this interpretation.[8] Underlying almost all current right-wing comparisons between Obama and Hitler is the sense that Nazism is fundamentally about race, a notion antifascists labored to burn into the minds of Americans from the 1930s through the 1960s. Stoked by a narrative of reverse racism, some on the political right arguably invoke Hitler because they feel racially marginalized by the Obama administration. The Tea Party's cries of fascism are not likely to convince many outside their ranks that the Democratic Party is the literal heir to the NSDAP. But such cries, combined with earlier hyperbole from the left, have worked to trivialize the term, further blurring its place in contemporary politics.

The fundamental novelty of recent rightist meldings of Hitler and Obama is their place in the cultural field: they are heard more loudly because left-wing antifascism has diminished in volume as the social movements that produced and sustained it recede from memory. As those who came of age in the thirties and forties pass on, and as the period becomes ever more remote from a vantage point of strip mall landscapes and an irony-driven consumer culture, it is more and more difficult to prevent fascism from becoming anything one wants it to be. The mass movements necessary for creating and maintaining an oppositional, anti-exceptionalist memory of the Second World War have been interrupted, and this presents incalculable challenges to the antifascist tradition outlined in this book. Yet the legacies of these movements have not vanished from the historical stage. Chris Hedges's *American Fascists* (2007), Michelle Goldberg's *Kingdom Coming* (2007), Philip Roth's *The Plot Against America* (2004), the film adaptation of *V for Vendetta* (2005), and Greg Pak and Mirko Colak's graphic novel *Red Skull Incarnate* (2012) point toward a possible future for antifascist cultural production in the twenty-first century. The new century unfortunately demonstrates a continuing need for antifascist voices. To hear and make sense of these voices, Americans must recognize their formidable antifascist tradition and begin calling it by name.

NOTES

Introduction

1. Connie Bradley, "Socialist? Better than a Fascist," *Chicago Sun Times,* October 27, 2008; Manos Angelakis, "Letter to the Editor," *The Record* (Bergen County, N.J.), November 19, 2008; Lon Speer, "Letter to the Editor," *Houston Chronicle,* September 5 2008; Harriet Dolin, "Why Sarah Palin Scares Me," *Augusta Chronicle,* September 17, 2008; Bruce Smith, "Take Back America? From Whom?" *San Antonio Express-News,* May 20, 2010. For a more elaborate liberal example, see Frank Schaeffer, "Sarah Palin: America's Lipstick Fascist," *Huffington Post,* September 5, 2008.

2. Thomas Butera, "The Road to Fascism," *Pittsburgh Post-Gazette,* September 23, 2008; Jeffrey Feldman, "Palin Rallies Ignite Widespread Talk of 'Fascism,'" *Huffington Post,* October 10, 2008.

3. Westbrook Pegler, *George Spelvin and Fireside Chats* (New York: Scribner and Sons, 1942), 3, 6, 58–61.

4. Arnold Forster and Benjamin Epstein, *Danger on the Right* (New York: Random House, 1964), 30–33.

5. Robert F. Kennedy Jr, "Governor Palin's Reading List," *Huffington Post,* September 15, 2008.

6. Palin's speech introduced the Pegler quote by saying that a writer once praised Harry Truman for using those words. Buchanan's memoir includes the same quote verbatim and also uses it to show that Pegler once admired Truman for his rural virtue. Pat Buchanan, *Right from the Beginning* (Boston: Little, Brown, 1988), 30–32. On Franco, see ibid., 97–99.

7. Sinclair Lewis, *It Can't Happen Here* (New York: New American Library, 2005), 70, 72, 162.

8. The argument of this book has been greatly aided by the use of electronic databases containing the searchable text of major newspapers and periodicals across the twentieth century. Using these sources, I found that from 1945 into the 1990s the words *fascist, fascism, Nazi,* and *Hitler,* as applied to U.S. politics and society, were overwhelmingly used by those on the left or by those on the right defending themselves against the charge.

9. William Buckley, "Riots Pose Dilemma for Conservatives," *Boston Globe,* April 19, 1968; Rowland Evans and Robert Novak, "West Germans Have Own George Wallace," *Boston Globe,* August 25, 1969. Reagan exclaimed to the convention, "Go back a few years to the origin of the terms and see where left or right would take us if we continued far enough in either direction. Stalin. Hitler. One would take us to Communist totalitarianism; the other to the totalitarianism of Hitler."

10. For the most explicit connections, see Daniel Bell, "The Dispossessed" (1962), 44–45, and "Intellectuals and the Discontented Classes" (1955), 134, both in Daniel Bell, ed., *The Radical Right* (Garden City: Anchor Books, 1964); Seymour Martin Lipset, *Political Man: The Social Bases of Politics* (Baltimore: Johns Hopkins University Press, 1981), 170–73.

11. While the Persian Gulf War was quite popular with the public, it was not because of George H. W. Bush's analogies between Hussein and Hitler, which brought him a great deal of criticism. In his memoirs, Bush wrote, "I caught hell on this comparison of Saddam to Hitler, with critics accusing me of personalizing the crisis, but I still feel it was an appropriate one." George Bush and Brent Scowcroft, *A World Transformed* (New York: Alfred Knopf, 1998), 375.

12. Henry Wallace, "Wallace Defines 'American Fascism,'" *NYT,* April 9, 1944.

13. Raymond Williams, *Marxism and Literature* (Oxford: Oxford University Press), 132.

14. These include Kirsten Fermaglich, *American Dreams and Nazi Nightmares: Early Holocaust Consciousness and Liberal America, 1957–1965* (Lebanon, N.H.: Brandeis University Press, 2006); Alan Mintz, *Popular Culture and the Shaping of Holocaust Memory in America* (Seattle: University of Washington Press, 2001); Jeffrey Shandler, *While America Watches: Televising the Holocaust* (Oxford: Oxford University Press, 1999); Peter Novick, *The Holocaust in American Life* (Boston: Houghton Mifflin, 1999); and Hilene Flanzbaum, ed., *The Americanization of the Holocaust* (Baltimore: Johns Hopkins University Press, 1999).

15. I allude here to the work of Benjamin Balthaser, Lizbeth Cohen, Michael Denning, Barbara Foley, Cheryl Higashida, Robin D. G. Kelley, Aaron Lecklider, Robbie Lieberman, William Maxwell, Julia Mickenberg, Bill Mullen, Paula Rabinowitz, Rachel Rubin, James Smethurst, Judy Smith, Alan Wald, and Kate Weigand.

16. Conservatives in the 1930s sometimes painted Franklin D. Roosevelt as a dictator, akin to Mussolini or Stalin, and during the Cold War there was a sustained attempt by figures ranging from J. Edgar Hoover to Arthur Schlesinger Jr. to conflate fascism and communism under the headings of totalitarianism or Red fascism. Yet even in the discourse of totalitarianism, the argument was usually that they shared the same methods yet their programs were different. Thus their respective status as left and right movements was preserved even within this formulation. Only with the publication of Jonah Goldberg's *Liberal Fascism* (2008) has the American right tried to revise history so radically as to actually claim that fascism was a left-wing, even liberal, movement.

17. Walter Benjamin, "Theses on the Philosophy of History," in *Illuminations: Essays and Reflections,* trans. Harry Zohn, ed. Hannah Arendt (New York: Schocken Books, 1968), 255.

1. European Precedents, American Echoes

1. Ernest Mandel, Introduction to Leon Trotsky, *The Struggle against Fascism in Germany* (New York: Pathfinder, 2013), 9.

2. Roger Griffin, *The Nature of Fascism* (London: Routledge, 1993), 8.

3. Trotsky, *The Struggle against Fascism,* 576–80. See also Otto Bauer, "Contradictions and Perspectives of Fascism," *ASQ* (September–October 1939): 21–23. Trotsky stressed that fascism in power tends to revert to Bonapartism, which positioned his analysis of its class politics more closely to that of the Comintern.

4. My reading of historical fascism is largely informed by major secondary works in the field of fascist studies. These include Stanley Payne, *A History of Fascism, 1914–1945* (Madison: University of Wisconsin Press, 1995); Ernst Nolte, *The Three Faces of Fascism:*

Action Française, Italian Fascism, National Socialism (New York: Holt, Rinehart, and Winston, 1966); Robert Paxton, *The Anatomy of Fascism* (New York: Alfred Knopf, 2004); Roger Griffin, *The Nature of Fascism,* 1993; Ian Kershaw, *Nazi Germany: Problems and Perspectives of Interpretation* (London: Edward Arnold, 1993); and Richard Bessel, ed., *Life in the Third Reich* (Oxford: Oxford University Press, 1987). In addition, I have drawn from a few seminal primary sources of fascist political rhetoric, including the speeches of Joseph Goebbels, assembled in Helmut Heiber, ed., *Goebbels-Reden, Band I: 1932-1939* (Düsseldorf: Droste Verlag, 1971); Adolf Hitler, *Mein Kampf,* trans. Ralph Manheim (Boston: Houghton Mifflin, 1971); and Benito Mussolini, *My Rise and Fall* (New York: De Capo Press, 1998).

5. Paxton, *Anatomy of Fascism,* 130.

6. Geoff Eley, *Forging Democracy: The History of the Left in Europe, 1850-2000* (Oxford: Oxford University Press, 2002), 242; Paxton, *Anatomy of Fascism,* 95-96.

7. Ibid., 5, 10, 102-3.

8. In Germany, Hitler dramatically purged the socialism from National Socialism during the so-called Night of the Long Knives from June 30 to July 2, when he ordered the murder of key *Sturmabteilungen* (SA) or Brownshirt, leaders. The SA was the central Nazi organization before the party's seizure of power, and many of its members still clung to the antibourgeois rhetoric of early Nazism even after Hitler was appointed chancellor in 1933. By 1934 their continued street violence became a political liability for the regime, particularly among conservatives and bourgeois, who craved order. By purging them, Hitler earned further respectability from these quarters and removed any substantive opposition to an alliance with established wealth from within his own party. See Bessel, "Political Violence and the Nazi Seizure of Power," in *Life in the Third Reich,* 10-14.

9. Eley, *Forging Democracy,* 242.

10. Hitler, *Mein Kampf,* 403.

11. Payne, *History of Fascism,* 242.

12. Hitler, *Mein Kampf,* 65.

13. Mark Christian Thompson, *Black Fascisms: African American Literature and Culture between the Wars* (Charlottesville: University of Virginia Press, 2007), 30.

14. Payne, *History of Fascism,* 71-79; Mussolini, *My Rise,* 32-50; Hitler, *Mein Kampf,* 161-69, 187-206.

15. Payne, *History of Fascism,* 90-92; Paxton, *Anatomy of Fascism,* 5.

16. Hitler, *Mein Kampf,* 280. Most historians are quick to point out that fascists cannot be defined by what they say, but by what they do (i.e., the institutions they create and the policies they pursue). But fascism is also an ideology not reducible to its institutional outcome: fascist "words" can be particularly instructive when trying to ascertain the nature of the national identity intended by its bearers.

17. Ibid., 132-35. Thompson synthesizes Theweleit and fascist misogyny in *Black Fascisms,* 30-31.

18. Payne synthesizes this debate in *History of Fascism,* 328-30.

19. Maria Hsia Chang, "'Fascism' and Modern China," *China Quarterly* 79 (1979), 553; Ho Chi Minh, *Ho Chi Minh Selected Writings, 1920-1969* (Honolulu: University Press of the Pacific, 2001), 54, 56, 303; Luis Taruc, *Born of the People: An Autobiography* (New York: International Publishers, 1953), 49; for an official example of "Japanese militarism," see Henry Wallace, *Our Job in the Pacific* (New York: American Institute of Pacific Relations, 1944), 39.

20. Paxton, *Anatomy of Fascism,* 172-73.

21. Griffin, *Nature of Fascism,* xii.

22. Payne, *History of Fascism,* 508, Paxton, *Anatomy of Fascism,* 176-77.

240 *Notes to Pages 18–31*

23. Griffin, *Nature of Fascism*, xii; Payne 511; Paxton, *Anatomy of Fascism*, 188.
24. Payne, *History of Fascism*, 516–17, 520.
25. Paxton, *Anatomy of Fascism*, 174–75, 241.
26. Ibid., 202, 205.
27. Mike Davis, *Late Victorian Holocausts: El Niño Famines and the Making of the Third World* (London: Verso, 2002), 5–7.
28. My notion of liberalism is deeply indebted to Nikhil Pal Singh's definition in *Keywords for American Cultural Studies*, ed. Bruce Burgett and Glenn Hendler (New York: New York University Press, 2007), 140–45.
29. Carl Schmitt, *The Crisis of Parliamentary Democracy* (Cambridge: MIT Press, 1988), 9–16.
30. Aimé Césaire, *Discourse on Colonialism* (New York: Monthly Review Press, 2000), 14.
31. Stefan Kühl, *The Nazi Connection: Eugenics, American Racism, and German National Socialism* (Oxford: Oxford University Press, 1994), 38–39.
32. Griffin, *Nature of Fascism*, 50; Payne, *History of Fascism*, 16. The positions of Sternhell and Lewis are synthesized in Roger Eatwell, "The Rise of Left-Right Terminology," in *The Nature of the Right: American and European Politics since 1789*, ed. Roger Eatwell and Noel O'Sullivan (Boston: Twayne, 1989), 30.
33. Eatwell, "Rise of Left-Right Terminology," 42.
34. Marcel Gauchet, "Right and Left," in *Realms of Memory: Rethinking the French Past*, Volume 1: *Divisions and Conflicts*, ed. Pierre Nora, trans. Arthur Goldhammer (New York: Columbia University Press), 241, 244.
35. Norberto Bobbio, *Left and Right: The Significance of a Political Distinction* (Chicago: University of Chicago Press, 1996), 58–59.
36. This definition of left and right is a reworking and elaboration of the definitions put forth by the cultural historian Marcel Gauchet regarding the French national context; from Bobbio's universal definition of left and right; and from Nikhil Pal Singh's notion of the American left and right. Gauchet, "Right and Left," 266, 277; Bobbio, *Left and Right*, 60–69; and Singh, "Culture/Wars: Recoding Empire in an Age of Democracy," *American Quarterly* 50.3 (1998): 476–77.
37. Avedis Derounian Papers, Drawer D2, folder "Gerald Winrod," and Drawer G2, folder "Christocrats." National Association for Armenian Studies and Research, Belmont, Mass.
38. Michael Denning, *The Cultural Front: The Laboring of American Culture in the Twentieth Century* (London: Verso, 1997), 6.
39. Raymond Williams, *Marxism and Literature* (Oxford: Oxford University Press), 122.
40. Ibid., 124.
41. Walter Benjamin, "Über den Begriff der Geschichte," in *Sprache und Geschichte: Philosophische Essays* (Stuttgart: Philipp Reclam, 1995), 153.
42. Walter Benjamin, "Theses on the Philosophy of History," in *Illuminations: Essays and Reflections*, trans. Harry Zohn, ed. Hannah Arendt (New York: Schocken Books, 1968), 254. Benjamin writes that the historical materialist must "blast a specific era out of the homogenous course of history—blasting a specific life out of the era or a specific work out of the lifework," ibid., 263.

2. From Margin to Mainstream

1. "The War Mongers," *Chicago Daily Tribune*, September 21, 1938.
2. In October 1936 Franco's general Emilio Mola boasted that he had four columns of

soldiers outside the gates of Madrid and a fifth column waiting for his command inside the city. The phrase was taken up by the liberal magazines the *Nation* and the *New Republic* to describe American fascists and became fully cemented in the public lexicon by Ernest Hemingway's play about the Spanish Civil War, *The Fifth Column* (1939). Dwight Bolinger, "Fifth Column Marches On," *American Speech* 19.1 (1944): 47–49.

3. George Gallup, *The Gallup Poll: Public Opinion, 1935–1971* (New York: Random House, 1972), 1:80, 92, 159, 112, 128–29.

4. Michael Denning, *The Cultural Front: The Laboring of American Culture in the Twentieth Century* (London: Verso, 1998), 9.

5. Frank Warren, *An Alternative Vision: The Socialist Party in the 1930's* (Bloomington: Indiana University Press, 1974), 3–4, 22–24, 28–31, 134–43; Paul Buhle, "Socialist Party," *Encyclopedia of the American Left,* 2nd ed., ed. Mari Jo Buhle et al., 767–74.

6. Robert McElvaine, *The Great Depression: America, 1929–1941* (New York: Times Books, 1984), 224–25, 262; Fraser Ottanelli, *The Communist Party of the United States from the Depression to World War II* (New Brunswick: Rutgers University Press, 1991), 47–48.

7. Stanley Payne, *A History of Fascism, 1914–1945* (Madison: University of Wisconsin Press, 1995), 108–10, 115.

8. Forty years ago the historian John Diggins published a book on American reactions to Mussolini that broadly surveyed the political left, right, and center. Entitled *Mussolini and Fascism: The View from America* (Princeton: Princeton University Press, 1972), it has apparently been the last word on the subject. No similar survey of American public opinion on Hitler, Franco, or fascism in general has followed, though there have been productive localized forays in this area. These include Andrew Nakorski, *Hitlerland: American Eyewitnesses to the Nazi Rise of Power* (New York: Simon and Schuster, 2012); and Stephen Norwood, *The Third Reich in the Ivory Tower: Complicity and Conflict on American Campuses* (Cambridge: Cambridge University Press, 2009).

9. Diggins, *Mussolini,* 224–31, 238.

10. Ibid., 144–48, 267; C. R. Hargrove, "Teutonic Discipline Rules Latin Italy," *Wall Street Journal,* March 22, 1927; "Italy: Pumping and Pruning," *Time,* February 20, 1933, 16; "Italy: Confidence," *Time,* April 2, 1934, 16–17.

11. "The Mussolini Plan," *Business Week,* February 15, 1933, 2.

12. Diggins, *Mussolini,* 166.

13. For an example of this view, see "Question of Price," *Wall Street Journal,* September 21, 1935.

14. Diggins, *Mussolini,* 166–68; Payne, *History of Fascism,* 224, 237–38.

15. The mainstream press often covered Nazi atrocities immediately after widely publicized protests by groups in the United States and abroad. For early treatments of Nazi atrocities and anti-Semitism in mainstream American publications, see "A Week's Vignettes of Nazi-Land," *Newsweek,* March 25, 1933, 13; Edmond Taylor, "German Terror? Here Are the Facts," *Chicago Tribune,* March 26, 1933; Ludwig Lore, "The Jews in Fascist Germany," *NR,* April 12, 1933, 236–38; Sidney Fay, "Nazi Treatment of the Jews," *Current History,* June 1933, 295–300; "Nazi Anti-Jew Drive Persists," *Wall Street Journal,* June 5, 1933; Dorothy Thompson and Benjamin Solberg, "Hitler and the American Jew," *Scribner's,* September 1933, 136–40; Robert Bernays, "The Nazis and the Jews," *Contemporary Review,* November 1933, 523–31; Verne Andrews, "Off to a Concentration Camp," *NR,* March 21, 1934, 155–57; "Prisoner of the Nazis," *Reader's Digest,* October 1934, 81–82; "Nazi Intolerance Grows Clearer," *Christian Century,* August 7, 1935, 1004.

16. "This Week," *NR,* April 5, 1933, 198.

17. Anonymous, "Prisoner of the Nazis," *NR,* August 8, 1934, 337–39; reprinted in *Reader's Digest.*

18. C. R. Hargrove, "Says Germany Is Improving," *Wall Street Journal,* February 14, 1934; "Almost Conciliatory," *Wall Street Journal,* May 18, 1933; "Germany: Hitler into Chancellor," *Time,* February 6, 1933, 20; Charles Hargrove, "The Nazi Regime: A Determined Effort," *Barron's,* February 5, 1934, 3; "Hitler Panacea Is Nationalism," *Wall Street Journal,* June 27, 1933.

19. "Storms That Fail to Clear," *Wall Street Journal,* July 18, 1934.

20. Qtd. in Diggins, *Mussolini,* 206.

21. John Spivak, "Who Backs the Black Legion?," *NM,* June 9, 1936, 9; Bruce Minton, "Fred Bass and the Norman Case," *NM,* December 17, 1935, 12–13; Walter Naughton, "Our American Institutions," *American Legion Monthly,* February 1941, 1, 38. For an example of Klan support in *American Legion Monthly,* see Marquis James, "And Then Came Forrest," August 1933, 18–19, 58.

22. John Stuart, "Bernarr Macfadden: From Pornography to Politics," *NM,* May 19, 1936, 8–11.

23. Crown Prince Wilhelm, "The Truth About My Life," *Liberty,* May 13, 1933, 34–38; George Sylvester Viereck, "The Web of the Red Spider," *Liberty,* June 17, 1933, 5–9; Bernarr MacFadden, "Democracy Is Doomed Says Dr. Goebbels," *Liberty,* October 16, 1937, 4; George Bernard Shaw, "Dictators: Let Us Have More of Them," Liberty, September 10, 1938, 6–7. On Viereck's imprisonment, see Tom Reiss, *New Yorker,* "The First Conservative," October 24, 2005.

24. Stuart, "Bernarr Macfadden," 11; Wilhelm, "The Truth About My Life," *Liberty,* April 22, 1933, 30.

25. "Government Regulating Mania," May 20, 1933, 4; "Death for Chronic Incurable Criminals," August 18, 1934, 4; "Defend the Child Labor Amendment," April 10, 1937, 4.

26. Wilhelm, "The Truth About My Life," April 22, 1933, 6. In the same series he wrote, "The boy who can box and swing a bat will have less difficulty in shouldering a musket than the poor pale bookworm bending his curved spine over dusty records" (April 29, 1933, 30); MacFadden, "Democracy Is Doomed."

27. For a few examples, see "Hearst's Hired Men," *NM,* July 23, 1935, 6; "Hearst's New Drive," *NM,* December 31, 1935; "This Week," *NR,* October 23, 1935, 284.

28. Rodney Carlisle, *Hearst and the New Deal: The Progressive as Reactionary* (New York: Garland, 1979), 9, 11–13.

29. Ibid., 82–84.

30. Ibid., 89–90.

31. Donald Warren, *Radio Priest: Charles Coughlin, the Father of Hate Radio* (New York: Free Press, 1996), 43, 111, 201; Payne, *History of Fascism,* 120, 217; Norwood, *Third Reich,* 196.

32. Norwood, *Third Reich,* 196, 208–10, 217–19; H. Rutledge Southworth, "The Catholic Press," *Nation,* December 16, 1939, 675–78.

33. Michael Kazin, *The Populist Persuasion: An American History* (Ithaca: Cornell University Press, 1995), 113–14. On working-class Roosevelt voters among Coughlin listeners, see American Institute of Public Opinion (AIPO), Press Release, January 8–9, 1938, and letter from William Lydgate (AIPO) to Avedis Derounian, May 14, 1940, Avedis Derounian Papers, Drawer G2, folder "Christian Front," National Association for Armenian Studies and Research, Belmont, Mass.

34. Warren, *Radio Priest,* 62–63, 87–94, 188–93; James Wechsler, "The Coughlin Terror," *Nation,* July 22, 1939, 93–96; Christian Front, "My Country"; "Great Pro-American Mass Meeting in Behalf of Free Speech and Americanism," May 24, 1939; "Christian Front Meeting, Tri-Boro Palace, Bronx, NY," May 3, 1939, Avedis Derounian Papers, Drawer G2, folder "Christian Front."

35. Warren, *Radio Priest,* 181–82.

36. Charles Coughlin, "Not Anti-Semitism but Anti-Communism," November 20, 1938; "Popular Front vs. Christian Front," February 21, 1937; "Czechoslovakia Problem," March 26, 1939; "Jews Support Communism," December 11, 1938 (radio addresses), accessed through *Father Coughlin,* CD produced by OTRCAT, Leneka, Kan.

37. "Defender of the Faith," *Social Justice,* July 1, 1940, 6; "Good Means—Bad End," *Social Justice,* July 15, 1940, 7.

38. "National Union for Social Justice, Bylaws," *Social Justice,* March 13, 1936, 7.

39. Warren, *Radio Priest,* 40–42, 60–79; Coughlin, "Rightists Go into Action," January 15, 1939 (radio address), accessed through *Father Coughlin* CD.

40. Coughlin, qtd. in Warren, *Radio Priest,* 113.

41. Coughlin, "Capital Cannot Do without Labor, Nor Labor without Capital," *Social Justice,* September 20, 1937, 2.

42. "Democracy," *Social Justice,* July 1, 1940, 10; "Here Are the Facts of the Spanish War," *Social Justice,* September 13, 1937, 5, 10.

43. Norman Thomas, *Fascism or Socialism?* (London: George Allen and Unwin, 1934), 42; Diggins, *Mussolini,* 213.

44. Diggins, *Mussolini,* 111–27; Marcella Bencivenni, *Italian Immigrant Radical Culture: The Idealism of the Sovversivi in the United States, 1890–1940* (New York: New York University Press, 2011), 29–33.

45. Upton Sinclair, *I, Governor of California, and How I Ended Poverty: A True Story of the Future* (Los Angeles: End Poverty in California, 1933), 20.

46. Joseph Tenenbaum, "Boycott: The People's Weapon against Fascism's Military Machines," *NL,* May 14, 1938, 8; "250,000 Jews Here to Protest Today," *NYT,* March 28, 1933, 4; "Protests: Nazi Anti-Semitic Atrocities Denounced Here," *Newsweek,* April 1, 1933, 5; Moshe Gottlieb, "The Anti-Nazi Boycott Movement in the United States: An Ideological and Sociological Appreciation," *Jewish Social Studies* 35, no. 3/4 (1973): 198–227.

47. Gottlieb, "The Anti-Nazi Boycott Movement," 217–18; "Meeting of the Executive Committee of the JLC," April 9, 1934, JLC Records, Holocaust-era Files, 1934–1947, reel 1, box 1, folder 9; "Report of Work Accomplished and Pending, July 18, 1934," reel 1, box 1, folder 12; *2nd Annual Convention of the Jewish Labor Committee,* October 27, 1935, reel 160; Tamiment Library, New York University.

48. *7½ Million Speak for Peace . . .* (New York: ALPD, 1939), 36, ALPD Papers, box 3, folder "ALPD, 1939"; "Report by Russell Thayer, Acting Executive Secretary," ALPD Papers, box 2, folder "ALPD, 1938," ALPD Papers, Peace Collection, Swarthmore College, Swarthmore, Penn.; Ottanelli, *Communist Party,* 173–74.

49. Ottanelli, *Communist Party,* 174; *Proceedings: Third U.S. Congress against War and Fascism* (New York: ALAWF, 1936), 8; "Emergency Legislation for Peace and Democracy," ALPD Papers, box 1, folder "ALAWF, 1937"; *Call to Action: American Congress for Peace and Democracy,* ALPD Papers, box 3, folder "ALPD, 1939."

50. *Program of the American League Against War and Fascism* (New York: ALAWF, 1933), ALPD Papers, box 1, folder "ALAWF, 1933."

51. James H. Hawkes, "Antimilitarism at State Universities: The Campaign against Compulsory ROTC, 1920–1940," *Wisconsin Magazine of History* 49.1 (1965): 41–54; LeRoy E. Bowman, "In the Public Schools," *Fight!*, April 1937, 8–9; Irving Adler, "Warping Minds for War," *Fight!*, April 1934, 13; "Peace Drive Mapped for Young Children," *NYT*, December 15, 1935, 30.

52. For rejections of the Popular Front and similar coalitions, see Karl Kautsky, "The United Front," *NL*, January 11, 1936, 5, 12; A. J. Muste, "Peace, Anti-Fascism, Stalinism," *New Militant*, August 17, 1935, 3; "Symposium on Important Problems of the Socialist Party," *ASQ* 5.4 (1936): 27–31. The Militants were willing to work with the communists on specific issues or events but refused to enter into any formal coalition.

53. Denning, *Cultural Front*, 6–7.

54. Under the banner of totalitarianism some liberals and socialists also engaged in this conflation, particularly after Stalin's show trials. However, when perusing the pages of periodicals like the *New Leader* and the *New Republic*, one cannot doubt that the contributors saw fascism as a far greater menace to democracy than communism, even after the Hitler–Stalin Pact.

55. Steven Casey, *Cautious Crusade: Franklin D. Roosevelt, American Public Opinion, and the War against Nazi Germany* (Oxford: Oxford University Press, 2001), 5–7; Ottanelli, *Communist Party*, 114; *People's Program for Peace and Democracy* (New York: ALAWF, 1938), ALPD Papers, box 2, folder "ALPD, 1938," 13.

56. For a few examples on the white left, see Otto Bauer, "The Essence of Fascism," *ASQ* 6.10 (1939): 10; Arnold Bartell, "Nazi Economics," *NM*, August 27, 1935, 27.

57. Penny von Eschen, *Race against Empire: Black Americans and Colonialism, 1937–1957* (Ithaca: Cornell University Press, 1997), 33.

58. Gerald Horne, *Race War: White Supremacy and the Japanese Attack on the British Empire* (New York: New York University Press, 2005), 43–59.

59. Robin D. G. Kelley, *Race Rebels: Culture, Politics, and the Black Working Class* (New York: Free Press, 1994), 128.

60. *People's Program*, 1938, 18.

61. ALPD Papers, box 1, folder "ALAWF, 1933."

62. Devere Allen, "Pacifism and its Critics," *ASQ* 5.9 (1937): 25.

63. Cecil Eby, *Comrades and Commissars: The Lincoln Battalion in the Spanish Civil War* (University Park: University of Pennsylvania Press, 2007), 3–5, 9, 13–15; *People's Program*, ALPD Papers, folder "ALPD, 1938"; *Constitution of the Joint Anti-Fascist Refugee Committee*, box 1, folder "Constitution," ALBA Collection, Tamiment Library; Amicus Most, "Men to Spain: The Eugene V. Debs Column," *ASQ* 5.9 (1937): 21–24.

64. ALPD, *People's Program*, 1938, 18.

65. Theodore Draper, "Arms and the People: Resistance or Surrender," *NM*, January 17, 1939, 6–8.

66. Casey, *Cautious Crusade*, 13–15.

67. *Program and Purpose of the ALPD* (New York: ALPD, 1939), ALPD Papers, box 3, folder "ALPD, 1939."

68. A minority on the left opposed even sanctions. At its Cleveland convention in 1936, the Socialist Party, small and decimated by that point, refused to endorse sanctions on the grounds that these were but a new form of imperialist rivalries. "Resolution on War," *ASQ* 5.5 (1936): 16. Perhaps the most significant noninterventionist organization of the left before 1939 was the socialist-pacifist Keep America Out of War Congress, founded in 1938,

with which Norman Thomas was affiliated. See Justus D. Doenecke, "Non-interventionism of the Left: The Keep America Out of the War Congress, 1938–41," *Journal of Contemporary History* 12 (1977): 221–36.

69. Casey, *Cautious Crusade*, 24–25.

70. "Ickes Canceled Talk Laid to Garner's Wrath," *Los Angeles Times*, January 8, 1939; Mary Elizabeth Pidgeon, "Wages," *Fight!*, March 1938, 15.

71. Mark Naison, "Remaking America: Communists and Liberals in the Popular Front," in *New Studies in the Politics and Culture of U.S. Communism*, ed. Michael Brown et al. (New York: Monthly Review Press, 1993), 45.

72. ALPD, *People's Program*, 1938, 18; ALPD, *Program and Purpose*, 1939; ALPD, *7 ½ Million Speak for Peace*, 1939, 39.

73. Chris Vials, "Red Feminists and Methodist Missionaries: Dorothy McConnell and the Other Afterlife of the Popular Front," in *Essays in Honor of Alan Wald*, ed. Paula Rabinowitz (Ann Arbor: Maize Books), in press.

74. Genevieve Tabouis, "Stalin's Ultimate Aims," *NR*, September 29, 1939, 1; for a similar view, see H. N. Brailsford, "The Russian Riddle," *NR*, October 11, 1939, 63–64.

75. Ottanelli, *Communist Party*, 198–99; "Soviet Chills and Fever," *NR*, June 23, 1937, 174; "Communist Imperialism," *NR*, October 11, 1939, 257–58; Louis Fischer, "Soviet Russia Today," *Nation*, January 6, 1940, 7. Ottanelli notes, however, that the majority of communists stuck with the party.

76. Robert Sherwood, *There Shall Be No Night*, in *The Ordeal of a Playwright: Robert E. Sherwood and the Challenge of War*, ed. John Mason Brown (New York: Harper and Row, 1970), 307.

77. "Resolution Concerning the Situation in Finland," December 2, 1939, ALPD Papers, box 3, folder "ALPD Press Releases, 1939."

78. Alice Payne Hackett, *70 Years of Best Sellers: 1895–1965* (New York: R. R. Bowker, 1967), 163–77.

79. For examples of the first position, see John Bodnar, *Blue Collar Hollywood: Liberalism, Democracy, and Working People in American Film* (Baltimore: Johns Hopkins University Press, 2006), 55–86; Larry May, "Making the American Consensus: The Narrative of Conversion and Subversion in World War II Films," in *The War in American Culture: Society and Consciousness during World War II*, ed. Lewis Erenberg and Susan Hirsh (University of Chicago Press, 1996), 71–102. For the second position, see Gary Gerstle, "The Working Class Goes to War," ibid., 105–27 and Nihkil Singh, "Culture/Wars: Recoding Empire in an Age of Democracy," *American Quarterly* 50.3 (1998), 475–81.

80. Gerstle, "The Working Class," 115; Charles Chamberlain, *Victory at Home: Manpower and Race in the American South during World War II* (Athens: University of Georgia Press, 2003), 5–9; Nelson Lichtenstein, "Class Politics and the State during World War II," *International Labor and Working-Class History* (Fall 2000): 264, 268–69.

81. George Lefebvre, *The Coming of the French Revolution*, trans. R. R. Palmer (Princeton: Princeton University Press, 1971), 178; *F.D.R.'s Fireside Chats*, ed. Russell D. Buhite and David W. Levy (Norman: University of Oklahoma Press, 1992), 292–93.

82. Henry Wallace, "The Price of Free World Victory," in *Democracy Reborn*, ed. Russell Lord (New York: Reynal and Hitchcock, 1944), 192, 194; Casey, *Cautious Crusade*, 42. Wallace's speech was dramatically adapted and read by Vincent Price on the radio program *Treasury Star Parade*, episode 79.

83. Casey, *Cautious Crusade*, xxi, 56, 87–94, 97–98. Office of Facts and Figures qtd. on 56.

84. Rolf Wiggershaus, *The Frankfurt School: Its History, Theories, and Political Significance* (Cambridge: MIT Press, 1995), 295, 299, 301, 305; Kellner, introduction to *Technology, War, and Fascism: The Collected Papers of Herbert Marcuse,* ed. Douglas Kellner (London: Routledge, 1998), 1:20–23; Franz Neumann, *Behemoth: The Structure and Practice of National Socialism* (Oxford: Oxford University Press, 1942), 14, 261–63.

85. Allan Winkler, *The Politics of Propaganda: The Office of War Information, 1942-1945* (New Haven: Yale University Press, 1978), 53–63, 84–95; Casey, *Cautious Crusade,* 156–57.

86. Thomas Dougherty, *Projections of War: Hollywood, American Culture, and World War II* (New York: Columbia University Press, 1999), 46; Winkler, *The Politics of Propaganda,* 58–59, 61.

87. Lee White, "What Pearl Harbor Means to Me," April 9, 1942 (radio address), accessed through *What Are We Fighting For?,* CD produced by OTRCAT, Leneka, Kan.

88. Carlos Bulosan, "Freedom from Want," *Saturday Evening Post,* March 6, 1943, 12–13.

89. Implicitly, Singh and Gerstle reject this view.

90. "Assignment USA," *Words at War,* February 22, 1944, accessed through CD, *Words at War,* Volume 1, OTRCAT, Leneka, Kan.

91. Gerstle, "The Working Class," 114.

92. On antiracist social science during the war, see ibid., 114. The works I refer to here are Lillian Smith's *Strange Fruit,* the best-selling work of fiction for 1944, and Richard Wright's *Black Boy,* fourth on the best-seller list nationally the next year, Hackett, *Best Sellers,* 169, 172. For the federal government and black contributions, see Lauren Rebecca Sklaroff, "Constructing G.I. Joe Louis: Cultural Solutions to the 'Negro Problem' during World War II," *Journal of American History* 89.3 (2002): 958–83.

93. Martha Biondi, *To Stand and Fight: The Struggle for Civil Rights in Postwar New York City* (Cambridge: Harvard University Press, 2003), 1; Lichtenstein, "Class Politics," 264.

94. For a few examples, see B. B. Friedland, "My Colored Troops are Fighters," *Pittsburgh Courier,* January 2, 1943; Randy Dixon, "Native Jamaican Flyer Proves Heroic Daredevil for British RAF," *Pittsburgh Courier,* May 8 1943; "U.S. Army Officer Praises Haitian Artillery Units," *Pittsburgh Courier,* May 8, 1943.

95. John R. Williams, "50,000 Hear Wallace," *Pittsburgh Courier,* July 31, 1943, 1, 4.

96. For examples from the *Courier,* see James M. Reid, "1942 In Retrospect Shows Gains Outweigh Losses;" Stanley Roberts, "Executive Orders are Not Getting Results," July 31, 1943; "Hope Lost," May 8, 1943. See also Singh, "Culture/Wars," 482.

97. Lichtenstein, "Class Politics," 264. For a sample of the cautious position, see "War Thoughts on Labor," *NR,* January 25, 1943, 103–4; for the more assertive stance, see George Schuyler, "Views and Reviews," *Pittsburgh Courier,* June 5, 1943; Stanley Roberts, "Poll Finds Race Overwhelmingly Pro-Labor," *Pittsburgh Courier,* July 24, 1943. The *Nation* and the *New Republic* urged more caution on labor than on civil rights.

98. Nihkil Singh, *Black Is a Country: Race and the Unfinished Struggle for Democracy* (Cambridge: Harvard University Press, 2004), 111; Ronald Takaki, *Double V: A Multi-Cultural History of America in World War II* (New York: Back Bay Books, 2000), 22–57; Chester Himes, *If He Hollers Let Him Go* (New York: Thunder's Mouth Press, 2002), 115; Alan Wald, *Trinity of Passion: The Literary Left and the Anti-Fascist Crusade* (Chapel Hill: University of North Carolina Press, 2007), 62–63, 249.

99. Coughlin, "Rightists Go into Action."

3. Beyond Economics, Without Guarantees

1. "Reichstag Fire Trial," *London Times,* September, 12, 1933 (emphasis added).

2. Michael Omi and Howard Winant, *Racial Formation in the United States: From the 1960s to the 1990s,* 2nd ed. (New York: Routledge, 1994), 69.

3. Dorothy Thompson, "Rebellion in Connecticut," *Boston Globe,* December 13, 1937; "Menace of Nazi 'Racism,'" *NYT,* November 21, 1937; "Christians Urged to Aid Reich Exiles," *NYT,* October 22, 1935; "State Church Assailed," *NYT,* June 17, 1935.

4. Bernard Stern, "Nazi Race Theories," *Fight!,* April 1934, 12; John Wexley, "White Supremacy," *Fight!,* April 1934, 7; Harry Ward, "Fascism and Race Hate," *Fight!,* July 1934, 4; Guy Endore, "Haiti and U.S.A. Occupation," *Fight!,* January 1934, 13.

5. *Equality*'s subtitle was "A Monthly Journal to Defend Democratic Rights and Combat Anti-Semitism and Racism."

6. "Thus Spake the Caveman," *NYT,* November 26, 1939.

7. For a few examples, see Larry Ceplair, *Under the Shadow of War: Fascism, Anti-Fascism, and Marxists, 1918–1939* (New York: Columbia University Press, 1987), 4; John Diggins, *Mussolini: The View from America* (Princeton: Princeton University Press, 1972), 219; Roger Eatwell, "Conceptualizing the Right: Marxism's Central Errors," in *The Nature of the Right: American and European Politics and Political Thought since 1789,* ed. Roger Eatwell (Boston: Twayne, 1989), 18–31; Stanley Payne, *A History of Fascism, 1914–1945* (Madison: University of Wisconsin Press, 1995), 127–28. Ian Kershaw summarizes and critiques this tendency among historians in *The Nazi Dictatorship: Problems and Perspectives of Interpretation,* 3rd ed. (London: Edward Arnold, 1993), 43–47.

8. For a few examples, see F. Britten Austin, "Salvaging the Workless," *Saturday Evening Post,* August 11, 1934, 16–17, 76–78; Alzada Comstock, "The Nazis and German Business," *Barron's Financial Weekly,* September 18, 1933, 3; "Germany," *Business Week,* July 7, 1934, 28–29; "Germany: 'National Revolution!,'" *Time,* March 13, 1933, 16–18; Harrison Brown, "Hitler's Age of Heroism," *Contemporary Review,* May 1933, 532–41; Ernst Henri, "Germany Moves toward War," *Living Age,* October 1933, 119–31.

9. C. D. H. Cole, "Fascism and the Socialist Failure," *Current History,* June 1933, 279–86; E. Francis Brown, "The American Road to Fascism," *Current History,* July 1933, 392–98; Calvin B. Hoover, "German Capitalism and the Nazis," *Current History,* August 1933, 533–40.

10. On the elites' enablement of fascism, see Ernst Nolte, *The Three Faces of Fascism: Action Française, Italian Fascism, National Socialism* (New York: Holt, Rinehart, and Winston, 1966) 19; Payne, *A History of Fascism,* 173–74; Robert Paxton, *The Anatomy of Fascism* (New York: Alfred Knopf, 2004), 22, 95–96, 108, 130. On the middle-class base, see Payne, *History of Fascism,* 95, 98, 118, 182; on the intensified exploitation of the working classes, see Payne, *History of Fascism,* 191, 226; Ian Kershaw, "Hitler and the Germans," in *Life in the Third Reich,* ed. Richard Bessel (Oxford: Oxford University Press, 1987), 49–50; Ulrich Herbert, "Good Times, Bad Times: Memories of the Third Reich," in Bessel, *Life in the Third Reich,* 97–110. Payne qualified that the wage reductions of the working classes were partly offset by an increase in fringe benefits, and Kershaw and Herbert qualified that reduced employment helped to offset the losses in Germany.

11. M. David Gould, "What Can We Expect from Hitler?," *Barron's Financial Weekly,* March 27, 1933, 13.

12. "Hitler at the Helm," *Barron's Financial Weekly,* February 6, 1933, 4.

13. Harold Ward, "The Middle Class Today and Tomorrow: Under Fascist Barbarism," *NM,* April 7, 1936, 33.

14. "Lewis Warns Steel Union of Fascist Danger," *CIO News,* December 12, 1937, 3; Stuart Chase, "A New Deal for America, III: The Road of the Fascists," *NR,* July 13, 1932, 225–26; Upton Sinclair, *I, Governor of California, and How I Ended Poverty: A True Story of the Future* (Los Angeles: End Poverty in California, 1933).

15. D. Z. Manuilsky, "On Fascism," in *Marxists in the Face of Fascism: Writings by Marxists on Fascism from the Inter-War Period,* ed. David Beetham (Totowa, N.J.: Barnes and Noble, 1984), 160.

16. Ernst Thälmann, "The Revolutionary Way Out and the K.P.D.," in Beetham, *Marxists in the Face of Fascism,* 163–65.

17. Earl Browder, "Forward in Struggle against Hunger, Fascism, and War!," the *Communist,* February 1934, 145–77.

18. Trotsky's views circulated in the United States in the booklet *Fascism: What It Is and How to Fight It* (New York: Pioneer Publishers, 1944); A. J. Muste, "Peace, Anti-Fascism, Stalinism," *New Militant,* August 17, 1935; "The Death Agony of Capitalism and the Tasks of the Fourth International," in *Trotskyism in the United States: Historical Essays and Reconsiderations,* ed. George Breitman, Paul Le Blanc, and Alan Wald (Atlantic Highlands, N.J.: Humanities Press, 1996), 139–40. Daniel Guerin's *Fascism and Big Business* (New York: Pioneer Publishers, 1939) largely reproduces the puppet master theory, albeit in a sophisticated way, with an excellent analysis of its appeal to the middle classes.

19. Beetham, introduction to *Marxists in the Face of Fascism,* 2–10, 25–39; Dave Renton, *Fascism: Theory and Practice* (London: Pluto Press, 1999), esp. chap. 6.

20. Vincenzo Vacirca, "The Essence of Fascism," *ASQ* 2.2 (1933): 44–45. Michael Denning observes this metaphor in the work of Welles and Hammett, in *The Cultural Front: The Laboring of American Culture in the Twentieth Century* (London: Verso, 1997), 375. It is also the guiding metaphor in Bertolt Brecht's play *The Resistible Rise of Arturo Ui* (1941). For nonliterary examples of the gangster idea, see Theodor Dan, "The German Catastrophe," *ASQ* 3.1 (1934): 29–37; Anonymous, "Kicking Hitler Upstairs," *NR,* May 10, 1933, 358–59; Keith Hutchison, "Ersatz Capitalism," *Nation,* December 30, 1939, 736–37; William E. Bohn, "Industrialists Hit by Nazism They Built," *New Leader,* May 21, 1938, 5.

21. John Spivak, "Germany's Al Capone," *NM,* January 7, 1936, 11.

22. Otto Bauer, "The Fascist Organization of Society," *ASQ* 6.11 (1939): 15–17; Friedrich Pollock, "State Capitalism: Its Possibilities and Limitations," in *The Essential Frankfurt School Reader,* ed. Andrew Arato and Eike Gebhardt (New York: Continuum, 1993), 71–94. Douglas Kellner summarizes this trend within the Frankfurt School in his introduction to Herbert Marcuse, *Technology, War, and Fascism: The Collected Papers of Herbert Marcuse,* ed. Douglas Kellner (London: Routledge, 1998), 1:10–11.

23. Norman Thomas, *Fascism or Socialism? The Choice before Us* (London: George Allen and Unwin, 1934), 43; Thedor Dan, "The German Catastrophe," *ASQ* 3.1 (1934): 29–37; Will Herberg, "Fascism on the American Horizon," *Workers Age,* June 20, 1936.

24. For the most systematic debunking, see Fraser Ottanelli, *The Communist Party of the United States: From the Depression to World War II* (New Brunswick: Rutgers University Press, 1991); and Barbara Foley, *Radical Representations: Politics and Form in U.S. Proletarian Fiction, 1929–1941* (Durham: Duke University Press, 1993), 44–85.

25. Georgi Dimitroff, *Working-Class Unity: Bulwark against Fascism* (New York: Workers Library Publishers, 1935), 13, 23, 77–79.

26. Ibid., 8, 12.

27. Arnold Bartell, "Nazi Economics," *NM,* August 27, 1935, 27; Karl Billinger (Paul W.

Massing), *Hitler Is No Fool* (New York: Modern Age Books, 1939), 89; Samuel Sillen, "Hitler and German Imperialism," *NM,* October 10, 1939, 24.

28. Victor Burtt, "Salvation by Delirium," *NM,* January 21, 1936, 25–26.

29. Mark Naison, "Remaking America: Communists and Liberals in the Popular Front," in *New Studies in the Politics and Culture of U.S. Communism,* ed. Michael E. Brown et al. (New York: Monthly Review Press, 1993), 58–59.

30. "The Negro in American Life," *NM,* July 29, 1941, 2; Franz Boas, "The Myth of Race," *NM,* July 29, 1941, 6.

31. William Gallacher and Earl Browder, *Anti-Semitism: What It Means and How to Combat It* (New York: Workers Library Publishers, 1943). See also Abraham Chapman, *Nazi Penetration in America* (New York: ALPD, 1939).

32. Miriam Allen De Ford, "Silver Shirts," *Fight!,* May 1934, 2, 7; Harry Ward, "Churches and Fascism," *Fight!,* April 1934, 4.

33. Langston Hughes, "Conversation," *Fight!,* October 1936, 21.

34. Dorothy McConnell, *Women, War and Fascism* (New York: ALAWF, 1935).

35. Steven Casey, *Cautious Crusade: Franklin D. Roosevelt, American Public Opinion, and the War against Nazi Germany* (Oxford: Oxford University Press, 2001), 36–37.

36. Henry Wallace, "The Genetic Basis of Democracy" and "The Danger of American Fascism," in *Democracy Reborn,* ed. Russell Lord (New York: Reynal and Hitchcock, 1944), 154, 260–61. Significant extended liberal treatments of fascism referenced here include Edgar Ansel Mowrer, *Germany Puts the Clock Back* (New York: Penguin, 1933); Raymond Gram Swing, *Forerunners of American Fascism* (New York: Julian Messner, 1935); Stuart Chase, *The New Western Front* (New York: Harcourt Brace, 1939); Lewis Mumford, *Men Must Act* (New York: Harcourt Brace, 1939); and William Shirer, *Berlin Diary: The Journal of a Foreign Correspondent, 1934–1941* (New York: Alfred Knopf, 1941).

37. In his review of Shirer's *Berlin Diary,* Samuel Sillen wrote, "He attacks not only the German rulers but the Germans as a people. . . . He speaks of their 'ingrained' militarism and their 'strange soul.' He indicts a whole people." "Mr. Shirer's Secret Diary," *NM,* July 15, 1941, 22.

38. Andrew Nagorski, *Hitlerland: American Eyewitnesses to the Nazi Rise to Power* (New York: Simon and Schuster, 2012), 6, 122; Steve Wick, *The Long Night: William L. Shirer and The Rise and Fall of the Third Reich* (New York: Palgrave Macmillan, 2011), 24, 66.

39. Mowrer, *Germany Puts the Clock Back,* 14, 30, 37–38; Shirer, *Berlin Diary,* 584–86.

40. Mowrer, *Germany Puts the Clock Back,* 22.

41. Will Herberg, "Black Legions of Fascism," *Workers Age,* June 20, 1935; Sinclair Lewis attacked the supposed anti-authoritarianism of the frontier mentality directly in his novel *It Can't Happen Here* (New York: New American Library, 2005), esp. 284–85.

42. W. Randy Dixon, "Aggressive Fighter for the Rights of Colored People throughout the World," *Pittsburgh Courier,* July 31, 1943, 5; Jerome Teelucksingh, "The Immortal Batsman: George Padmore the Revolutionary Writer and Activist," in *George Padmore: Pan-African Revolutionary,* ed. Fitzroy Baptiste et al. (Kingston: Ian Randle, 2009), 2–20.

43. Alan Wald, *American Night: The Literary Left in the Era of the Cold War* (Chapel Hill: University of North Carolina Press, 2012), 151–52.

44. George Padmore, "The Second World War and the Darker Races," *Crisis* 46.11 (1939): 327.

45. George Padmore, "Hitler, Mussolini and Africa," *Crisis* 44.9 (1937): 262.

46. On overall trends in the black press, see Penny Von Eschen, *Race against Empire:*

Black Americans and Anticolonialism, 1937–1957 (Ithaca: Cornell University Press), 33; for Padmore's wartime critique, see "Anglo-American Plan for Control of Colonies," *Crisis* 51.11 (1944): 355–56.

47. Seyla Benhabib, *Critique, Norm, and Utopia: A Study of the Foundations of Critical Theory* (New York: Columbia University Press, 1986), 173.

48. Beetham, introduction to *Marxists in the Face of Fascism,* 41–42.

49. Thomas, *Fascism or Socialism?,* 42; Billinger, *Hitler Is No Fool,* 89.

50. Ernst Toller, "We Are the Plowmen," *NM,* October 27, 1936, 5–6.

4. Resuming the People's War

1. *Congressional Record: Proceedings and Debates of the 83rd Congress, Second Session* 100, no. 6 (Washington, D.C.: U.S. Government Printing Office, 1954), 7389.

2. Qtd. in "McCarthy Cooling-Off Period Seen," *Hartford Courant,* June 14, 1954.

3. Michael Kazin, *The Populist Persuasion: An American History* (Ithaca: Cornell University Press, 1995), 185–86.

4. David Caute, *The Great Fear: The Anti-Communist Purge under Truman and Eisenhower* (New York: Simon and Schuster, 1978), 32; Joel Kovel, *Red Hunting in the Promised Land: Anticommunism and the Making of America* (New York: Basic Books, 1994), 12.

5. Gallup polling from 1950 to 1954 consistently revealed that a larger share of the public had an unfavorable opinion of McCarthy and his methods rather than a favorable one, with a few momentary exceptions (May 1950, June 1953, and March 1954); George Gallup, *The Gallup Poll: Public Opinion, 1935–1971* (New York: Random House, 1972), 2:912, 1003, 1135, 1150, 1154, 1164, 1203, 1220, 1225, 1247.

6. "McCarthy Protests Pour into the *Times,*" *NYT,* October 28, 1952.

7. For a few examples, see Albion Ross, "Fascists Put Off Plans in Germany," *NYT,* December 16, 1954; Blanche Appelton, "McCarthy View from Japan," *NYT,* June 23, 1954; Drew Pearson, "Europe Sees U.S. Going Fascist," *Washington Post,* June 25, 1953; Drew Middleton, "British Compare McCarthy, Hitler," *NYT,* March 5, 1954; William Henry Chamberlin, "Reign of Terror?," *Wall Street Journal,* March 29, 1954.

8. "Dreary Business Ended," *Atlanta Constitution,* reported in *NYT,* "Editorial Excerpts on Condemnation of McCarthy," December 4, 1954; Alson J. Smith, "The McCarthy Falange," *Christian Century,* December 29, 1954, 1580–83.

9. For labor leaders, see "Rieve Issues Warning," *NYT,* June 21, 1953; "Clothing Unionist Assails McCarthy," *NYT,* June 21, 1953; for clergy, see "Donegan Decries McCarthy Tactics," *NYT,* March 1, 1954; Foster Hailey, "A Catholic Bishop Berates McCarthy," *NYT,* April 10, 1954; for Democratic politicians, see "Roosevelt Terms McCarthy 'Phoney,'" *NYT,* April 8, 1954; "Harriman, in Maine, Berates McCarthy," *NYT,* March 27, 1954.

10. Carey McWilliams, *Witch Hunt: The Revival of Heresy* (Boston: Little, Brown, 1950); Cedric Belfrage, *The American Inquisition, 1945–1960* (Indianapolis: Bobbs-Merrill, 1973).

11. For the Salem-Inquisition-HUAC link, see Belfrage, *The American Inquisition;* Brenda Murphy, *Congressional Theatre: Dramatizing McCarthyism on Stage, Film, and Television* (Cambridge: Cambridge University Press, 2003), chaps. 4 and 5. A vast array of literary criticism on Arthur Miller's *The Crucible* also addresses this link and is best synthesized in Susan Haedicke, "Arthur Miller, A Bibliographic Essay," in *The Cambridge Companion to Arthur Miller,* ed. Christopher Bigsby (Cambridge: Cambridge University Press, 1997), 261–62.

12. David Everett, *A Shadow of Red: Communism and the Blacklist in Radio and Television* (Chicago: Ivan Dee, 2007), 317, 321.

13. "Two Debate Issue of McCarthy and His Critics," *Chicago Daily Tribune,* May 12, 1954; William Schamm, prologue to William Buckley Jr. and Brent Bozell, *McCarthy and His Enemies* (Chicago: Henry Regnery, 1954), xii; Committee on Un-American Activities, U.S. House of Representatives, *Preliminary Report on Neo-Fascist and Hate Groups* (Washington, D.C.: Committee on Un-American Activities), December 17, 1954.

14. Arthur Miller's exposure to such talk while working at the Brooklyn Naval Yard during the Second World War was the inspiration for his novel *Focus,* published in late 1945. Arthur Miller, introduction to *Focus* (Syracuse: Syracuse University Press, 1997), v.

15. Lizbeth Cohen, *A Consumers' Republic: The Politics of Mass Consumption in Postwar America* (New York: Alfred Knopf, 2003), 100–109.

16. Michael Denning, *The Cultural Front: The Laboring of American Culture in the Twentieth Century* (London: Verso, 1998), 46. Sherwood and Archibald MacLeish were the two most important figures in formulating the general direction of American wartime propaganda in the early days of the war. Allan Winkler, *The Politics of Propaganda: The Office of War Information, 1942–1945* (New Haven: Yale University Press, 1978), 9.

17. On McCarthy's attack, see *Major Speeches and Debates of Senator Joe McCarthy, Delivered in the United States Senate, 1950–1951* (Washington, D.C.: U.S. Government Printing Office, 1953), 243. The notion that the OWI was riddled with Communists (most famously, Owen Lattimore) was also a recurring theme in the Senators speeches. See ibid., 7, 73–75, 125–33. For the twenty-first-century, right-wing perspective on Sherwood and the OWI, see M. Stanton Evans, *Blacklisted by History: The Untold Story of Joe McCarthy and His Fight against America's Enemies* (New York: Crown Forum, 2007), 87–90.

18. Robert Sherwood, *Roosevelt and Hopkins, an Intimate History,* rev. ed. (New York: Harper and Brothers, 1950), 83, 127–31, 367–68.

19. Elmer Davis, *But We Were Born Free* (Indianapolis: Bobbs-Merrill, 1954), 19–20, 93.

20. Pepper quoted in Bob Blauner, *Resisting McCarthyism: To Sign or Not Sign California's Loyalty Oath* (Stanford: Stanford University Press, 2009), 4.

21. Wright Patman, foreword to *Fascism in Action: A Documented Study and Analysis of Fascism in Europe* (Washington, D.C.: U.S. Government Printing Office, 1947), v, 88, 110.

22. Amartya Sen, *Poverty and Famines: An Essay on Entitlement and Deprivation* (Oxford: Clarendon Press, 1981), 52. Preventable famine is also the means by which Stalin killed the majority of his victims. See *Stalinist Terror: New Perspectives,* ed. Getty Arch and Roberta Manning (Cambridge: Cambridge University Press, 1993).

23. George Gallup, *The Gallup Poll: Public Opinion, 1935–1971,* Volume 1: *1935–1948* (New York: Random House, 1972), 382, 453, 492, 499, 555, 617.

24. Catherine Merridale, *Ivan's War: Life and Death in the Red Army, 1939–1945* (New York: Metropolitan Books, 1996), 337.

25. Ibid., 41–42.

26. Kovel, *Red Hunting in the Promised Land,* 12.

27. Martin Walker, *The Cold War: A History* (New York: Henry Holt, 1993), 31, 38–39.

28. Robert Messenger, "Last of the Whigs: Churchill as Historian," *New Criterion* 25.2 (2006): 22; Alice Payne Hackett, *70 Years of Best Sellers, 1895–1965* (New York: R. R. Bowker, 1967), 36–37, 179.

29. Winston Churchill, *Triumph and Tragedy* (Boston: Houghton Mifflin, 1953), 140.

30. On the enormity of Operation Bagration, see Merridale, *Ivan's War,* 263–98.

31. Winston Churchill, *The Hinge of Fate* (Boston: Houghton Mifflin, 1950), 499, 759–65; Churchill, *Triumph and Tragedy,* chap. 9.

32. *Triumph and Tragedy,* 683.

33. Kovel, *Red Hunting in the Promised Land,* 49.

34. Winston Churchill, *Closing the Ring* (Boston: Houghton Mifflin, 1951), 188–89, 467, 503–5, 535–52; Churchill, *Triumph and Tragedy,* 283–306.

35. Churchill, *Hinge of Fate,* 219, 220.

36. Churchill, *Closing the Ring,* 51.

37. This figure was presented by the Ethiopian government at the Paris Conference of 1946. A. J. Barker, *Civilizing Mission: A History of the Italo-Ethiopian War of 1935–1946* (New York: Dial Press, 1968), 316.

38. N. J. Crowson, *Facing Fascism: The Conservative Party and the European Dictators, 1935–1940* (London: Routledge, 1997), 36, 99, 185.

39. *Major Speeches and Debates of Senator Joe McCarthy,* 212, 226, 235. As a more pragmatic conservative, Churchill did not portray the outcome of the Yalta talks as a betrayal but as a diplomatic and military necessity given the reality of the war. *Triumph and Tragedy,* 402.

40. Robert Paxton, *The Anatomy of Fascism* (New York: Alfred Knopf, 2004), 211.

41. Les Adler and Thomas Paterson, "Red Fascism: The Merger of Nazi Germany and Soviet Russia in the American Image of Totalitarianism: 1930s–1950s," *American Historical Review* 74 (April 1970): 1047–51.

42. Truman quoted in Adler and Paterson, "Red Fascism," 1055; J. Edgar Hoover, "Red Fascism in the United States Today," *American Magazine,* February 1947, 24.

43. Murphy, *Congressional Theatre,* 77.

44. Mickey Spillane, *The Mike Hammer Collection,* Volume 2: *One Lonely Night, The Big Kill, Kiss Me Deadly* (New York: New American Library, 2001), 78.

45. Adler and Patterson, "Red Fascism," 1052–53.

46. Arthur Schlesinger Jr., *The Vital Center: The Politics of Freedom* (London: André Deutsch, 1970), 53; Hannah Arendt, *The Origins of Totalitarianism* (Orlando: Harcourt, 1985), 322.

47. Arendt, however, avoids such crudities, finding the origins of totalitarianism in the deep structures of the West, most important, imperialism. In her prefaces, added in 1967, she noted that while the contemporary USSR remained a one-party dictatorship, Khrushchev effectively "de-totalitarianized" its political system.

48. For a few examples, see Ian Kershaw, *Nazi Germany: Problems and Perspectives of Interpretation* (London: Edward Arnold, 1993), 19–29, 38–39; Paxton, *Anatomy of Fascism,* 212.

49. Paxton, *Anatomy of Fascism,* 212–13.

50. Caute, *The Great Fear,* 253–54.

51. George Kennan, *Memoirs, 1925–1950* (Boston: Little, Brown, 1967), 1:176–77.

52. Christopher Simpson, *Blowback: America's Recruitment of Nazis and Its Effects on the Cold War* (New York: Collier Books, 1988), 68–70.

53. Ibid., 190; Walker, *Cold War,* 92.

54. Simpson, *Blowback,* 4, 8, 19, 25, 40, 46–77.

55. Ibid., 9–10, 207.

56. Ibid., 262–63. Gallup Poll data on Americans' attitudes toward Spain in the late 1940s and early 1950s show a significant minority in opposition to official policy on Franco. *The Gallup Poll,* 2:613–14, 813, 986.

57. Mark Shiel, "Hollywood, the New Left, and FTA," in *"Un-American" Hollywood: Politics and Film in the Blacklist Era,* ed. Frank Krutnik and Steve Neale (New Brunswick: Rutgers University Press, 2007), 210.

58. Everett, *A Shadow of Red;* Murphy, *Congressional Theatre;* Paul Buhle and Dave Wagner, *Hide in Plain Sight: Hollywood Blacklistees in Film and Television, 1950–2002* (New York: Palgrave Macmillan, 2003). For a similar dynamic in academia, see Blauner, *Resisting McCarthy,* 140–41.

59. Everett, *A Shadow of Red,* 192.

60. Ibid., 107–8; Buhle and Wagner, *Hide in Plain Sight,* 4–5.

61. Everett, *A Shadow of Red,* 197.

62. Murphy, *Congressional Theatre,* 2–5.

63. Kazin, *Populist Persuasion,* 165–92. On the wealthy backing for McCarthy and McCarthyism, see Michael Rogin, *The Intellectuals and McCarthy: The Radical Specter* (Cambridge: MIT Press, 1967).

64. Kazin, *Populist Persuasion,* 109–34.

65. Samuel Sillen, "Our Time," *Masses and Mainstream,* December 1951, 1–6.

66. Alan Wald, *American Night: The Literary Left in the Era of the Cold War* (Chapel Hill: University of North Carolina Press, 2012), 3–7, 17–19.

67. For a good contemporary overview of the Marxist debate over McCarthyism, see Art Sharon, "The Opposition to McCarthyism," *Fourth International,* Spring 1954, 39–43. For sophisticated instances of the socialist debate, see Julius Falk, "McCarthy and McCarthyism: The New Look at America's Post War Reaction," *New International,* January–February 1954, 26–38; Murray Weiss, "The Problem of Smashing McCarthyism," *Fourth International,* January 1954, 3–9, and the *Militant* for December 7, 1953.

68. On Derounian's best-seller status, see William Petersen, "The Native Fascist Threat," *Commentary* 3.3 (1947): 294.

69. Unfortunately, Derounian's research in the early 1950s was never published in monograph form. Avedis Derounian Papers, boxes 11 and 23, National Association for Armenian Studies and Research, Belmont, Mass.

70. John Roy Carlson, *The Plotters* (New York: E. P. Dutton, 1946), vii, 244.

71. Ibid., viii–ix, 334–36, 348–49.

72. Avedis Derounian Papers, box 5, Drawer B2, and Drawer C2 (especially the folders "AMVETS" and "American Veterans Committee"). Quote from "Statement on Fascism by the National Planning Committee of the AVC," Quarterly Meeting, New York City, November 9–11, 1946. Founded during the war with much promise, the American Veterans Committee after 1945 was rent by infighting between Cold War and Popular Front liberals and perished within a few years. See Robert Tyler, "The American Veterans Committee: Out of the Hot War and into the Cold," *American Quarterly* 18.3 (1966): 419–36.

73. Avedis Derounian Papers, boxes 17 and 23, especially letter from John Roy Carlson to James Conant, April 7 1953 (box 23), and letter from Carlson to Dr. Kempner, March 8 1952 (box 23).

74. Rolf Wiggershaus, *The Frankfurt School: Its History, Theories, and Political Significance* (Cambridge: MIT Press, 1995), 411.

75. Ibid., 408.

76. Theodor Adorno et al., *The Authoritarian Personality* (New York: Norton, 1982), 22–23.

77. Ibid., 5–6.

78. Ibid., 51, 113.

79. For a discussion of Adorno's writings on pseudoconservatism, see Wiggershaus, *Frankfurt School,* 419–20, quote on 419.

80. Adorno, *The Authoritarian Personality,* 7.

81. Ibid., 155.

82. On *The Authoritarian Personality* and the academy, see William Hixon Jr., *The Search for the American Right Wing: An Analysis of the Social Science Record* (Princeton: Princeton University Press, 1992), xii. For a sampling of positive reviews, see *Christian Century,* April 26, 1950, 532; *New York Herald Tribune,* May 7, 1950; *American Political Science Review* 44 (1950): 1005. In *The New American Right,* the essays by Lipset and Viereck firmly reproduce the totalitarianism conflation.

83. Murphy, *Congressional Theatre,* 20, 24, 60–64.

84. Belfrage, *The American Inquisition,* 65, 151.

85. This was particularly evident in 1947 in the examination of Hans Eisler. See *Thirty Years of Treason: Excerpts from Hearings before the House Committee on Un-American Activities, 1938–1968,* ed. Eric Bentley (New York: Viking Press, 1971), 73–109.

86. Irwin Shaw, *The Troubled Air* (New York: Random House, 1951), 292–93.

87. Bentley, ed., *Thirty Years of Treason,* 259.

88. Ibid., 784.

89. Belfrage, *The American Inquisition,* 253–54.

90. Murphy, *Congressional Theatre,* 5.

91. For a sampling of positive reviews, see *Chicago Sunday Tribune,* October 25, 1953; *Nation,* December 19, 1953, 177; and *NYT,* November 8, 1953.

92. "Conversation with Ray Bradbury," in Ray Bradbury, *Fahrenheit 451* (New York: Ballantine, 2001), 182.

93. In 1952, for instance, he published in the *California Quarterly,* the literary journal for the ailing Hollywood left. Buhle and Wagner, *Hide in Plain Sight,* 75.

94. Paul Lazarsfeld and Robert Merton, "Mass Communication, Popular Taste and Organized Social Action"; Irving Howe, "Notes on Mass Culture"; Theodor Adorno, "Television and the Patterns of Mass Culture," all in *Mass Culture: The Popular Arts in America,* ed. Bernard Rosenberg and David Manning White (Glencoe: Free Press, 1957).

95. Buhle and Wagner, *Hide in Plain Sight,* 426; Steve Neale, "Swashbuckling, Sapphire, and Salt: Un-American Contributions to TV Costume Adventure Series in the 1950s," in *"Un-American" Hollywood,* 198–200.

96. Ibid., 198.

97. The theme of anti-Semitism is most clear in "The Wanderer."

98. Neale, "Swashbuckling," 202.

99. Qtd. in Wald, *Trinity of Passion,* 216. On Miller and the Holocaust, see Joyce Antler, "The Americanization of the Holocaust," *American Theatre* 12.2 (1995): 16–20; Edward Isser, "Arthur Miller and the Holocaust." *Essays in Theatre* 10.2 (1992): 155–64; Lawrence Langer, "The Americanization of the Holocaust on Stage and Screen," in *From Hester Street to Hollywood: The Jewish American Stage and Screen,* ed. Sarah Blacher Cohen (Bloomington: Indiana University Press, 1983), 213–30; Janet Balakian, "The Holocaust, the Depression, and McCarthyism: Miller in the Sixties," in *Cambridge Companion to Arthur Miller,* 115–38.

100. Arthur Miller, "Why I Wrote *The Crucible,*" *New Yorker,* October 21, 1996, 158.

101. In his published commentary on *Incident at Vichy,* for example, he applies its lessons on human agency and indifference to the failure of many to act on behalf of African Ameri-

cans in the United States. Arthur Miller, "Our Guilt for the World's Evil," *NYT Magazine,* January 3, 1965, 10–11, 48.

102. Christopher Bigsby, *Arthur Miller: A Critical Study* (Cambridge: Cambridge University Press, 2005), 145; Christopher Bigsby, *Arthur Miller: 1915–1962* (Cambridge: Harvard University Press, 2009), 116–24, 346, 358, 554; Wald, *Trinity of Passion,* 228.

103. For a few examples, see David Bronson, "*An Enemy of the People:* A Key to Arthur Miller's Art and Ethics," in *Critical Essays on Arthur Miller,* ed. James Martine (Boston: G. K. Hall, 1979), 55–71; Enoch Brater, "Ethics and Ethnicity in the Plays of Arthur Miller," in *From Hester Street to Hollywood,* 123–36.

104. In 1957, for instance, he asserted that McCarthyism was "a political, objective, knowledgeable campaign from the far Right [that] was capable of creating not only a terror, but a new subjective reality." Qtd. in A. P. Foulkes, *Literature and Propaganda* (London: Methuen, 1983), 87.

105. Wald, *Trinity of Passion,* 215.

106. Arthur Miller, *You're Next!,* 6, Arthur Miller Papers, box 63, Harry Ransom Center, University of Texas, Austin.

107. Bigsby, *Arthur Miller, 1915–1962,* 438; Bigsby, *Critical Study,* 149–50.

108. Marion Starkey, *The Devil in Massachusetts: A Modern Inquiry into the Salem Witch Trials* (New York: Alfred Knopf, 1949), ix–x.

109. Arthur Miller, *The Crucible* (New York: Penguin, 1995), 5–6.

110. Ibid., 6.

111. Arthur Miller, "It Could Happen Here—and Did," in *The Theater Essays of Arthur Miller,* ed. Robert Martin and Steve Centola (New York: De Capo, 1996), 298.

112. Miller, *The Crucible,* 11, 40.

5. Brownshirts in the Twilight Zone

1. Arthur Olsen, "Nazi Criminals Still a Problem," *NYT,* January 10, 1960.

2. "Smear Church with Nazi Sign in Ypsilanti: Swastikas Appear in More U.S. Cities," *Chicago Tribune,* January 11, 1960; Sydney Gruson, "Vandalism Ebbs in West Germany," *NYT,* January 15, 1960; Oscar Handlin, "Grown-Up Juvenile Delinquents Wage Anti-Semitic War," *Boston Globe,* January 12, 1960.

3. For examples of this position, see William Henry Chamberlin, "Jews in Germany: Adenauer Moves Swiftly to Run Down the Instigators of Synagogue Desecration," *Wall Street Journal,* January 13, 1960; "Germans Nab Red Leader of Nazi Students," *Chicago Daily Tribune,* January 17, 1960; Roscoe Drummond, "German Leaders Can Be Trusted," *Boston Globe,* January 9, 1960.

4. Speech reprinted in Thomas Dodd, *Freedom and Foreign Policy* (New York: Bookmailer, 1962), 76–80.

5. Curtis Pepper and Robert Massie, "Eichmann on Trial," *Newsweek,* April 17, 1961, 49.

6. Daniel Bell, "The Dispossessed," in *The Radical Right,* ed. Daniel Bell (Garden City: Anchor Books, 1964), 44–45; Seymour Martin Lipset, *Political Man: The Social Bases of Politics,* 1960 (Baltimore: Johns Hopkins University Press, 1981), 169–72.

7. Kirsten Fermaglich, *American Dreams and Nazi Nightmares: Early Holocaust Consciousness and Liberal America* (Waltham, Mass.: Brandeis University Press, 2006), 58–123.

8. Jeffrey Shandler noted this trend in the television dramas of the period in *While America Watches: Televising the Holocaust* (Oxford: Oxford University Press, 1999), 42, 137.

9. Pepper and Massie, "Eichmann on Trial," 41–49; "A Model Prisoner's Regimented Day: How Eichmann Has Spent Months in Jail," *Life,* April 14, 1961, 24–27; Harry Golden, "'A Stranger to the Human Race,'" *Life,* April 21, 1961, 43–46, 51. Pepper and Massie wrote, "As a member of the black-shirted SS elite guards he climbed steadily upward through the ranks, holding fast to his blind belief that *Befehl ist Befehl* (an order is an order)," "Eichmann on Trial," 42.

10. Hannah Arendt, *Eichmann in Jerusalem: A Report on the Banality of Evil* (New York: Penguin, 2006), 48.

11. Marianna Torgovnick, *The War Complex: World War II in Our Time* (Chicago: University of Chicago Press, 2005), 65–66.

12. Fermaglich found this to be particularly true for readers of Stanley Milgram's obedience experiments. See *American Dreams,* 92, 111.

13. Joel Kovel, *Red Hunting in the Promised Land: Anticommunism and the Making of America* (New York: Basic Books, 1994), 9–11.

14. Alan Mintz, *Popular Culture and the Shaping of Holocaust Memory in America* (Seattle: University of Washington Press, 2001), 11–12.

15. Mintz, *Popular Culture,* 11; Fermaglich, *American Dreams,* 9.

16. Manning Marable, *Race, Reform, and Rebellion: The Second Reconstruction in Black America, 1945–2006,* 3rd ed. (Jackson: University Press of Mississippi, 2007), 17–31; Mary Dudziak, *Cold War Civil Rights: Race and the Image of American Democracy* (Princeton: Princeton University Press, 2000), 154.

17. Fermaglich, *American Dreams,* 4–6.

18. T. H. Tetens, *The New Germany and the Old Nazis* (New York: Random House, 1961), 235–43; "We Belong to the West," *Time,* January 4, 1954, 18.

19. Elke Reuter and Detlef Hansel, *Das kurze Leben der VVN von 1947 bis 1953: Die Geschichte der Vereinigung der Verfolgten des Naziregimes in der sowjetischen Besatzungszone und in der DDR* (Berlin: Edition Ost, 1997), 32–42.

20. Lutz Niethammer, *Deutschland danach: Postfaschistische Gesellschaft und nationales Gedächtnis* (Bonn: Dietz Verlag, 1999), 56–57; Heinrich Best and Axel Salheiser, "Shadows of the Past: National Social Backgrounds of the GDR's Functional Elites," *German Studies Review* 29.3 (2006): 589–602.

21. Alf Lüdtke, "'Coming to Terms with the Past': Illusions of Remembering, Ways of Forgetting Nazism in West Germany," *Journal of Modern History* 65:3 (1993): 547–49.

22. Rolf Wiggershaus, *The Frankfurt School: Its History, Theories, and Political Significance,* trans. Michael Robertson (Cambridge: MIT Press), 446.

23. Theodor W. Adorno, "What Does 'Coming to Terms with the Past' Mean," in *Bitburg in Moral and Political Perspective,* ed. Geoffrey Hartman (Bloomington: University of Indiana Press, 1986), 115.

24. Norbert Frei, *Adenauer's Germany and the Nazi Past: The Politics of Amnesty and Integration,* trans. Joel Golb (New York: Columbia University Press, 2002), xiii–xv.

25. Wolfram Hanrieder, *Germany, America, Europe: Forty Years of German Foreign Policy* (New Haven: Yale University Press, 1989), 161, 172–76.

26. For an emblematic example, see Jack Raymond, "Yesterday and Today," *NYT,* November 19, 1961.

27. Federico Finchelstein, "The Holocaust Canon: Rereading Raul Hilberg," *New German Critique* 96 (Fall 2005): 7.

28. Raul Hilberg, *The Destruction of the European Jews* (New York: Harper Colophon Books, 1979), 701, 704–11.

29. Gavriel Rosenfeld, "The Reception of William L. Shirer's *The Rise and Fall of the Third Reich* in the United States and West Germany, 1960–62," *Journal of Contemporary History* 29.1 (1994): 95, 101.

30. Ibid., 100–101. Excerpts from *Rise and Fall* appeared biweekly in *Look* from March 15 to May 10, 1960, and daily in the *Boston Globe* from March 12 to March 24, 1961.

31. Rosenfeld, "Reception," 95–96, 100–103; Gavriel Rosenfeld, "The Controversy that Isn't: The Debate over Daniel J. Goldhagen's *Hitler's Willing Executioners* in Comparative Perspective," *Contemporary European History* 8.2 (1999): 259; Steve Wick, *The Long Night: William L. Shirer and the Rise and Fall of the Third Reich* (New York: Palgrave Macmillan, 2011), 228, 231.

32. William Shirer, *The Rise and Fall of the Third Reich* (New York: Fawcett Crest, 1985), 46, 81; Terence Prittie, "The Rise and Fall of Hitler," the *Atlantic,* December 1960, 108; "Again, Götterdammerung," *Time,* October 17, 1960, 108.

33. Shirer, *Rise and Fall,* 201, 261.

34. Ibid., xi, 1248–88.

35. Ibid., 1223–88.

36. Catherine Merridale, *Ivan's War: Life and Death in the Red Army, 1939–1945* (New York: Metropolitan Books, 2006), 4.

37. Shirer, *Rise and Fall,* 1092–93, 1225–29, 1235–44, 1248–50, 1266–67, 1274.

38. Ibid., 1119, 1129.

39. Ibid., 1130.

40. Ibid., 722–23. Ironically, Shirer cites Churchill's history in order to make this point, noting how the latter claimed Stalin's move as "at the moment realistic in a high degree."

41. Ibid., 133.

42. Rosenfeld, "Reception," 102.

43. Ibid., 103.

44. Rosenfeld, "The Controversy," 253–54, German detractor qtd. on 253.

45. Ibid., 254.

46. Bosley Crowther, "Hollywood's Producer of Controversy," *NYT Magazine,* December 10, 1961, SM76.

47. Martin Walker, *The Cold War: A History* (New York: Henry Holt, 1993), 130, 156–57.

48. Judith Doneson, *The Holocaust in American Film* (Philadelphia: Jewish Publication Society, 1987), 104; David Binder, "World Premiere for 'Nuremberg': Kramer's Film Gets Mixed Responses in West Berlin," *NYT,* December 15, 1961; "Movie of Nuremberg Trial Stirs Germans," *Los Angeles Times,* December 16, 1961.

49. Mintz, *Popular Culture,* 92; Doneson, *Holocaust,* 106. For a sampling of positive reviews, see Bosley Crowther, "Nuremberg Judgment: Kramer Hands Down a Fine, Forceful Film," *NYT,* December 24, 1961; Philip Hartung, "The Screen: Who Shall Judge?," *Commonweal,* December 15, 1961, 318–19; "Bitter Question of Man's Guilt," *Life,* December 15, 1961, 121–23.

50. Mintz summarizes this strand of criticism and builds on it. See *Popular Culture* 92–97.

51. Doneson, *Holocaust,* 106; Harris Dienstfrey and Jason Epstein, "Two Views of 'Judgment at Nuremberg,'" *Commentary,* January 1962, 57; Crowther, "Hollywood's Producer," 79.

52. Crowther, "Hollywood's Producer," 80.

53. Dienstfrey and Epstein, "Two Views," 60–61.

54. See Mintz, *Popular Culture,* 103–4; Doneson, *Holocaust,* 99–100, quote on 99.

55. Dienstfrey and Epstein, "Two Views," 58.

56. Mintz, *Popular Culture,* 103.

57. From the standpoint of Cold War politics, Montgomery Clift's performance as the witness Rudolph Petersen is perhaps the most problematic moment of the film. Petersen is from a communist family and is also revealed to be mentally deficient. This is more than simply a poor representation of the European left: the equation of mental deficiency and Bolshevism replicates the figure of the *Untermensch,* a Nazi construction that held communism to be the natural political choice for the racially degraded. Ironically, *Judgment at Nuremberg* makes the communist a sympathetic figure to Cold War audiences by reviving a staple of Nazi propaganda.

58. For conservative defenses, see Russell Kirk, "Goldwater, Fascism Poles Apart," *Los Angeles Times,* August 27, 1964; "Into an Intellectual Vacuum," *Wall Street Journal,* August 4, 1964. Goldwater himself belatedly hurled the charge of fascism at his opponents toward the end of his campaign. See Charles Mohr, "Goldwater Calls Rivals 'Fascists,'" *NYT,* October 14, 1964.

59. Some of the most lucid commentary in this vein includes Walter Dean Burnham, "The Goldwaterite Revolution," *Commonweal,* August 7, 1964, 531–34; David Danzig, "The Radical Right and the Rise of the Fundamentalist Minority," *Commentary,* April 1962, 291–98; "Antidote to Extremism," *Christian Century,* July 29, 1964, 955–56.

60. Bell, "Dispossessed," 19–22, 44–45; Lipset, *Political Man,* 127–29, 172–73.

61. Ibid., 169–72.

62. "In the Cow Palace: 'Toads' and 'Brinklies,'" *Newsweek,* July 27, 1964; "Guest Editorial: Ugly Campaign," *Chicago Tribune,* September 8, 1964.

63. "Goldwater: The World Reacts," *Newsweek,* July 27, 1964, 37; "Can Anyone Stop Goldwater Now?," *Newsweek,* June 15, 1964, 27.

64. Emmet John Hughes, "On Goldwaterism," *Newsweek,* July 27, 1964, 17.

65. "Thunder on the Far Right: Fear and Frustration Rouse Extremists to Action Across the Land," *Newsweek,* December 4, 1961, 19; "Brown Sees Fascism in Goldwater's Speech," *Los Angeles Times,* July 17, 1964; "Republican Mayor Says Goldwater Is a Fascist," *NYT,* July 19, 1964; "Bishop Lauds Barry, Raps Europe's Press," *Chicago Tribune,* July 24, 1964. According to the later piece, the editorial board of the *Methodist Recorder* concluded that Goldwater's platform contained "the seeds of fascism."

66. Lisa McGirr, *Suburban Warriors: The Origins of the New American Right* (Princeton: Princeton University Press, 2001), 36, 129, 131, 158, 176–85.

67. Gordon Sander, *Serling: The Rise and Twilight of Television's Last Angry Man* (New York: Dutton, 1992), 13, 17, 41, 49–50.

68. Ibid. 52–54, 64.

69. Ibid., 30, 63, 69–70. Andrew Falk, *Upstaging the Cold War: American Dissent and Cultural Diplomacy, 1940–1960* (Amherst: University of Massachusetts Press, 2010), 169.

70. Ibid., 120, 204.

71. Letter to Ms. Linda Villamor, February 24, 1965, and letter to Mr. Alden Schwimmer, February 3, 1965, Rod Serling Papers, box 13, folder "Political File," Thayer Library Special Collections, University of California-Los Angeles.

72. Letters to Robert Nichols, January 25, 1966, and March 11, 1966, Rod Serling Papers, box 13, "Political File."

73. For example, at a campus speech in November 1967, he stated, "We can love our fellow man—but we can deny him housing because this finicky morality of ours decides for us that the right of property is of the essence while a man's right to live out of squalor must

be secondary. Thou shalt not kill . . . but thou *shalt* kill communists or suspected communists or pseudo-communists or agrarian land reformers or peasants or anyone who will not accept our form of government, our way of life, our values." "Speech at Redlands University," November 16, 1967, 5, Rod Serling Papers, box 14, folder "Speeches."

74. Rod Serling Papers, box 7, folder "Radio Scripts, 1947–1950."

75. Philip Roth, *I Married a Communist* (New York: Houghton Mifflin, 1998), 39.

76. Jenny Edkins, *Trauma and the Memory of Politics* (Cambridge: Cambridge University Press, 2003), 34, 39–40.

77. Toward the beginning of the episode, Serling appears before the camera and states, "Portrait of a bush-league Führer named Peter Vollmer. A sparse little man who feeds off his self-delusions and finds himself perpetually hungry for want of greatness in his diet. And like some goose-stepping predecessors, he searches for something to explain his hunger, and to rationalize why a world passes him by without saluting." Serling takes the theme of the psychologically profiled, marginalized Nazi even further in his television script for the program *Insight* entitled "Hate." Here, the marginalized, power-craving neo-Nazi turns out to be a self-hating Jew.

78. Danzig, "The Radical Right," 295, 297.

79. Letter from Eugene Seeman to Rod Serling, January 11, 1966; letter from Rod Serling to Eugene Seeman, March 22, 1966, Rod Serling Papers, box 10, folder "Angry Letters."

80. Don Presnell and Marty McGee, *A Critical History of Television's* The Twilight Zone, *1959–1964* (Jefferson, N.C.: McFarland, 1998), 141.

81. McGirr, *Suburban Warriors,* 173.

82. Speech delivered at Ithaca College, May 1, 1967, Rod Serling Papers, box 14, folder "Speeches." In the original script, Vollmer's anticommunism is even more pronounced, as are references to the Holocaust. Yet, given that these two subjects are still quite visible in the episode, the edits could have been an attempt by Serling to avoid semantic overkill. Rod Serling Papers, box 9, "He's Alive."

83. Daniel Horowitz, *Betty Friedan and the Making of the Feminine Mystique: The American Left, the Cold War, and Modern Feminism* (Amherst: University of Massachusetts Press, 1998), 4.

84. Betty Friedan, *The Feminine Mystique* (New York: Norton, 1963), 37, 305–6.

85. Fermaglich, *American Dreams,* 75, 77–78.

86. Friedan, *The Feminine Mystique,* 186.

87. Ibid., 38; Horowitz, *Betty Friedan,* 49.

88. Kate Weigand, *Red Feminism: American Communism and the Making of Women's Liberation* (Baltimore: Johns Hopkins University Press, 2001), 3; Horowitz, *Betty Friedan,* 10, 47–48, 52–53. The slogan *Kinder, Küche, Kirche* actually originated in Wilhelmite Germany and was not widely used by the Nazis, though in broad strokes it fairly characterizes their blatantly patriarchal policies.

89. For a sampling of her political thought in *Smith College Associated News,* see "This Is What We Believe," March 14, 1941; "Education in Emergency," April 15, 1941; "The Right to Organize," October 21, 1941; "War Against Fascism," October 24, 1941; "Labor Education Described by Smith Summer Workers," October 28, 1941; "In Answer to Mr. Davis," November 18, 1941.

90. Bettye Goldstein, "Smith in the War," *Smith College Associated News,* January 9, 1942.

91. Friedan, *The Feminine Mystique,* 206–8, 305.

92. Ibid., 254.

6. United Front against Genocide

1. "Penny Nakatsu, A Japanese American, Speaks Out against Fascism," *BP,* August 2, 1969.

2. "Oscar Rios of Los Siete Speaks at UFAF Conference," *BP,* August 2, 1969; "Father Earl Neil Speaks," *BP,* August 9, 1969.

3. "Chairman Seale Sums Up Conference," *BP,* August 2, 1969.

4. Herbert Aptheker, *Manuscript of a speech delivered at the National Conference for a United Front Against Fascism, July 18, 1969,* Michigan State University Special Collections, Radicalism, East Lansing.

5. I refer here to the conclusion of Mark Christian Thompson's *Black Fascisms: African American Literature and Culture between the Wars* (Charlottesville: University of Virginia Press, 2007), 172–77.

6. Hilene Flanzbaum, introduction to *The Americanization of the Holocaust,* ed. Hilene Flanzbaum (Baltimore: Johns Hopkins University Press, 1999), 1–17.

7. Robert Self, "The Black Panther Party and the Long Civil Rights Era," in *In Search of the Black Panther Party: New Perspectives on a Revolutionary Movement,* ed. Jama Lazerow and Yohuru Williams (Durham: Duke University Press, 2006), 22.

8. Giorgio Agamben, *Homo Sacer: Sovereign Power and Bare Life,* trans. Daniel Heller-Roazen (Stanford: Stanford University Press, 1998), 9–10. This discussion of the dual system, fascism, and *homines sacri* is a synthesis of two separate pieces from Nikhil Singh, "The Afterlife of Fascism," *South Atlantic Quarterly* 105:1 (2006), 76–79, and "Liberalism," in *Keywords for American Cultural Studies,* ed. Bruce Burgett and Glenn Hendler (New York: New York University Press, 2007), 41–45.

9. My discussion of liberalism and fascism departs from that of Agamben, who, in my view, unduly collapses the difference between the two.

10. Hughes quoted in *Proceedings: Third U.S. Congress against War and Fascism* (New York: ALAWF, 1936), 8–9.

11. William Patterson, "Language and Liberation Struggles," *BP,* January 17, 1970; William Patterson, "The Black Athlete and Democracy U.S.A.," *BP,* December 13, 1969; "Robert Williams Speaks at Panther Benefit," *BP,* December 27, 1969; Robert Williams, "Do You Know?," *Black America* (undated, 1965), 13, Social Protest Collection, carton 5, reel 15, Bancroft Library, University of California at Berkeley. In this piece from 1965, Williams wrote, "The racist Minute Men are becoming a fascist vanguard that will some day be turned loose on all Afro-Americans and white Americans who get out of line."

12. Robert Self captures this historiographical trend in "The Black Panther Party," 15–55. In tracing a black antifascist tradition, I do not seek here to deny the existence of the protofascist, intellectual current which Mark Christian Thompson identifies in his book *Black Fascisms*—but I do want to place it in context. When most African Americans writers, journalists, and intellectuals rejected European fascism in the 1930s and 1940s, they tended to oppose it with a civil rights agenda that included trade unions, social democracy, a broad anticolonial solidarity, and even socialism—that is to say, an agenda more aligned with the left than with fascist racialism.

13. W. E. B. Du Bois, *Color and Democracy: Colonies and Peace* (New York: Harcourt, Brace, 1945), 9–10, 57, 101.

14. Peter Geismar, *Fanon* (New York: Dial Press, 1971), 39.

15. Frantz Fanon, *The Wretched of the Earth,* trans. Constance Farrington (New York: Grove Press, 1986), 101.

16. Frantz Fanon, *Black Skin, White Masks,* trans. Richard Philcox (New York: Grove Press, 2008), 70–71.

17. Aimé Césaire, *Discourse on Colonialism,* trans. Joan Pinkham (New York: Monthly Review Press, 2000), 36–37.

18. Hannah Arendt, *The Origins of Totalitarianism* (Orlando: Harcourt, 1985), esp. 221–22.

19. Jeffrey Ogbar, *Black Power: Radical Politics and African American Identity* (Baltimore: Johns Hopkins University Press, 2004), 18, 20, 44.

20. "Rockwell and Co.—They Speak for All White," April 1962; "How Youth, Aged 13, Faced Assassination by a Nazi," July 5, 1963; "Nazi Rockwell: Only Total Terror Can Stop Negro," *Muhammad Speaks,* August 28, 1964.

21. Civil Rights Congress, *We Charge Genocide: The Crime of Government against the Negro People* (New York: Civil Rights Congress, 1951), xi; Office of the United Nations High Commissioner for Human Rights, "Convention on the Prevention and Punishment of the Crime of Genocide," www2.ohchr.org.

22. *We Charge Genocide,* 4–5, 153–54.

23. Carol Anderson, *Eyes Off the Prize: The United Nations and the African American Struggle for Civil Rights, 1944–1955* (Cambridge: Cambridge University Press, 2003), 180.

24. *We Charge Genocide,* 3.

25. Ibid., 7.

26. Anderson, *Eyes Off the Prize,* 186–87, 194, 202.

27. Mary Dudziak, *Cold War Civil Rights: Race and the Image of American Democracy* (Princeton: Princeton University Press, 2000), 58, 63.

28. "We Charge Genocide," *Muhammad Speaks,* June 1962.

29. "Race Murder in Southwest Africa," *Muhammad Speaks,* July 15, 1962; "Goering, Father of Nazi Thug, Helped Exterminate Blacks," *Muhammad Speaks,* July 15, 1962.

30. "We Charge Genocide," *BP,* February 7, 1970. The Civil Rights Congress petition is quoted at length in "Genocide Leads to Fascism and War" and "We Charge Genocide," both in *Anti Fascist Front,* July 18–20, 1969, Thomas J. Dodd Research Center, University of Connecticut, Storrs.

31. For the Klan's use of Aryanness and its praise of the SS and the SA, see "Yesterday, Today, Tomorrow" (1958), Social Protest Collection, reel 22, carton 6, folder 38.

32. *We Charge Genocide,* 4.

33. Kenneth O'Reilly, *"Racial Matters": The FBI's Secret File on Black America, 1960–1972* (London: Free Press, 1989), 158–71.

34. Ibid., 200.

35. Ibid., 215–21, quote on 225.

36. William Buckley, "Riots Pose Dilemma for Conservatives," *Boston Globe,* April 19, 1968; Rowland Evans and Robert Novak, "West Germans Have Own George Wallace," *Boston Globe,* August 25, 1969; Joseph Alsop, "Seeds of Fascism in Our Land," *Boston Globe,* October 7, 1968.

37. Tom Wicker, "Clashes Mar Wallace Rally in Detroit," *NYT,* October 30, 1968; Aldo Beckman, "Shouting Match with Hecklers Ends Wallace Talk in Texas," *Chicago Tribune,* October 17, 1968; "Wallace Scorns Nazi Salutes," *Hartford Courant,* October 13, 1968.

38. Sara Davidson, "Street Clashes Greet Wallace at N.Y. Rally," *Boston Globe,* October 25, 1968; William Kling, "3500 N.Y. Cops Guard Wallace," *Chicago Tribune,* October 25, 1968; Dan T. Carter, *From George Wallace to Newt Gingrich: Race in the Conservative Counter-*

revolution, 1963–1994 (Baton Rouge: Louisiana State University Press, 1996), 19–21; Wallace quoted on page 20.

39. "Wallace Scorns Nazi Salutes."

40. Carter, *Wallace to Gingrich*, 2–3.

41. Ibid., 35.

42. "Declaration of Principles: American Independent Party," July 8, 1967; "National Platform of the American Independent Party," August 1972; "Support George Wallace for President in '68," Social Protest Collection, reel 91, carton 25, folder 5; "The Difference Between National Socialism and Communism"; "I am an American Nazi," Social Protest Collection, reel 91, carton 25, folder 7.

43. Robert Paxton, *The Anatomy of Fascism* (New York: Alfred Knopf, 2004), 202.

44. Friends of George C. Wallace, "What You Can Do 'That Government of the People, by the People, for the People Shall Not Perish from the Earth,'" Social Protest Collection, reel 73, carton 20, folder 12.

45. Carter, *Wallace to Gingrich*, 6.

46. Ibid., 23, 30.

47. Michelle Alexander, *The New Jim Crow: Mass Incarceration in the Age of Colorblindness* (New York: New Press, 2010), 9, 43–44; Sabina Tavernise, "Life Expectancy Shrinks for Less-Educated Whites in U.S.," *NYT,* September 20, 2012.

48. O'Reilly, *Racial Matters,* 244–45, 261–62, 295, 325.

49. David Barber, "Leading the Vanguard: White New Leftists School the Panthers on Black Revolution," in *In Search of the Black Panther Party,* 234.

50. "Panther Conference," *Old Mole,* July 4–17, 1969.

51. Ibid., *Anti Fascist Front,* July 18–20, 1969.

52. *BP,* July 20, 1967.

53. "Petition for Decentralization of Police," *Anti Fascist Front,* July 18–20, 1969.

54. U.S. House of Representatives, Committee on Internal Security, *Gun-Barrel Politics: The Black Panther Party, 1966–1971* (Washington, D.C.: U.S. Government Printing Office, 1971), 48–50.

55. *The Barb* interview of Bobby Seale and David Hilliard, reprinted as "Our Enemies' Friends are also our Enemies," *BP,* August 9, 1969.

56. "Roberta Alexander at Conference," *BP,* August 2, 1969.

57. "UFAF Conference," *Old Mole,* August 1–14, 1969.

58. Stanley Aronowitz, *Honor America: The Nature of Fascism, Historic Struggles against It and a Strategy for Today* (New York: Times Change Press, 1970), 26.

59. Barber, "Leading the Vanguard," 225.

60. Ibid., 225, 235–38.

61. "UFAF Conference," *Old Mole,* 3.

62. *Gun-Barrel Politics,* 60.

63. Ibid., 78. Paul Alkebulan, *Survival Pending Revolution: A History of the Black Panther Party* (Tuscaloosa: University of Alabama Press, 2007), 47; "Dallas, Texas NCCF Disbanded," *BP,* February 20, 1971.

64. Federal Bureau of Investigation, BPP, North Carolina, Bufile Number 105-165706, To Director FBI, From SAC Charlotte, RE: Charlotte airtel to Bureau, 8/19/70 (September 21, 1970), 2, http://vault.fbi.gov.

65. To Director, FBI, from SAC Charlotte, Charlotte Division Monthly Summary, May 6, 1970, 1–2, http://vault.fbi.gov; To Director FBI, From SAC Charlotte, RE: Black Panther

Party, April 22, 1971, 26, http://vault.fbi.gov; "Seattle NCCF Medical Corps Treats Walla Walla Prison Inmate," *BP,* March 6, 1971. The report of April 1971 is dated after the National Committees to Combat Fascism graduated to a BPP branch. However, it is based on documents from late 1970s found by agents in the debris of the NCCF office following a fire there.

66. "Charlotte Division Monthly Summary," 2; John E. Moore, "People of the Community vs. the Slumlords and Fascist Pigs of Winston-Salem," *BP,* March 28, 1970.

67. Ogbar, *Black Power,* 94.

68. To Director, FBI from SAC Charlotte, "RE: Charlotte airtel to Bureau, dated 8/30/70," September 4, 1970, 4, http://vault.fbi.gov; To Director, FBI, From SAC Charlotte, "Re: Charlotte airtel to Bureau, dated 7/7/71," July 19, 1971, 3, http://vault.fbi.gov.

69. To Director, FBI, From SAC Charlotte, "Re Director's airtel to SAC, Albany, dated 5/17/71," June 23, 1971, http://vault.fbi.gov; To, Director FBI, From SAC Charlotte, Sept 24, 1970, http://vault.fbi.gov.

70. Kirsten B. Mitchell, "Black Panthers Online Reports of the Activities of the Group in Winston-Salem," *Winston-Salem Journal,* January 30, 2000.

71. "Jury Acquits Panthers of Murder Charges," *Hartford Courant* (AP), July 1, 1971; "Man Charged in Shooting of Policeman Bound Over," *Hartford Courant,* October 2, 1970; "Police Jail Black Militants in Raids in New Orleans," *NYT* (AP), November 2, 1970; Andrew Blake, "Chief Counts Dropped in New Bedford," *Boston Globe,* March 30, 1971; "New Orleans Police Seize Guns in New Panther Raid," *NYT* (UPI), November 30, 1970; "2 Militants Guilty in Bomb Slaying of Policeman," *Hartford Courant* (AP), April 18, 1971.

72. George Jackson, *Blood in My Eye* (New York: Random House, 1972), 118–19, 127–77.

73. Letter from Loretta Young to Huey Newton, ca. early 1973, Huey P. Newton Foundation Records, series 2, box 4, folder 1, Stanford University Libraries, Department of Special Collections, Stanford, Calif.

74. Kathleen Cleaver, "Racism, Fascism, and Political Murder," *BP,* September 14, 1968.

75. Eldridge Cleaver, "Students and Education against Fascism," *Anti Fascist Front,* July 18–20, 1969.

76. Bobby Seale, "Message to all Progressive Forces," *BP,* January 3, 1970.

77. "October 1966 Black Panther Party Platform and Program," *BP,* June 10, 1968.

78. "Sterilization: Another Part of the Black Genocide," *BP,* May 8, 1971; Charlotte O'Neal, "Fascism in America's Institutions," *BP,* March 28, 1970.

79. "Robert Williams Speaks at Panther Benefit," *BP,* December 27, 1969; William Patterson, "Language and Liberation Struggles."

80. Lorena Oropeza, *¡Raza Sí! ¡Guerra No! Chicano Protest and Patriotism during the Viet Nam War Era* (Berkeley: University of California Press, 2005), 16.

81. Mike Davis, *Late Victorian Holocausts: El Niño Famines and the Making of the Third World* (London: Verso, 2002), 7.

82. Oropeza, *¡Raza Sí!,* 6, 73–74, 84; Vijay Prashad, *Everybody Was Kung Fu Fighting: Afro-Asian Connections and the Myth of Cultural Purity* (Boston: Beacon Press, 2001), 126–49; Ogbar, *Black Power,* 159–74.

83. On Bulosan and Tsiang, see Chris Vials, *Realism for the Masses: Aesthetics, Popular Front Pluralism, and U.S. Culture, 1935–1947* (Jackson: University of Mississippi Press, 2009), 110–48.

84. On the Native American movement, see Social Justice Collection, carton 7, reel 23, folders 6–13.

85. Some examples, not referenced below, include, "Chicanos Demand Judge in San Jose Be Ousted," *Adelante,* October 14, 1969; "Free the Schools," *Ya Basta!,* October 4, 1969; "It Happens Every Day," *Ya Basta!,* October 1970; "The Preparation for Fascism!" *La Causa Legal Defense Fund* (newsletter), (no month) 1975.

86. Untitled, *Basta Ya!,* September 6, 1969.

87. Daniel Gorostiza, "2 More La Raza Deaths—for What?," *Basta Ya!,* August 1970. For a similar example, see "The Fascist Pigs Must Withdraw from Our Communities," *La Chispa: Chicano Community News Service,* February 19, 1971.

88. "Brown Beret 13-Point Political Program," *La Causa,* December 1970.

89. "National La Raza Unida Party Priorities," October 6, 1972, Social Protest Collection, reel 23, carton 7, folder 18.

90. Oropeza, *¡Raza Sí!,* 137, 166–67; Edward J. Escobar, "The Dialectics of Repression: The Los Angeles Police Department and the Chicano Movement, 1968–1971," *Journal of American History* 79.4 (1993): 1499–1500.

91. Escobar, "Dialectics of Repression," 1493–95, 1501–3.

92. "Law and Order," *La Causa,* December 1970.

93. Oropeza, *¡Raza Sí!,* 6–7, 79.

94. Ralph Guzman, "Mexican American Casualties in Vietnam," *La Raza* 1.1 (1970): 12–15; "Chicano Moratorium," *La Raza* 1.1 (1970): 5–11.

95. Qtd. in Oropeza, *¡Raza Sí!,* 154.

96. Hortencia Bussi de Allende, "No to Fascism!" and "¡No al Fascismo!," *La Raza* 2.1 (1974): 40–43, 44–47.

97. "Muslim Brothers Rise against Marcos Fascism," *Kalayaan International* (December 1971/January 1972), 3–4; cover image, *Kalayaan International* (October/November 1971); images, *Ang Katipunan* (March 1–15, 1979), 1, 7–8.

98. "Fascism!," *Getting Together* 1.5 (1970): 2.

99. "Chinese American History," *Getting Together* 1.3 (1970): 3; see also "Hoover's Yellow Peril," *Getting Together* 1.2 (1970): unpaginated.

100. "Hoover's Yellow Peril"; "Yellow Peril," *Getting Together* 1.1 (1970): unpaginated; Asian-American Political Alliance, "Concentration Camps U.S.A.," Position Paper, June 28, 1968, Social Protest Collection, reel 23, carton 7, folder 20.

101. *Getting Together* 1.1 (1970): unpaginated.

102. Ibid.

103. Asian-American Political Alliance, "Concentration Camps U.S.A."

104. Huey Newton, "Intercommunalism" and "Uniting against a Common Enemy," in *The Huey Newton Reader,* ed. David Hilliard and Donald Weise (New York: Seven Stories Press, 2002), 184–89, 234–39.

7. Queer Antifascism

1. Box 2, folder 6, Gran Fury Collection, New York Public Library, New York.

2. Avram Finkelstein, telephone interview with author, March 17, 2012; Douglas Crimp, "AIDS: Cultural Analysis/Cultural Activism," in *Cultural Analysis, Cultural Activism,* ed. Douglas Crimp (Cambridge: MIT Press, 1998), 7.

3. Kai Hammermeister, "Inventing History: Toward a Gay Holocaust Literature," *German Quarterly* 70.1 (1997): 18–26; Erik Jensen, "The Pink Triangle and Political Consciousness: Gays, Lesbians, the Memory of Nazi Persecution," *Journal of the History of Sexuality* 11.1–2

(2002): 319–49; Deborah Gould, *Moving Politics: Emotion and ACT UP's Fight Against AIDS* (Chicago: University of Chicago Press, 2009), 165–72; Les Wright, "Gay Genocide as Literary Trope," in *AIDS: The Literary Response,* ed. Emmanuel Nelson (New York: Twayne, 1992), 50–68; Gregory Woods, *A History of Gay Literature: The Male Tradition* (New Haven: Yale University Press, 1998), 247–56; R. Amy Elman, "Triangles and Tribulations: The Politics of Nazi Symbols," *Journal of Homosexuality* 30.3 (1996): 1–11; Dorthe Seifert, "Between Silence and License: The Representation of the National Socialist Persecution of Homosexuality in Anglo-American Fiction and Film," *History and Memory* 15.2 (2003): 94–129.

4. "En Route: Gay Culture Around the World," *Advocate,* January 21, 1986, 36–37, 113.

5. Seifert, "Silence and License," 96, 100, 123; Jensen, "Pink Triangle," 330, 339–42.

6. Jensen, "Pink Triangle," 344–45; Seifert, "Silence and License," 108.

7. Jensen, "Pink Triangle," 342.

8. Stuart Marshall, "The Contemporary Political Use of Gay History: The Third Reich," in *How Do I Look? Queer Film and Video,* ed. Bad Object-Choices (Seattle: Bay Press, 1991), 87.

9. Les Wright, for instance, calls the discourse surrounding the pink triangle "the language of political paranoia." "Gay Genocide," 51.

10. Gert Hekma et al., "Leftist Sexual Politics and Homosexuality: A Historical Overview," *Journal of Homosexuality* 29.2–3 (1995): 20–21.

11. Günter Grau, "Persecution, 'Re-education' or 'Eradication' of Male Homosexuals between 1933 and 1945," in *Hidden Holocausts? Gay and Lesbian Persecution in Germany, 1933–1945,* ed. Gunter Grau, trans. Patrick Camiller (Chicago: Fitzroy Dearborn, 1995), 1–4.

12. Claudia Schoppmann, "The Position of Lesbian Women in the Nazi Period," in *Hidden Holocausts?,* 8–15.

13. Richard Plant, *Pink Triangle: The Nazi War against Homosexuals* (New York: Henry Holt, 1986), 80, 143, 149.

14. Grau, "Persecution," 5; Plant, *Pink Triangle,* 149.

15. Plant, *Pink Triangle,* 154, 165, 179.

16. Grau, "Persecution," 6–7, 18–23.

17. Plant, *Pink Triangle,* 13–14, 181; Richard Plant, "East German Gay Laws: Years Ahead of West," *Outweek,* June 6, 1990.

18. W. U. Eissler, *Arbeiterparteien und Homosexuellenfrage: Zur Sexualpolitik von SPD und KPD in der Weimarer Republik* (Berlin: Rosa Winkel, 1980), 37–38, 49–51, 53–54, 62.

19. Will Roscoe, "Mattachine, 1948–1963," in *Radically Gay: Gay Liberation in the Words of Its Founder,* ed. Will Roscoe (Boston: Beacon Press, 1996), 43, 54.

20. Daniel Hurewitz, *Bohemian Los Angeles and the Making of Modern Politics* (Berkeley: University of California Press, 2007); Aaron Lecklider, "H. T. Tsiang's Proletarian Burlesque: Performance and Perversion in The Hanging on Union Square," *MELUS* 36.4 (2011): 87–114.

21. Allan Bérubé, *Coming Out under Fire: The History of Gay Men and Women in World War II* (New York: Free Press, 2000).

22. Harry Hay, "Preliminary Concepts: International Bachelors' Fraternal Order of Peace and Social Dignity, Sometimes Referred to as Bachelors Anonymous," in *Radically Gay,* 63–64.

23. Stuart Timmons, *The Trouble with Harry Hay: Founder of the Modern Gay Movement* (Boston: Alyson Publications, 1990), 141.

24. Eissler, *Arbeiterparteien,* 106–14; Alexander Zinn, "'Die Bewegung der Homosexuellen': Die soziale Konstruktion des homosexuellen Nationalsozialisten im antifascistichen Exil," in *Die Linke und das Laster: Schwule Emanzipation und linke Vorurteile,* ed. Detlef Grumbach (Hamburg: MännerschwarmSkript Verlag, 1995), 38–84; "La révolution des homosexuels," *Fag Rag* (Summer 1972), 18.

25. William Shirer, *The Rise and Fall of the Third Reich* (New York: Fawcett Crest, 1985), 48, 64, 79–80, 172–73, 307, quotes on 172–73.

26. Timmons, *Harry Hay,* 72–73.

27. Harry Hay Papers, series 1, box 1, folder 8, San Francisco Public Library, San Francisco.

28. Ibid.

29. Harry Hay, "Homosexuality and History . . . an Invitation to Further Study," in *Radically Gay: Gay Liberation in the Words of its Founder,* ed. Will Roscoe (Boston: Beacon Press, 1996), 94–119.

30. Carl Harding, "Deep Are the Roots," *Mattachine Review* (March–April 1955): 4–7.

31. For a few examples in *Mattachine Review,* see Peter Jackson, "The Tender Trap" (June 1957): 6; "German Police Shield Victim of Extortion: A Factual Case Report," February 1958, 29; Wolfgang E. Bredtschneider, "About the Prejudice against Homosexuality," October 1957, 5–10; "Bibliography of Books on the Homosexual (and Related) Subjects," August 1957, 24–29.

32. Martin Meeker, "Behind the Mask of Respectability: Reconsidering the Mattachine Society and Male Homophile Practice, 1950s and 1960s," *Journal of the History of Sexuality* 10.1 (2001): 79–81, 87–88.

33. For early awareness, see A. E. Galbraith, "Die Insel" *ONE* 1.1 (1953): 4–7; Jack Argo, "The Homosexual in Germany Today," *ONE* 3.6 (1955): 9–10; for a later usage of Nazism in *ONE,* see James Kearful, "The New Nazism," *ONE* 11.5 (1963): 5–12.

34. Education Division of ONE, Incorporated, "History and Organization," *Institute for Homophile Studies, Catalog for 1968–1969,* 6–8. Social Protest Collection, Bancroft Library, reel 27, carton 8, folder 11.

35. "Complete Listing of Courses Given, 1956–1968," *Institute for Homophile Studies, Catalog for 1968–1969,* 11–15.

36. For an emblematic example of the colonial paradigm, see Carl Wittman, "Refugees from Amerika: A Gay Manifesto," Fall 1970, Social Protest Collection, reel 28, carton 8, folder 17; "On Our Identity as Faggots," *Magnus: A Journal of Collective Faggotry* (Summer 1976): 3–4, 9; Social Protest Collection, reel 28, carton 8, folder 18.

37. My observations of gay liberation are based on a survey of materials from 1969 to 1973 produced by the Berkeley-based Gay Students' Union, Gay Switchboard, Gay Liberation Front, Committee for Homosexual Freedom, Students for Gay Power, and the magazines *Free Particle, Fag Rag,* and *Pride of Lions.* Social Protest Collection, series 2, reel 27, carton 8, folders 6–9, 12–15; also reel 28, carton 8, folders 16–18; these observations also extend to a survey of the Boston-based *Fag Rag* from 1975 to 1977.

38. Jensen, "Pink Triangle," 329; for a vivid example of Anita Bryant as fascist, see Doug Ireland, "Open Season on Gays," *Nation,* September 15, 1979, 207–9.

39. Andreas Salmen and Albert Eckert, *20 Jahre bundesdeutsche Schwulenbewegung, 1969–1989* (Cologne: Bundesverband Homosexualität, 1989), 24–25, 45–47; Elmar Kraushaar, "'Nebenswidersprüche': Die neue Linke und die Schwulenfrage in der Bundesrepublik der siebziger und achtziger Jahre," in *Die Linke und das Laster: Schwule Emanzipation und*

linke Vorurteile, ed. Detlef Grumbach (Hamburg: MännerschwarmSkript Verlag, 1995), 145.

40. Salmen and Eckert, *Schwulenbewegung,* 29, 33, 37, 40–41; Kraushaar, "Nebenswidersprüche," 144, 146.

41. "Die Männer mit dem Rosa Winkel," March 1975, 3–8; and "Rosa für Schwule," March 1975, 9–15, both in *Info / Homosexuelle Aktion Westberlin* (my trans.).

42. Letter from Maynard Smith, August 12, 1988; letter from Keith Mandel, July 1, 1989; Richard Plant Papers, box 1, folder 9, New York Public Library. For sample citations in the gay press, see Jonathan Ned Katz, "Signs of the Times: The Making of Liberation Logos," *Advocate,* October 10, 1989, 49; Rev. Irene Monroe, "Black, Queer, and in Nazi Germany?," *Windy City Times,* March 3, 2010, 10; Lev Raphael, "Deciphering the Gay Holocaust," *Harvard Gay and Lesbian Review* (July 1, 1995): 16–20; Lucinda Zoe, "The Black Triangle," *Hag Rag: Milwaukee's Lesbian Feminist Newspaper,* January/February 1992; "The Final Solution," *New York Native,* November 20, 1989; Lawrence Mass, "The Swastika and the Pink Triangle: Nazis and Gay Men," *Christopher Street* 9.11 (1987): 46–52.

43. "Memoirs of the Holocaust," *Gay Tide* 3.1 (1975): 6–7, 10; "The Men with the Pink Triangle," *Christopher Street* 1.8 (1977): 4–10; "Nazis' Forgotten Victims: Gays: Wiesel Helps End Jews' Silence on Shared Agony," *NYT,* November 7, 1989.

44. Letter from Robert Hawkins and Rose Walton (undated), Richard Plant Papers, box 1, folder 9.

45. The periodical of the HAW listed Egmont Fassbinder as its contact person in 1975 (see *Info,* March 1975, 2). For the correspondence between Plant and these individuals, see Richard Plant Papers, box 1, folders 10, 12, 15, and 20; and box 3, folder 12.

46. Rüdiger Lautmann, "Hauptdevise: 'bloβ nicht anecken.' Das Leben homosexueller Männer unter dem Nationalsozialismus," Richard Plant Papers, box 1, folder 20. The HAW's founding document stated, "We see that the repression of sexuality serves to secure political and economic power. Simultaneously, the discrimination against socially marginal groups represents a steam valve for oppressed classes and strata and is encouraged as such by the ruling classes" (qtd. in Kraushaar, "Nebenswidersprüche," 146, my trans.).

47. Plant, *Pink Triangle,* 26, 31–33, 63, 67, 77, 99–102.

48. Ibid., 52, 80, 114–16, 125, 143, 149

49. Letter from Egmont Fassbender, February 26, 1976, Richard Plant Papers, box 1, folder 10 (my trans.).

50. Letter from Richard Plant to Erich Henschel, September 16, 1978, Richard Plant Papers, box 1, folder 15 (my trans., ellipsis in original).

51. Didi Herman, *The Antigay Agenda: Orthodox Vision and the Christian Right* (Chicago: University of Chicago Press, 1997), 4–5; Steve Bruce, *The Rise and Fall of the New Christian Right: Conservative Protestant Politics in America, 1978–1988* (Oxford: Clarendon Press, 1988), 49, 68, 101.

52. Hal Lindsey, *The Late Great Planet Earth,* 1970 (Grand Rapids: Zondervan, 1971), 184.

53. Chris Hedges, *American Fascists: The Christian Right and the War on America* (New York: Free Press, 2006), 29–32; Michelle Goldberg, *Kingdom Coming: The Rise of Christian Nationalism* (New York: Norton, 2006), 17, 163–64; Stephen Glain, "Backward Christian Soldiers," *Truth Out,* web, accessed February 10, 2011; Laurie Goodstein, "Evangelicals Are a Growing Force in the Military Chaplain Corps," *NYT,* July 12, 2005; Neela Banerjee, "Religion and Its Role Are in Dispute in the Service Academies," *NYT,* June 25, 2008.

54. For example, the first-person narrator of a pamphlet published by the American Nazi Party argues "The CROSS is the symbol of Western, Christian civilization. I believe America was founded as a Christian nation." American Nazi Party, *I Am an American Nazi*, San Francisco (undated, ca. 1960s), Social Protest Collection, reel 91, carton 25, folder 7.

55. Herman, *Anti-gay Agenda*, 190–91; Chip Berlet and Matthew Lyons, *Right-Wing Populism in America: Too Close for Comfort* (New York: Guilford Press, 2000), 253.

56. Rousas John Rushdoony, *The Institutes of Biblical Law*, 1973 (no location listed: Presbyterian and Reformed Publishing, 1977), 60–62, 99–100.

57. Ibid., 77–78, 294, 425, 586, 588.

58. Herman, *Anti-gay Agenda*, 190–92.

59. Berlet and Lyons, *Right-Wing Populism*, 252–53.

60. Craig Rimmerman, *From Identity to Politics: The Lesbian and Gay Movements in the United States* (Philadelphia: Temple University Press, 2002), 126.

61. Theodor Adorno et al., *The Authoritarian Personality* (New York: Norton, 1982), 51; Goldberg, *Kingdom Coming*, 51, 73–74; Herman, *Anti-gay Agenda*, 76–82, 126–27.

62. Herman, *Anti-gay Agenda*, 69–74.

63. Enrique Rueda and Michael Schwartz, *Gays, AIDS, and You* (Old Greenwich: Devin Adair, 1987), 9, 12.

64. Katz, "Signs of the Times," 49.

65. Jeffrey Shandler, *While America Watches: Televising the Holocaust* (Oxford: Oxford University Press, 1999), 155.

66. Alvin Goldfarb, review of *Bent, Theater Journal*, October 1980, 398–99.

67. Lannon Reed, *Behold a Pale Horse: A Novel of Homosexuals in the Nazi Holocaust* (San Francisco: Gay Sunshine Press, 1985), 101.

68. Rimmerman, *From Identity to Politics*, 88, 93, 96.

69. Qtd. in Stephen Engel, *The Unfinished Revolution: Social Movement Theory and the Gay and Lesbian Movement* (Cambridge: Cambridge University Press, 2001), 48.

70. Gould, *Moving Politics*, 122–38; William F. Buckley Jr., "Crucial Steps in Combating the Aids Epidemic: Identify All the Carriers," *NYT*, March 18, 1986; Burger qtd. in Rimmerman, *From Identity to Politics*, 61.

71. Larry Kramer, *Reports from the Holocaust: The Story of an AIDS Activist* (New York: St. Martin's Press, 1994), 263.

72. Charles Kreloff, telephone interview with author, May 7, 2012; Avram Finkelstein, telephone interview.

73. Finkelstein, telephone interview; ACT UP New York Records, reel 153, boxes 193–94, New York Public Library.

74. Kreloff, telephone interview; Finkelstein, telephone interview.

75. Examples include "En Route," *Advocate*; Arnie Kantrowitz, "Friends: Gone with the Wind," *Advocate*, September 2, 1986, 42–47; Katz, "Signs of the Times"; Miles Michael, "In Fascist America," *New York Native*, September 29, 1986, 18–19; Ronald Gans, "Putting the Fire Out This Time," *New York Native*, August 4, 1986, 12; Jeffrey Nickel, "The Fascisms of Patrick Buchanan," *New York Native*, March 23, 1992, 27–31; Herb Spiers, "Fighting the AIDS Beast: Strategies and Consequences," *Windy City Times*, June 23, 1988, 36; DAGMARR (Dykes and Gay Men against Racism and the Right Wing),"Gays Urged to Be Educated about KKK and Nazis," *Windy City Times*, September 11, 1986, 10.

76. Michael, "In Fascist America," 18; Norberto Bobbio, *Left and Right: The Significance of a Political Distinction* (Chicago: University of Chicago Press, 1996), 59.

77. John Gallagher, "The Rise of Fascism in America," *Advocate*, November 3, 1992, 37–43.
78. Tony Kushner, *A Bright Room Called Day* (New York: Theater Communications Group, 1994), quotes on 27, 61.
79. Ibid., 155.
80. Ibid., 70–71.
81. Ibid., afterword, 172, 174, 177, 179.
82. Ibid., 79–80.
83. Ibid., 106.
84. Kreloff, telephone interview.
85. Roger Griffin, *The Nature of Fascism* (London: Routledge, 1993), xii.

Epilogue

1. U.S. Department of Homeland Security, Extremism and Radicalism Branch, *Rightwing Extremism: Current Economic and Political Climate Fueling Resurgence in Radicalization and Recruitment,* April 7, 2009, 2, 4.
2. Ginger Thompson, "Extremist Report Draws Criticism, Prompts Apology," *NYT,* April 16, 2009.
3. See the Southern Poverty Law Center database, "Hate Incidents," www.splcenter.org; Kathleen Belew, "Theatres of War: Mercenaries, Paramilitarism, and the Racist Right from Vietnam to Oklahoma City," PhD diss., Yale University, 2013.
4. Southern Poverty Law Center, *Intelligence Report,* "Active Hate Groups in the United States since 2011" and "Patriot Groups," Spring 2012, 43, 50.
5. Joshua Green, "Why Is This GOP House Candidate Dressed as a Nazi?," *Atlantic Monthly,* October 8, 2010; Judy Thomas, "Tea Party rejects NAACP's Racism Claims, But Concerns Still Exist," *Kansas City Star,* July 16, 2010, web, accessed November 23, 2012.
6. Jonah Goldberg, *Liberal Fascism: The Secret History of the American Left, from Mussolini to the Politics of Meaning* (New York: Doubleday), 9.
7. For example, Goldberg refers to a small section of John Diggins's *Mussolini: The View from America* (1972) to suggest that liberals were the sole American supporters of Mussolini. He ignores the remainder of Diggins's book, which argued that liberal sympathy was isolated and short-lived and that the most tenacious support for Il Duce came from businesspeople and conservatives. Diggins, incidentally, is almost the only source for Goldberg's claim that the left supported European fascism. He also misrepresents the history (and historiography) on Nazi Germany and, to cite but one of many errors, claims that W. E. B. Du Bois used the Nazi swastika on the cover of "his magazines" beginning in 1924. In fact, the *Crisis* never used the swastika on its cover but did, starting in 1915, five years before the Nazi Party was founded, use a symbol of Hindu and Buddhist spirituality to divide the text of its articles. The *Crisis* dropped the symbol around 1924, precisely when the NSDAP began to be known to the outside world and the symbol became associated with Nazism. See ibid., 9, 26–31, 58–59, 66, 100–101, 103.
8. Ibid., 56.

INDEX

Abraham Lincoln Brigade, 54
ACT UP. *See* AIDS Coalition to Unleash Power
Adenauer, Konrad, 127, 133, 139; administration of, 128, 135, 204
Adorno, Theodor, 112–14, 134. See also *Authoritarian Personality, The*
Adventures of Robin Hood, The (TV series), 119–20, 153
Advocate (Los Angeles magazine), 227
Agamben, Giorgio, 4, 164
AIDS Coalition to Unleash Power (ACT UP), 194, 198, 224–25
AIDS crisis, 194, 195–96, 198, 223–25, 226–27
Alexander, Roberta, 177
Algren, Nelson, 153
allegory, 108, 117–25
Allen, Devere, 53
Allende, Hortencia Bussi de, 190
Amendola, Giovanni, 104
America First Committee, 2, 97
American Civil Liberties Union (ACLU), 35, 49, 92, 116, 171
American Independent Party, 94, 170, 171–73
American Indian Movement (AIM), 186
American Jewish Committee, 112
American Jewish Congress, 47–48
American League Against War and Fascism, 17, 34, 47, 49–57, 58
American League for Peace and Democracy. *See* American League Against War and Fascism
American Legion, 40, 111, 233, 234
American Nazi Party, 146, 147, 167, 172–73, 217

American Socialist Party, 33, 34, 79; Militants, 34, 244n52; Old Guard, 34, 53, 81
American Socialist Quarterly, 73, 79, 81
American Veterans Committee, 112, 253n72
anticommunism, 44, 92, 94–95, 97–107, 111, 115–17, 121–25, 130–31, 147. *See also* antifascism (as an analytic/theory)
antifascism, definition, 5
antifascism (as an analytic/theory): American exceptionalist strains, 85–86; diagnosis of anticommunism, 94, 97, 129, 130–31; and anti-imperialism, 86–87, 163–64, 166–68, 182–83; atavism analysis, 88–89; class politics of, 72–85, 98, 114, 119–20, 122–25, 129, 136–37, 153, 160, 213; and economic reductionism, 72–84, 88–89, 137; and feminism, 83, 115, 155–58; gangster metaphor, 77–79, 80; and homosexuality, 115, 206; international nature of, 72–73, 85; intersectional nature of, 8, 70–72, 80–84, 112–15, 122–25, 148, 156, 158, 206–8, 214; Luther to Hitler thesis, 85–86, 138–39; nationalism analysis (*see* nationalism: antifascist analysis of); psychoanalytic turns, 80–81, 112–15, 129–31, 148–49, 153, 222; puppet master theory, 75–77, 78, 79; proto–Cold War strains, 85–86; as queer analytic, 199–200, 206–8, 212, 214, 222, 225–27; racial analysis, 70–71, 76, 81–87, 113, 122, 124–25, 129, 131, 150–54, 160, 166–67, 168, 182–85, 207; scholarship on, 72, 74, 77; sense of time, 72, 87–89, 158, 231–32; spatial metaphors, 164–65, 166–67, 169, 182–83, 189, 192. *See also* anti-intellectualism; anti-Semitism; liberalism; social fascism

271

Index

antifascism (U.S. to 1945): in 1920s, 46–47; advocacy of armed force, 30–31, 50, 53–56, 157; and African Americans, 35, 52–53, 67–69, 86–87, 166; and anti-imperialism, 50, 51–53, 57–58, 64; and anti-racism, 70–71, 81–84; and civil rights, 57; efforts against fascism abroad, 31–33, 47–48, 51–56, 59–69; and feminism, 57, 83; impact, institutional, 33, 56–57, 59, 62, 69; impact, public opinion, 6–7, 32, 34, 47–48, 51, 59–60, 69, 192, 241n15; intersectional praxis, 8, 33, 47, 49, 80, 83–84; isolationist strand, 244n68; and Italians, 47; against militarism, 49–50, 55, 60–61; and nationalism, 7, 50, 53, 64–65, 80; and domestic political reaction, 4, 7–8, 47, 49, 56, 62, 71; public understanding of, 8. *See also* anti-Semitism; Holocaust; liberalism (Enlightenment)
antifascism (U.S. after 1945): as academic discourse, 112, 115, 129, 146, 215; and African Americans, 117, 160–65, 167–70, 174–85; and anti-imperialism, 167–68, 177, 183, 189–90, 192; and Asian Americans, 159–60, 161, 164, 185, 190–92; as coalition-building strategy, 175–79, 186, 190; Cold War incompatibility, 99–100, 127, 129, 132, 136–39, 141–45, 168–69; and feminists, 155–58, 177–78; and gays and lesbians, 161, 193, 194–201, 205–14; impact, institutional, 91, 192; impact, public opinion, 7, 8, 91, 94, 129, 146–48, 192, 198, 232, 236; and Latinos, 161, 185–90; and McCarthyism, 90–95, 108–12, 115–17, 121–25, 143, 149; against militarism, 94; as residual culture, 27–28, 136; and 1960s right wing, 128–29, 146–54; right-wing cooptation of, 6, 11, 235–36, 238n16; in twenty-first century, 232–36; and white radicals in late 1960s, 161, 176, 177–78. *See also* anti-Semitism; Holocaust; liberalism (Enlightenment)
Anti-Fascist Alliance of North America, 47
anti-imperialism. *See* antifascism (as an analytic/theory); antifascism (U.S. to 1945); antifascism (U.S. after 1945)

anti-intellectualism, 94, 109–10, 115, 118, 123
anti-Semitism, antifascist efforts against, 47–48, 66, 80–82, 129, 131, 135, 144, 156–58. *See also* Holocaust (U.S. perceptions)
appeasement, 30, 55, 56, 57, 103, 138
Aptheker, Herbert, 160, 165, 177
arditi, 16
Arendt, Hannah: *Eichmann in Jerusalem*, 128, 130; *The Origins of Totalitarianism*, 105, 167, 252n47
Armenian genocide, 111
Aronowitz, Stanley, 177
Asian-American Political Alliance (AAPA), 159, 191–92
"Assignment U.S.A." (radio adaptation), 66
Atwood, Margaret, 216
Authoritarian Personality, The (Adorno et al.), 112–15, 130, 208, 219

Baldwin, James, 159
banality of evil, 130
Barbusse, Henri, 73
Basta Ya! (newspaper), 186, 187
Bauer, Otto, 73, 78
Beck, Glenn, 235
Beetham, David, 77
Behemoth (Neumann), 63
Behold a Pale Horse (Reed), 222–23
Bell, Daniel, 93, 115, 129
Benét, Stephen Vincent, 150
Benjamin, Walter, 11, 16, 28, 107, 196, 229, 231, 240n42
Bent (Sherman), 199, 213, 220–22, 223
Berlin Diary (Shirer), 59, 85, 135–36, 139, 249n37
Best Years of Our Lives, The (film), 95–98, 125
Billinger, Karl. *See* Massing, Paul
Biondi, Martha, 67
Black Legion, 40, 56
blacklist (McCarthy era), 91, 95, 108, 117, 119, 135, 149
Black Panther (newspaper), 181–84
Black Panther Party (BPP), 159–63, 170, 174–85, 192
Blackshirts, origins of, 16, 36

Blood in My Eye (Jackson), 181
Boas, Franz, 81, 84
Bobbio, Norberto, 22
Bonapartism, 13, 75
book burning, 118
Bowers v. Hardwick, 223–24
Bradbury, Ray, 118
Brecht, Bertolt, 123, 137, 228, 229
Bright Room Called Day, A (Kushner), 1, 194, 227–32
Broadway, 108
"Brooklyn Boys," 43
Browder, Earl, 82
Brown Berets, 185, 186, 188
Brownshirts (SA, *Sturmabteilung*), 39, 239n8
Buchanan, Pat, 2–3, 237n6
Buck, Pearl, 60
Buckley, William F., 5, 95, 146, 171
Bulosan, Carlos, 65, 185
Bush, George H. W., 5, 6, 18, 174, 238n11
Bush, George W., 3, 6, 215
business press (U.S.), 37–39, 75
But We Were Born Free (Davis), 98

Cannon, James, 68
Capra, Frank, 60, 141
Captain America (comic), 128
Carlson, John Roy. *See* Derounian, Avedis
Carmichael, Stokely, 178
Carter, Asa, 172
Catholics (United States), support for fascism, 37, 42
Causa, La (newspaper), 188, 189
Central Intelligence Agency, 107, 112
Césaire, Aimé, 21, 165, 166–67, 175
Chamberlain, Neville, 30, 103, 138
Chase, Stuart, 76, 84
Chicago Daily Tribune, 30
Chicago Defender, 68, 87
Chicago School (U.S. proletarian literature), 153
China, 17, 51, 54–55
Christian Front, 43, 151
Christian Mobilizers, 43
Christian Reconstructionism (Rushdoony), 217–19

Christian right: fascist tendencies, 2, 94, 200–201, 215–20, 234; as represented by antifascists, 196, 198, 215–16, 226–27
Churchill, Winston, 97, 99, 101–4, 135, 136, 138, 252n39, 257n40
Civil Rights Congress (CRC), 165, 167–70
civil rights movement: backlash against, 94, 170–71; Cold War strategy, 169; impact on antifascism, 68, 131, 137, 143, 149, 153–55, 161, 163; the long civil rights movement, 67, 165–66; interrupted by McCarthyism, 131–32; in Second World War, 67–68
Cleaver, Eldrige, 182–83
Cleaver, Kathleen, 182–83
Cold War: antifascist incompatibility with, 99–100, 127, 129, 132, 136–39, 141–45, 168–69; as dominant culture, 26, 107; shift away from McCarthyite strategy, 132; origins of, 98–100; rehabilitation of former Axis enemies, 97, 100–107, 108, 127–28, 134. *See also* anticommunism; blacklist; liberals; McCarthyism; totalitarianism (discourse)
collective security, 53, 57
Comintern. *See* Communist International
Committee to Defend America by Aiding the Allies, 35
Communist International (Comintern), 50, 72, 76
Communist Party Germany (KPD), 76, 201, 204, 228
Communist Party Opposition, 79
Communist Party U.S.A. (CPUSA): black belt thesis, 207; and gay and lesbian movement, 204–5; institutional impact, 35–36, 56–59; myth of ideological uniformity, 79; in postwar period, 110, 119, 121, 167, 175–76, 204–5; and Second World War, 50, 57–59, 69; Third Period, 49–50, 82, 181; united front groups, 34, 49–57; and the USSR, 35–36. *See also* American League Against War and Fascism; Comintern; liberals; Molotov-Ribbentrop Pact; Popular Front
concentration camps, as meme, 38
conservative dictatorship (Europe), 13–14
Conservative Party (U.K.), 31, 102–3

274 Index

conservatives (U.S.): in 1960s, 146–47, 154; in twenty-first century, 5, 6; views of fascism abroad before 1942, 30–32, 36–46, 56
corporatism, 44
Corwin, Norman, 65, 84, 148, 149
Coughlin, Charles, 32, 42–46, 69, 81, 109, 124, 200, 217
Crimp, Douglas, 194, 195
Crucible, The (Miller), 120, 122–25

Daughters of Bilitis, 210; *The Ladder,* 209
Davis, Elmer, 63, 64, 98
democracy. *See* liberalism (Enlightenment)
Denning, Michael, 32, 50–51
Department of Homeland Security (U.S.), 233
Derounian, Avedis, 111–12, 234; *The Plotters,* 111–12; *Under Cover,* 59–60
Desert Fox (film), 110
Destruction of the European Jews, The (Hilberg), 128, 135–36
Diggins, John, 46, 235, 241n8, 269n7
Dimitrov, Georgi, 72, 79–80, 165, 175, 207
Discourse on Colonialism (Césaire), 166–67
Dodd, Thomas, 127
Double V campaign, 68–69
Dragon Seed (Buck), 60
Du Bois, W. E. B., 165, 166, 175

Edkins, Jenny, 151
Eichmann in Jerusalem (Arendt), 128, 130
Eichmann trial, 128, 130, 131
Eisenhower administration, 91, 134
End Poverty in California (EPIC), 47
Epstein, Jason, 143
Equality (magazine), 71
Ethiopia, Italian invasion of, 102; reception in U.S., 31, 36, 37, 38, 52, 86–87
Eugene V. Debs Column, 54

Fahrenheit 451 (Bradbury), 118
Falwell, Jerry, 196, 201
Fanon, Frantz, 165, 166
Farrell, James T., 153
Faschismustheorie, definition, 73
fascism: definition, 13, 216; as defined in 1930s, 73; the "fascist minimum," 24; and liberalism, 19–21, 45–46; mislabeling, 2, 5, 6, 24, 156, 230, 235; as right-wing phenomenon, 22–24, 31. *See also* gangster metaphor of fascism; social fascism; spatial metaphor of fascism
fascism (Europe): and conservatives, 14, 18; economic policies, 38, 44; and elites, 13–14, 239n8; expansionism, 51; and historians, 13, 17–18, 105, 139; gender politics, 16; and the left, 14–15, 32–33; middle-class basis, 14, 72; militarism, 16–17; origins of term, 17; persecution of homosexuals, 199, 201–4, 219; postwar resurgence, 18; and racism, 15–16, 21, 168. *See also* Hitler, Adolf; Franco, Francisco; Mussolini, Benito; nationalism
fascism (Japan), 17
fascism (U.S.): historians' views of, 17–19; potential in 1930s, 45–46, 56; and militarism, 21, 217; postwar resurgence, 3, 18–22, 94, 146–48, 170–74, 200–201, 215–20, 234; religious tendency, 217; and war veterans, 111–12, 234
Fassbender, Egmont, 213
Faulk, John Henry, 95
Federal Bureau of Investigation (FBI), 159, 170–71, 179, 180, 182, 188
Feminine Mystique, The (Friedan), 129, 132, 155–58
Fermaglich, Kirstin, 156
fifth column, origin of term, 31, 241–42n2
Fight! (magazine of ALAWF/ALPD), 73, 80, 82, 181
finance capital, 80
Finkelstein, Avram, 26, 224–26, 231
Finland, Soviet invasion of, 58
Fish, Hamilton, 56
Flanders, Ralph, 90–92
Foucault, Michel, 4, 183–84
Four Freedoms (Roosevelt), 62, 67
Franco, Francisco (U.S. views): conservative and rightist support, 37, 42, 43, 46, 53–54; post-1945 controversies, 108, 252n56; postwar leftist critiques, 110
Frankfurt School, 63, 73, 78, 87, 112–15, 157. *See also* Adorno, Theodor; *Authoritarian*

Personality, The; Horkheimer, Max; Marcuse, Herbert; Neumann, Franz; Pollock, Friedrich
Friedan, Betty, 129, 132, 155–58
Friends of Democracy, 35, 112

gangster metaphor of fascism, 77–79, 80, 120
Gays, AIDS, and You (Rueda and Schwartz), 220
gay and lesbian movement (Germany), 199, 201, 203, 204, 211–13
gay and lesbian movement (U.S.): AIDS activism, 194–98; impact on antifascism, 198, 201; archive-building, 203, 213, 223; gay liberation, 209–10; homophile movement, 205–9, 210; trans-Atlantic connections, 204, 211, 212–13
gay and lesbian press (U.S.), 226–27
gay Holocaust: controversies over, 198–99; emergence of concept, 198, 203; historical basis, 202; literary genre, 199, 220–23
genocide: as political concept, 161, 163–64, 167–70, 182, 183–84, 189–90, 199, 210; United Nations definition, 168
German American Bund, 36, 43, 56, 104, 151
Germany, East (GDR), 133, 204
Germany, Nazi Period. *See* fascism (Europe); Hitler, Adolf; Nazi Germany (U.S. views)
Germany, West (FRG), 106, 112, 126–28, 133–35, 139, 204, 211–12
Gernreich, Rudi, 205–6
Gerstle, Gary, 66–67
Getting Together (newspaper), 190, 191
Gingrich, Newt, 174
Glaeser, Ernst, 81
Glazer, Nathan, 115, 130
Goldberg, Jonah, 5, 235, 238n16, 269n7
Goldberg, Michelle, 215, 216, 219, 236
Goldwater, Barry, 129, 146–48, 258n58
Gramsci, Antonio, 51, 73, 87
Griffin, Roger, 12, 13, 18
Guerin, Daniel, 248n18

Hampton, Fred, 175
Handmaid's Tale, The (Atwood), 216
Hargis, Rev. Billy James, 146
Hay, Harry, 199, 205–8
Hays, Arthur Garfield, 92, 116–17
Hearst, William Randolph, 40, 42
Hedges, Chris, 215, 216, 236
Heger, Heinz, 203–4, 211, 212
"He's Alive" (Serling), 151–55, 259n77, 259n82
High Noon (film), 119
Hilberg, Raul, 128, 135–36
Hilliard, David, 176, 179
Himes, Chester, 69
Hirschfeld, Magnus, 71, 201, 204, 209
Hitler, Adolf, 15, 16, 124, 172, 188–89, 239n8; as viewed by U.S. conservatives, businessmen, and rightists, 30–32, 36, 38–46, 75
Hitler-Stalin Pact. *See* Molotov-Ribbentrop Pact
Hochhuth, Rolf, 128
Holocaust, scholarship on, 10, 135, 144, 184
Holocaust (German perceptions), 134
Holocaust (U.S. perceptions): amnesia, 94, 101, 132; centrality to antifascism, 88, 129; civil rights, dependence on, 131; controversies over Gentile victims / application to Gentiles, 138, 144–46, 156, 184–85, 198–99, 219, 225; denial, 218; early narratives, 38–39; and Betty Friedan, 155–58; impact on gay and lesbian politics, 194–98; early 1960s memory boom, 128–32, 135, 137–38, 156; and Arthur Miller, 120–21; impact on people of color movements, 161, 183–85, 189–90; psychologizing trends, 129–30; and Rod Serling, 149, 154; unproductive dominant narratives ("Americanization"), 163, 214–15, 221–23. *See also* genocide
Holocaust: The Story of the Family Weiss (TV series), 214, 221
Hollywood. *See* motion picture industry (U.S.)
Hollywood Anti-Nazi League, 34, 119
Hollywood Ten, 91
homophile movement. *See* gay and lesbian movement
homo sacer, 164–65, 173, 223

Homosexuelle Aktion Westberlin (HAW), 211–13, 214, 267n46
Hoover, Herbert, 37
Hoover, J. Edgar, 104, 175, 182, 191
Horkheimer, Max, 87, 112
House Committee on Un-American Activities (HUAC), 91, 92, 95, 115–17, 121, 191
Hughes, Langston, 82–83, 165

Ickes, Harold, 34, 49, 56, 84
If He Hollers Let Him Go (Himes), 69
imperialism (European), 19, 20, 64, 68, 86–87, 99, 167, 184–85
intercommunalism, 192
Internal Security Act of 1950, 106, 191–92
Institute of Homophile Studies, 209
Institutes of Biblical Law (Rushdoony), 217–18
Iott, Rich, 234
Islamofascism, 6
isolationism, 55–56, 97
Italy, fascist period. *See* Mussolini, Benito
It Can't Happen Here (Lewis), 3–4, 74, 79, 226, 249n41
I Wor Yuen, 185, 190–91

Jackson, George, 181
Japan: as fascist state, 17; as viewed by African Americans, 52; racialization of, 60–61, 63, 67; Roosevelt and, 62–63
Japanese American internment, 19, 67, 160, 191–92
Jewish Labor Committee, 34, 47–48, 81
Joe Palooka (comic), 59
John Birch Society, 146, 154
Johnson, Lyndon, 171, 175
Joint Anti-Fascist Refugee Committee, 34, 54
Joint Boycott Council, 48
Judgment at Nuremberg (film), 128, 132, 134–36, 140–45, 258n57

Kalayaan International (newspaper), 190
Kautsky, Karl, 88
Kazin, Michael, 44
Keep America Out of War Congress, 244–45n68

Kennan, George, 91, 100, 106–7
Know Your Enemy: Japan (film), 60
Keynesian economics, 78, 125
Khaki Shirts, 36
Korean War, 106, 127, 168–69
Kovel, Joel, 99, 131
Kramer, Larry, 199
Kramer, Stanley, 132, 134–36, 140–45
Kreloff, Charles, 26, 224–26, 232
Ku Klux Klan, 40, 56, 168, 170–73, 217
Kushner, Tony, 199, 227–32

labor unions, 35, 47, 56, 68–69, 97, 125
Late Great Planet Earth, The (Lindsey), 216–17
Lautmann, Rüdiger, 203, 213
law and order right, 37, 39–42
left wing, definition, 22–23, 65
Let the Record Show . . . (art installation), 195–98, 228
Lewis, John L., 69, 76
Lewis, Sinclair, 1, 3–4, 249n41
Liberal Fascism (Goldberg), 5, 235, 238n16, 269n7
liberalism (Enlightenment): as antithesis of fascism, 20, 85; and capitalism, 20, 122–24; definition, 19–20; differences from fascism, 20; as dual system, 19–21, 164–65, 182–83, 234; as facilitator of fascism, 8, 13, 21; and Four Freedoms (Roosevelt), 62; left-wing repurposing of, 20, 56; and race, 19, 20, 163–65, 182; explicit rejections of, 147–48, 172, 217; and spatial concept of fascism, 164–65, 167, 169, 182–83; and totalitarianism discourse, 105; U.S. fascist uses of, 45–46, 172–73
liberals (U.S.): and antifascist organizations, 34–35; support for Cold War, 93, 95, 100, 105, 150; and communists, 34, 49, 50, 53, 57; definition of, 19; support for Mussolini, 36
Liberty (magazine), 41–42
Lindbergh, Charles, 2, 56, 97, 98
Lindsey, Hal, 216–7
Lipset, Seymour Martin, 115, 129, 146, 254n82

Luce, Henry, 91; "American Century," 62, 64, 65
Luther to Hitler thesis, 85–86, 138–39

MacFadden, Bernarr, 40, 41–42
MacLeish, Archibald, 63, 64
Mandel, Ernest, 12
Mann, Abby, 140, 141
Manuilski, D. Z., 76
March on Rome, 36
Marcuse, Herbert, 63
Marshall, George C., 103
Marshall, Stuart, 200
Martin, Geoff, 226
Marxism, Western, 87–88
Mass Culture (1957 anthology), 118
Masses and Mainstream, 110
Massing, Paul, 81, 88–89
Mass Psychology of Fascism, The (Reich), 177–78
Matsui, Haru, 73
Mattachine Review, 208–9
Mattachine Society, 205–6, 207–9
Mauldin, Bill, 93
McCarran Act. *See* Internal Security Act of 1950
McCarthy, Joe, 90–95, 97, 98, 103–4, 109, 250n5
McCarthyism, 90–95, 103–4, 108, 110, 115–17, 121–25, 130, 131–32
McConnell, Dorothy, 57, 83
McCormick, Robert, 30, 56
Mein Kampf (Hitler), 15, 16
Menefee, Selden, 66
Michael, Miles, 226–27
Milgram, Stanley, 129
Miller, Arthur, 119, 120–25; *The Crucible*, 120, 122–25; *An Enemy of the People*, 122; *Focus*, 121, 251n14; *A View from the Bridge*, 121; *You're Next!*, 121, 122
Mission to Moscow (Davies), 59
Molotov-Ribbentrop Pact, 57–59, 86, 138, 225
Moon Is Down, The (Steinbeck), 60, 141
Moral Majority, 201, 215
motion picture industry (U.S.), 64, 104, 108
Mowrer, Edgar, 84, 85–86

Muhammad Speaks, 167, 169, 175
multiculturalism, 3, 21, 223
Mumford, Lewis, 84, 85–86
Munich Agreement (1938). *See* appeasement
Murphy, Brenda, 115, 117
Mussolini, Benito, 15, 36, 38, 44, 47, 52, 104, 172. *See also* fascism (Europe); Ethiopia, Italian invasion of; Partito Nazionale Fascista
Mussolini, Benito (U.S. views): in Churchill's history, 102; by conservatives, businessmen, and rightists, 31, 36–38; by Italians in the U.S., 47; by liberals and leftists, 36, 46–47, 86

Naison, Mark, 56
Nakatsu, Penny, 159–60, 165, 191
Napolitano, Janet, 233, 234
Nation (magazine), 35, 54, 73, 79, 84
nationalism: antifascist analysis of, 4, 7, 76, 79–80, 82, 83, 85, 111, 113, 130–31, 146, 153–54, 212; antifascist use of, 64–65; fascist, 15–16; right-wing (U.S.), 4, 7, 23
National Association for the Advancement of Colored People (NAACP), 49, 58, 169
National Committees to Combat Fascism (NCCF), 161, 174–75, 178–81, 186
National Union for Social Justice (NUSJ), 43, 44
Nation of Islam, 167
Nazi Germany. *See* fascism (Europe); Hitler, Adolf
Nazi Germany (U.S. policy toward): Roosevelt administration, 53, 55–56, 62–63; postwar recruitment of ex-Nazis, 106–7
Nazi Germany (U.S. views): by conservatives, businessmen, and rightists in the 1930s, 30–46; consumer boycott, 48; by liberals and leftists in the 1930s, 38, 46–48; myth of Nazi homosexuality, 206, 209, 221; in postwar period, 118, 126–28; as totalitarian, 104–5. *See also* Holocaust (U.S. views); Hitler, Adolf
negative dialectics, 87
Neumann, Franz, 63

278 *Index*

Neutrality Acts, 53, 55
New American Right, The (Bell et al), 115. See also *Radical Right, The*
New Deal: antifascists and, 6, 34–35, 49–50, 56–57, 66, 76, 181; as hegemonic force, 26; legislation, 35, 56, 61; rollback of, 97. See also Roosevelt, Franklin D.
New International (magazine), 110
New Leader (magazine), 73, 81
New Masses (magazine), 73, 78, 80–81
New Museum of Contemporary Art, 195
New Republic (magazine), 35, 38, 54, 63, 73, 84
Newton, Huey, 175, 192
New York Native (magazine), 226–28
"Nightmare at Noon," 150
Nixon, Richard, 171, 173–74, 175, 182, 188, 190
Nolte, Ernst, 18
North American Committee to Aid Spanish Democracy, 54
Novak, Robert, 5, 171
Nuremberg trials, 106, 139, 141, 195; perceptions of inadequacy, 126–28, 135, 142

Obama, Barack, 235–36
Odets, Clifford, 206
Office of Facts and Figures (OFF), 63
Office of Price Administration, 61, 69, 97
Office of War Information (OWI), 35, 63–65, 98, 152, 251n17
"On a Note of Victory" (Corwin), 65
ONE, Inc., 209
One World (Willkie), 65
Origins of Totalitarianism, The (Arendt), 105, 167, 252n47
Ortega y Gasset, José, 118

pacifism, 53–54
Padmore, George, 86–87
Palin, Sarah, 1–3, 217, 237n6
Pan-African Reconstruction Association, 52
Paragraph 175 of German Penal Code, 201, 204, 212
Partito Nazionale Fascista (PNF), 18, 36
Patman, Wright, 98
Patterson, William, 165, 169, 184

Paxton, Robert, 18–19, 105, 172–73
Payne, Stanley, 18
Pegler, Westbrook, 2
Pelley, William, 36
People's War, the, 59, 61–69
Pepper, Claude, 98
pink triangle: controversies over, 198–99, 225; Nazi origins of, 194; as reclaimed symbol, 194–98, 211–12, 224–26; trans-Atlantic migration, 204, 211–15
Pink Triangle, The (Plant), 213–14
Pinochet, Augusto, 190
Pittsburgh Courier (newspaper), 68, 86, 87
Plant, Richard, 199, 202, 212–15, 221, 223
Plot Against America, The (Roth), 216, 236
Political Man (Lipset), 115, 129, 146
Pollock, Friedrich, 63, 78
Pope Pius XI, 42
Popular Front (Comintern), 50, 76, 79–80
Popular Front (U.S.), 6, 50–57, 63, 64–65, 80–82; postwar afterlife, 92–94, 109, 125, 129, 136, 149–50, 153, 156–58, 160, 161, 175–77, 178, 207–8
populism: as antifascist target, 3–4, 109–10; uses by the left, 59; in literature, 3–4; uses by the right, 2, 44, 91, 109, 147
Progressive Labor / Worker-Student Alliance, 177
Provisional Committee for the Defense of Ethiopia, 34, 52
Plotters, The (Carlson), 111–12
puppet master theory, 75–77, 78, 79

racism, origin of term, 70–71
Radical Right, The (Bell et al.), 115, 146
radio industry, 59, 64, 108
Raiders of the Lost Ark (film), 5
Rand, Ayn, 97
Randolph, A. Philip, 69
Rankin, John E., 122
Reagan, Ronald, 5, 147, 174, 215, 230, 237n9
Reconstructionism, Christian (Rushdoony), 217–19
"Red Fascism in the United States Today" (Hoover), 104
Red Skull Incarnate (Pak and Colak), 236
Reed, Lannon, 221, 222–23
Reich, Wilhelm, 177–78, 209

Renton, Dave, 77
Republican Party (U.S.), 173–74, 234
residual culture, 26–28, 136, 139
Revolutionary Action Movement (RAM), 165, 170
Riesman, David, 115, 130
right wing, definition, 22–24
Rise and Fall of the Third Reich, The (Shirer), 128, 132, 134–39, 206
Robertson, Pat, 201, 218
Robeson, Paul, 117, 159, 169
Rockwell, George Lincoln, 146, 167
Röhm purge, 39
Roosevelt, Franklin D., 34, 49, 51–52, 55, 56, 62–63, 84. *See also* Four Freedoms; New Deal
Roper, Billy, 234
Roth, Philip, 150, 216, 236
Rubin, Marty, 226
Rueda, Enrique, 220
Rushdoony, Rousas John, 217–19
Russo-Japanese War (1904–1905), 52

Sanford, R. Nevitt, 112–13, 219
Sartre, Jean-Paul, 125
Schlafly, Phyllis, 146
Schlesinger, Arthur, 105
Schmitt, Carl, 4, 20, 164
science fiction, 118, 149
Seale, Bobby, 160, 176, 179, 183
Second World War: African Americans and, 67–69; military strategy (U.S.), 62–63; racial crosscurrents (U.S.), 67–68; and sexuality, 205; Soviet contribution / losses, 99, 101, 138
Second World War (postwar memory), 10–11, 27, 95–98, 100–107, 110–12, 119, 126–31, 134–36, 138, 141, 151–52
Second World War (U.S. propaganda, 1941–45): free world / slave world narrative, 60–61, 141–42; imperial tendencies, 62; internationalist tendencies, 65; left-liberal impact on, 59, 61–69; patriotic nature, 64–65, 68; "the People's War," 59, 61–69; politics of unity, 68–69; and race, 60–61, 66–69; Roosevelt's emphasis on Europe, 62–63; scholarly debates over U.S. propaganda, 61

Senate Internal Security Subcommittee (SISS), 91, 92
Serling, Rod, 129, 148–55, 258–59n73
Shachtman, Max, 79, 110
Shaw, Irwin, 116
Sherman, Martin, 199, 213, 220–22
Sherwood, Robert, 58, 63, 84, 95, 97–98, 125
Shirer, William, 84, 85; *Berlin Diary,* 59, 85, 135–36, 139; *The Rise and Fall of the Third Reich,* 128, 132, 134–39, 206, 249n37
Siete de la Raza, Los, 160
Silence = Death graphic, 194–96, 224–25, 228
Silence = Death Project, 194, 196, 197, 199, 224–25
Sillen, Samuel, 70, 249n37
Silver Shirts, 36
Sinclair, Upton, 47, 76
Singh, Nikhil, 22–23, 164
Smith, Gerald L. K., 92, 200, 217
Social Democratic Party of Germany (SPD), 85, 88, 201, 204, 229, 231
social fascism, 76
Socialist Party (U.S.). *See* American Socialist Party
Socialist Workers Party (U.S.), 34, 68, 77, 110
Social Justice (newspaper), 43–44, 46
Southern Poverty Law Center (SPLC), 233–34
southern strategy, 173–74, 175, 234
Spanish Civil War, 32, 53–55, 57, 110, 121
spatial metaphor of fascism, 164–65, 166–67, 169, 182–83, 189
Spillane, Mickey, 104–5
stabbed-in-the-back myth, 103–4
Stalin, Josef, 35, 57, 94, 98–99, 251n22
Starkey, Marion, 122
state capitalism, concept, 78–79
Steinbeck, John, 60, 141
structure of feeling, 8, 84, 105, 113, 181
Student Nonviolent Coordinating Committee (SNCC), 178
Students for a Democratic Society (SDS), 177, 178
Sturmabteilung (SA). *See* Brownshirts
Sweezy, Maxine, 98

Taft-Hartley Act, 97
Tea Party (political movement), 6, 24, 114, 234–36
television industry, 108, 149, 155
Tetens, T. H., 128, 133, 134–36
Thälmann, Ernst, 76
There Shall Be No Night (Sherwood), 58
Theweleit, Klaus, 16
Third Period analysis (Comintern), 76, 181
Third Reich. *See* fascism (Europe); Hitler, Adolf; Nazi Germany (U.S. views)
Thomas, Norman, 34, 46, 54, 70, 79, 88, 245n68
Thompson, Dorothy, 84
Thompson, Mark Christian, 260n12
Toller, Ernst, 89
totalitarianism (discourse), 6, 94, 95, 100–101, 104–6, 121, 132, 133–34, 135, 139, 238n16, 244n54
trade unions. *See* labor unions
trauma theory, 151
Trotsky, Leon, 13, 73, 77, 238n3
Trotskyists (U.S.), 77, 110. *See also* Cannon, James; Socialist Workers Party
Truman, Harold, 91, 104; administration of, 91, 107, 142
Tsiang, H. T., 185
Twilight Zone, The (TV series), 148, 151–55

Union of Soviet Socialist Republics (USSR), 33, 34, 35, 50, 57–58, 98–99, 101–2, 104, 105, 138, 204
United Front Against Fascism (UFAF, conference), 159–61, 165, 170, 175–78, 186
United Nations, 169; convention on genocide, 168
U.S. National Catholic Welfare Conference, 42

Vacirca, Vincenzo, 73, 77, 78
V for Vendetta (film), 236
Viereck, George Sylvester, 41
Vietnam War, 189
Vladeck, Baruch, 48

Wald, Alan, 86, 110, 121
Walker, Gen. Edwin, 146
Wallace, George, 94, 171–74
Wallace, Henry, 7, 34, 60, 62, 68, 84, 92
Wallant, Edward Lewis, 129
Wall Street Journal (newspaper), 39
Ward, Harry F., 75
We Charge Genocide (UN petition), 167–70, 175
Weinstein, Hannah, 119
Wheeler, Burton, 56
whiteness, 4, 82–83, 124–25, 167
Why We Fight (film series), 60–61, 141
Williams, Raymond: and residual culture, 26–28, 136, 139; and structure of feeling, 8, 84, 105, 113, 181
Williams, Robert, 165, 184
Willkie, Wendell, 65
Wilson, Sloan, 130
Winrod, Gerald, 24, 25, 200, 217
Wissenschaftlich-humanitäre Komitee (WHK), 201, 204, 206
Women, War, and Fascism (McConnell), 83
Workers Age (newspaper), 79
World War II. *See* Second World War
Wright, Richard, 153
Wyler, William, 95

Yellow Power, 185, 190–92

CHRIS VIALS is an associate professor of English at the University of Connecticut–Storrs, where he also served as interim director of American Studies. His work looks at American literature and history, social class, race, popular culture, social movements, and political economy. He has also been quite active on the issue of academic labor throughout his career. He is the author of *Realism for the Masses: Aesthetics, Popular Front Pluralism, and U.S. Culture, 1935–1947* (2009). His work has also appeared in *Criticism, Against the Current,* and *Science and Society,* among other venues. He received a PhD in English (American Studies concentration) from the University of Massachusetts Amherst in 2006. He lives with his wife, Cathy, in Willimantic, Connecticut.